Appeal and Attitude

INDIANA SERIES IN THE PHILOSOPHY OF RELIGION
MEROLD WESTPHAL, GENERAL EDITOR

Appeal and Attitude
Prospects for Ultimate Meaning

Steven G. Smith

INDIANA UNIVERSITY PRESS
BLOOMINGTON AND INDIANAPOLIS

#606508906
i12696237

Publication of this book is made possible in part with the assistance of a Challenge Grant from the National Endowment for the Humanities, a federal agency that supports research, education, and public programming in the humanities.

Indiana University Press
601 North Morton Street
Bloomington, IN 47404-3797 USA

http://iupress.indiana.edu

Telephone orders   800-842-6796
Fax orders   812-855-7931
Orders by e-mail   iuporder@indiana.edu

© 2005 by Indiana University Press

The paper used in this publication meets the minimum requirements of American National Standard for Information Sciences—Permanence of Paper for Printed Library Materials, ANSI Z39.48-1984.

MANUFACTURED IN THE UNITED STATES OF AMERICA

Library of Congress Cataloging-in-Publication Data

Smith, Steven G.
   Appeal and attitude : prospects for ultimate meaning / Steven G. Smith.
      p. cm. — (Indiana series in the philosophy of religion)
   Includes bibliographical references and index.
   ISBN 0-253-34645-2 (cloth : alk. paper)
   1. Values. 2. Attention. 3. Attitude (Psychology) 4. Philosophical theology. I. Title. II. Series.
BD435.S722 2005
128'.4—dc22

                                                                                      2005015762

1 2 3 4 5   10 09 08 07 06 05

To Elise

Contents

PREFACE

I take the most basic philosophical question to be, What ultimately warrants and constrains our thoughts, utterances, and actions? So far I seem to have made my best progress with this question by working out applications of the concept of the spiritual, deriving the sense of "spirit" centrally from the old moving-air metaphor of a movement from within (breath) integrally related to a reception of movement from without (wind).[1] A spiritual being is one whose prospects of meaningful life are determined by the state of its relationships with other beings, most importantly by the degree of reciprocal affirmation in those relationships. Qualifying myself as spiritual, aerated by awareness of other beings whose relevance to me exceeds any grasp of them I can form, I take up position in a field of relationships requiring rectification and recognize in that issue of rectification an unconditionally superordinate claim embedded in every meaning that touches me. From that superordinacy derives the force of all normative claims on thought and action.

The general program of affirming beings in relationship provides an ultimate warrant and constraint validating any and all rules of engagement one might conscientiously follow. But it leaves dark how *these* beings are the ones with whom engagement is actual or possible—not just *these kinds*, but *these*: the amazing mise-en-scène, not merely of a picture or play, but of my life.

The point of the world, one might say, is to be wild; a spiritual subject cannot dictate the world's content. We brush up our principles so that we can deal in the best way with whatever actually comes up. But how does "coming up" occur? It is not true either that subjects notice and attend equally to each and every being that comes within their experiential reach or that the actual entry of beings into a subject's experience is purely random and wild. Clearly, a drastic selection takes place from among possible recognitions. The selection is organized by physical process, habit, culture, and choice; and the selection can be better or worse.

In practice, the question, What are we dealing with? is usually more pressing than the reflective question, Why this? But critical reflection on how our encounters get their content is mandated by our responsibility to beings on a larger spatiotemporal scale. If I give all my attention to a pet cat while humans starve on the street outside my house, my cat-doting is wrong; I am failing as the administrator of my attention. The roots of my failure lie in my subjective counterpoint to the presented scene, an arrangement I have made of the world I am acting in.

Raised in this way, the issue of attention is very difficult indeed. What appeals will we be subjected to? What will all the implications of these appeals be, and what will our whole response be? How can we overcome each day's innumerable temptations of dullness or doting? Any communicated appeal that makes our experience *coherently* meaningful—most graspably of all, one that organizes our experience around the center point of a single supreme appeal, like a philosophical or religious teaching—will be enormously attractive in promising to free us of conflicts and confusions in our response to the appeals of all the beings in our world. But even if we recognize a supreme appeal, we still face the formidable problem of acting well in concrete situations. We are still at the mercy of appearances and impulses. Thus, our own orientation in dealing with beings is a matter of great interest. Might I adopt a general attitude in relation to the world on the basis of which interactions would tend to go in the best way to the extent that they depend on me? May I not hope that with the right attitude I might be equal to the challenge of appeals? Among the most potent of communicated appeals will be those that offer such an attitude.

In the present inquiry, "appeal" and "attitude" come into focus as the most pertinent general concepts for understanding encounterable beings and intentional respondents as live issues, that is, in the full dynamism of a bad, good, or better relationship shaping between them rather than in the frozen roles of "object" and "subject." The concepts of appeal and attitude take on a significance that is more than rhetorical or psychological: they become the warp and woof of meaningful experience as such, and the axes of normative thinking.

In chapter 1 I propose that meaningful experience occurs when some being takes priority over other beings in a subject's attention, at least for a moment—for example, while in a state of distraction I notice a friend across the room—and the subject commits to addressing that being in a certain way. The subject of meaningful experience has a touchstone and an orientation. To understand a particular kind of meaningfulness, then, one wants to be able to specify both the *appeal* of a being—how that sort of being can enter compellingly into a subject's experience—and the priority-sustaining *attitude* that a subject can take in relation to such an appellant. To specify an ultimate meaningfulness, like that of a religious or philosophical ideal, it is necessary to specify a maximally commanding claim on a subject and a maximally justified orientation of the subject—that is, a supreme appeal (something like "God" or "reality" or "the Other") and a sovereign attitude (something like "faith" or "reason" or "responsibility").

In chapter 2 the analysis is linked to a question of cultural history: How is it that we have come to feature appeals in our thinking, and where is appeal thinking leading us? The literatures of the classical age (Karl Jaspers's "Axial

Age"—the mid-first millennium BCE in China, India, Persia, Greece, and Israel) are noteworthy for their explicit attention to the prospect of a supreme appeal; indeed, all the religions of the "world religion" type and the classical philosophies are supreme appeal moves geared to command the attention of mentally free individuals. That this individual-directed structure of meaning is cross-cultural explains the possibility of cross-cultural "classics." (There are five translations of the *Daodejing* in my local bookstore.) The supreme appeal premise involves a number of serious difficulties, however, which appeal thinking must wrestle with. How can a concrete appeal adequately represent an infinitely worthy appellant? How can a supreme appellant be established in one ontological location rather than another—for instance, in the future rather than in the past, or outside of time rather than in it? How can a finite subject respond adequately to an infinitely exigent appeal? How can the supreme appeal be adequately inclusive in its outreach, and how can the community of its respondents be adequately inclusive? These issues must be in play in any searching interpretation or evaluation of a line of thinking, insofar as a fundamental principle of that thinking is a supreme appeal.

Although it is beyond any one book to give a comprehensive historical account of appeal thinking, chapters 3 and 4 trace two especially important lines of development in modern thought, one philosophical and one religious. I start in both domains with Kant, whose account of pure practical reason is a preeminently influential deployment of an explicit appeal motif. I show how a family of intellectual alternatives, till now under-recognized in their character as rivals and complements to each other, grows out of modern-classic complexes of early twentieth-century neo-Kantian philosophies (Rickert, Buber, Heidegger) and theologies (Bultmann, Gogarten, Barth). I take readings of the current state of the discussion by critically engaging Jean-Luc Marion's philosophy of appeal and Jay McDaniel's theology of full openness.

The great appeals have always included ideal attitudes like faith and rationality. In chapter 5 I explore the basic motivations of our concept of attitude to show why attitude is so important an object of concern in its own right. Here it is important to work out distinctions between attitude, with its distinctively direct relevance to the justification of the subject, and intentional capacity, emotion, and experience. To sustain these distinctions it is crucial to bear in mind that an attitude is always both a pose (an actual positioning of a subject in relation to the world that is determined at least in part by external factors) and a poise (a self-maintained stability).

Chapter 6 discusses sovereign attitude ideals that are centerpieces of the classic philosophical and religious teachings: benevolence and filial piety in Confucianism, tranquility in the Upanishads, devotion in the *Bhagavad Gita*, logos-reasonableness and civic piety in Greek philosophy (along with varieties of detachment in Hellenistic philosophies), and righteousness and mercy in Israelite prophecy. As with the notion of supreme appeal, deep-rooted problems attend the notion of sovereign attitude. How can a subject take a *justified* attitude without thereby turning away from a supreme appellant's always-active challenge to live *more* rightly? How can a devout subject choose between the diverse and divergent sovereign attitude claims of past-oriented piety, future-oriented faith, and present-oriented love? Or how can such claims be harmonized?

In chapters 7 and 8 I review an increasingly lucid discussion of basic attitude issues in modern philosophy (beginning this time with Leibniz and Spinoza) and theology (with Kant and Schleiermacher). The philosophical discussion concerns the life-rectifying powers of a more receptive sort of basic attitude (a "feeling" or "attunement") versus a more active sort (a "disposition"), the possibility of a basic attitude prescription that escapes the distortion of either a receptive or active bias (a "comportment"), and the possibility and benefit of entering appreciatively into diverse basic attitudes (as in Dilthey's and Jaspers's inventories of world-intuitions). Modern theologians, meanwhile, explicitly compose normative bundles of diverse basic religious attitudes (such as hope and love) and begin the process—which I carry forward another step—of theorizing the personal and collective possibility of such a difficult synthesis.

My constructive conclusion in chapter 9 affirms the continuing relevance of appeal and attitude ideals to our normative discourse by defending an ideal of responsible, communally inspired life against fundamental alternatives that have philosophically interesting expressions: idealism, positivism, relativism, noncommittalism, and absolute nondualism. I give ideals of "reality" and "responsibility" the sense of appeal and attitude horizons stretched out by the alternatives and issues I have brought forward. These ideals cannot realistically be sustained by an individual alone; a maximally inclusive community of individuals is required to sustain them.

* * *

For their critical responses to various portions of this work, I thank Kristen Brown, Steven Galt Crowell, Laura Franey, Charles Scott, Elise Smith, Bill Storey, Sandy Zale, and the Indiana University Press readers. I would like also to thank Jan Allison, Catherine Freis, Tom Henderson, and Allison Mays for research help, and Millsaps College for the inspiration and discipline of its Core Curriculum as well as for material help with bringing the project to completion.

Appeal and Attitude

one Appeals

The Question of Appeals

How will we live? With experience we learn that this most basic of questions gets addressed and shaped by particular beings, relations, and events on various scales of complexity. We want to understand the question in order to comport ourselves in it in the best way. An understanding requires a construal of the situation. A construal must be constructed. A construction must start somewhere and in some manner. To philosophize is to seek understanding by starting this construction entirely afresh, openly, as free of prejudice as possible. But there are many ways of starting afresh, depending on which beings, relations, and events seem to require attention.

What claims your attention? What is meaningful? If you are in doubt about the meaningfulness of X, with reference to what character and context of X do you determine that X is meaningful? When X and Y are rivals for your attention, on what basis do you respond to X rather than, or more than, Y? We can readily say what *you* do: you "value" (or "evaluate") them according to criteria implied by your interests. But what do X and Y contribute to that process? And how have past Xs and Ys contributed to the formation of what we are now calling your interests? The central focus of these questions is not on

1

you alone but on what other beings offer you. If we suppose that the questions concern only your own measure of satisfaction or frustration in relation to X and Y, we reduce their normal seriousness; if you insist on construing them in that way, as though nothing were vitally at stake for you in their reality or in the reality of your relationship to them, we find you to be somehow impaired— jaded, cynical, narcissistic, or excessively controlling.

A seriousness-impaired interpretation of our issues of attention is unfortunately the norm of the subjectivist modern philosophy of "value." On this view, complementary to the "value-free" objectivist view of what is available for encounter, beings acquire meaningfulness only when they are picked out, taken over, and formed by the desires, emotions, plans, and cognitive requirements of subjects. Yet it is obviously reasonable to ask how beings themselves capture a subject's attention. After all, our world is generally more like a colorful bazaar full of invitations to experience than like the grim sort of store where an item will appear only if you specifically request it at the counter. To speak of invitations to experience is to emphasize the possible and actual discontinuities in experience; we allow that beings are not already in our grasp or picked out by our own projection but that in some way they interrupt us, calling us over. They appeal to us. We find ourselves attending to them, or even committing to them, *because* they are appealing or have appealed to us and not merely because fears or desires are prompting us to keep track of them as means to an ulterior end. We say "X is appealing" or "X is more appealing than Y" to credit X for a power of bringing this about. We say experience of X is "meaningful" (or X "matters") to draw a contrast with purely utilitarian experience in which the distinct character of X plays no essential role, whatever logically discriminable "meaning" X may bear.

Following the lead of Levinas, Jean-Luc Marion has recently made telling use of the idea of appeal in his account of supremely meaningful kinds of experience.[1] Both thinkers properly emphasize that the subject of appeal does not exercise that mastery of experience that philosophy has typically wanted to establish for the subject. But in reserving appeal for a preeminent appellant, an exceptionally transcendent Other, Levinas and Marion break away from the ordinary worldly level of appealing and thus obscure the footing that their special appeal-events have in worldly life; they miss a chance to give a livelier, more adequately interactive general account of experience that would keep in check philosophy's tendency to homogenize experience by imposing general meaning requirements (forms, ideas, alterity, givenness); and they miss vital connections in meaningful experience between issues of ideal priority and issues of empirical fact. My aim here is to show a way of deploying the idea of appeal that can lead to a richer and better integrated yield of insight in all these areas.

The literal center of appeal-talk is a communicative act, specifically a somewhat urgent request, but our usage allows any being to be credited with appealing to anyone. I take this allowance as a primary clue. Although communicative appealing is dominant in our everyday life—indeed, it is communicative appealing that imposes on us the category of appeal when we reflect on how contents of experience can be superordinately meaningful—still we are not required to define appealing as a fully communicative act. Instead, we can expand our understanding of the commanding meaningfulness of communicative activity by first establishing in more basic terms what it means for a being, any being, to present something of interest to a subject. Let us therefore understand "X appeals to S" as "X makes available to S any sort of basis for S's voluntarily attending to X" and then go on to see how, building on that broad platform, we can locate the different kinds of appeals, including our commanding ideals, in an inclusive system of meaningful experience that accords with the inclusiveness of our seriously X-affirming concept of meaningfulness.

The Appellant Being and the Appellate Subject

A subject's attention may be drawn to (1) a concretely existing encountered being, (2) a form of beings, and (3) a manifestation of the subject's own disposition in regard to a being. These are three dimensions of appeal realizing. (If there is, arguably, a fourth—for instance, in a primal appeal of Being to consciousness—still the meaning generated in that dimension must be realized in the first three dimensions if it is to play the part of an appeal in a subject's life.)[2]

(1) It is worth scrupling in this context to speak of "beings" rather than "things." A "thing" in the ordinary wide sense found in the terms "something," "anything," and "nothing" is simply any item I can refer to, regardless of the real conditions of its obtaining as a unity in the world or in my consciousness or discourse. Calling an item a "thing" construes it as a correlate of intention. But I can also respond to any item, even "nothing," as a *witness* to it, not merely referring to it but perceiving or envisioning it focally, and in that stance, I call it a "being."[3] As I register the properties of the being together with my relevant contextual knowledge and my specific reactions to the being, the theme of the experience is the determination of the content of my awareness by an actuality. This appeal *of the being* is the least pliable layer in the appeal experience. It is distinct in principle from enjoyments and projections that may belong to the whole phenomenon of the "directive" (in Lingis's term) that I accept in relation to the being and yet are predominantly shaped by me at my own discretion.[4] Even an imaginary or intellectual being produced by my own mental activity has its own nature of which I can be a witness. For example, I can consciously attend to the impression made on me by a beach photograph in a vacation advertisement.

(2) I also *think* about *kinds* of beings, surveying possibility. I can compare the general attributes of "vacation" and "work," for example. "Vacation" has the item-like specificity of a Platonic form—it can confront my mind objectively—but it also has a generality that gives me mental room to maneu-

ver, so that its meaning cannot coincide with any particular attestation of the first-level sort (unless I objectify it for the sake of treating it in that way). The theme of this experience is the more or less balanced partnership of thought-forms and thought-freedom with the forms and contingency of actuality. The "meanings" of propositions relating to beings and the experienced import of beings are mixed together in it.

(3) I can also attend to something that is least object-like, my own motivation. Do I really want to take a vacation? How do I feel about other possible uses of the money it would cost? What suffering might I relieve? Manifest here in a background way is a stirring of desire or will—which could be construed as an appellant being in its own right, if I were to turn my attention to myself to that degree, though usually I will not—and my response to this stirring is a volitional movement. The theme of this aspect of the experience is my relationship with my own active core as qualified by an appeal. I am poised at the point where an appealing prospect could become part of *my* appealing in the sense that I am committed to wanting it and asking for it.

In sum, then, an advertised beach vacation appeals to me as a three-dimensional prospect comprising, in the simplest analysis, a certain beautiful beach (the actual beach pictured or an impression given by the picture), the general idea of a vacation, and a stance toward vacations and toward this vacation. Any of these aspects might dominate my attention at a given moment. All are essential to the whole experience. But the preeminent focus of an appeal experience as such is the concrete being that appeals to me. The appellant being exercises a certain rulership in my life, imposing a harmony between us in the form of the appeal.

Being appealing or having appeal involves more than the bare event of eliciting a reaction; it means being attractive, having the drawing power of seeming to offer something to the perceiver that the perceiver would thrive in accepting and supporting—a good. A partnership is involved: there must be an offer by the appellant being and an answering construal by the appellate subject. (The appellate subject's construal of the appellant may have *almost nothing* to do with an appellant's real nature, as in psychotic delusion, or with an appellant's real good, as in rape or theft.) Considered externally, as an objective question about the relation between a being and a subject, a being might or might not exert attraction; from this point of view we can investigate neutrally the conditions under which an appeal is effective. Considered from the appellate subject's point of view, however, the attraction *has been* and *is being* exercised, and the question that faces me when I am under appeal is how I am motivated and how I shall conduct myself in relation to the good that is promised me. The good might be accessible directly or only indirectly; it might be actual or virtual (if the being appeals as the token of an ideal, for example); it might be disingenuously disguised; it might be amplified to a fantastic extent by its resonance with my strongest desires or fears. In any case, all questions concerning how I and the appellant really are or are not good for each other are centrally pertinent insofar as the appellant is addressed in its appeal to me, though always inflected by the appeal itself.

An appeal may offer a benefit of its own—like the tingling tranquility induced by a beautiful surface that makes it hard for an observer to turn away—but its specifically appealing power lies in *referring* to a good, not in *being* a good. I cite as a very pure illustration of this principle the chord struck at the beginning of the Beatles' recording of "A Hard Day's Night."[5] Possessing barely enough extension to be identifiable as a musical event, the chord is not an element that one wants to listen to again and again for its own sake, but it compels our entry into the song.[6] An appeal is a threshold-hook like that opening chord or like the view at the top of a slide before the slider takes the plunge. The invitation to experience is the front edge of the experience and not yet the main part, although it projects something essential about the character the main part will have. Its theme is the choice of a certain flourishing prior to the realization of that flourishing. Thus, an appeal is peculiarly interesting in being potentially decisive. When there is a discernible flourishing just in the heeding of a certain appeal—for instance, in a humane response to a fellow human being's appeal for help—then the appeal itself can be seen as the highest good and most important part of an experience. Even so, it is just the edge. The importance of experiencing the appeal still depends on a thriving to which the appeal promises to lead—in that case, some practical realization of human fellowship. (Our real flourishing itself is often not present to us in the subjectively exciting zone of appeals; we realize it en route.)

Just as the good promised by the appeal is other than the appeal and significantly independent of it, the central intentions of the appellate subject are free in relation to the appeal's exerted charm. To be "brainwashed" or "carried away" is not to be the subject of an appeal. Nor can subjection to appeal simply coincide with the general carrying along of the subject in the ordinary flow of experience, earlier events leading to later events according to the momentum and form of a larger process. Appeals presuppose this ligature of experience, but their own peculiar requirement is not to prolong a flow. Even an overwhelmingly exigent appeal is presented as an "if" rather than a "then." The subject that *would* flourish with the appellant is still mainly a prospective subject; the quality of its existence is tasted but not wholly established in the reception of the appeal.

Since an appeal's success depends on the subject's concurrence with it, an appellant is always vulnerable, and an appellate subject is correspondingly responsible for the appellant as its upholder. The responsible subject is vulnerable in turn to developments that are determined by the appellant or that affect it. Obviously, there are great differences in cases; a peanut butter and jelly sandwich that appeals to me at lunchtime has a vastly different vulnerability than a person applying to me for a job. But we can trace the lines of the same general structure in both sorts of case. Representing the sandwich maker's effort to be of service (and, in the background, the efforts of plants to distribute their seeds), the sandwich needs to attract an eater just as a job applicant needs to inspire confidence in an employer. The being depends on that success in the sense that its effects in the world otherwise would fail to correspond with its genetic principles and form. I, encountering the sandwich or the job applicant, become vulnerable in turn: I may be subjected to an aroused but not satisfied hunger or the disappointing rapid loss of a tasty item as I consume it; I may regret sending an applicant away. The appellant is a blackmailer: "If you leave me, you will be a loser." In my immediate appeal-vulnerability, I implicitly confront issues of eventual real vulnerability, such as to hunger or work breakdown, or to a state of affairs that makes me sick or wastes my time.

The degree of experience-forming freedom that I retain in relation to an appellant is a variable that can powerfully affect our goodness for each other (although in an obvious, basic way the import of the appellant depends on my *not* being free of its claim, and its meaningfulness for me is in inverse proportion to my indifference to it).[7] Whether the well-being of the appellant and the appellate subject are really connected—whether there is what we will acknowledge as real need in the case, not merely the momentary stipulated dependency of the appeal—and whether the appellate subject is really under practical obligation to the appellant are different questions than simply whether an appeal will register as an appeal. But the experiential doorway to those issues is opened in every case by an appeal's presentation of the contingencies of partnership between the appellant and the appellate subject.

As an experiential doorway, an appeal is only ambiguously an "experience" by the standard of evidential fulfillment. Nor is an appeal a "value," whether intuited or constructed; the subject of appeal as such is not in command of experience to that extent.[8] Nor is an appeal a defined rule, a "norm," even if it often obviously implies more. Appeal experience is an entangling involvement with unknowns. An appeal could even lead to the undoing of an already-constituted experience (which is the point of appealing against someone's action, or against an earlier legal judgment in court).

Although an appeal is the promise rather than the delivery of a good, we assume for any acknowledged appeal the possibility of a real affinity between the appellate subject and the appellant, such that an actualized relationship *would* foster the flourishing or affirming of both under the aegis of the appealing form. It is through such assuming that our basic maps of possible goodness are drawn. There is always an implicit comparison and competition in the offer of flourishing: a good partner for me is better, offers more, than alternatives—perhaps even as much as a chance for one or both of us to be perfected or to surpass ourselves in some experienceable way. This means that the idea of all beings in the world actually appealing to a subject all at once is incoherent. Beings are appealing seriatim, even if sometimes in big bewildering bouquets. When appeals jostle against each other, the appellate subject must be somewhat unsettled.

In fact, we do perceive beings unsettlingly; composing a coherent good out of our responses to appeals is a great problem. Articulate approaches to this problem take the form of an argument (in which the assembled appeals are "claims") or a story. Within such a frame, each appeal's offer of good implicitly looks ahead toward a satisfactory conclusion. We are able simultaneously to accept and to relinquish active relationship with a particular appeal in good conscience, given that it points down a passable road. We realize a profound well-being simply in placing ourselves within a harmoniously composed appeal-world (even if we are only submitting to that world experimentally, as you might be trying out the conceptual mise-en-scène of a new philosophical work).

At stake for the subject with each new appeal is discovery and gain; with already-known appeals, rescue and retention. In a stranger's call for help, for example, I see both dimensions starkly: a new opening to relationship with an individual, and a familiar demand to protect human well-being and the fabric of interpersonal concern. So begins an interesting story, the human weight of which I already feel. If I construe the situation ethically rather than narratively, as an argument of general import, I see the same two dimensions in its basic syllogism. The claim of the major premise, "Human well-being should be protected," reminds me of an established appeal of the sort we call an ideal, in this case a responsibility to aid; the major premise holds appeal particularity to a minimum. The minor premise, "This person's well-being is threatened," presents the claim of the new particular that has captured my attention. Rational argument always aims to secure interintentional concurrence by marshalling the full force of broadly established generic appeals, and yet the significance of an argument always depends on its application, which requires that the occurrent appeal of the particular be lodged in the minor premise.

The link between appeal and goodness might seem to suggest that the class of appellants is not nearly as extensive as the class of identifiable phenomena, since much that is identifiable does not promise me good. I reckon with many beings toward which I am evaluatively neutral and many beings that repel or threaten me. Nevertheless, any being that figures in my experience in any way at all must in an important sense be attractive to me, for I would not notice a being if my attention were not in some way drawn to it, to start with, and then sustained by it, however briefly. Even if we think of experiencing in the most predatory way, with the subject as the active taker of information and the objects of experience as passive resources—or, alternatively, of the objects of experience as assailants and the subject as their helpless victim—we still must assume a "givenness" of the objects to the subject and an opening of opportunities of experience by them. Even the most misleading and exploiting appeal gives some sort of nourishment. Every being I am able to notice offers me a direction in which to aim my interest, and so, just insofar as experience as such is good, every being I can experience promises me good. Furthermore, every being I can experience poses for me a practical question of relationship. I have a part in determining the effect that the experienceable being will have on my life. (To lack that capacity is to be the victim of a serious disorder.) By coming to my attention, a being auditions for a role in what could be anything from obsession to dismissal.

But do beings really "audition"—or "offer" or "pose"? Does the anthropomorphism of such expressions betray an illegitimate assumption in calling objects of experience "appellants"? Conceiving meaningful experiences as encounters with the appeals of beings implies a component of meaningfulness that we can call "intrinsic," meaning that is *formed by* a being—to be accepted and answered by a free subject—as distinct from meaning that is produced just in the fulfillment of the subject's intentional proposals for experience. But does an ordinary experienceable being actually form? A being *is* centered, to be sure, insofar as it is formed and findable; but *does* it center—that is, does it maintain and manifest its own character?

I will address this question here only on the basis of the concept of meaningful experience and for the sake of elucidating that concept, not (except incidentally) as a problem in metaphysics and not as subject to the different treatments it would require in different scientific domains. I answer, then, that in whatever counts as meaningful experience of X, X has not only a bare identifiability but an integrity and even a propriety insofar as its properties hold together independently of the experiential subject's preferences and acts. On this basis it is possible to speak of "X itself." X can sustain the subject's attention and be the referent of questions about "X itself" because it is formative. To mark the extra dimension that a "meaningful experience" has in comparison with experiences that are registered only to be filed away, so to speak, one can distinguish between X's *fulfilling* a subject's intentions, which is necessary for X to take any place in experience at all, and X's *answering* a subject's intentions. In fulfilling intentions, X figures only as material of experience, whereas answering to intentions involves an active relationship between X and the subject. X's fulfilling intentions leaves open the question of what the subject's experience, in which X is one identifiable constituent, is *really of* or *about* (for example, X might be interchangeable with thousands of other items in an induction of a general pattern); X's answering intentions determines that the experience is of and about X, whatever else is going on. In the second situation, we speak of a call-like "appeal" of X in consideration of X's ongoing formation of our responsive apprehension of it. When a being is centrally understood, not as what we already know it to be, but rather as whatever it might turn out to be, it breaks into our experience in the way a heard call interrupts one's thoughts, as an entering wedge of further developments and questions—an "object" thrown against us.[9]

To represent beings that are not persons as appellants would amount to an objectionable anthropomorphism if experiences and principles specific to interpersonal relations were imported without justification into relations of a non-personal kind. But the idea that experienceable beings, as such, appeal—which, on my hypothesis, is inseparable from the idea of meaningful experience—does not rest on that mistake. A crucial difference remains between asserting that an experienceable being centers—that is, exists independently as a center of perceptible occurrence—and asserting that such a thing intends—that is, adjusts its own orientation in relation to other beings. To be sure, everything that we experience as alive or lifelike does adjust its own orientation responsively, but that is not a necessary condition for intrinsic meaning. The stony insistence of a stone is a kind of intrinsic meaning also. We can mean a great deal when we speak of "the stone itself" (though not as much as we can mean by personalizing a being).

The appeal of a meaningful being would be an act, according to the grammar of the verb *appeal*, yet I have admitted that the centering and relationship-enabling accomplished by a being, just as a being, is not any sort of intending overture. The act-aspect of meaningful experience that we turn to in speaking of an appeal might be conceived more accurately as an eventfulness.[10] A being "strikes" us, we say, or "gets" our attention; with this act-language we note that the meaningfulness of the being begins at a certain time and in a relatively abrupt way, with important effects thereafter. The initiation of our notice of the being is a sort of summons, for we experience an invitation to a relationship—insofar as a possibility of relationship is part of what is apprehended—and already a preliminary installation in that relationship, a changed life containing that relationship, and a prospect of seeing all this through.

The World of Appeals

As the foregrounding of a single being, an appeal brings an attractive simplification, vividness, and wholeness to a subject's experience—and this experiential resolution can happen in different, even conflicting ways. Suppose that ten people have been looking out from an observation deck at a mass of vegetation when at a certain moment they all see a bright yellow bird land in the bushes. One of the viewers, a physicist, goes on thinking steadily about energy fields without taking particular notice of the bird qua bird; another, a botanist, pursues an examination of plant relationships and fits the bird into the ecological system as a potential seed-carrier. The other appellate subjects, however, are birders, and theirs is the purest experience of appeal saliency as they are suddenly focused, alert and curious, engaged by the bird, eager to see what it will do next. From their perspective, the physicist and botanist miss the bird, while from the scientists' perspective, the birders overlook a phenomenal expression of natural principles and therein a larger, more enduringly important appeal.[11]

Is an appeal always a veil, then, as well as a revelation? Is there always loss as well as gain in an appeal's articulation of a world? The foregrounding of a being does always relegate other beings to the background, but we can distinguish between relatively mind-opening and mind-closing ways in which this can happen. From the perspective of the scientists in the bird example, the birders miss a larger, more complex object in their fascination with a smaller, simpler one. The vividness and wholeness in the bird jolt them in a way that narrows their awareness. Yet the birders are not all alike in this. Some look for birds, perhaps only for certain favorites, in order to enjoy a relatively simple, pleasurably intense feeling of color, form, and a personal bond with a fellow animal. Others are more interested in a larger system of ornithology. One of the birders in the group knows enough about the ecology of the area to see the plant system in relation to the bird, *through* the bird, as fully as the botanist is able to see the bird through the plant ecology. Another is a nature writer for whom the yellow bird's arrival will make an incident in a narrative. Each of these experiencers can manage the seductions of individual appeals in such a way as to participate in the weaving of a densely interesting world fabric. Thus, we may never assume without further examination either that an appeal discloses reality adequately or that it distorts it.

The power of an appeal goes beyond the surge of representational satisfaction in a vivid whole. It has larger essential themes of ontological depth and cosmological extension. When I am the subject of an appeal, I am made aware of a real relation of compossibility between myself and a being. This relation is an objective reality that has a past, a present, and a future. Existence and the world are revealed to have already been such that this being and I can coexist. We can coexist both in the sense that the existence of one does not preclude the existence of the other, and in the richer sense that the meaning or directedness of one is compatible with the meaning or directedness of the other. The emplacement of each being in all the categories and structural interconnections of reality is in play in this relating of meanings, for appeal is generalizing as well as individualizing: *this* bird appeals to me as *a* bird, an animal, a member of a natural system, and so forth, while I am appealed to not only "personally" but as a birdwatcher, a biologist, and so forth. With the preliminarily successful impingement of the appeal, it becomes possible to show how I and the other being can coexist. This showing may lead to new learning about what or who I and the other being are. (The ambitious worldview projects of religion and science foster perception of the appeals of individual beings as always also presenting the appeal of a universal order.) Besides information, a set of promises and questions for the future of our relationship has been introduced. I know that the relationship can never in the future be entirely stripped of meaning, yet no present judgments on the nature and significance of the relationship can be immune from revision. Nor can I control consequences. For all I know, the relationship may turn out to be a violently transformative one. The cheerful idea that I and the other are compossible does not imply much protection.

The world around the subject and the appellant, the comprehensive exhibition of compossibility, is shaped anew by each appeal. The appeal contains a humble "and": I am invited to live with all the beings I am already engaged with in any way *and* with the appellant, which is different enough from everything else to be noticeable and to affect the composition of the world. As an appeal establishes itself, however, the balance of power tilts toward the appellant. Now I am asked to accept the appellant, centrally, *and* all other beings as they fall into place around it. The appeal "makes a difference" touching everything. My life has a new center. Whether the life entailed by full affirmation of the other is as whole or wholesome as alternate lives remains to be seen, as does the degree of violence involved in my separation from life as it was. In any event, my new life does have a distinct orientation, and this is a fundamental good. When I am not in the presence of a foregrounded appellant, I lack the most meaningful way of taking bearings in a world.

If the objective theme of appeals is compossibility, the subjective theme is my own awakening. I am revealed to have already been, and to presently and prospectively be, so constituted and attuned that the appealing being can register in me, qualifying my intending, "reaching" me. But this qualification is enigmatic. In being drawn to the appellant, I experience a preliminary confirmation of my own existence in the relationship with the other, but I am also subjected to potentially upsetting questions pertaining to the true nature and prospect of the relationship. I do not know exactly what I am involved with. Indeed, insofar as another being is "given" to me to experience, that is, really released for me to possess in representation and so to characterize on my own initiative, I am separated and screened off from the "giver," which lurks outside of my experience "anonymously" (as Marion puts it).[12] Nor can I know exactly what the relationship's effect on my own character and quality of experience will be. *How* will I be "reached"? Perhaps I will be "claimed" in some fashion, or checked, or exposed. I may even be led to question whether any attribute that I usually associate with the pronouns "I" or "me" is real and understood rightly. Love or enlightenment may remake me drastically.

The negative implications of an appeal could turn out to be more important than the positive ones, depending on the actual career of a relationship or trajectory of an awakening. Chaos, extinction, and horror are essential larger themes of appeal as much as harmonious compossibility is.

* * *

To sum up our findings so far: the meaningful entry of a being into a subject's experience is at least implicitly solicitous and at least minimally attractive and therefore is aptly conceived as an appeal. A being's appeal is not the whole or the core but rather the active edge of its meaning: we locate the appeal in the event of a being's eliciting the attention of a subject. This event occurs on the appellate subject's edge also, in the sense that discoveries will be made regarding aspects of the subject that will be "reached" and thus stimulated or exposed. To reckon intently with appeals, then, is to think on the edge of experience as it occurs, open to what will develop both on the appellant's side and on the appellate subject's side. (This kind of thinking must differ greatly from any phenomenology, analysis, or speculative construction that is oriented to closing accounts with its objects.) At the same time, the meeting of the appellant's and appellate subject's edges makes a center and an orientation in life for the subject.

The various hallmarks of appealing that we have identified are menu items or recipe ingredients for meaningful as opposed to merely comprehensible or pleasant experience. To what extent appealing actually occurs and how the orientation established by one appeal reception will relate to orientations implied by other appeals are always real and open questions.

We have not yet explicitly acknowledged the ultimately riveting figure of appeal, the face, which reflects back to me my own form of life and so confronts me with a uniquely relevant vividness and wholeness and presents me with incomparably momentous issues of compossibility. More than a being, the face is a communicator. It perceives and ponders me; it formulates propositions that I could entertain and respond to. To appreciate this preeminent form of appeal, it is necessary to shift into the communicative frame of reference.

Communicated and Comprehensive Appeals

As we enrich our model of appealing by adding factors involved in the deliberate making of an appeal by a conscious communicator, let us bear in mind that the order of thinking we follow here reverses the actual order in which we find the meaning of our experience always already determined by communication.

A communicated appeal might consist of nothing but a self-positioning or posturing by the appellant to actualize or to inflect somehow the appeal that proceeds from her or his objective existence, as by standing in front of a man and staring at him to get his attention. A communicated appeal normally consists, in part, of this embodiment of the appeal by the appellant but also, in part, of something detachable from the appellant's actuality, namely, the message, a representation *about* and *of* some actuality or actualities. A person might appeal by crying, "Help!" or by saying at a meeting, "The union calls on the owner to address the issue of overtime pay," or by placing a magazine ad that shows seabirds killed by oil spills, or by leaving a ring under a pillow. In each case, a representation aims to bridge the gap between mere information offering and meaningful experience. As a representation *about* something, the appeal takes advantage of the possible generality and richness of symbolism. As a representation *of* an appealed-for, it projects some of the intrinsic attraction of a being. As a being in its own right, it projects its own appeal, as, for example, a well-wrought linguistic utterance projects the style and power of a complex gesture toward many possible interlocutors and referents. To the extent that the communicative appeal actually succeeds as an appeal, it "reaches" its hearer. To the extent that its success is that of an honest broker, it is an event of the meaningfulness of the appealed-for to the appealed-to. To the extent that it capitalizes on the powers of symbolism, it captures a large portion of the world and of the appellate subject's mind—conceivably even the whole of world and mind ("Listening not to me but to the Logos it is wise to agree that all things are one," ventures Heraclitus).[13]

Appeal mediated by communication can be infinitely indirect. If the stakes of appeal are the highest, it may be understood that the presentation of such an important appeal is *obliged* to be infinitely indirect. For example, the appeal of holiness to an orthodox Jew is mediated by a vast number of turgid Talmudic discussions of such topics as the conditions under which boiling milk is rendered unusable by contact with a particle of olive.[14] In a quite different but potentially complementary religious scenario, it is understood that access to the highest appeal is gained only by an extraordinary act (perhaps of "faith") apart from which the appeal itself cannot genuinely be heard. The extraordinary act must be solicited by extraordinary means of communication such as riddles, irony, or symbolism.

Communicators can never be certain that a communicative appeal will succeed. They must contend with the unresponsiveness of their audience and, on their own side, with limitations of their communicative ability, unresolved issues in motives and relationships, and the discouraging complexities of message formation. To overcome these problems, an appeal must succeed initially by impressing; it must be a *tremendum*. One yells "*Help!*" One doesn't merely ask, "When will overtime pay be forthcoming?"; one summons the company owner before the bristling bar of the whole union membership. One doesn't merely say, "Oil spills must be prevented"; one shows heart-wrenching pictures of oil-covered gulls. One doesn't merely say, "I love you," one offers a costly present. One doesn't merely say, "This wrongdoing must stop"; one threatens hellfire. Insofar as communicators have discretionary freedom in forming their appeals and are responsible for whether or not they succeed, they are obliged to express their appeals with maximum effectiveness. This implies, besides meeting the audience's basic intelligibility requirements, a continual escalation of appeals—as far (in the absence of countervailing factors) as shock tactics, whether in the form of an over-saturated direct appeal or as a provocatively oblique allusion. In a second phase, the sustaining of an appeal that has begun to succeed requires snare tactics, like the intriguing composition of a metaphor or picture, or an inescapable, illimitable dialectic generated by a concept or argument. The virtue of an appeal in this phase is to be captivating, *fascinans*.

Impressive and captivating results can be produced by communication processes for which no one individual is responsible, such as in the development of a language or of a language-like system of fetishized commodities, when the formation process is driven by differentials in the responses of the subjects involved. We can speak here, on the analogy of Darwinian natural or sexual selection, of communicative selection of appeals.

Imperatives are a class of designedly forceful appeals. The heightened appeal force in imperatives comes not from the impact of the appeal presentation's immediately presented qualities, but from a cognitive thickness of combined foreground and background in its sense. An imperative reminds the appellate subject of a somewhat determined order of things and presumes on the subject's commitment to that order. Disregarding the imperative would mean not merely turning away from an appellant but tearing oneself out of a fabric of relationship. The background consideration is appealing in its own right—or at least is ideally stipulated as appealing, so that we are prepared to respond to its appeal whenever there is need to do so.

Message appeals exploit an extra dimension of appeal-force in the generality of their symbolism. The generality within my own experience (according to which I perceive *a* bird as *one of* the birds, *one of* the animals, etc.) gets linked in the communicable sense of words to every other subject's actual and possible experience of generality. When I speak or make a judgment concerning a being, I cannot but refer universally in whichever contexts the sense of the term opens up.

The generality of words is motivated in the first place not solely by the sheer power of referring that they grant the subject, with an implied indifference to any particular object of reference ("bird" meaning "no matter which bird"), but also by the impressiveness and incontinence of their appealing ("bird" meaning everything to do with all birds, actually and potentially). This can be shown by a thought experiment. First, say the word *man* or *woman* with all the feeling and richness of experience you can bring to mind, and notice how the reverberations of the word reveal that you have placed yourself in the force field, as it were, of a vast and complex appellant. Then say any other common word, such as *chair* or *walk* or even *or,* in a similarly intent and open way. The reverberations will be weaker, probably, but they will be fascinating and they will lead into an infinity of possible permutations of experience. That is how words get their first force of meaningfulness; that is what we are estranged from when we come to feel that words are mere counters. The generality in the meaning of any word registers as a disclosure of an impressive structure of relevance (not redundancy) in the world.

Appeal communicating is distinctively incontinent. Whereas a flower simply blossoms, its appeal inherently restrained by its actual attributes, human poetry embellishes flowers endlessly. But it must be noted that in a Darwinian order of natural selection the difference between these two situations of appeal is not absolute or simple. The flower has indeed already become physically embellished in order to appeal more effectively to the plant's friends and enemies. That is why it is so red. Red! Even before humans painted their lips, they grew enticingly large, reddish, paintable lips. Any macro-organism exists as the product, in part, of its appeals. Such appeals, even if not consciously communicative, are subject to the exigencies of communication to such an extent that we can easily see the principles of attractiveness and incontinence at work among all living beings in their extremes of size, number, and surface design. Much of what we experience as the exuberance of nature is the fruit of this principle. Human culture is bound to be exuberant, likewise, insofar as its articulation is fostered by an analogous process of selection.

A great constraint on intentional communion that checks the incontinence of communicative appealing is the principle of sustainable fellowship among subjects. We explicitly invoke it as "reasonableness" or "fairness." Appeals that are not adequately affirming of their recipients and of the ensemble of possible recipients are liable to be overridden, sooner or later, by the appeal of this principle. Just as the *tremendum* and *fascinans* principles of attraction have a natural analogue and basis in natural selection, so the principle of fairness has an analogue and basis in ecological balance. Unlike the principles of attraction, however, the principle of fairness is categorically superior to other appeals. Fairness is not contingently dominant by virtue of a greater vividness or sweeter fit, leaving the question open for each succeeding moment as to which being shall hold the interest of the subject of appeal, but rather it presents itself as the *final* determination (or as an unconditional part of any total determination) of the subject's relations. The appeal of fairness has this distinctive force as a function of the way interintentional relationships frame the experience of the world that is had by interintentionally responsive beings. Fellow intenders affect the formation of one's own intentions centrally and comprehensively in three ways: (1) *originally*, determining one's identity according to what is called the "social constitution of the self"; (2) *most actively*, in that fellow intenders pose the most profound and extensive challenge to a subject trying to ascertain what is going on in any present moment; and (3) *ultimately*, insofar as the continuing concurrence of fellow intenders is a condition of the validity of any intention.

When a person speaks to me, then, I am confronted with a partly hierarchical, partly scattershot array of appeals, including the perceptible appeals of body, clothing, gesture, voice, and smell; the appeals of the beings that are represented by the message of the utterance and the appeals of the forms of the representation; organizing these, the practical appeals of the ongoing activity in which the encounter is embedded and of activities that are promised; ruling these, the specific inflection of the ongoing coordination of all intenders made by my interlocutor and myself together; ruling this, the principle of fairness as we understand it and other generally normative appeals that likewise subsist in actual intentional performances without being restricted to them. Appeals of this last kind belong to "objective spirit," according to the Hegelian conception, or "culture" as we more usually say.

The active edge of the meaning of human culture is found in the impressiveness, beauty, and fairness of life-organizing appeals we have developed that are commonly called *ideals*. We have given our ideals every possible appeal-power, embodying them in the most imposing and fascinating individuals, sanctioning them with the concurrence of whole communities, building up their material basis, guarding against their logical closure, and articulating them so intensively and extensively as to make them intellectually and practically inescapable. Our variously specified ideals of *justice* proceed more or less directly from the interintentionally binding appeal of fairness. *Truth*, a double-barreled general appeal of intellectual coherence and real disclosure— its theme, our togetherness with all real being and beings in our fullest self-conscious self-realization—is a superlatively strong ideal as well. (Augustine argued that truth compels our regard so strongly, with its unrestricted, perfectly reliable power to determine the character of beings and experiences, that we would have to accept it as our God if there were not a greater, necessarily truth-including God.)[15] Those who appeal to others to respect the truth bring a well-nigh irresistible claim to bear on their hearers, given the compelling premise that subjects are always in a healthier condition in engaging things as they are.[16] Submitting to the ideal of truth convenes us in a discipline.

As I stare off into space reflecting on the power and glory of the ideal of truth, a yellow bird flashes by and my eyes fly with it. A perceptual stimulus has momentarily interrupted the appeal of a grand ideal. I can also see at this or any other moment, however, that the categorically superior appeal of a best general way of having experience allows me, indeed requires me, to heed the appeal of a concrete being. The meaningfulness of this bird is amplified by the meaningfulness of truth, which we elucidate by the interintentional negotiations of a priori inquiry; in turn, the meaningfulness of truth is grounded by the meaningfulness of a bird, which is filled in by empirical inquiry. The structure holding both kinds of meaningfulness together is the realization of other beings' relevance to us and ours to them—not merely our disposition to feel that way about other beings or a general power of responding affirmingly to them or of opening to their self-giving (as with Marion's inflections of the subject as the "addressed," the "receiver," and the "gifted"), but the actual affecting or the prospects of affecting each other for better or worse that our experience of meaningfulness registers.[17] In this manner, we may conceive a world of meaningfulness accommodating all kinds of experience and inquiry, a world articulated, not ruptured, by the various transcendences of beings and intentions.

The Structure of Appeal Experience: Conclusions

We began a fresh elucidation of the question "How will we live?" by standing at the crossroads, so to speak, where a responsive subject encounters plural beings and possibilities. We abstracted from most of whatever might already be true of beings, relations, and events in order to attend to the new formation of all things in, and as a direct consequence of, appealing. What do we achieve by proceeding in this way?

In the first place, we allow for a certain dis-orientation. The essence of the appeal is to interrupt. The appellant is sovereign as surprise. Of course, this aspect of appeal experience could be exaggerated. A colorful bazaar world is not purely chaotic. Every appeal depends on already-established enabling structures of being, knowing, and valuing, as does the practically crucial possibility of harmonizing appeals. Still, appellant and appellate are supremely *interesting* versions of "object" and "subject" because they are constituents of openings in experience. Our powers are galvanized by participation in new-making. This activation of our powers is in itself part of our flourishing or good. (It follows that ideals of appellant being and appellate subjectivity are supremely powerful influences, even if not the only strong influences, on all our specifications of being and subjectivity.)

In a second respect, appeal does establish order and orientation, for the appellant being is superordinate to all else in the appellate subject's experience as long as the appeal holds sway. This occurrent experiential primacy of an appellant is not the same thing as real importance; obviously, I am most often appealed to by beings that are not really of the greatest importance for me, or for us, in principle. (We design and value special occasions in which appeal and real importance are understood to coincide—for instance, in the splendor of a wedding.) The difference between experiential and real preeminence is, in itself, both disorienting and orienting for the subject that is cognizant of it: disorienting because the good that is the point of the appeal cannot reliably be found within the appeal, but also orienting to the extent that the subject is able to take a position with respect to this very issue.

Appeal experience prompts the appellate subject to two empowering realizations. One is a critical recognition of the difference between appeal and goodness, which is a linchpin of practical intelligence and responsibility. The other is recognition of opportunities to participate in the constitution of structures that embrace and jointly amplify appeals and goods—to work out an understanding, for example, of the substance of the beauty and goodness of a beloved, and to enlarge one's practical commitment to the love. Ideals express and advance both sorts of realization. Their generality makes appellants virtually interchangeable with each other within classes and enables an intellectual positioning of classes of appellants within a larger cognizable scheme, which promotes the subject's critical freedom. But their generality also amplifies appeals and goods by providing for the richest possible relevance of all appeals and goods to each other in larger classes and schemes.

The specification of the *ultimate* ideal in principle, the ideal of ideals, is, on the philosophical drawing board, straightforward: the ultimate ideal must be the maximized flourishing of beings and relevance of beings to each other. But what could constitute maximal flourishing and relevance? What experience, argument, or story could make a concretely compelling specification of that abstract ideal? What real events and arrangements could satisfactorily address the great issues of compossibility that a great appeal must raise? Here enter religious suppositions as to the nature of a greatest appealing (a revelation), a greatest appellant (a divinity), a greatest appeal-content (holiness), a greatest good (salvation), and a greatest state of the appellate subject's realizing (devotion). Such suppositions must interest us as long as we are willing to be open to appeals, and they offer capstones for the rational architecture of ideals. But they threaten us in that they may be inadequate, false, and inept. And religious appeals come in ungovernably competing versions, each in its concrete presentation answering, rather than merely fulfilling, the intention to seek a greatest state, each eliciting a unique response in its concrete relation to a different appellate subject or community.

Is it possible to test and evaluate a greatest appeal? The devotees of a great appeal often deny this possibility. Yet an appellate subject retains freedom not only to decline or accept an appeal but also to taste its qualities while thinking comprehensively about its promised good. A religious ideal formally guarantees that there will be no dissatisfaction in carrying out this examination, but the examination itself is not suspended. We also know that appeals, powerful as they are to interrupt a flow of experience, are always interruptible in turn. One appeal's promise of access to a great good can be checked by the competing promise of another that may present a better prospect and track record of compossible thriving. Moreover, there is the possibility that subjection to rival appeals will produce more than a simple change or alternation of attentions and allegiances: a compelling argument or story may bring about a compounding of appeal-experience, so that it will become possible to consider and respond to multiple appeals in a spirit that is foreign to none of them. (Such has been the hope of many dialogues of "faith" and "reason" in Western religious reflection and also of much interreligious dialogue.) These are among the most important of all reasons to be optimistic about the feasibility of philosophy of religion or any other project, if there is another, of comparable evaluative ambition.

To place ourselves in the best position to evaluate the greatest appeals, we must trace as perspicuously as we can the most compelling shapings of the appellative structure of meaningful experience. I will venture to tell an appealing story about this. The story mainly unfolds in chapters 2–4 (complemented by the parallel chapters 6–8). I address a strategically chosen set of texts and thinkers, interrogating them selectively and assessing them in a deliberately maintained and not uncontroversial perspective (the *pneumatological* perspective of a subject or community whose paramount concern is pursuit of the greatest rightness in relations among beings). This approach is not the best way to do justice to the singular and complicated aims of each of these texts and thinkers or to the thick meaning of their cultural contexts. But it is still worth taking. Any student of these texts, thinkers, or cultures will be better equipped to engage any of them for having learned to appreciate their positions in the scene of appeal and attitude thinking. And no way of construing these positions could claim ultimate precedence over the pneumatological way.

two

Appeal in the Axial Age

Where can I flee from Your presence?
If I ascend to heaven, You are there;
if I descend to Sheol, You are there too.

—Psalm 139.7–8[1]

The ten thousand things ranged all around us, not one of them is worthy to
be singled out as our destination.

—Zhuangzi[2]

The Axial Age Revolution in Appealing

When we feel it necessary to try to establish our fundamental orientation, we appeal to great appeals like God, reality, humanity, the Earth, reason, love, and hope. Our appealing action has of course been shaped and to some extent aimed by a history. (Notice that I construe what we have been doing and are doing as an *action* rather than as, say, *activity*; I mean to speak purposefully and directively, though without trying to insist on a perfected mastery of our action or a perfected interpretation of it.) If we are to have the greatest possible lucidity in this supposed action of ours, we need an assessment of representative formulations of appeals, appeal situations, and appeal-power that have been made in our history, particularly those that have had "classic" force. In a corresponding phase of the second main part of the present work, I will develop an interpretation of classic attitude conceptions of the Axial Age (chapter 6). There I will aim to show more fully how the appeal ideal involves issues of response that must be interpreted in the category of attitude—concerning, for example, the inner determination of subjectivity that enables a Yahwist to face up to the lord of the universe and a Daoist master to be oriented to none of the "ten thousand things" but rather to "the boundless."[3] But many important considerations can be uncovered by tunneling from the appeal side, as it were, asking about models of appealing and inherent problems in appealing.

In this chapter I will concentrate on one part of the history of appeal thinking. My main premise is that *we inherit from Axial Age thinkers and texts an understanding of the possibilities of appeal that gears our directive thinking —our "normative" thinking, when in legislative mode—toward a supreme appeal.* Although the whole range of relevant data far exceeds the scope of this or any single study, since what is in question is nothing less than the structure of the appearing of meaningfulness, certain points can nevertheless be made strategically to frame larger issues pertaining to the ideal of supreme appeal. It will be useful for many humanistic purposes to acquire a structured, debatable overview of the cross-cultural intellectual and spiritual matrix in which classic philosophical and religious claims are made about the conditions of supreme meaningfulness.

* * *

The term "Axial Age" was proposed by Karl Jaspers to draw attention to the synchronous appearance in the mid-first millennium BCE of most of the foundational intellectual and spiritual teachers of the Old World civilizations— including Zarathushtra, the Hebrew writing prophets, the Greek philosophers, the Upanishadic sages, the Buddha, Mahavira, and the first great writers of Confucianism and Daoism.[4] What parallel social developments in the Old World civilizations enabled these religious and philosophical fruits to ripen together?[5] The rise of the new thinking probably depended on a combination of prosperity and disunity in the affected societies: at a time of serious threats to social order, there existed a class of people able to devote themselves to an ideal reformulation of good order. Subsequently, the new thinking could not have endured had there not been a complementary relationship between its conceptions of accessible ultimate reality and individual responsibility, on the one hand, and the governing strategies of the societies that officially adopted them, on the other.

Be all that as it may, a practical factor that was clearly of enormous importance in the formation of Axial Age appeals and attitudes was a new development of literacy. Overflowing from the authoritarian channels of state and religious business, often promoted by trade, literacy created a revolutionary communicative situation in which messages of "wisdom" or "truth" could travel freely and compete with each other for attention.[6] Relatively independent patrons could ask purveyors of wisdom for increasingly refined articulations of the conditions of worthy individual existence, even theories of *one* strategic adjustment of life that would solve all problems forever. Meanwhile, *any* free individual could influence the thinking of a public by publishing teachings, and *any* individual hearer could browse anonymously and latch onto ideas in an ideological marketplace—which gave a newly powerful sense to "freedom" and "individuality."[7] Our generally credible "philosophies" and "religions" (that is, "world religions") were born in this marketplace, and the reasons and revelations they offer still presuppose it.

Jaspers was interested above all in the relationship of the Axial Age to our contemporary existence. Why should the teachings of that time remain the axial "classics" around which our reflection continues to revolve? What is the significance of the fact that such teachings were generated in all the literate civilizations? Borrowing the premise of a center point of human history from the Christian "B.C./A.D." scheme, Jaspers claimed that the ideas and methods of the mid-first millennium BCE should be acknowledged as central and decisive for the kind of life that is most deserving of *any* human being's consideration and therefore as constituting the axis of a common world history (in a way that Europe's "modernity" does not).[8] For the radical questioning of the Axial Age breaks through the limits of custom and myth to bring about a direct confrontation between thinking individuals and Being as a whole. These thinking individuals—as modeled and challenged by the classic sages, philosophers, and prophets—experience a terrifying insecurity in the face of boundless possibilities from which they are no longer sheltered but also a new power and self-confidence in their thinking.[9] What would be the impact of such a development on the understanding of appeal? Or how might a new conception of appeal be instrumental to that development?

The dynamics of appeal seems to have been a prominent theme of communication fully as long as there has been thematic communication. Our oldest surviving stories make much of the presentations, rivalries, and consequences of appeals. The Mesopotamian epic of Gilgamesh, originating in the early third millennium BCE, dwells on the attention-worthiness of its hero ("Gilgamesh the tall, magnificent and terrible . . . his beauty was consummate") and his works ("He built the rampart of Uruk . . . See its wall like a strand of wool, view its parapet that none could copy!"), includes the gods' hearkening to human cries, pits female sex appeal and the charms of the city against the appeal of the wild life in Enkidu's seduction ("Every day [*in Uruk*] there is a festival . . . and there are harlots, most comely of figure, graced with charm and full of delights"), and motivates the adventures of Gilgamesh and Enkidu by their attraction for each other. The bitter lesson of the impermanence of all goods that strikes Gilgamesh when Ishtar, angry at him for spurning her, causes Enkidu's death, is finally confirmed in the theft of his remedy, the plant of immortality, by a serpent drawn by its scent.[10] Words like "sublime" or "imperative" or "poignant" will not be found in the epic, but it does not lack an appeal vocabulary: it speaks of beauty, shining, fragrance, and greatness. In its later part, it makes Gilgamesh move the hearts of those he meets with his "hollow cheeks."[11] Vision is an important modality of appeal, but the story is interested also in hearkening, smelling, and pondering. The ideal of justice is implied by an indictment of Gilgamesh for abusing his royal power in Uruk.[12]

We see the same limitation in the surviving Bronze Age literature of India. The vocabulary of appeal qualities is remarkably smaller than ours, even though much attention is paid to the seeing and hearing of what is impressive. *Rig Veda* hymns evince much interest in the stirring of the appellate heart, especially in hymns to the intoxicating soma: "Where there are joys and pleasures, gladness and delight, where the desires of desire are fulfilled . . . there make me immortal."[13] There is no absolutely privileged mode of appeal—the "Aryans" or "shining ones" are second to none in their appreciation of what shines, and the *Rig Veda* writers are known as "seers," but at the same time it is possible to construct a theology of sacred voice and sound from certain passages—nor is there any one wholly dominant appeal.[14] A hymn may greatly magnify a god, particularly Indra, but the relevance of the god's impressive qualities is always limited in being tied to specific actions and events in the god's legend and usually to specific practical contexts in the life of worshipers.

The Gilgamesh narrative does coordinate the various powerful appeals of charismatic characters like Gilgamesh and Enkidu, of sex, of urban civilization, of gods and goddesses, of adventure, and of immortality so that they make coherent sense together and even imply a major theme: life is best lived zestfully with friends but in any case must be lived subject to mortality and the assessments of justice. Thanks to this unity, the Gilgamesh epic is an impressive story. But the story's unity is not achieved by affirming a single dominant appeal. It entertains the possibility that immortality could hold such appeal, but this possibility is ultimately dismissed. What is affirmed is that we have to find our way amidst diversely potent appeals. As rival appeals vie for attention, so also appellate subjectivity is conceived as a manifold of engaged responsiveness: it would strike a jarringly modern note to be told something like "Enkidu found Gilgamesh appealing," implying that Enkidu weighs appeals in an inner center.

For the Bronze Age literary forerunners of what we think of as philosophy and religion, as for the Gilgamesh epic, it is axiomatic that human life is subject to many compelling appeals—many amazing apparitions of beauty, offers of power, incursions of scruple and regret. Is it not precisely this variety that makes life an interesting challenge? What could be more worthwhile than giving the fullest possible recognition to all the appeals that are powerful enough to dominate us and managing our responses to these appeals most adroitly? Hence, Bronze Age worship is polytheistic, and Bronze Age wisdom is transmitted in the form of a treasury of wise observations. Gods and teachings are situationally, but never universally, supreme. Appeal situations can be understood systematically—this is what divides civilized thinking from a completely open susceptibility to "momentary deities"—but there is no one master situation.[15]

The hallmark of an Axial Age appeal, however, is that it represents itself as supreme and comprehensive. In comparison with the ordered array of appeals in the Gilgamesh epic (or the Egyptian *Coming into Day*, or the Indian *Rig*

Veda, or the Chinese *Classic of Odes*), the new kind of appeal is more drastically unifying. Thus:

> Listening not to me but to the Logos [that is, the Word] it is wise to agree
> that all things are one. (Heraclitus)[16]

> He who knows the always-so has room in him for everything . . .
> To be of heaven is to be in Dao [that is, the Way].
> Dao is forever and he that possesses it,
> Though his body ceases, is not destroyed. (Laozi)[17]

> To the end that you may take thought, and . . . understand that I am he:
> Before me no god was formed, and after me none shall exist—
> None but me, Yahweh; beside me, none can grant triumph.
> (Second Isaiah)[18]

> The finest essence here—that constitutes the self of this whole world; that is
> the truth; that is the self. And that's how you are [*tat tvam asi*], Shvetaketu.
> (*Chandogya Upanishad*)[19]

The Logos (as controller of Heraclitus's "one"), the Way, Yahweh, and Brahman are inescapably compelling *once one understands*. Now there must be a
dominant intellectual modality of appeal, so that the appellate subject is free
from the contingency and diversity of sense experience. In the *Bhagavad Gita*,
an Axial Age addition to India's Mahabharata epic, the hero Arjuna is made to
see a blazing image of the uniquely full reality of divinity and to *tremble* before
it, but the scene is intended as a metaphor for a profound access of understanding; bodily sense alone could never establish that uniqueness and depth.[20]

What could have led in a specifically appellative way to this great simplification of positing a supreme and comprehensive appeal, which goes so much
against the grain of pluralistic appeal experience? Two noteworthy trends are
visible in ancient literature. They have deeply conflicting implications for the
meaning of a supreme appeal, and yet their conflict is often disguised, if not
actually mediated, by their intertwining.

1. One trend is clearly *intellectual:* the ancient sages participate in a
competitive refinement of reflection and explanation that leads to the discovery of positions of ever-greater intellectual leverage with ever-more-powerful
principles. In appreciating this evolution we should not dwell so much on the
technical advantages of rationalization that we overlook the sheer impressiveness of the intellectual discoveries. The leverage is exerted upon, not merely
by, the sages. Heraclitus submits to the Logos.

What the sages submit to transcends the world. Thus, response to a supreme appeal is an adventure of leaving the world. Gilgamesh arguably had
some implicit idea of attempting this adventure, only to be turned back by the
disappointingly ordinary gatekeeper, Uta-napishtim; Bronze Age Egyptians
already looked ahead to an encounter and reconciliation with a world-order-
ing principle of truth and justice, *maat,* upon their death.[21] One may wish to

interpret the realizing of *maat*, the Logos, the Way, Brahman, or the lordship of Yahweh purely as an event in the inwardness of the appellate mind, but however the locus of transcendence is understood, a crucial consequence for the appellate subject is liberation from worldliness. (Indeed, the question must arise whether the main point of submitting to a supposed supreme appeal is nihilistic—whether that intellectual affirmation expresses a resentful negation of the pulls of actual appeals.) The supreme principle will be tested in worldly experience, which it must successfully interpret, but its appeal-power is extraordinarily heightened by its independence and better-than-worldly simplicity.

The intellectual evolution of a transcendent supreme appeal can be traced in all the civilized literatures: in the Vedas, where early recognition of cosmic order (*rita*) and speculation on the seemingly unknowable origin of all things ripen into the Upanishadic affirmation of the essential Self;[22] in the Greek world, where Hesiod's systematic organization of older creation motifs in the *Theogony* is succeeded by the centralizing Ionian physics, starting with Thales' derivation of all things from water, and the imperatively unifying concepts of justice (*dike*) and destiny (*moira*) are taken up in the speculation of Anaximander and in the reflective tragedies of Aeschylus, Sophocles, and Euripides;[23] in classical Chinese writings, where Heaven as a universal structure of events displaces a high god;[24] and in the Hebrew Bible, where the Israelite god for whom earlier prophets speak is conceived in and after the Babylonian exile, as by Second Isaiah, as sole master of the universe. The purely intellectual motivation of these developments is not hard to recognize, since the Axial Age proposals cater directly to our reflective curiosity.

2. The other great trend of appeal consolidation in the ancient world is *practical* and primarily political. As governments attempt to control larger areas, binding culturally diverse and even inimical populations together, neither custom nor the forceful personality of a leader is sufficient to maintain good order. It is necessary to have rationalized law, to expand the charisma of an individual monarch into the institutionalized glory of a regime, and to anchor government in a view of reality that is correspondingly centralized.

The unification of Upper and Lower Egypt in the third millennium BCE, for example, was supported by a remarkable theological declaration that all Egyptian gods are derived from Ptah, a god associated with the new capital of Memphis. This proposal accommodates the divine rulerships of Horus and Seth and the contributions of Atum, Thoth, and Osiris within Ptah's work as a primal thinker and speaker of all things. To exercise this hegemony over the sprawling array of Egyptian religious appeals, including world-creator claims for Atum, Ptah must be positioned in an abstract, philosophically interesting space, virtually equated with "heart" and "tongue" as general principles: "So were all the gods born . . . for it is through what the heart plans and the tongue commands that every divine speech has evolved."[25] In the Vedic literature of India we can see how priests' appreciation of what they themselves do led similarly to an absolutizing of the appeal of "what the heart thinks and the tongue commands," "brahman" as word of power or prayer coming to be identified with Brahman as ultimate reality.[26] But this parallel idea was not so directly coupled with the fortunes of monarchy, though it undoubtedly helped to maintain the social privileges of the north Indian priestly class. In the culture of dynastic Egypt, as generally in the ancient Near Eastern states, the politics of monarchy was more dominant.

Another Egyptian text famous for its philosophical and religious interest, Akhenaten's proto-monotheist hymn to the solar divinity Aton, was composed to strengthen royal authority against the priests of Amun and other cults during the fourteenth century BCE. In the hymn, Akhenaten's enthusiasm in beholding a universal principle of beneficent power is inseparable from his self-presentation as preeminent among humans:

> You yourself are lifetime, one lives by you.
> All eyes are on [your] beauty until you set,
> All labor ceases when you rest in the west.
> When you rise you stir [everyone] for the King,
> Every leg is on the move since you founded the earth.
> You rouse them up for your son who came from your body,
> . . . the Lord of [Upper and Lower Egypt] . . .
> *Akhenaten* . . .[27]

As the unique "son of God," Akhenaten's entitlement to political deference is refracted through and amplified by the glory of a paramount divinity. The political point of the hymn requires that its appeal-content be predominantly worldly; it dwells on human experience of the day-night cycle, animals and plants, procreation, farming, and geography. When it approaches a transworldly plateau of insight into the essence of life, the that-by-which-life-is-possible—"You yourself are lifetime, one lives by you"—it does not press further toward transcendental logic in the manner of Heraclitus or toward metaphysical substance in the manner of the *Chandogya Upanishad*; instead, it veers immediately back to the world to confirm and expand on its political relevance.

As the sun shines on all Pharaoh's subjects, so the same sky or "Heaven" embraces and stipulatively unifies all subjects of the ancient Chinese government, according to a theory offered by the Zhou rulers to justify their displacement of the Yin (Shang). A Zhou ode to the legendary sage-king Wen shows the same mixture of philosophical and political advantage, for a predominantly political purpose, in the use of sky appeal:

> King Wen is on high; oh, he shines in Heaven!
> Zhou is an old people, but its Mandate is new . . .
> The Mandate is not easy to keep . . .
> Display and make bright your good fame,
> And consider what Yin had received from Heaven.
> The doings of high Heaven have no sound, no smell.
> Make King Wen your pattern, and all the states will trust in you.[28]

The "Mandate of Heaven" that confers legitimacy on every Chinese imperial government lacks tangibility (sound or smell)—it is *abstract* so that it can stand *above* claimants to cultural and political authority in the right way, warranting some against others, impossible to challenge in turn.

Somewhat different political factors push the Israelite figure of Yahweh toward a comparable abstract comprehensiveness. First there is the heritage of wandering; Yahweh makes surprising appearances to the patriarchs as the same god who is remembered to have appeared under different circumstances: "I am Yahweh, the God of your father Abraham and the God of Isaac," he informs Jacob in a dream.[29] Next there is the problem of Israelite weakness in relation to neighboring peoples; a god more concretely correlated with Israel could not be expected to overcome the might of Egypt, for example, so that it is crucially reassuring when Moses' appellant defines himself enigmatically as "I am who I am."[30] Finally, there is the federalism of the Israelite tribes assumed in the old covenant formula, "Hear, O Israel, Yahweh is our God, Yahweh alone." Yahweh overarches tribal differences without canceling them.[31]

In spite of their abstractness, the discourses of Heaven and of Yahweh focus relentlessly on the worldly actions that must be performed—acts of filial and civic piety, of honest work, of traditional sacrifice—if good order is to be sustained, and so they revolve around the worldly administration. The appeal of the divinity is yoked to the idealized splendor of the king. This approach is intended not, of course, as an idolatrous reduction of divinity, but for the sake of practicality and responsibility: only as subject to the commands of a prime agency are humans drawn fully into the work of the best world-making; only as subject to the judgments of a prime court are all humans fully accountable for their actions. For purposes of devotion, the divinity itself is addressed as the ultimate and most real ruler, either through the instrumentality of the human king or independently. The worldly axis of collective life, in any case, is the government. The exigencies of government fund the general understanding of the divinity's activity; the divinity may be identified as a supreme appellant of the kind that a king is, personally commanding and calling to account. The appeal is powered by the perception of the reins of the whole campaign of life being gathered into the hands of one agency:

> In ancient times those who created writing took three horizontal lines and connected them through the center to designate the king. The three horizontal lines represent Heaven, Earth, and humankind while the vertical line that connects them through the center represents comprehending the Way. As for the one who appropriates the mean of Heaven, Earth, and humankind and takes this as the thread that connects and joins them, if it is not one who acts as a king then who can be equal to this [task]? Therefore one who acts as king is no more than Heaven's agent. He models himself on Heaven's seasons and brings them to completion. He models himself on Heaven's commands and causes the people to obey them. (Dong Zhongshu, 2nd century BCE)[32]

With this sort of supreme appellant one keeps faith. This sort of supreme appellant is trusted for one's salvation. This sort of appellant prevails over others by imposing the conditions of the appellate subject's partnership with it on that subject's dealings with any other being. "He who has put himself in the wrong with Heaven has no means of expiation left" (Kongzi).[33] The partnership is understood on the model of the strongest possible family tie, the parent-child or marriage relation: "I fell in love with Israel when he was still a child; and I have called [him] my son ever since Egypt," professes Yahweh.[34]

It is quite otherwise with the supreme appeal that is formulated through an intellectual evolution. This appeal maintains its supreme position by explaining; it alters the meaning of any rival appeal so as to bring it under its own principle. It can have massive worldly implications—as the great simplifications of the Ionian physicists were pregnant with natural science, for example—but it is not intrinsically practical in the way the politically formulated supreme appeal is. It is activated primarily in reflection and in reflective communication, both of which depend on relative immunity from worldly concerns. As it is not directly practical, neither is it directly personal. The exposure of the appellate subject to the appellant being involves neither loyalty nor hope but only access to the rewards of clear and consistent perception.

One can imagine stark conflict between these two types of supreme appeal, as perhaps in a militant Yahwist exhorting a reclusive Vedantist to pitch in with the Mosaic social project (buoyed by hope for perfect success in the day of a Davidic messiah) while the Vedantist calmly unravels each of the Yahwist's claims as a species of world-illusion. Conflicts like this do actually occur in various guises. But combinations of the appeal forms are common as well. Loyalty to Yahweh is bolstered by ontological, cosmological, and axiological reflection; clear perception of Brahman is guarded by loyalty to a historical and functional community.

A notably smooth blend of supreme appeal motivations underlies the Chinese Axial Age philosophies of Confucianism and especially Daoism. These schools of thought took over the political concept of the mandate of heaven but modulated the discourse on legitimate kingship to a discourse on righteous and enlightened life as accessible to any thinking individual. The king's task of managing worldly affairs remains a featured topic, but with the complete generalization of the practical point of application it becomes possible for a reader of the *Daodejing* to become wholly absorbed in the deep interpretation of reality. "Dao never does, yet through it all things are done. If the barons and kings would but possess themselves of it, the ten thousand creatures would at once be transformed"[35]—in such a formulation it is hard to determine whether one or the other of the two major types of supreme appeal is dominant. It sounds both philosophical and political. Is it equally impressive philosophically and politically? Could it be?

We can address this question by examining the structure of such an appeal's prospects for success. To be supremely comprehensive, an appeal must relate to the whole of meaningful experience. This relating involves an inside-out extension of the appeal to the rest of experience and an outside-in centering of all experience on the appeal. It is characteristic of the intellectually motivated supreme appeal to impress us most acutely in its extension, as it explanatorily projects its forms on the world; the referring of actual experience back to it as time goes on is its test phase, more sober than enthusiastic. Meanwhile, it is characteristic of the politically motivated supreme appeal to impress most acutely in its centering, that is, in the prime agent's gathering of the reins of the worldly campaign, and to be tested in the projection of that agent's purposes and strategies to new territories. Thus we can ask whether the *Daodejing* waxes in appeal-power more in the extension of principle or more in the centering of practice. It is clear in this case that the answer depends on the hearer. One hearer could be a metaphysically fascinated subject of intellectual appeal, while another could be a politically ambitious subject of practical appeal.

The intellectual appellate subject is disengaging from the actual world, while the practical appellate subject is plunging into it. These opposite actions cannot be explicitly intended at the very same time. Thus the blending of supreme appeals in the *Daodejing*, or in any other teaching in which these two kinds of appeal can be found, corresponds, not with a unified consciousness in the appellate subject, but instead with an alternation. The teaching will provoke debate between representatives of the philosophical and the devout perspectives; it will sustain oscillations within individual minds. Any formula that tries to consolidate the supremacy of an appeal by building a bridge over the opposition of these strategies of comprehension—"God is great, [and] God is good"—must contain at least implicitly a linking "and" that discloses the opposition.

This irreducible divergence of supreme appeal rationales introduces the broader topic of the potentially very serious difficulties that supreme appeal thinking makes for itself.

Classic Issues of Supreme Appeal

In an open marketplace of communicative appealing, supreme appeals are sure to be formulated, and yet maintaining a supreme appeal is not easy. It will be useful for future reference to survey the more important problems inherent in that premise that the classic supreme appeal proponents are obliged to wrestle with.

1. *The problem of adequate representation of the appellant by the appeal.* A major Bronze Age appellant was typically understood as a deity; a deity was represented as an extraordinarily powerful agent in narratives and a noteworthy physical presence in pictures. For example, Egyptian *maat* was portrayed as a queen wearing a special ostrich feather that she used to weigh the

hearts of the dead in a scale of righteousness. Such imagery was always palpably suitable, for the particular thrust of the representation could be seen as corresponding to the thrust of the principle or power represented—as in this case the feminine majesty of Maat brings home to her viewer the integrity of truth. Obviously there were discussions among patrons, priests, and artists about better and worse ways to portray gods, but it would be foolish to denounce a given story or picture as inadequate when virtually any representation (if not perversely designed) gives its audience a fair chance to attend to the appellant it represents.

The question of adequacy cannot be handled so easily with a purportedly supreme appeal, however. Compared with the gods of polytheism, the supreme appellant is more remote from worldly qualities, more ethereal in presentation, necessarily the object of a more abstractive work of understanding. Every finite being fails to tally with it in a most important way. Without the checks and balances of polytheism, a mistake about such an appellant can have more serious consequences. We can be hurt more by our intellectual and communicative limitations in this situation. To attain what seems like a necessary minimum of concreteness in our supreme reference point, we might lapse into a totalizing kind of idolatry much more dangerous than idolatry can ever be on the premise of competing great appeals.

Axial Age teachers acknowledge these problems with a new rhetoric of circumspection. "The Way that can be told of is not an Unvarying Way," cautions Laozi.[36] "Of the Logos which is as I describe it men always prove to be uncomprehending," says Heraclitus.[37] In Second Isaiah, Yahweh removes himself from our grasp: "To whom can you compare me or declare me similar? . . . As the heavens are high above the earth, so are my ways high above your ways."[38] The Upanishadic insight is said to be beyond the ken of the learned class.[39]

The claim of the supreme appellant cannot be straightforwardly and completely apprehended; naive trust in any concrete token of the supreme appeal is a pitfall that must be avoided. Moreover, the apparent good promised by the appeal can go sour: the ancients came to realize that the astrological interpretation of heaven's appeal spawns an oppressive fatalism, for example, and moderns have come to realize that the monarchist interpretation of the practical appeal of unified government is closely allied with sexism.[40] (The intellectual appeal of the autonomous individual subject may have a sexist affinity as well, though this is more controversial.)[41] We are best advised, therefore, to understand our relationship with the supreme appeal as a journey on a way to a conclusion that cannot yet be completely specified. In a simile used by the *Chandogya Upanishad*, the reception of the supreme teaching is like having bandages removed from one's eyes after being led away from Gandhara; at that point one does not yet see Gandhara, but one is able to ask one's way there.[42] "*Phusis* [reality] is accustomed to hide itself," says Heraclitus, implying that the Logos-oriented philosopher is in the hunt for truth rather than in possession of it.[43] What could be seen as a discrediting unreliability in supreme appeal is made a dynamic and authenticating principle within it.

2. *The problem of adequate response by the appellate subject.* How can an appellate subject be authentically captured by a transcendent appellant? How can the right journey into mystery be discriminated from wrong ones? Appellate subjects can be sure they are on the right journey if they apply the right *algorithm* of interpretation to their experiences. "Asking one's way to Gandhara" might involve the cultivation of extraordinary states of consciousness as in Indian disciplines, rational or empirical inquiry as in Greek philosophy or Daoism, classical scholarship in the Confucian sense, or prophetic attention to a covenant with the lord of the universe in the Israelite manner. Each of these very different modes of intellectual discipline attests the comprehensiveness of a supreme appeal by applying itself to experience unlimitedly and rewardingly. Commitment to the supreme appellant becomes inseparable from commitment to the discipline; the ideal of the discipline can be the supreme vehicle of the supreme appeal. The most successful discipline will enact and prove the superiority of that appeal in every situation by trumping finite appeals and exposing defects in rival claimants to appeal supremacy.

Axial Age texts offer models of authentic appellatehood also in the dimension of style: on the surface, the riddling wit of the Daoist sage, the Confucian's enthusiasm for learning, the intellectual luxuriance of the Upanishadic writer, the dialectical tenacity of the Greek philosopher, the mordant misanthropy of the Hebrew prophet whom Israel continually disappoints; at a deeper level, the fundamental attitudes achieved and prescribed by the model appellate subjects. A strong style is requisite because of the exceptional demand and vulnerability that a supreme appeal imposes on a subject. Style enables the teachers to uphold their own appellate position and then mediates that advantage to their audience. If the prescribed style resonates with impressive individual style, we see that individual freedom and distinctiveness need not be annihilated by subjection to such an overwhelmingly imposing appellant.

An algorithm and style that are understood as universally sustainable, "objectively valid" in a stronger sense than would otherwise be available, can sponsor high-handed and brutal treatment of those who disagree. Avoiding this pitfall requires clarity about the relation of appellate subjects to real good and to the real inclusiveness of the appellate community.

3. *The problem of the appellate subject's relation to the promised good.* The gap between an appeal token or moment of appeal and the shared flourishing that the appeal promises is extremely large when the appellant is transcendent. This problem is partly solved in the projection of a strong subjective style by the teacher in the role of model appellate subject. Being like Kongzi, for example, seems a good life. But the *Analects* themselves acknowledge that Confucian life, even though it is confidently geared toward the greatest gen-

eral flourishing, does not necessarily produce all the flourishing one might wish for in a particular situation. "Wealth and rank are what every man desires; but if they can be obtained to the detriment of the Way he professes, he must relinquish them. Poverty and obscurity are what every man detests; but if they can only be avoided to the detriment of the Way he professes, he must accept them."[44] In fact, Axial Age teachers are often represented as persecuted, which has the double rhetorical advantage of proving the toughness of their way of being and of dramatizing the disparity between the supreme appellant and the ordinary world. Appreciating the supreme appellant requires that one reckon goodness more deeply (in heart and mind) and more extensively (in the cosmos and in history) than human subjects ordinarily do.

The most persecuted of all Axial Age teachers as a class seem to be the writing Hebrew prophets, for theirs is the most vividly, turbulently political version of supreme appeal. They are in constant jeopardy in relation to their fellow citizens, their rulers, rival prophets, and events generally because the algorithm of their appellate journey involves enforcing norms of righteousness, love, and covenant history upon actual decisions that their contemporaries are making or trying to make. The world's uncooperativeness forces great inconveniences and indignities on prophets—the exile of Elijah, Hosea's marriage to a harlot, Jeremiah's yoke-bearing, Ezekiel's 390-day prostration, and the affliction of Second Isaiah's "suffering servant" representing the historic affliction of the whole people of Israel as the servant of Yahweh.[45] The crucifixion of the Christian savior seems to risk this reverse-credibility of supreme appeal by pushing it to an extreme, yet the flourishing of Christianity (also with its cult of martyrs) proves there can be great power in contrasting actual evil with postulated good.

4. *The problem of the appellant's ontological location.* The supreme appeal's promised good cannot be fully meaningful to me if I cannot understand how in principle an appellate subject comes into real relation with the supreme appellant. Even if we all agree that the supreme appellant belongs on an ontologically extraordinary "level"—say, as Creator rather than one of the creatures, or as Being rather than one of the beings, or as Emptiness rather than any sort of fulfillment—we will still have important uncertainties about how to find it and respond to it, attenuating its appeal, if we do not make a determination of *where*, in some deeper-than-spatial sense, it is. Are we always already in relation with it? Is it most properly the real correlate of an *intensive* experience, like a brilliantly composed picture, as a contemplative would suggest—a present possibility? Or is it most properly the real correlate of an *extensive* experience, like a vast piece of music, as a historically minded prophet might suggest—a goal to work toward, hope for, continuing an action already under way? If it calls from the past, does it call from a stabilized past or a restless, haunting past? If it calls from the future, does it call from an excitingly open future or a prefigured future?

The primary rubrics for the appellant give important but sometimes misleading clues in this regard. "Creator," for example, seems to locate the Abrahamic God in the ontological *background* as a first cause of all that we experience and value.[46] The central positive response to such a god would be gratitude and a practical concern for continuity. And ancient Israelite theology does run in this channel in repeating its assertion that Yahweh created the nation of Israel by leading them out of Egypt and giving them their laws. "I [Yahweh] am your God who brought you out of the land of Egypt, the house of bondage: You shall have no other gods beside Me," begin the Ten Commandments.[47] But the classic Hebrew prophets cite this creation as an auxiliary consideration for their more urgent appeals relating to ethical and political possibilities of the moment and sometimes also to messianic hopes for the future. Second Isaiah, for one, recalls the storied power of Yahweh over the waters of the Red Sea primarily to lend force to his optimism about an imminent restoration of Israel:

> Thus said [Yahweh], who made a road through the sea and a path
>   through mighty waters,
> Who destroyed chariots and horses, and all the mighty host . . .
> Do not recall what happened of old, or ponder what happened of yore!
> I am about to do something new; even now it shall come to pass,
>   suddenly you shall perceive it:
> I will make a road through the wilderness and rivers in the desert.[48]

The apocalyptic strain in later Hebrew prophecy moves the apparent site of divine power farther off into the unknown future, its openness all the more impressively determined by detailed imagery, as in Ezekiel's description of a last battle against evil in the oracle of Gog and Magog.[49] But this is not the only biblical trend: the ripe reflection of the book of Job most crucially locates God in the past, for the weightiest part of the answer Job receives lies in God's rhetorical question, "Where were you when I laid the foundations of the earth?"[50]

An analogous uncertainty helped to motivate classic Chinese debates on the Way of Heaven. Does right response to Heaven consist primarily of acknowledging and respecting a continuity with the past of the ancestors (as a traditionalist appeal to the "rites" implies), or of actualizing the moral possibilities of human nature in the present (as Kongzi and Mengzi argued), or of building an ideal society (as the Legalists thought)?[51] Since it is proverbial that Chinese Heaven "does not speak" to us directly, we are thrown on our own resources in determining how to comport ourselves under Heaven's appeal.[52]

It is easy to say formally that an ultimate appellant must saturate all meaningful ontological locations. But the supreme appeal may not actually be able to register so fully—as, for example, with the end of accepted prophecy in the late biblical period, Yahweh disappeared from the arena of live present encounter in one important way. Even apart from limitations of this sort, it is unclear how human appellate subjects could act coherently on so broad an understanding, and it remains debatable whether one such location ought to dominate or even preclude the others.

5. *The problem of the inclusiveness of the appellate community.* The supreme appeal ought to be everyone's supreme appeal. To some extent this issue is addressed by the transcendent perfection in the conception of the appellant. If Yahweh, for example, is understood to be ruler of the entire universe, then necessarily Yahweh is the rightful lord of every possible appellate subject. Or if Heaven is the way all things spontaneously go, then no one could be exempt from its pattern. There is a vital communicative concern, however, that everyone understand and respond rightly to this one appellant— supposing a spiritual linkage between the teacher and all fellow subjects, or even a merely social linkage—without a guarantee that everyone will be capable of apprehending the appeal.[53] On the contrary, the very notion of a certain mandatory discipline seems to guarantee that supreme appeal insiders will be divided from outsiders, even within a single culture that notionally pledges itself as a unit to right piety or right reason.[54]

Heraclitus can be taken as proposing that "the one" is inherently what people can understand in common; the quest for consensual objectivity and the journey to the supreme appellant are identical. This is a great procedural strength of "logic" as Logos-appeal. But the use of logic does not actually produce an impressive consensus on important matters. The history of philosophy makes logic look more like a framework for chronic disagreement than a royal road to agreement.

The Confucian and Israelite programs reach for the appropriate ideological inclusiveness by making a point of conserving traditions. Kongzi references the ancient "rites" and the sage-kings of yore, Yao, Shun, and Yu; a "covenant theology" that forms the ideological backbone of Israelite prophecy is woven of reminders of divine appeals made in connection with Noah (the covenant of the rainbow with all humanity), Abraham (the covenant to sustain the people of Israel), Moses (the covenant of laws), and David (the covenant to sustain the kingdom).[55] Analogous to the Israelite four-covenant scheme is the four-yoga scheme of Hinduism as classically discussed in the *Bhagavad Gita*, where a certain preeminence is accorded to the way of devotion (bhakti yoga) but valid places are granted also to the ways of intensive self-control (raja yoga), philosophy (jnana yoga), and the fulfillment of worldly duties (karma yoga).[56]

What about *social* inclusiveness? The classic teachings of supreme appeal all have the revolutionary feature that they can be read as available and applicable to any human being in principle—or so they are commonly read today— but were they actually aimed at all human beings? In the Axial Age civilizations, awareness of the supreme appeal became part of the social standard of an educated person, but that standard was inseparable from restrictions of literacy and leisure, firstly in the specialized activity of the Axial Age teachers and their followers, and secondly as those teachings were taken up by a ruling elite. The earliest Axial Age thinkers formed small countercultural groups within or at the margins of their societies. There is evidence of participation by women, especially in Greek and Indian philosophy, but not of a sincere or effective program to overcome sexual inequality.[57] The Hebrew writing prophets give the impression that the whole people of Israel is continually confronted with Yahweh's self-revelation, but even though prophets did preach publicly, it seems most likely that serious monotheist theology was reserved to the same small circles that transmitted the prophetic texts, analogous to the early cells of philosophers and seekers in China, India, and Greece. The transcendent supreme appellants recognized by these small communities were conceived in such a way as to sustain the communities against the mainstream in their incongruousness—to sustain them, in effect, outside the world, which made them quietist as well as radical, esoteric as well as universalist. The key appellate subjects were, in their own estimation, the very ones who had taken up relationship with the extraordinary appeal. The transpersonal understanding of goodness they reached remained in their custody.

Not until the mass movements of proselytizing Judaism succeeded by Christianity, bhakti Hinduism, Mahayana Buddhism, and Islam did a presumption for unfettered sharing of supreme appeal begin to be effective. But the ideally catholic communities created by these movements have not been able to escape the insider/outsider division created by the exigencies of discipline on the one side and unreduced social inequalities on the other. They have had to concede the imperfect inclusiveness of the appellate community and rationalize it by a theory of multiple truth—asserting, for example, that divinity must be understood differently by the educated, using reason, than by the uneducated, relying on imagination—or by a law of karma that balances opportunities for enlightenment across a succession of lifetimes.[58]

6. *The problem of the inclusiveness of the appeal.* A supposed supreme appeal that simply eclipsed the appeals of worldly beings or required total insensitivity to other appeals would produce objections: how could this appellant be attractive and promise good in a way that has *nothing* to do with how other beings are attractive and promise good? Or how could the attraction and goodness promised by this appellant really be greater than the whole sum of attraction and goodness promised by *all* other appellants or the largest compossible set of such appellants? Some otherworldly ideologies, including early Christianity and Buddhism, are able to draw paradoxical strength from their categorical rejection of worldly appeals. (Accordingly, they are denounced by some observers as world-hating.)[59] But most of the durable candidates for supreme appeal meet these objections by including the appeals of finite things within the infinite appeal—by discovering the divine harmony of Beauty in all things insofar as they are beautiful, as in Platonism, or the grace of a Heavenly Way, or a creator God in all worldly beings.

[People] supposed that either fire or wind or swift air,
or the circle of the stars, or turbulent water,
or the luminaries of heaven were the gods that rule the world.
If through delight in the beauty of these things people assumed them to
    be gods,
let them know how much better than these is their Lord,
for the author of beauty created them.
And if people were amazed at their power and working,
let them perceive from them
how much more powerful is the one who formed them.
For from the greatness and beauty of created things
comes a corresponding perception of their Creator.
    (The Wisdom of Solomon)[60]

The imperative of inclusion suggests an agenda for systematic cosmology in Axial Age traditions. But the imposition of the formula of inclusion on the subordinate appeals tends to homogenize them and mask the actual appellants. For us there is historical charm in reading a medieval breviary account of how various species of animals exemplify God's wisdom and love, for instance, yet modern naturalist work on animals opens up to much wider, more interesting horizons. Ironically, a community of supreme appeal becomes dangerous precisely in the apparent success it has in giving substance to its assumption of inclusiveness. The world it sees is the whole real world; the history it is able to tell is the whole of meaningful history; the membership it can imagine exhausts eligibility. The humility enjoined by the Axial Age sages is always liable to be overbalanced by the urgent-seeming work of filling in an appearance of all-inclusiveness.

Another problematic side of the inclusiveness of a supreme appeal is that it necessarily includes too much reality, evil as well as good; an appeal of this form should perhaps be seen as a sinister seduction rather than as a gateway to true flourishing. According to a latter-day polytheist, John Cowper Powys, "Our attitude toward the First Cause need not be religious. It *ought not* to be so, unless we are consciously forgetting the evil side of this Ultimate Being and thinking only of its good side. It is best to worship the 'little gods' and defy the First Cause. Thus, what we should really aim at is to become idolaters."[61] In spite of much mythological and theological attention paid to the problem of evil in Zoroastrian and Abrahamic monotheism, the implied acceptance of evil remains an important limitation of God's appeal.

7. *The problem of abstractness dissolving appeal.* A striking feature of Akhenaten's new monotheist iconography is the privileged position it grants the king himself, as though the real upshot of the clearing out of lesser appeals on behalf of a highly abstracted supreme appeal might be the destruction of external appeal altogether. An Egyptologist observes of a typical image in the Akhenaten style:

In the old type of scene in which [the king] and the deity faced each other on either side of the rectangular frame, a balance was preserved among all the elements, human or inanimate, which went into the makeup of the vignette. Now, however, after the metamorphosis of the god and his gravitation to the top of the scene in the form of an unobtrusive disc, the king's figure remains the largest single element in the scene and, in addition, he now occupies the central position. All eyes, therefore, naturally focus on him, and that is precisely the intent of the arrangement.[62]

There is a similar implication, though at a higher level of abstraction, in the Qur'an's story of the birth of monotheism: Abraham sees the beautiful stars set, then the more beautiful moon, then the most splendid of all heavenly bodies, the sun, and concludes that no visible thing can be worthy of worship, only Him who created everything.[63] What holds center stage in the end is Abraham's own judgment, apart from any being actually appealing to him.

The problem of abstractness might be seen as an alternate aspect of the previously discussed problem of adequately representing a supreme appeal. To distrust any concrete token of the supreme appellant is to be driven back to the power of our understanding as a check on perceptual or imaginative credulity. But it is also to be driven back to our own understanding as the one occupant of supreme appeal space that cannot be dislodged—in other words, to be driven into our own embrace, dissolving the difference between appellate and appellant. Without a difference between appellate subject and appellant being, without a promised good greater than the good otherwise accessible to the appellate subject, the point of appeal vanishes and with it the fundamental principle of meaningful experience. Thus it seems, as Feuerbach would argue later, that "the consciousness which the understanding has of its own perfection" is inevitably our god, but it must be disguised somehow as an Other to sustain its appeal to us.[64] Axial Age transcendentalism bares its humanism in the prayer Euripides gives Hecuba in *The Trojan Women*: "You that support the earth and have your seat upon it, whoever you may be, so hard for human conjecture to find out, Zeus, whether you are the necessity of nature or the mind of mortal men, I address you in prayer! For proceeding on a silent path you direct all mortal affairs toward justice!"[65]

The Upanishads grasp this nettle directly by asserting that salvation lies in the knowledge of salvation; the distance between appellant and appellate subject is cancelled: "Knowledge is the eye of the world, and knowledge, the foundation. *Brahman* is knowing. It is with this self consisting of knowledge that [the seer Vamadeva] went up from this world and . . . became immortal."[66] So long as the inquiring self is still on its way to becoming this nondual "self consisting of knowledge," however, philosophical and religious appeals persist as a function of an apparent dualism.

Higher than the sense objects is the mind;
Higher than the mind is the intellect;

> Higher than the intellect is the immense self;
> Higher than the immense self is the unmanifest;
> Higher than the unmanifest is the [cosmic] person;
> Higher than the person there's nothing at all.
> That is the goal, that's the highest state.[67]

The image of one who does have full knowledge of Brahman can be supremely appealing to us in our goal-directed orientation: "Be a man who [sees that Person], who knows this . . . a man who dallies with the self, who finds pleasure in the self, and thus an active man. He is *brahman!* and of those who know *brahman*, he is the best!"[68]

A theistic countercurrent to nondualism, signs of which appear in the *Shvetashvatara Upanishad* and the *Bhagavad Gita*, contends that the supreme discipline is devotion rather than knowledge (or intensive self-control or socially dutiful works) precisely because a Beloved has the superior power of appeal to call the subject toward and into itself. "Not through sacred lore, [austerities, almsgiving,] or sacrificial rites can I be seen in the form that you saw me," says Krishna after the great theophany of the Gita; "by devotion alone can I, as I really am, be known and seen and entered into, Arjuna."[69] This approach is dedicated to preserving and exploiting the appeal structure of meaningful experience. It seems, however, that appeals to the gracious Lord, whether on a path of bhakti or of Abrahamic monotheism, are liable to be completely dominated by exigencies of human desire and judgment—in practice, dominated by the desires and judgments of particular religious leaders. When the appeal is so abstract, what can push back against an appellate subject's willful shaping of it?

***

That the Logos, the Way of Heaven, Brahman, Yahweh, and other Axial Age supreme appeals differ importantly from each other sets up the problem of conflicting ultimate truth-claims in an inclusive culture. We have seen that within this well-known problem and within each appellate community and stated appeal there lurks a variance between theoretical and practical interpretations of supreme appeal, and that a number of other possibly inelimin-able problems in appeal-appellate relations are associated with the presumption of supreme appeal.

The Appeal of Appeal Itself

Appealing is itself, in an important sense, the main point of the classic religious and philosophical initiatives of the Axial Age. Perennial issues of order and power are now framed, animated, and ruled by consciously recognized appeals. Ultimates of order and power for which names previously existed—

destiny, Heaven, *El* the high god—become fully activated for appellate subjects, commanding their lives, saturating their horizons of meaningfulness. The empowerment of human beings as "rational" or "spiritual" is thought to be achieved in this centered, deepened, broadened subjection to appeal, a newly lucid commitment that is not to be identified simply with ordinary confidence in the accuracy of beliefs, the efficacy of practices, or the consistency of order.

It is commonly said, with good reason, that Axial Age ideologies are concerned with "salvation," yet it is a mistake to construe the appeals we have been discussing, even the political ones, as too closely bound to any individual's worldly interest. The Axial Age type of salvation is far different from bodily healing or victory in battle, though it may encompass such goods. The supreme appellant is lifted clear of the appealing *of* its devotees; it does have power and confer benefits, but its supreme intrinsic greatness sustains any subject's attention unconditionally and so conquers any suspicion that the represented appeal of the Logos, the Way, Brahman, or Yahweh reflects only the incontinent flattery of anxious, greedy human appellants.

> Pythagoras is said to have been the first to call himself a philosopher . . . He likened the entrance of men into the present life to the progression of a crowd to some public spectacle. There assemble men of all descriptions and views. One hastens to sell his wares for money and gain; another exhibits his bodily strength for renown; but the most liberal assemble to observe the landscape, the beautiful works of art, the specimens of valor, and the customary literary productions. So also in the present life men of manifold pursuits are assembled. Some are influenced by the desire of riches and luxury; others, by the love of power and dominion, or by insane ambition for glory. But the purest and most genuine character is that of the man who devotes himself to the contemplation of the most beautiful things, and he may properly be called a philosopher. (Iamblichus)[70]

It is characteristic of Axial Age traditions to distinguish between true philosophy and religion within the circle of supreme appeal, and manipulative "magic" and "superstition" outside it. Although we have found reason to characterize the relationship with a supreme appeal as a journey, nevertheless, in comparison with the worldly instrumentalism and mythological supernaturalism that dominated earlier thinking, the Axial Age appeals announce an *arrival*: the supreme appellant has been seen only in a mirror, dimly, to use a Christian writer's expression, but still appellate subjects are sure that what they see dimly has uniquely and sufficiently great meaningfulness.[71]

A false arrival? Life in this world does go on, its prospects of good ever-changing, ever-diverging. Supreme appeal claims could deceive us profoundly about our situation. There now seems little room to doubt that historically such claims have promoted a kind of reasoning that is insensitive to the intrinsic meaningfulness of actually existing beings and so have produced, in Weber's expression, a general disenchantment of the world.[72] A strange consequence of this disenchantment is that the category of appeal has become marginalized in the rational interpretation of meaningfulness, which now most often refers, not to appellatecy, but to quasi-physical vectors of desire and need or purely functional exigencies; religions and philosophies are evaluated primarily as *explanations* of experience; appeal-experience as such is left over as an "affective" surplus.[73] Still, insofar as we continue to reach for a true, fully justified understanding of our situation—insofar as our communication is oriented to perfecting a communion of responsible beings—the premise of supreme appeal continues to structure even our criticisms of the supreme appeal premise.

As heirs of the Axial Age, we live in a regime of supreme appeal. This assertion indicates something important about the meaning of our "classics" and thus of a large phase of cultural history we live in. However, the specific currents and edges of our most acute normative thinking today reflect a modern phase within that larger phase. To understand the state of appeal issues today, it is necessary to understand the structure of a modern discussion in philosophy and theology that flows largely from a bold reformulation of the supreme appeal premise made at the height of the European Enlightenment by Immanuel Kant. In the next two chapters we will take stock of philosophical and theological developments of the Kantian initiative.

three

The Appeal in Modern Philosophy

Philosophy and the Truth Ideal

Virtually from its beginning, Western philosophy has manifested a conflicted relationship with the ideal of a supreme appeal. The most important work in philosophy today for our purposes derives from Kant's interpretation of this situation. Before discussing Kant's contribution, I will indicate the nature of the problem Kant inherited.

As a gambit of and on behalf of knowledge, philosophy has a vested interest in the truth ideal. If philosophy fails to represent a supremely impressive appeal of truth, then it cannot be the authoritative vehicle of our hope of comprehending reality thoroughly and evaluating it fairly. Accepting truth as its highest good commits philosophy to find a way to construe being as such and knowing as such as good. Characteristically, philosophy serves the good of truth, being, and knowing by mounting an unrestricted critique of the appearances of ordinary experience. However, this move generates a pitfall at the start: a sour-grapes view of experience as the mother of illusion, an adversarial attitude toward the world and, consequently, a bias toward unworldly referents and an attenuated view of reality (seen most extremely in the Being-ball to which Parmenides reduces reality).[1] Worse, philosophy finds that it cannot carry out the critique of appearances without turning its critical weapons against its own supposedly superior construals of reality, so that the signal of its appeal breaks up (to use a radio metaphor) and a truth crisis ensues, reopening the question of how we are to recognize and respond to a supreme good.

One classic truth crisis is occasioned by Plato's conception of forms. To counter popular prejudices on the one hand and sophistical abuses of reasoning on the other, Plato develops an account of eternal forms as the enablers of being and referents of true judgment.[2] These forms have commanding importance precisely because they constitute the fundamental solution to the problems of being something and knowing something—they are *good for* being and knowing, providing for their requisite perfections. Accordingly, Plato has Socrates say, in the *Parmenides*, that he certainly wants to affirm forms for logico-mathematical concepts (likeness, unity, plurality) and basic moral and aesthetic principles (rightness, beauty, goodness) that are indispensable if there is to be any thinking of perfection at all.[3] He is unsure about forms for worldly beings (humanity, fire, water), apparently because it is not evident that worldly kinds of things can have determinate perfections. But he is quite sure, on the other hand, that he does not wish to affirm forms for utterly out-of-focus objects like hair, mud, dirt that seem not to exhibit any positive relation to being and knowing. How could paying attention to forms in that murky region advance the greater cause of responding to the appeal of truth? Plato then makes Parmenides suggest that Socrates will see the significance of such things as hair, mud, and dirt when he outgrows his youthfully narrow idealism. But doubt has now been raised about the status of the forms in general, for it has been revealed that philosophical construals of truth, being, and knowing are infected with contingencies of appearance and valuation. Truth must be the Good, and the Good must be what the philosopher can recognize and affirm. But appealing to being as such or knowing as such does not suffice to motivate recognition or affirmation, nor is any one reference set of beings and knowings justified against others.

A related and more extensively discussed aspect of the Platonic truth crisis is that by making the forms transcendent of common experience in their appealing perfection of being and knowableness—so that appeals to them and from them would be rationally decisive in principle, as the contents of common experience cannot be—Plato gets the paradoxical result that the forms are, as Aristotle noted, strangers to change and so inapplicable to our world.[4] Platonism flies beyond the world to make contact with a truth that cannot include the world's materiality and so cannot ascertainably yield the individuated and dynamic truth proper to this world. This is another sign that the perfection principle is not yet responding adequately to a supreme appeal. (Aristotelians still have a problem of being alienated from the world, in spite of their advanced conception of a form-matter partnership in nature, inasmuch as their supreme being is separate from the world and their supreme knowing and human flourishing belongs to the philosopher who detaches from the world in contemplating this divinity.)[5]

A second classic crisis is produced by the modern subjectivity-centered philosophy of Descartes. Here the Platonic standards of ontic and epistemic perfection still rule the pursuit of truth under the aegis of form-determining "innate ideas" given by a natural light to every mind, but philosophy now undermines these standards in the opposite way, stopping short of the world instead of overshooting it. Cartesian thinking secures truth in a system of appearances correlative to an "I think," an ego that can always be sure at least of how things seem to it. In its confirmation and cultivation of interiority, Cartesian thinking is haunted by the issue of exteriority. The ego is sunk in a world of its own that differs incalculably from the world "out there." Thus, a guarantee of objective reality must be sought in an extraordinary relationship with an extraordinary being, God; and the chief significance of the divine being that Descartes is able to identify is not that it is perfect, as the Platonic metaphysical tradition (and another of Descartes's arguments also) requires, but rather that it indubitably exists *outside* the philosopher's consciousness, a dazzling Infinite present to the finite mind, which the finite mind could not have produced on its own.[6] Descartes pauses at the end of his third Meditation to "admire and adore" this impressive and beautiful . . . idea of his![7] The idea may be claimed to be more than an idea, verily an event of transcendence, and yet, however earnestly this claim is made, the idea of "the Infinite" is really only specifiable as a general idea of the subject's response situation and capacity.[8]

The Cartesian crisis in the philosophical appeal of truth was reshaped by Kant still more explicitly as an issue of our response to a supreme claim. Because Kant laid this card on the table, his position remains a central touchstone for reflection on life as life-under-appeal.

The Appeal of Pure Practical Reason: Kant

Pursuing the epistemologically radical implications of Cartesianism, Kant checks the theoretical appeal of truth by demonstrating in his *Critique of Pure Reason* that the coherence of experience is a function of the subject's own spontaneity rather than an ascertainable property of reality external to the subject. He makes thought's agreement with its own demands the main theme of knowledge and undercuts the traditional (and still essential) standard of truth as thought's agreement with reality. The supreme appeal of truth leads only to a negative fulfillment: neither naively realistic knowledge nor metaphysically inferred knowledge of beings as they are in themselves is possible. If Kant's result itself counts as metaphysical knowledge, it gives only a weirdly hollow satisfaction to anyone seriously heeding the appeal of truth. We still have a universal "theory" in the sense that we have principles of interpretation and explanation that apply to everything in our experience, but the application does not reach beyond a phenomenal surface. All the late-modern, fundamentally Kantian proposals of an a priori determination of the content of our experience by some sort of cognitive framework are under the same limitation.

Kant's main positive move is to draw attention to the appeal of moral conscience, which he conceives as the active principle of fairness or "good will," "pure practical reason," the one reality we *can* know, inasmuch as it is our own reality, the exercise of our freedom in practice. It is not an object to be grasped and measured; it is manifested in the world only ambiguously through our conduct. Nevertheless, it claims to rule our life in the world. It produces our one *objectively necessary susceptibility* to appeal, "respect": "This [moral] law . . . being the form of an intellectual causality, i.e., the form of freedom . . . is at the same time an object of respect, since, in conflict with its subjective antagonists (our inclinations), it weakens self-conceit" and constrains self-love.[9] It is "a tribute we cannot refuse to pay to merit."[10]

Pure practical reason determines goodness by sovereignly imposing the formal demand of fairness on all our choices. Thus the appeal of the freedom of pure practical reason is superordinate both experientially in the feeling of respect and operationally as a norm of deliberation, and it inspires Kantian answers to questions of global or centrally pivotal meaningfulness in all realms of experience. In theoretical experience, it calls for an affirmation of noumenal freedom of the will in conjunction with a perfect causal determinism in phenomena; in aesthetic experience, it explains the thrill of sublimity as an indication of our own infinitely important rational purposiveness; in religious experience, it prompts a rejection of passively grateful or wishfully hopeful attitudes toward a supreme cause.[11] None of these claims are robust within the nonmoral contexts in which they are made—you cannot demonstrate free will as an inference from empirical observations, or rational purposiveness as an inference from emotional stimulation, or the badness of pious deference strictly from a phenomenology of devotion—but they show up in these contexts as indicators of the dominant practical principle.

The Kantian primacy of practical reason implies that a supreme appeal cannot be "objective" in the sense that it is simply presented from outside the subject of appeal. A supreme appeal must involve not only a response by the subject but a participation of the subject in the generating of the appeal. Kant holds that the noumenal subject *makes* the appeal, that the supreme appeal is only the subject's call to itself, experienced as the subjection of the empirical creature of inclinations to the purely rational self. This unlimited self-respect creates, as an echo of the crisis in knowledge caused by the segregation of experiential appearances from noumenal realities, a crisis in practical responsibility: is the meaning of responsibility not lost if we take direction from ourselves only? This difficulty has both an individual form, in the apparently selfish ideal of my responsibility to my own true nature, and a collective form, in the apparently chauvinist ideal of a human responsibility restricted to humanity ("respect always applies to persons only").[12] But if we want to say that we *are* in a relationship with an appellant really exterior to ourselves, how can that exteriority be verified and interpreted without disobeying Kantian strictures on knowledge of what is outside ourselves? To the extent that I do become acquainted with beings other than myself, necessarily as "phenomena," won't my subjection to appeals be dissipated?[13]

Since the good promised and administered by practical reason is a world-engaged flourishing, the practical supreme appeal applies to every fulfillment one could righteously hope for. Kant allows that virtuous subjects have a subjectively necessary hope of attaining as much happiness as they have made themselves worthy of. The "highest good" for the appellate subject is the synthesis of virtue with this reward. But the highest good is only a real possibility if there exists a power capable of bringing about morally appropriate life-outcomes. *This* matter is clearly *not* just between the human agent and his or her own conscience, since a human agent lacks such power.[14] Only God holds it, if anyone does. So moral agents necessarily hope a divine Other will reward them, and this division of responsibilities threatens to compromise the Kantian appellate subject's necessary autonomy.[15] Kant insists that the demands of morality are uniquely, objectively necessary, so that nothing can be taken away from the paramount status of virtue's appeal, and nonmoral appeals are unequivocally subordinated to the supreme moral appeal, yet thanks to the "highest good" argument the identity of the Kantian supreme appellant now oscillates between an ideal, purely virtuous self and a self that is responsive to all the appeals of the world and benefited by God. Is Kant's narrowly moral version of the single supreme appeal program not feasible, then? These difficulties carry forward in Kantian thinking.

* * *

A glance at Kierkegaard at this juncture can enhance our appreciation of the power of the main lines of the Kantian approach. Kierkegaard should be credited with initiating important departures from Kant, considering his effects on twentieth-century thought, but his position can also be interpreted as a neo-Pauline Christian variation on Kant's. Kierkegaard accepts the Kantian demand for a self actively responsible *for* its own sincere good will, and he places this demand in relation with a divine Other *to* whom the self is responsible and *by* whom authenticity and goodness are defined, not merely formally but in actuality. The Kantian appeal structure is already split, as Kant's "dialectic of pure practical reason" shows, between two life-defining appeals: one *made* by a self that despairs of attaining happiness in the world while under the constraints of moral duty; and one *perceived* by that self in the transworldly possibility of virtue's full reward, the "highest good," which is in God's power. Kierkegaard magnifies this split by portraying the situation of the human self as even more radically desperate and by identifying the adequate ground of personal existence as a Wholly Other whose love is greater than reason.[16] The

Kierkegaardian themes of a supreme transrational appeal and a radically self-redefining *decision* (in contrast to a rational *judgment*) as the authentic acknowledgment of appeal will be taken up by many of the most significant post-Kantian appeal thinkers of the twentieth century. But Kierkegaard's substitution of faith and God-dependence for reason and autonomy does not change the basic structure of the Kantian appeal position. The Kierkegaardian knight of faith listens to a voice in his head just as the Kantian man of reason does.[17] And his hopes for flourishing rest on reciprocation from a postulated supreme power.

***

Kant leaves us in a contradictory situation. Philosophy is now about *valuing* more than about *knowing*, and everything in experience is interpreted in relation to the will's solicitation by a commanding transcendence. Perhaps not since the eroticism of Plato's *Phaedrus* and *Symposium*—or Augustine's new Platonism of Christian love—has a philosophical appeal been so directly shaped by an experiential structure of appeal. On the other hand, in Kant's world the paramount appeal is, oddly, just our own to ourselves (though shadowed by that of a God who presides over happiness), and it is always the formal appeal of a rational "one" embedded in existing selves rather than the concrete appeal of a *He* or *She* or *You*.[18] So the role of appeal in experience is both infinitely wide and infinitely narrow. By the Kantian logic of the a priori, it is so wide *because* it is so narrow: only the essential requirements of the subject would necessarily be applicable and valid throughout the subject's world. Moreover, the appeal is over us *because* it is in us, exterior in the relevant way because it is interior in the relevant way. So Kantians do not live in a world of many substantial appeals. Accordingly, philosophy is set up with new clarity as the technique of human reasoning rather than as a guide to reality.[19] Kantians are well oriented to carry on as responsible individuals in the "disenchanted" modern world described by Weber, and, if their position is given a social and practical twist, to undertake creation of the new world demanded by socialism.[20]

Three Post-Kantian Paths: Rickert, Buber, and Heidegger

A century after Kant, the idea was well advanced that Western philosophy's quest for truth had been or soon would be rendered superfluous by the work of the positive sciences. This could be seen as a fulfillment of the negative implications of the Kantian critique of theoretical reason. While workers in the positive sciences seemed able to keep up a reliable production of new disclosures and articulations of reality, philosophers continued to manufacture pseudo-disclosures in their typically unbridled attempt to realize everything that the appeal of all-reality *could* involve—not omitting, of course, to discredit each other's claims. Many thought that philosophy's questions would soon be resolved or dissolved by a truly scientific physics, biology, psychology, or economics. If philosophy tried to satisfy a distinctive need by forming an all-inclusive "worldview" (*Weltanschauung*) in the most reasonable manner, this ideal was undermined by a historical and social-scientific consciousness that could explain the dependence of rival "worldviews" on personal temperament or social-historical context.

In the larger world, meanwhile, everyone in Europe or under its influence faced the twin threats of an inhuman materialist science and technology, and a suffocating idealist cultural complacency. The First World War fulfilled both threats cataclysmically. Philosophers responded with new counter-materialist and counter-idealist attempts to articulate the appeal of truth. There are numerous important varieties of this development, but here I propose to compare several in which a relatively pure appeal-concept becomes prominent in such a way that the position associated with it sticks out as a major alternative and point of reference for subsequent discussion. These are the "value philosophy" of the Southwest Neo-Kantians as maturely represented by Heinrich Rickert's *Gegenstand der Erkenntnis* and *System der Philosophie*, "dialogical" philosophy as represented by Martin Buber's *I and Thou*, and Martin Heidegger's ontological version of phenomenology as represented by *Being and Time*.[21] Each of these positions tries consciously to go to the heart of appealing in order to disclose the general nature of the offer and reception involved in superordinately meaningful experience. Each develops a Kantian legacy by bringing forward a possible implication of the appeal of practical reason to shine like a beacon in the disorienting darkness of positivism.

(1) *"Value philosophy"* interprets the Kantian primacy of practical reason in the most constructive, theoretically enterprising way, offering a re-Kantianized version of Hegel's concept of "objective spirit": we confront the transcendent source of unconditional meaning not merely in a single abstract law of freedom, as expressed by Kant's categorical imperative, but (most articulately and adequately) in a culturally rich world of goals, standards, and channels of freedom formed in relation to the various cognitive, practical, and aesthetic challenges of worldly life in its historical development. The ruling appeal of our own freedom is expressed by the language of "values." The greatest task of thought is to construct the most valuationally adequate total worldview. The appeal of fulfillment is assigned simply to the open ideal of maximal fulfillment; God plays no essential role.

(2) *Dialogical philosophy* transposes the Kantian division between phenomena (appearances of things as we are able to apprehend them) and noumena (things in themselves) into a dichotomy between the "primary words" of "I-It" and "I-You." Saying "I-It" maintains a manageable system of experience; saying "I-You" acknowledges the presence of a being as independently and commandingly appealing. Thus, the sphere of contact with noumenal reality

is generously enlarged beyond the rational self-discovery of the Kantian subject to admit various kinds of actual encounter and relatedness, and therewith a fuller meaning of responsibility. God is located in all encounter as its uttermost depth and breadth.

(3) Heidegger's *phenomenological ontology* centers on the existential-ontological meaning of Kant's demonstration of the finitude of reason. The conscious existent's essential involvement in error and mortality discloses the most original structure and dynamics of the Being of beings in its temporalization. Kant's strictly moral call of conscience is transposed to a summons to understand being "authentically" in a resolute anticipation of death. Being displaces both reason and God as a supreme appellant.

I hope to show that these three positions are dramatically related, not merely diverse. They draw power, individually and collectively, from their oppositions. In this respect, too, they radiate from Kant. They exhibit the possibly unrivaled power inherent in the Kantian approach, a power responsible for that approach's dominance in late-modern intellectual history. My account will pit the positions against each other to tease out their strengths and weaknesses.

* * *

Value philosophy. Neo-Kantianism makes a bold attempt to overcome, on idealist lines, the fundamental limitation of idealism in regard to truth, namely, that it suppresses the exteriority of the real by subsuming reality within the operations of consciousness. On Rickert's view (derived from Windelband and Lotze), the consciousness of truth is transcended by the *value* of truth.

Knowledge is ordinarily thought to differ from mere belief in that the content of knowledge depends crucially on the known as distinct from the knower. Without this dependence, knowledge claims would not have their distinctive justification. In light of the Kantian critique of cognition, however, Rickert holds that no known thing could really transcend consciousness, at least not in its knowable content. The "facts" naively enshrined by positivism as norms of knowledge are always already shaped by factors of a wholly different and radically normative kind—that is, by ideals intrinsic to theoretical consciousness. On the other hand, theoretical consciousness cannot simply justify itself. To what, then, is theoretical consciousness responsible?

Rickert opens the possibility of a meaningful relation of consciousness to a transcendent factor by dividing real existents from "irreal" items such as meanings and values. Meanings and values are to be conceived, not as existing, but as "holding" (*gelten*). The irreals are not postulated ad hoc; they are methodically established when philosophy, fulfilling its distinctive truth-mission of forming a most-adequate conception of the universe (*Weltall*), develops all warranted categorical enrichments of our understanding of what is—including subjectivity as well as objectivity, ideal as well as actual existence, and "valid" irreality as well as existing reality.[22]

Like the phenomenologist Husserl, Rickert rejects psychologism: the meaning or validity of a thought cannot be reduced to the characteristics the thought has as a psychological actuality. But Rickert thinks that Husserlian phenomenology's attempt to ground logical content and validity in an ideally clarified intuitive "givenness" of ideal objects fails to correct the radical error of trying to derive meaning and validity from objects of any sort whatsoever. Phenomenology is but a refined positivism. For Rickert, the independent factor that assures meaning and validity in our experiential judgments must be sought in a transcendent non-objective, non-ontological, axiological *order* given to consciousness. A judgment of truth has the meaning of "truth" fundamentally because a being has been characterized in such a way that its apparent real material is subjected to the "theoretical form" of the "theoretical value" of truth.[23] "In this reversal of traditional opinion" about the truth-constituting relation between thought and reality, says Rickert, "lies our 'Copernican' standpoint: the knowing I-subject does not 'revolve around' *reality*, thereby becoming theoretically *valuable*, but rather 'revolves around' theoretical *value* insofar as it wants to know *reality*."[24]

The true "object" of knowledge, in which the meaning of truth is presented, is an imperative to be "acknowledged" rather than a thing to be perceived. Idealism's basic point against any sort of realism, that it is impossible to find justifications in how things are apart from the apprehension and judgment of things, cannot be gainsaid.[25] Thus, the only philosophically viable way to secure a relation between thought and something transcending thought, as the ideal of truth requires, is to honor the value of that very requirement, ordering truth-judgments by it—so that, for example, we posit that a true content holds for any object of a specified type or for any subject whatever. Acknowledging that we answer to values in our cognitive life leads to an honest affirmation that our will participates in the making of cognitive judgments. We *decide* and *act* for knowledge; cognition is a "practical comportment" (*Verhalten*).[26]

Rickert's position appears to make the most of the subjectivism inherent in the concept of "value," keying meaningfulness to choosing. To some extent this situation is disguised by the projection of identifiable, reliably operative, and so quasi-objective "values" out of the subjectivity of choosing—although these values are distinguished from existing beings by the telltale property that they come in pairs of contraries, which manifests their connection with affirming and negating acts of will.[27] Neo-Kantian value theory claims to be lucid, then, about the relationship between freedom and structure that commanding meanings imply. But a strange implication of Kant's original position comes back to haunt us here: Isn't real exteriority dissolved, and responsibility with it, when the subject is ultimately subjected to nothing other than its own experiment of freedom? Rickert thinks that the necessary exteriority is assured by locating values outside of living consciousness. They *apply* to choosing without being *generated by* or *distilled from* acts of choosing. That is why we can always meaningfully ask whether a valuation is objectively valid.[28]

Values are inherently *more meaningful* than existing things as such:

> The essence of what exists . . . is that it does not concern us, it *only* exists. We represent it. It is simply there . . . A value, in contrast . . . draws us into its circle, does not let us rest . . . we feel ourselves grasped and summoned in our spontaneity . . . Everything that merely exists has something in common in comparison with that which possesses the character of value, and thus the world is organized in two sharply distinguished spheres which must be strictly held over against each other conceptually, notwithstanding all the relations and associations that obtain between them.[29]

Ushering us into the realm of meaningfulness in this sweeping way, value philosophy is a magisterial appellant of the value situation; it shows us not only the general character of value but also its main regions and kinds (theoretical, moral, aesthetic, religious; personal vs. nonpersonal; individual vs. social; contemplative vs. active).[30] On the widest reading it embraces *any* meaningful experience, validating *anything* by which we are or might be "grasped and summoned" so long as we can answer for the participation of our "spontaneity" in the transaction.

In another important way, however, Rickert's value philosophy is limited and reserved. Philosophy is properly a theoretical, rational pursuit. It can demonstrate the necessity of the theoretical value of truth and its derivatives. The philosopher is aware that non-theoretical values obtain also; it is necessary to map these and to ascertain the subject's formal possibilities of valuation in relation to them, all for the sake of forming a picture of life that is *truer* in being free of intellectualistic distortion. But philosophy cannot carry its methods of establishing truth over to the establishing of beauty, righteousness, and holiness.[31] Appeals in these domains solicit affirmation differently.

* * *

Dialogical philosophy. Whether Rickert's values are genuinely independent of consciousness or not, the account of I-You relation given in Buber's *I and Thou* clashes with Rickert's value theory insofar as Buber's "You" appeal-motif pins the transcendence in the subject's relation with reality to an actual other being, not to an irreal. The "I" always finds meaningfulness in saying "You" to another being; as a You-sayer, the I cannot but vouch for the unadulterated reality of the encounter. Bound to the other *as* other *and* as itself, the subject, Buber says, is "seized by the power of exclusiveness."[32] Rickert would interpret You-saying as a non-theoretical proposition governed by an ethical, religious, or possibly aesthetic value rather than as a judgment of reality. Buber, however, means to "translate" a non-theoretical experience into a reality claim.[33]

Buber criticizes idealism directly:

> Some men who in the world of things make do with experiencing and using
> have constructed for themselves an idea annex or superstructure in which
> they find refuge . . . At the threshold they take off the clothes of the ugly
> weekday, shroud themselves in clean garments, and feel restored as they
> contemplate primal being or what ought to be—something in which their
> life has no share.[34]

> A world of ideas and values . . . cannot become present for us . . . All the
> prescriptions that have been excogitated and invented in the ages of the
> human spirit . . . have nothing to do with the primally simple fact of
> encounter . . . All this has its place in the It-world and does not take us one
> step—does not take the decisive step—out of it.[35]

So much the worse for values. But Rickert's work and *I and Thou* have
important features in common. Rickert, like Buber, wants to show a relation
of the subject extending beyond an immanent realm of representations; he
understands the subject's relation with transcendence to be sited in actual
beings and thoughts, though not fulfilled in any "thing" or "thought" as such;
he grounds cognitive experience in a *Verhalten* that is not passively contemplative; and he divides experience into two great "spheres," one marked by
intrinsic meaningfulness. Buber, like Rickert, roots his privileged category of
meaning in a form of subjective activity—in his case, the attitude (*Haltung*) of
"I-You" saying —and treats the actualities in an encounter as contents embraced by a categorically commanding form, which he calls "the a priori of
relation."[36] A Buberian counterpart to the Rickert sentence already quoted
would run: "The self does not perceive an Other, thereby finding itself in
relation, but rather the self enters relation and thereby finds itself with an
Other." Moreover, Buber affirms a supreme norm of "perfect relationship"
comparable to the Platonic Good or Kantian pure reason: "[I]n every You
we address the eternal You."[37] This claim protects "I-You" saying from what
Rickert would call the characteristically aesthetic value-limitation of seeking a
perfection of experience in the present particular to the exclusion of the rest
of reality.[38]

Buber has been criticized for adhering to the epistemological formalism
of idealism.[39] There are several deep reasons why that formalism would persist
in his project.

(1) Although Buber opposes idealism in holding that the exteriority that
pierces the shell of I-It experience is the present actuality of the Other being,
he also moves back toward idealism in holding that the I and You of "I-You"
saying do not exist outside the meaning-form of relation.[40] That meaning-form
is said to be inseparable from the present actuality of Others, yet we seem to be
required to focus on the ideally general sense of "I-You" saying if it is to be
elevated and enforced as a fundamental norm of thought and valuation, as
"the a priori of relation."[41] Furthermore, Buber's claim that relation is realized

in a basic "word" trades on the generality of sense that language possesses by virtue of the way in which speaking *offers* and *transfers* meaning from one subject to another. (It is noteworthy that Buber's critic Levinas, after first shifting the focus of the dialogical appeal argument in his own work toward the concretely existing face of the other human being, later explicated the meaning of the face as a general structure of communicative generosity, "Saying.")[42]

I observe that idealism at some level is unavoidable in any piece of discursive reasoning. The I of diverse You-sayings is the I qualified in the same way, and the meanings achieved in You-saying are of a common kind. In a philosophical book on *I and Thou*, the thematic generalities of "I" and "You" must supersede the particularities of real beings. It may also be said, however, that Buber's use of indexical personal pronouns counteracts this supersession. The respect in which "I" refers differently from "consciousness" and "you" refers differently from "it" is not less important than the respect in which the references in those pairs are alike.

(2) Buber's sharp distinction between You-meaning and It-meaning creates two dilemmas in his presentation of beings. On the one hand, if he were to describe the You-appeal of a tree, he could in no clear way avoid a theoreticizing or aestheticizing It-representation of it. Thus, the tree testimony he does give remains circumspectly abstract and inevitably leaves the impression that what mainly matters in a tree encounter is how the subject is seized by it rather than anything about the tree itself.[43] If, on the other hand, Buber tries to tell us something *about* the tree, he must address it as an It and so consign it to inactuality, which implies that neither scientific knowledge of nature nor religious affirmation of the created as such is a relationship with actuality at all.[44]

(3) Buber's most profound affinity with idealism lies in his essentially religious concern with the problem of wholeness and authenticity in the self, the self whose "*one* great faith-experience," he says, was the original root of his dialogical philosophy.[45] In *I and Thou*, actual Others pass before us fleetingly, for the most part, as auxiliaries to this dominant theme. Socrates, Goethe, and Jesus, exhibited as great role models of I-saying, are just minimally identified by who and what they said You to, as though the idea of being generally like them is sufficiently inspiring.[46]

* * *

Phenomenological ontology. Heidegger's *Being and Time*, like Buber's *I and Thou*, takes up the question of the self's authenticity and tries to shift the question's center of gravity away from idealist subjectivism and value theory. But the core question for Heidegger is that of the meaning of the Being of beings, the immanently extraordinary ground of the meaningfulness of all thoughts and things; and the appeal that Heidegger wants to heed and convey is that of Being as such in its disclosures. He believes that the meaning of Being and the basic structures of the self's existence in the world are presupposed by any meanings that are specific to I-You relation.[47]

Heidegger finds our relationship with reality in an active orientation that he calls "care" (*Sorgen*) (§41).[48] "Care" expresses the fundamental relevance of everything in the world and the wholeness of the world. It seems a subject-oriented expression, but Heidegger claims its meaning is not derived from the concept of a subject; rather, the meanings of subjectivity and selfhood are derived from it (§64). What binds the world together is a primordial relatedness of beings from which all significance derives (§18). "Truth" most primordially belongs to the disclosedness of beings, another essential aspect of a world and of a subject's existence (§44). The subject, which Heidegger calls *Dasein* (literally, "there-being"), is continually "there" *for* disclosures. But the main proper concern of Dasein and the guiding element in interpreting the constitution of its being is the meaning of its *own* being *as* a disclosure of the Being of beings. Dasein is in a cognitively privileged relation to Being as such in certain attunements, such as objectless angst, that part the curtains of Dasein's everyday absorption in finite concerns so that the difference of the ground of being from beings is realized. This difference registers, not as a sunny plenitude of Being purified of limitations, but rather as a relative lucidity of the finite being realizing its factical "thrownness" in the world and anticipating its extinction. Only in these darker ways does the understanding being engage most understandingly with the ultimate to-be-understood. Heidegger calls a realization of this sort "authenticity" and the opening of access to it the "call of conscience" (§§54–60). "The call of conscience has the character of an *appeal* (*Anruf*) to Dasein by calling it to its ownmost potentiality-for-Being-its-Self; and this is done by way of *summoning* (*Aufruf*) it to its ownmost Being-lacking" (269). This appeal is maximally compelling in principle because, like the Kantian moral claim, it "comes *from* me and yet *over me*."[49]

Just as Buber's You-saying must bypass determinate representation to honor the "living present" of relation, Heidegger's call of conscience is absolved from any utterable message: "*conscience discourses solely and constantly in the mode of keeping silent*" (273). "That which calls the call, simply holds itself aloof from any way of becoming well-known, and this belongs to its phenomenal character. To let itself be drawn into getting considered and talked about, goes against its kind of Being" (274–75). It is "uncanny" because it reveals that Dasein is essentially incomparable with anything in its experience (277). The call of conscience cannot be reconciled with the dogma that whatever really is must be objectively present (275).

This climactic appeal argument in *Being and Time* is built on a broader base of appealing already contained in Heidegger's distinctive conception of phenomenology. Heidegger so much stresses the inquirer's active response to disclosures that he makes the concepts of phenomenon and question converge. His rule is to follow where the phenomenon leads—not merely to report an apprehension of it, but to keep going into it and after it, beyond the preliminary work of removing the obstructions of prejudice through which we first saw it glimmering. "Phenomenon" is not "image"; any particular presentation or representation is to be taken as a summons to explore depths and contexts; that is, a phenomenon is to be acknowledged as just the leading edge of a meaning—an appeal. Heidegger's ideal of exploring radically and comprehensively what is shown leads him ineluctably to the appeal of the preeminent phenomenon, Being as such:

> What is it that phenomenology is to "let us see"? What is it that must be called a "phenomenon" in a distinctive sense? What is it that by its very essence is *necessarily* the theme whenever we exhibit something *explicitly*? Manifestly, it is something that proximally and for the most part . . . lies *hidden* . . . but at the same time it is something that belongs to what thus shows itself, and it belongs to it so essentially as to constitute its meaning and ground. (35)

By this reasoning, phenomenology and ontology are one. The logic of Heidegger's position is appellate; it owes as much to the sense of "phenomenon" as intriguing transcendence as to any metaphysical commitment to grounding or totalizing. Phenomenological ontology can be defined, therefore, as the adequate response to being maximally appealed to. The appeal-structure in Heidegger's thinking becomes increasingly obvious in his later work, where he is often heard in this vein: "Man alone of all beings, when addressed by the voice of Being, experiences the marvel of all marvels: that what-is *is*."[50] "Man is the shepherd of Being . . . whose dignity consists in being called by Being itself into the preservation of Being's truth."[51] "From . . . the presence of what is present, there speaks the duality of [Being and beings]. There speaks from it the call that calls us into the essential nature of thinking."[52]

In his 1947 "Letter on Humanism," Heidegger attacks value philosophy as inadequately responsive to appeal: "Every valuing, even where it values positively, is a subjectivizing. It does not let beings: be. Rather, valuing lets beings: be valid—solely as the objects of its doing."[53] This way lies nihilism. From Rickert's point of view, however, Heidegger makes the double mistake that he sells values short, mistaking the nature and force of their transcendence, and also fails to offer a critically tenable alternative to value-oriented idealism. The way beings can be allowed to be, *meaningfully*, is not by peremptorily asserting a relation of the subject's awareness of them with some non- or trans-rational factor in them, but rather by responsibly acknowledging an ordering of the subject's awareness of them by the purest truly commanding ideals, such as the ideals of truth and impartiality. From Buber's perspective, Heidegger's ontology lets beings be solely as the objects of *its* theoretical doing, substituting its own transcendental apparatus for that of idealism. Since Heidegger's appealing Other is impersonal, universal Being, his position is monologically enclosed, soundproofed against the appeals of actual other beings and emergent situations.[54]

Heidegger's ontology is meant to be responsive to an impersonal Being, yet in *Being and Time* he holds so tenaciously to the clue of the human relationship with Being that he mimics idealism in restricting intrinsic meaningfulness to subjectivity. This comes out in his claim that Dasein is distinguished from all other beings in its Being being an issue for it, in having a "self," and in being essentially the "clearing" of Being's disclosure.[55] The ontological importance of the phenomenon of "care" and world-constituting "relevance" relegates nonhuman beings to the satellite role of "equipment."[56] And the most explicit appeal of Heidegger's argument turns out to be a "call of conscience," as we have noted. Thus the question of Being, though surpassingly inclusive in principle, has an intensely anthropocentric, evidently Kantian focus.[57] Even when Heidegger gets rid of the more obvious anthropocentric features of *Being and Time* in his later work, he persists in positing an ultimate *centered* meaning-of-everything, reflecting basically an idealist (and so, arguably, anthropocentric) stance. "Idealism" to this extent may be inescapable in philosophical thought; but in that case, Heidegger's claim to offer a radical alternative is misleading.

* * *

I have sketched three sorts of fundamental philosophical appeal distinguished by a prominent appeal motif: idealist, dialogical, and ontological. I chose arguments that were offered at a sensitive moment in the history of Western thinking as regards the feasibility of any a priori discourse on truth and reality. Each made a deliberately heightened appeal. I will not pause to examine all the historical antecedents and consequences that are relevant to a full assessment of their significance, although a larger historical case will emerge as my argument develops. To draw certain conclusions about intellectual appeals that are important for our inquiry at this stage, I will discuss two closely related features, one positive and one negative, that these three appeal strategies share.

These appeals are all *amazing*, wonder-inducing, by virtue of the prime appeal motifs they revolve around. It is probably hardest to make this case for Rickert's philosophy of values since *value* is a heavily soiled, workaday concept and so, in this context, a suspect one. But in his concern to separate values from subjective and objective actualities alike, Rickert has pointed toward something that is not easy to conceive. Values do not exist, although they are "not nothing." The priority of the *quaestio iuris* (issue of justification) to the *quaestio facti* (issue of fact) is the only proof we have that they are operative. They rule even being and truth, and there is nothing to them other than their ruling. Anyone who quickly dismisses values as a hypostatization of human valuations is missing a mystery embedded in valuation itself as it distinguishes itself from factual preference—the mystery of what we get involved in when we ask seriously whether a thought or action is right. Admittedly, we often fail to stabilize our answers to that sort of question, but neither are we simply lost in asking it. How are we fundamentally to explain the measure of ideal effectiveness that our discourses on justice and truth *do* have? In the perspective of systematic philosophy, Rickert's values occupy a transcendent niche in being, much as do other metaphysically explanatory ultimates (forms, monads, etc.), and they are cognitively challenging in that metaphysical way; but unlike other such ultimates, they are defined non-ontologically and so are even less amenable to objectifying discourse. "What are they?" is an infelicitous question to ask about "them." But what then are we really asked to ask? The question seems to concern *how* we are "summoned" to act in relation to other beings.[58]

Heidegger's Being-of-beings, Being-that-is-not-a-being, Being-that-is-*there*-in-our-being, is a stunning and elusive theme as well. It must be presented to us in the character of an appeal because it is neither "in our way" in the manner of concrete beings nor intellectually tractable in the manner of ordinary referents of discourse. One's sense of the question of Being wobbles in and out of tune while speaking or hearing of it. It is a sort of deep space-time that we inhabit essentially implicitly, farther from recognizability than the space-time of our subjective life as such. Yet we are bound to probe toward it in the course of inspecting most intently the physical and psychical realms.

The I of Buber's You-saying also comes in and out of tune in relation to the extraordinary You. "This, however, is the sublime melancholy of our lot that every You must become an It in our world . . . Only it is not always as if these states took turns so neatly; often it is an intricately entangled series of events that is tortuously dual."[59] It is difficult to understand the You in Buber's discourse even while quiveringly or conscientiously inhabiting Buber's living present, because the objectifying surface of language holds no room for this meaning. Once one realizes that the meaning of You is only reached in addressing another being with the full intent of co-presence, the You theme becomes the centerpiece of an amazing general view of meaningfulness—as amazing as if I found out that the air I breathe is actually produced at each and every moment by someone else exhaling.

It must also be seen, however, that the heightened appeals of value philosophy, dialogical philosophy, and phenomenological ontology are all *too strange* in an important way. Each engages in a certain excess and becomes incredible. And yet each achieves a pneumatologically significant result in its excess.

Value philosophy. Rickert's idealist values are strangely constructionist. They are destined not only by his manner of discovering them (his project of rounding out the universe) but by the very grammar of his discussion of them to inhabit some sort of "realm." Represented as quasi-entities, they are "out there" somewhere, so that philosophy is obliged to locate them in conceptual space and provide for their necessary combinations with thoughts and things in valuation. Thus, they share to some extent in the weaknesses of metaphysical Platonism that Aristotle criticized: they are estranged by definition from the things they were invented to explain.

The value of truth is an especially odd construct, for the primary motivation to look to values is to look beyond reality, to heed the appeal of the interruption of our experience of reality by gleamings of qualitatively superior possibility; whereas the point of the ideal of truth is to bind our awareness to reality. The normative superiority of the ideal of truth is a matter of thought coming right, flourishing, and being fulfilled in a relation with its real object. At issue are the potentialities of thought and of the reality it would know, and nothing else; all truth appeals are grounded in these. The truth-ideal can be represented as a *structure* of thought-in-relation-with-reality, and this structure surely embraces more than any finite set of thinking acts. But such a structure is more plausibly understood as the ideally complete unfolding of knowing initiatives than as a subjection of thought to a transcendent irreal factor. Only as an immanent telos of representational acts as guided and sustained by realities is the ideal of truth able to exert normative force in an appropriately standard way. If truth-seekers were just those who notice values and try to make thoughts and things conform to them, they would be an elite group of specialists within the community of subjects; but truth-seeking is part of normal human consciousness, not the exclusive province of philosophers.

Rickert can answer such objections, of course, by further explaining the peculiar properties of values, but their notional separateness continues to cause a strain in our understanding. The account is off-center. It could be justified only by showing how the adoption of the value figure of speech in philosophical discourse can bring essential implications of valuation into helpful focus—how, for instance, representing a problem of conflicting ethical and aesthetic valuations as a problem of the relation between the values of justice and beauty can be perspicuous, or how canvassing values is necessary to get hold of all the ingredients we need to assemble a more rewarding culture. But value talk is, in fact, troublesome to the degree that it aggravates such difficulties by taking separate and incommensurable points of reference instead of centering in the valuing subject.[60]

The value concept threatens to betray not only the realities we would know but also the choice we make to be so engaged. For the valuing subject is properly to be appreciated as *free*, whereas value talk seems to try to pour our valuing into hard molds. (Jaspers's concept of appeal is aimed against just this sort of betrayal.)[61] If a value is to be defined strictly as an authentic expression of freedom, in something like the way Kant tied worthiness to the exercise of pure practical reason, then the focus of our attention should shift back to that freedom and away from its always-questionable crystallizations. As an act of the subject, however, valuing cannot be categorically adequate to the appeal of *truth*, since the point of the most robust ideal of truth is to bring subjects to encounters with reality—not merely to counsel them how to be, and not merely to coordinate them with each other.

Having lodged these complaints, I must affirm that a major cause of the weakness of Rickert's account of truth is at the same time a great, potentially decisive strength: the oddly objectifying discussion of values is one in which all subjects are invited to participate quite fully. For values are *negotiable*. We have them on the table to define and use as we collectively see fit; their diversity reflects the diverse possibilities of valuing that we bring to any discussion. In that aspect, the concept of values represents effectively the superordinate appeal of the fellowship of intenders. These paradoxically discussible "irrealities" are an optimistic projection into our collective possibility. To characterize truth as a value is to posit that nothing may be said or believed about truth or fact that is not fair, and to trust that something eventually can be said that *will* be fair. The trumping of the realistic appeal of truth by the appeal of fairness, on this account, will not of course seem right to everyone, but at least this line of thinking leads to the important question of the right order of appeals.

Dialogical philosophy. Buber's understanding of the subject's relation with reality is strangely polarized. I-You relation is presented as the salvation of a subject in desperate straits—a sudden union with reality preceded and followed by a basic estrangement. He admits that You-saying and It-saying are "intricately entangled" but maintains that they are "tortuously dual," as though a subject oscillates between dedication and indifference. Buber's standards of authentic You-saying are extremely rigorous as well as rapturous: I say "You" *only* when I am seized by the "power of exclusiveness," when "nothing else is present but this one, but this one cosmically . . . measure and comparison [having] fled."[62] This is an *exceptional* event. There cannot be an "experience" (an *Erfährung*, a having-learned-about) of a being addressed as You, only a present "encounter."[63] Buber imposes this unexpected restriction on the category of experience because he understands the I of You-saying to be a uniquely actual, unified, fully human, redeemed self in contrast to the everyday utilitarian self of It-saying.[64] Reaching for a perfected relation, Buber misses the continuous and pervasive soliciting of the subject by all the beings that come into its experience. While there is indeed a "power of exclusiveness" and a transcendence of inert objectivity in any successful appeal, still a subject can very well attend to a being's appeal sincerely and at the same time continue to weave a fabric of "experience," measuring its own openness to various beings according to a program of coherent life in the world. The subject does give something of itself in attending to an appeal, but the subject need not become, even momentarily, the fully consecrated devotee of an appellant. If the reception of every appeal had to meet Buber's standards for "encounter," there could be no coherent sequence either of directly experienced or of communicated appeals, and most of what we justifiably think of as meaningful experience and communication could not be recognized as such.[65]

It seems, however, that by adopting a speech model of appeal, Buber does impressively convey the superordination of the appeals of interintentional fellowship to all other appeals. For our working answers to the question of what constitutes ultimately acceptable relationship—in a word, our spirits—do constitute the directive axes of our experience, and although the causes and effects of spirits are not confined to actual interintentional encounters, such encounters are their one wholly necessary condition of origination and full realization. A present, active orientation to encounter is the engine of spirits in any cultural context. Activity in encounter (spirit spiriting) transcends culture (spirit spirited) in the sense that subjects retain a prerogative to make spirits new according to the emerging exigencies of relationship, although this point should be balanced by recognition that meaning-formation always proceeds from a previously achieved posture, a valid form of fellowship.[66] (Rickert, we know, would invoke the guidance of values here in a describable order, but he also has a more specific claim that parallels Buber's claim about the power of exclusiveness in You-saying: according to Rickert, we find ourselves dealing with a true "individual" in the eminent sense, that is, a singularly compelling and indivisible being, only in relating our perception of a being to a *value* that forbids its segmentation or submersion in generality.)[67] In *I and Thou*, Buber gives some suggestive examples but no sustained account of the forming of I-You saying by spirits. This is because his main aim is to shake the complacency of a culture deeply sunk in its enlarged It-world, alienated from the You.[68]

Phenomenological ontology. Heidegger's ontological appeal is a strangely radical exercise in phenomenology. It goes so deep into the core of phenomenality that its connections with actual phenomena and with familiar genres of rational question (scientific, ethical, aesthetic) become tenuous. The appeal of Being dominates the inquiry in such a way as to disallow the appeals that beings make in their relative independence. (The same result came from Parmenides' attestation of Being-itself on the basis of an extreme requirement of perfect thinkableness.) Beings are de-realized, as a consequence, and Being takes on one or the other of two unwelcome aspects: that of the abstract common denominator of speculatively homogenized beings, and that of an exotic pseudo-being. In response to the complaint that his center of inquiry seems distant from the center of meaningfulness in experience, Heidegger affirms that there is indeed a distance between the commonsense perspective of "fallen" everyday experience and the radically disclosive experience of the call of conscience. How then are we to understand a truth value in everyday experience? In "On the Essence of Truth," Heidegger goes so far as to identify the apprehension of the accessible natures of concrete beings as *error*, a mode of "insistence" hiding Being's own truth.[69] Being's appeal is thus epistemologically overweening, intolerant to a strange degree.

Heidegger's positive achievement in pneumatological perspective is to give fellowship an ontological anchorage by showing that Being is properly elucidated, not as an abstract common denominator or exotic existent, but rather as the being-*there* and being-*with* of concrete intenders. "Resoluteness [i.e., the authentic response to Being's appeal] brings the Self right into its current concernful Being-alongside what is ready-to-hand, and pushes it into solicitous Being with Others."[70] It is far from clear how fellowship qualifies the meaning of Being for Heidegger, but at least he has indicated a mode of thinking that could sustain spiritually robust claims.[71]

* * *

Each of the philosophical appeals we have examined has been placed in deliberately maximized tension with the fabric of ordinary experience. Each confronts ordinary discourse in a quasi-prophetic stance, one of contradiction and summons. The implication is that a rare, precious, and authoritative insight is offered—something akin to religious revelation, the most compelling appeal conceivable. Are there perhaps religious *motivations* behind these appeal formulations that have not yet been defined? We can judge this better once we have studied overtly religious appeals. Just in what we have seen so far, however, we have learned some important things about the ideal of a most compelling appeal, an ideal that is integral to philosophy and religion alike, preceding their differentiation.

A great appeal will amaze; it will press against us the edge of a most-meaningful experience, like the sharp bow of a great ship slicing through water, in the form of an extraordinary conception. It will be able to justify itself by offering an important contribution to the supreme project of fellowship. A great appeal may also be expected to overreach and vex itself—and not merely because of the predictable incontinence of appeal communicators—for a great appeal places us under strain by attempting, in a necessarily unworldly way, to decisively interrupt and enrich our experience while at the same time also securing the broadest-based, deepest-rooted solidarity with the world we continue to live in. Necessarily most complex in what it purports to represent, it will achieve the maximum of attractive power by a great oversimplification; thus will it cut with an edge and hold a focus for attention.

The general ideal of truth, our prime example thus far, aims to represent each being and ensemble of beings as belonging to the real totality and to thought at the same time. But we can explicitly address the all-reality horizon of the various encounterable beings only in the most tenuous notional way, and only by running the risk of dismissing concrete appeals in favor of an ersatz universal Appeal. Unavoidably, then, our concept of truth does, after all, function for us typically as a self-managing, self-mirroring value of some sort, the appeal of reality being eclipsed by the appeal of our own powers to ourselves— whether as a realm of standardly attractive values, or in the guise of a general form of encounter, or as an adventure of ontological interpretation.

An adequate account of meaningful experience cannot, however, restrict the source and power of appealing to the subject, nor can it resolve meaning in a single supreme being. It is true that a being as an appellant is more meaningful than a being as a piece of information, but it is not true that a being-as-more-than-information can only be a vehicle of choice or the bearer of a value or the site of a deeper ontological apprehension. Idealist and ontologizing accounts each have their warrant in that beings really are interesting and really do matter in mediating our relations to our own powers and to a guessed-at deeper ground of being. Nevertheless, it belongs to a quite ordinary and irrefutable conception of meaningfulness that beings are interesting and matter also for what they are in themselves. From this perspective, idealist and ontologizing appeals must be redeemed by refracting them through real beings.

Buber accomplishes this by departing from third-person discourse. The a priori norm of You-saying refers essentially to the addressing of a real individual. Buber does not escape from the idealist trap in truth-appealing; in his thought, as we saw, the real individual is addressed as You just insofar as he, she, or it is the bearer of Youhood, and in this imposition of a unitary form of affirmation on the plurality of encounters, Buber rejoins the idealist philosophers of value. But his discourse continues to crack open this shell, taking advantage of the unique capacity of the second-person pronoun to unite concrete ostension with a radical exteriority to consciousness, all under the aegis of intimately challenging relationship.

A discourse that presents a great appeal cannot preserve its credibility if it fails to embody the heeding of the appeal. It cannot stand pat. How, though, can a rational discourse adhere actively to appeal other than by turning itself into exhortations, imitating prophecy? It would have to maintain the stance of rational inquiry and an objective engagement, but it would also have to press beyond any of its representational results before they solidify. It would have to keep arguing and interpreting. Heidegger, a brilliant example in this regard, portrayed his thinking of Being as essentially "on the way."[72] He stated very early that the essence of his approach must be "expressed precisely in the 'how' of our persisting in it . . . An incessant enactment of our concern for achieving primordiality is what constitutes primordiality."[73] He paid the price, as we saw, of de-realizing concrete beings, but his model of interminable analysis established that Being is not to be accessed and represented like beings.

Have we yet seen an adequate elucidation of the *concept* of appeal? Each of the approaches we have surveyed implies a distinctive apprehension of the essence of appealing.

To theorize as a thing what is essentially unlike a thing, as in Rickert's account of values, is to embed in the fabric of objectifying discourse tokens of that which inapprehensibly animates it as meaningful. Peculiarly difficult puzzle-objects of the highest significance have been postulated. Whenever anything in our experience substantially appeals to us, one or more of these mysterious appeal-things will be found attached to it. The theme of these appeal-things is always the rectification or perfection of existing beings. But they transcend existents. To be related to existents through them is to be spiritually excited in an idealist way, oriented to what could be.

To attempt to bottle the practical seriousness of a particular address and encounter of another being in a general theory of meaning, as Buber did with You-saying, is to turn *you* or *I* toward *that* other being, using the indexical force of personal pronouns to produce kinesthetically, as it were, an orientation to a basic situation of meaningfulness. In this case, the spiritual excitement is intensely present. The surplus of meaning in the appeal-fired experience does not point to another frame of reference.

Heidegger's digging down, in the most radical archaeology possible, to the fundamental eventfulness out of and in which all specific meaningful events occur examines you and I as pinned to our existence in the figure of Dasein, "being there." Phenomenological ontology finds out at ever-deeper levels how it is with us, what our true health and constitution are, and brings us peculiarly concerning news like that of a medical report. The spiritual excitement here lies in realizing what all along has been the unsuspected true state of affairs.

We have seen three major kinds of appeal. It is not obvious that any one of them could be dissolved or assimilated to another. It does appear, from the philosophical debates of the last century, that they can challenge each other endlessly. In their diversity, the three positions realize a dramatic tension that is internal to the Kantian position that they develop and adjust. To call their relationship "dramatic" is to say that we would miss or impair their revelatoriness if we tried to eliminate or subordinate any of them. But it is also to suggest that they can coexist in a stable, meaningful larger form. Can they indeed?

The Appeal of Donation: Marion

Our contemporary, Jean-Luc Marion—the first philosopher, according to François Laruelle, "to found the whole of his problematic as well as his method on *the appeal as appeal*"—offers not only a uniquely concentrated and inclusive discussion of appealing but also a test of the continuing force of the post-Kantian alternatives we surveyed in the preceding section.[74] As I will show with reference primarily to his work *Being Given*, Marion effectively inherits and refigures all three of those alternatives and the dramatic relationship among them.[75]

Marion adheres to phenomenology as the one possible path remaining for first philosophy, given the impossibility of validating knowledge claims either in a metaphysically objective way or egologically.[76] To be a phenomenologist is to try to achieve a purer disclosure of meanings (including the meanings that sustain metaphysical claims and critiques) by cultivating their most authentic, most "originary" presentations. The phenomenologist is obliged to perform one or more across-the-board "reductions" to lift the phenomena clear from ordinary experience—to distinguish their essential lines from their nonessential variations, for example, or to locate them in relation to the sense-giving activity of consciousness (Husserl), or to think them within their ontologically radical enabling by Being-as-differing-from-any-being (Heidegger). Marion proposes that by performing an explicit reduction of all phenomena to their *donation*, their sheer giving/givenness—this reduction having been implied, he argues, in the emphasis Husserl and Heidegger placed on intuitive and ontological donation, respectively—we will understand the fundamental character of all phenomena more adequately (Book 1).[77]

Donation is not required to be presented as an intuitive fulfillment or as a configuration of being. By a proper alignment of our attention that Marion calls "anamorphosis," referring to the optical trick of the anamorphic image, we can register the giving and givenness of what is shown—whatever enters our experience in any way—as what is given (117, 123–31). The "reduction" of donation, bracketing off all supposed transcendences—which in this context means clarifying the independence of donation from a real giver, or a real recipient, or a real gift—discloses the *irreal* essence of phenomenality: there is a showing of something insofar as there is a giving, not insofar as there is a real existence (39–51). A giver, recipient, or gift taken as a real cause or effect is made part of a system of exchange rather than accepted as a participant in genuine gratuitousness (74–81).[78] The true given "exercises [of] itself the initiative of making itself visible" (133) and arrives in my life contingently, as a fait accompli (139-41), on the basis of a depth or ground (*fond*) of its own which is not a background (*arrière-fond*);[79] it is received or not depending on how I am disposed (109). I become the "receiver" (*attributaire*, "appointee") of the phenomenon, a witness to it, without any claim to possess or produce it in the manner of a constituting ego (p. 249).

Marion's revision of phenomenology is inspired in large part by Levinas, who had pointed beyond intuition and being in tracing the ultimate source of meaningfulness to a moral appeal of face-to-face relation with the other person.[80] Levinas argued that this appeal transcends consciousness and being inasmuch as the meaning of moral obligation is precisely that the Other commands me prior to any initiative or self-possession whatsoever—thus, prior to any intentional constitution and unencompassed by any representation of alterity or value—and that my obligation of concern for the other determines the meaning of being before any event in being is effected.[81] Levinas was, for phenomenology, the Buber within the gates, the thinker who would push to the extreme the implications of the exteriority of the other being in terms of the "unforeseeableness" of the Other, or the "height" of the Other above the plane of intentional relations, or the "anarchy" or "immemorial" age of the Other's claim. Meanwhile, as we have already indicated, Levinas was unhappy with Buber's position in a phenomenologist's way: "The I-Thou relation in Buber retains a formal character: it can unite man to things as much as man to man. The I-Thou formalism does not determine any concrete structure."[82] Like Buber and Kant, Levinas made a single great division between unconditionally supreme meaningfulness and meaningfulness of every other sort. Like Buber and unlike Kant, he found a warrant for this division in actual relationship with other beings, allowing reason to play a role in determining meaning and value only insofar as it can function as a witness and servant of encounter. Like Kant and unlike Buber, he restricted the supreme appeal and superordinate meaningfulness to interhuman relations, but he framed this restriction as a phenomenological response to the face in which speaking begins.[83]

Marion revises Levinas, in turn, by integrating the special meaning of the ethical relation into a general phenomenology in such a way that (a) the meaningfulness of appeal and response is not confined to one part or dimension of experience but is appreciated in its universality, insofar as it belongs to donation; and (b) the superordinate meaningfulness that properly belongs to a specifically ethical or religious appeal and response can be understood as an intensification and privileged revelation of the universal meaning of donation, on which it depends.[84] This revision makes for a more methodologically defensible general phenomenology, Marion thinks: "At no moment was it necessary, when describing the given phenomenon, to have recourse to situations of intersubjective or ethical relations. The description was always able to stick strictly to intentional immanence."[85] But the general phenomenology of donation is also, in effect, a general revelation of gratuitousness that will support a more universally receptive response to the world, for the exceptional status of ethical meaning in Levinas's account implies a great unlikeness and conflict between that which can redeem and that which needs redeeming, between an irreal good and a neutral or even evil reality.[86]

Marion locates Levinas's main ethical point in an account of special phenomena called "saturated." Phenomena do not all offer the same degree of donation (*Being Given*, Book 4).[87] Some are evidently impossible to synthesize or sum up in the usually necessary way, or are dazzling or unbearable (like the sunlight for Plato's cave dwellers). The subject is aware of being at their mercy. Marion's four categories of saturated phenomenon are the *event*, most manifestly a great historical event, provocative of endless discussion; the splendid *idol*, such as an impressive painting whose self-manifestation absorbs me individually; the sorrowing, anxious, or joyful affections of the *flesh*; and the *icon*, whose visage I am not capable of visually mastering but rather must endure (228–33). Finally, Marion finds the ultimate possibility of phenomenality, a saturation to a second degree, in the category of *revelation*, combining the powers of all four of these types. Revelation is exemplified by the intense unworldliness-in-the-world of Christ (234–41).

The theme of appeal makes its appearance in *Being Given* as the status of the subject-as-witness-of-phenomenality is raised from the generic "receiver" to the more special "gifted" (*adonné*, "devotee"), corresponding to the radicalizing of the impact of the self-giving of the phenomenon in the saturated phenomenon (366). "Each type of saturated phenomenon inverts intentionality [and] therefore makes a call [*appel*] possible, even inevitable . . . [the *appel* is] the undeniable *par excellence*" (267, 283). To speak of appeal is to say that the witness of the phenomenon is most momentously engaged. The appeal gives birth to the gifted as one who receives wholly (268). The gifted receives what is given so radically as to take from it the excess of donation as such, and in doing so it receives its own ultimate determination (282). The gifted has a doubly extreme responsibility, on the one hand in being deprived of an intuitive or intellectual grasp of the appellant's being (since the appellant, as radical giver, is "anonymous"), and on the other hand in being burdened with the "positive indifference" of love with respect to all the possible ways of mediating the appeal's manifestation and responding to it (306–307).

Thus, Marion has made a discrimination among phenomena without giving up the generality of donation:

> Though paradoxical, or precisely for that very reason, the saturated phenomenon should in no way be understood as an exceptional, indeed vaguely irrational (to say it plainly, "theological"), case of phenomenality. Rather, it accomplishes the coherent and rational development of the most operative definition of the phenomenon: it alone appears truly as itself, of itself, and on the basis of itself, since it alone appears without the limits of a horizon or reduction to an [I] . . . It is purely and simply a matter of the phenomenon taken in its full sense, in short, of the phenomenon's normative figure, in relation to which the others are defined and declined by defect or simplification. (218–19)

And so the appeal, as Laruelle suggested, is revealed as the *one* theme—the appropriately radical, full, and inclusive theme—of a philosophy of meaningful experience. We can see now how Marion would answer the charge of anthropomorphism that might be directed against an appeals account of experience. The "privileged phenomenon" of interpersonal appeal is minimally meaningful in the relevant way because it participates in the universal structure of donation; meanwhile, it has its distinguishing maximal meaning as a maximization of donation. That is, the amazing entry of the other person into my experience as one with whose status and intentions I, as a new and different "I," must be concerned is amazing as a radical and great donation.

The amplitude and dimensionality of donations, insofar as donation admits of degrees, seemingly must vary as a function of the physical, intellectual, and spiritual capacities of donation's witnesses. The relevance of these powers is crucial in a proposition that introduces the notions of the appeal and the devotee: "To be sure, any 'to whom/which' ['*à qu(o)i*'] will be enough to welcome what gives itself, but only a 'to whom' (and never a 'to which') can assume the full role of receiver—presenting what gives itself in such a way that it shows itself in the world" (265). More specifically, the "self" that appeals to me in the situation that would ordinarily be deemed one of appeal is phenomenologically founded on the "self" involved in any appearance whatsoever; for all phenomenal showing, *if* it is phenomenologically received, is a self-showing (*se montrer*). The anthropomorphism or animism of an appeal to appeals (or in the use of a reflexive verb) is rooted in nothing less fundamental than the disposition to address "the things themselves," that is, to seek sources and standards of meaning without relying primarily on metaphysical or worldview constructions.

Marion reaches saturated phenomena (in Book 4) only after working out more basic and universally applicable "determinations" of donation—various aspects of the gratuitousness of giving, the gift, and receiving. This is a risky approach in that our sense of the meaningfulness of the donation that is being discussed, and indeed of the point of the whole program of a "reduction" of donation, is long suspended. A critic might well worry that Marion's reduction actually empties experience of all significant content (72).[88] But the point of the exercise becomes more apparent in the saturated phenomena, which appear to be just the sorts of things that most deeply concern us (even if not everyone's gallery of "saturated phenomena" would hold the same items as Marion's); and we find that the phenomenological way has now been cleared so that we no longer have reason to discount testimony to these "excessively" impressive phenomena and we do have a license to appeal to them as interpretive keys to the meaningfulness of all phenomena. In the account of donation, we have an appropriate philosophical elucidation of appealing; in the concept of revelation, we have an appropriate philosophical indication of supreme appeal (as a possible meaning-structure).[89]

* * *

Now I shall offer criticisms of Marion's project in relation to the three major alternatives of appeal philosophy that I have already outlined. I will be testing the premise that he inherits and renews all three of those alternatives and that his most significant gains and difficulties are new inflections of theirs.

Phenomenological ontology. Marion shares with Husserl and Heidegger the presumption of a pristine or "originary" or most-basic meaning, a meaning that determines all the ordinary meanings *we* mean because, as the enabling ultimate source and standard of our meanings, it must be prior to them; the philosopher cannot hope to dictate it but only to assist at its appearance. A basic problem with this presumption is the unresolved relation in which it holds realism and idealism. It insists on finding rather than making, and elevates describing over arguing, so as to assume the whole virtue of a realist stance; but it does this in a resolutely idealist way, either by gearing itself to the perfectly accessible datum, which must be immanent to consciousness (Husserl), or by articulating a perfect unification of all things, such as the event of being (Heidegger). Thus, phenomenology is at risk of missing, on the one hand, realism's power (against an uncritical idealism) of recognizing that beings are only partially accessible and deeply diverse, and, on the other hand, idealism's power (against an uncritical realism) of detecting and appropriately allowing for the constructive operations of formal principles in experience. Supposing that Marion's donology overcomes certain important limits in Husserl's egology and Heidegger's ontology, it still holds to immanence and wields a global thesis the meaningfulness of which cannot be specified nonarbitrarily. By rejecting, under the rubric of "metaphysics," *all* consideration of cause, effect, and subsistence, it exempts itself from the burden of figuring out what is really going on in the world, what really holds benefit or harm for what else, and what our multiply schematic, complexly interested, late-capitalist, mammalian minds are up to. What is offered is strictly a first philosophy, to be sure; but one can justifiably expect a first philosophy to give a rewarding orientation for worldly inquiry rather than collapse in on itself in an edifying vision (whether the vision be Marion's Christian-agapic one or Heidegger's pagan-heroic one).

The distortion inherent in Marion's pursuit of a primordial certainty and wholeness in phenomenality is manifest in the attenuation of the meaning of appeal in his discourse. In immanence, the appeal reduces to a variety of odd states it inflicts upon the subject. We are told that it decenters the subject, changing the "I" to a "me-to-whom," dispossessing the subject of all properties the "I" would own; that it overhangs the subject with an ungraspable claim; that it is always previously established. The appeal in no way conveys or points to information about the real being of the appellant (a paramount point being always that appeal's meaningfulness transcends determinable being). Actually, though, who or what an appeal represents is an essential interest of appeal. Marion excludes from view what makes an appeal appealing, the good it promises, except insofar as its good coincides with the good of universal donation; but a universal donation that is not individually specified offers an utterly ambiguous prospect as regards goodness. It can sponsor evil and good equally.[90]

Marion's presentation of the universally experienceable sense of appeal has a kind of virtual anchorage in the examples, often religious and artistic, by which he conveys something of what his position *might actually* mean, but he does not provide a template of meaningful worldly life comparable to what *Being and Time* offered in its categories of care, fallenness, and resoluteness. In this he remains phenomenologically radical and avoids sliding into theology, but he also exerts only the slightest pressure on our interpretation of worldly life. Yet Marion's donology could be credited with a formidable power in showing that our experience is utterly pervaded by a prime constituent of meaning, pure gratuitousness, that might otherwise be referred to a questionable divine being or overlooked altogether. And it could be said, adapting my earlier comment on Heidegger, that Marion performs a vital pneumatological service in displaying the donological credentials of the supremely appealing enterprise of fellowship.

Dialogical philosophy. Marion makes still more patent the extremely strange position that a philosopher of "exteriority" is in. The figure of exteriority assumes certain rules and bounds "inside" which all experience falls and then proceeds to violate those rules and bounds in order to expand experience. Thus, Buber would not allow that the "encounter" with the other being amounts to an "experience" at all, since experience must be entirely "had."

And Levinas elaborately anti-locates the Other in relation to consciousness and being on the assumption of a rather tyrannical regular constitution of all meanings intentionally or ontologically. But when the ungraspable aspect of the other being's appearance is identified as the other's essence, the strange consequence is that the other cannot be individually identified at all, but instead becomes a generic Other interchangeable with all other Others. This is but an inversion of the idealist reduction of everything to contents of consciousness or configurations of being.

To avoid a total blackout of the Others in an exteriority-driven account, it is necessary to describe kinds of Other-encounter in such a way that it becomes apparent how exteriority qualifies our experience. Thus, *I and Thou* makes various suggestions about the You-saying conditions of wholesome personal and cultural development. In *Totality and Infinity*, Levinas evokes the moral transcendence in ordinary human relationships, notably erotic and familial ones.[91] In *Being Given*, Marion follows Levinas's precedent by describing parent-child relations, claiming, for example, that the father's gift of the family name in response to the newborn's appeal presupposes a fundamental and irremovable anonymity in the appealing child.[92]

Dialogical philosophy's commitment to the exteriority principle also puts it on a difficult argumentative footing insofar as it must set aside accepted rules of demonstration. Many people simply do not understand what Buber is getting at in *I and Thou* or feel no loss in transposing his descriptions and evaluations into the experiential frame of reference he says he means to exceed. If a sane listener cannot follow the exceptional gestures of the exteriority thinker, or has no reasons of an accepted kind to try to do so, how can any pretense of rational communication or adequate appealing on behalf of all-reality be maintained? Or, supposing that the Other *is* beheld as Other, what assurance could there be that one is seeing a truth accurately, as with the sharper focus obtained by squinting, rather than seeing an illusory artifact of the strange Othering gesture, like stars produced by rubbing one's eyes? Marion addresses this difficulty with his notion of anamorphosis. The devotee of an appeal is stationed and pointed on the right line to see the phenomenon at the angle at which radical donativity is disclosed. But Marion's optical metaphor, by itself, only raises without answering the question of how a subject becomes properly responsive to appeals. It would seem that a donological answer ought to be worked out at least on the scale of Heidegger's account of the call of conscience.

The best way to elude the exteriority dilemma is to sidestep philosophical theorizing and seek meaning pragmatically in actual You-saying. In addressing You—not "a You," but *You*—the other being, or rather You, are invited to declare what, or in this case who, You are. And yet perfect immediacy is chimerical: any appealing or witnessing must be mediated by intellectual and communicative structures. It is a question, then, not of sidestepping theory altogether, but of rightly deploying theory as an auxiliary of practice. In this light we can see the relevance of Marion's proposals even as wholly abstracted from actual You-saying. The very concept of donation is an enabling device for conscious receptiveness to a being's self-manifestation. Although Marion portrays donation as an affection rather than as a venture of conception, our initial exploration of appeals revealed that an appeal must involve construal as much as affection inasmuch as it links the actuality of an appearance with projections (inferences, and even plans) regarding realities to which the appearance is taken to refer. Donation as a primordial meaning-event that might or might not animate consciousness, depending on anamorphosis, must be completed by a worldly, purposeful construal that might or might not apply to the relation with the other being, depending on how interaction actually goes.

Value philosophy. Given the importance of the Heideggerian prototype of phenomenology for Marion, and given Heidegger's categorical rejection of the constructivism and subjectivism of neo-Kantian value theory, it is surprising to find Marion using just the sorts of arguments to disclose donativity that Rickert used to define the true nature of meanings and values—for example, the argument that the meaning of a painting is indifferent to its factual realizations.[93] But Marion reactivates this idealist argument in the new frame of reference established by his "third reduction" to radical givenness, that is, in an effort to go beyond ontologism of the Heideggerian as well as of the pre-Kantian kind.[94] In any case, Marion's project shares with Rickert's the crucial limitation that it posits a structure of putative goodness in which the substance of real flourishing of beings and of real benignity in relation remains almost unguessable. The connections between the irreal form of meaningfulness and the real contents of experience are to be filled in however we like. Marion and Rickert both stress the meaningfulness of the "individual" as such in meaningful experience, Marion laying greater emphasis on the "self" of *se donner* and *se montrer*; but both explain this meaningfulness as supervening from irreality. Individuals count only as vehicles. There is no indication that the world is enriched by the existence of a particular cat or tree.

Although Marion proceeds by an immanentist reduction and Rickert by heterological expansion, their projects share the crucial goal of transcending *being*. Both embrace the requirement of a non-ontological or "irreal" source of meaning, and both make this move as a way of forming a most-adequate response to a very broad kind of appeal appreciated especially in its interruptive, commanding aspect. They agree that actuality, as such, cannot ground the superordinate appeals of meaningful experience, not even the meaningful evidentness of evidence.[95] If I think an actual thought or encounter an actual being and find it meaningful, that is because my soul is made to vibrate in relation with an irreal condition that can in no way be grasped as an object and, partly for that reason, can unreservedly be affirmed as a *way* of dealing with objects—a way of happy and/or fair coexistence like beauty, truth, justice, or generosity.[96] The disagreement with Heidegger is clear: Heidegger believes that the delineation of such a way must fall into subjectivism, a form of alienation from Being's disclosure, if it is not thought as a way opened and led by Being, that is, rooted in what *is* going on. For their part, Rickert and Marion maintain that an ontological interpretation of the way is alienated from the utterly non-objective ultimate sources of meaningfulness, pure gestures of some sort that refuse to coincide with what is. From the perspective of Buber's acknowledgment of the Youhood of actual beings, however, the neo-Kantian and donological critiques of objectivity overshoot the target; their irrealities are general, abstract, and remote.

Since Rickert and Marion go to equally great lengths to locate their prime referents elsewhere than in being, one wonders to what extent the results of idealist value theory and post-post-idealist donology might be compatible, or even convergent.

Both Rickert and Marion deploy in close association a principle of unity and a principle of plurality of appeals. There is unity insofar as Rickert makes out a "realm" (*Reich*) of non-actual "holding" (*gelten*) of meanings and Marion affirms donation in the phenomenality of all phenomena. Yet for Marion the various phenomena are not simply identical insofar as they are meaningful (that is, as interchangeable illustrations of donation), but rather they are *differently meaningful* precisely because it is an aspect of "being given" that a being *gives itself* from itself, on the basis of itself. If Marion seems sometimes to tremble on the verge of claiming that what ultimately *is given* in every phenomenon is just the Ur-event of donation itself, he need not make that claim; he can maintain a meaning pluralism in basically the same way that Rickert does, by construing each concrete meaning-presentation as a union of value-form (for Marion, donativity) with existing content. Rickert organizes meanings by metaphysical realms and value categories but otherwise believes that philosophy should be completely open to all meaning-material. Philosophy's task is to sort out the universal conditions of meaningfulness for the sake of responding more intelligently to the unforeseeable concrete meanings that nature and culture generate.[97]

Rickert distinguishes directly commanding meanings as "values," while Marion distinguishes the conspicuously gratuitous "saturated phenomena." It seems from Marion's perspective that Rickert operates at an abstract and derivative level and risks a false objectification in affirming generic values such as truth, pleasure, and holiness without a basis in a radical phenomenological investigation. It seems from Rickert's perspective that Marion gets more appeal-force from his saturated phenomena than they are able to provide just as concrete faits accomplis and that Marion could more honestly justify his choices of example and attest the true dimensions of their meaning by taking up the discourse of values. In any case, Rickert and Marion both claim that the subject is intrinsically non-indifferent toward these commanding meanings. They share a Kantian excitement in activating this more-than-actual subjectivity of non-indifference, this "good will." Both look beyond the various occasions of non-indifference to the form of a supreme climax of meaningfulness, the ultimate object of strictly philosophical valuation, which Rickert formally designates as "full-fillment" (*Voll-endung*) and Marion as "revelation," and then beyond that form to a *realization* of supreme meaningfulness that can be an object of faith but not of philosophical demonstration.[98]

Rickert and Marion are committed to a non-ontological location of the sources and standards of meaningful experience because they wish to participate philosophically in a gesture that cannot coincide with the real. How is such a move to be understood? Their "irrealizing" strictures imply some negation of the compulsion of reality, some opening of an otherwise-than-what-occurs-as-such or an otherwise-than-what-is-experienced-as-such. For now I will use the open term "irrealizing" to refer to this kind of move, which they make in different ways.

Rickert's irrealizing is undoubtedly Kantian. Values relate directly to willing acts of the subject, primarily in judgments and choices. Dominant values register as "oughts." The subject complies with them by willing in conformity with them. This submission is ultimately a spontaneous expression of autonomy, for the value-responsive subject submits just to its own *valid* form of willing as distinct from its real acts and inclinations.[99] Thus, Rickert's gesture is fundamentally that of freedom. As non-indifferent to validity, as sensitized to the issue of the meaning of life, my will is always other than my real will—that is my negative freedom—and yet is capable, on the other hand, of forming itself perfectly—that is my positive freedom. Freedom in Rickert is not as insistently self-centering and self-announcing as in Kant or Fichte, however; it is more diversely deployed in the life-worlds studied by the cultural sciences. Indeed, freedom is somewhat masked as a philosophical motive by Rickert's strategy of gaining access to values by a methodical expansion of the concept of the universe rather than by a Kantian plunge inward into the self-shaping of reason. The heterological expansion of the universe makes theoretical room for something-positively-other-than-the-real but gives no justification for a particular sort, or *this* sort, of other. We are left with the spontaneity of free willing as the best answer to the question of Rickert's basis for affirming an irreal.

In contrast, the subject of Marion's "phenomenological act" observes its own being-affected. Judgments and choices are secondary; reception is primary. Thus, Marion's irrealizing cannot be centered in the subject's own activity as implied by the Kantian principle of freedom. Rather, his efforts to disengage irreal giving from real causation point to a principle of universal gratuitousness or—to use a theological word that seems always on the tip of the donological tongue—grace. The superordinate appeals come from the external "good will" of self-offering phenomena (or perhaps ultimately from whatever offers *them*) rather than from the internal "good will" of freely poised practical reason. What I meet is what is first other-than-real, and then, as its witness or receiver or devotee, I become other-than-real with it.

Could it be determined that either Marion or Rickert have adopted the right priority in irrealizing—that one appeal really overrides the other? Alternatively, could Marion's and Rickert's arguments be reduced to one argument for a primal irrealizing that can assume the aspect of free will or grace, depending on one's position and the direction of one's attention in the transactions of life? Then, having escaped the limits of either of the one-sided situations characterized by the provocative contrast between irrealizing and reality—the situation in which I am to be free to enter the reality-system from my irreal inwardness, or the situation in which an Other is to be admitted to relate to the reality-system from "outside" it—would there remain any important reason not to identify this all-enabling irrealizing with the "event of Being"? Alternatively, could the two kinds of irrealizing be treated as complementary and combined without a synthesis?

Buber chose the second alternative. One of his formulas for meaningful experience is the joining of will and grace (58).[100] The subject of encounter, the I of I-You relation, is (ir)realized as a being of "will" that is (a) distinct from the bundle of desires, satisfactions, and calculations that obtain at any moment in "experience"; and (b) able to apply to an actual decision or deed all the energy and import of excluded possibilities (55–56, 101). The encountered being is (ir)realized as an Other that arrives without conceptual mediation, "in no system of coordination," in splendid insubordination sustaining a free *reciprocity* without which the self cannot will freely (62, 81, 100). Buber calls the "readiness" of the self to enter into relation with this gracious Other the "innate You" (78). Active I-You reciprocity is located "between" I and You and identified with "spirit" and meaningfulness (56, 89).[101]

Superficially like Heidegger and unlike Rickert and Marion, Buber does resort to the category of ontology to distance his claims from idealist subjectivism. At one point he builds up the category of the ontological in an inclusive movement similar to Rickert's heterological construction of the world-all:

> This reality understood as existing being, as existing being into which all that is psychic and all that is cosmic and all that is opposite and all that is inclusive of the two is embedded, this *ontologism* we can, with all foresight and self-limitation, set up for a moment as a third to the two . . . which unites them. But careful! . . . What we are discussing is a problem, not an answer.[102]

Yet Buber does not define I-You relation as an inclusive event of being. It appears that he holds back from doing this in *I and Thou* because his conception of meaningfulness is strictly tied to the over-against structure, the *Gegenüber*, and the pluralistic relation-structure of "between." He will not shift to a supposedly more fundamental question (like Heidegger's question concerning the meaning of being) that would neutralize the directly challenging confrontation of the Other's irrealizing in relation with that of the self. The appeal associated with such a position could not be as strong.

I conclude that Buber's position holds a distinctively strong philosophical appeal insofar as it offers to accommodate the profoundly appealing claims of autonomous freedom (Rickert) and phenomenal gratuitousness (Marion) together. By holding these two claims together without reduction or synthesis, Buber's position gives them their most dramatic mise-en-scène and at the same time allows the best answer to the supremely strenuous appeal of justice as it applies to the formation of first philosophy. For two understandings of justice are in contention here. Justice for a Kantian is always formed as an iteration of freedom. The manifestations of beings provide content for ethical experience, while the principle of consistency in willing provides the form. For Marion, however, the loving intelligence of the subject inundated by phenomenal givings must be occupied in composing a most-appreciative total response. On Marion's path to justice, the Kantian priority of willing to experience is reversed. The actual flourishing of beings rather than the perfection of willing dominates the realization of justice.

Must we choose between respect and love? It seems an inescapably compelling proposition that the most just response, that is, the most adequate heeding of appeals for the sake of coexistence, is one that gives each perspective a turn (insofar as turns are desired or needed) and a share (insofar as sharing is possible) in directing our life.

* * *

The radiation of Kantian appeal implications through neo-Kantian value theory, dialogical philosophy, and phenomenological ontology suggests a large structure that will recur in this investigation. It is an array of alternative stances oriented to the most basic dimensions of being to which we can direct our attention—that is, respectively, to the not-yet-constituted, the event of constituting, and the already-constituted; or, put differently, to possibility, actuality, and reality; or to the future, the present, and the past. The future, open to proposals, is where appeal *leads*. Value-philosophy is an articulate way of responding to a cognitively supreme appeal of which the center or thrust lies somewhere in the range of the not-yet-constituted, appealing especially to determine our free will as it takes advantage of possibilities of shaping the world. The present, which is the zone of constituting and active negotiation, is where appeal *grasps* us, as dialogical philosophy articulates. The past—or, better, the status of the already-constituted—is the zone in which an appellant figures as an important *source* for our life and thus an object of *acknowledgment*, the response to which Heidegger's ontology is geared (most explicitly in his later thinking-as-thanking).[103] The juxtaposition of these post-Kantian philosophies is thus an intellectually powerful reflection of one of the most basic dramatic structures of our life and a promising way to address the adequacy and inclusiveness issues that are inherent in the premise of supreme appeal. A similar intellectual structure will appear when we are drawn again into the drama of the claims of future, present, and past in examining the post-Kantian discourses of revelation.

The Appeal in
Modern Theology

Religious Appeal and the Ideal of Revelation

We began our investigation of appeals by considering the appeals of beings as though a solitary subject had just begun a life and entered a world and could freely observe how his or her attention spontaneously follows objects of outer and inner perception. That pristine scenario never actually obtains, but the idea of it indicates a layer of meaningful experience that is important at all times. This layer of experience is all the more credible phenomenologically since it holds not merely fixed "givens" that serve as docile building blocks for claims about life and the world but rather *rattlings* of our experience by implicit *questions* and *issues* of real identity and real relation among beings—including the crucial practical issue of what will turn out to be conducive to one's own flourishing and the flourishing of other beings in relationship. Beings appeal by offering goodness, putting at stake the roles they and we will have in the shaping world.

Beings offer prospects that become appeals as we incline to them. We impute appeals to them of what we take to be their own sort. Beings as such do not *confront* or *call*, strictly speaking—even if it is worthwhile to think of them as doing something like this in order to overcome the false idea that we are basically uninvolved with them. But when another being intentionally presents something to my perception so as to elicit my response, then appealing in a fuller sense occurs. Issues of identity and relation presented at this level of appeal apply to communicating partners in the enterprise of collective life. The implications of responding to a call one way rather than another involve a subject in friendship and enmity, loyalty and betrayal, legitimacy and outlawry. Appeal in this fuller sense is freighted with spiritual seriousness, and its interruptive power is accordingly greater. Even if its content is a meek request, it has the cutting-edge form of a demand.

The appeals of cultural ideals are related to interpersonal appeals, for they draw on our active involvement in collective living. They lack the momentarily sharp exigency of a call (unless they happen to be presented by someone's actual call, or in an arresting aesthetic object), but they have an extra seriousness of their own in representing the experience and prospects of a whole community and a farther-reaching effect on the appellate subject's relations with practical and intellectual possibilities. The formal ideals of justice and truth, notably, are universally and unconditionally binding. More fleshed-out ideals of a best practice or fullest knowledge can be compelling as supreme appeals; Axial Age teachings are stuffed with such content.

Is it possible to go any higher on a scale of appeal-power? Evidently certain kinds of appeal can exert supreme authority in a given context, like the appeal of a fellow human being to be treated with respect in any actual interhuman transaction. And life-organizing cultural ideals are inescapably authoritative. *Religion,* conceived strictly as a comprehensive valuation or guided way of life, involves no appeal beyond a cultural ideal in that sense. It seems, however, that a *religious person*—one who intends to be religious, understanding religiousness as a state more pervasively binding and promising than contingent associations with worldly beings can be and more powerfully motivating and guiding than everyday compliance with a cultural order can be—is necessarily interested in discerning a unique religious grade of appeal. (I leave open the question of the extent to which a given culture allows for or promotes this intention in its members. I assume that all the so-called world religions have supported it and been shaped by it.) Thus, religious appeals must by definition be incomparably strong.

Understood in this way, religious appeals must fulfill some possibility of appeal-power that is greater than those that belong generically to call-appeals and ideals. One possibility, at least, fits this prescription: to be the *sole* compelling appeal and thus an unchallengeable supreme appeal. Interpersonal appeals can be supremely exigent in everyday life, but there are always two lines of practical escape from them: one may, at whatever cost, reject such an appeal on its own merits; or one may heed another person or ideal ("I could not love thee, dear, so much, / Lov'd I not honor more").[1] Such is the complexity of life that no call or ideal is sheltered from competition on that plane of appeal, even one that plausibly presents itself as supreme. But a religious appeal is understood to be a great simplifier of appellate loyalty. The religious subject is a *devotee*. The religious object is "holy, holy, holy," that is, intrinsically *most great*, not merely formally supreme. It is true that a devotee could have a change of heart at any time: as long as life continues, a different greatest appellant could appear or the apparently greatest appellant could disappear. It must be remembered also that the subject's power of withdrawal is always essential to the appeal's remaining an appeal rather than a coercion. Nevertheless, a religious ideology posits that such a change of heart is normatively precluded by the recognizable maximal greatness of the appellant, or by the irresistible power exerted by the appellant over the devotee by whatever means (perhaps as the granting of a superlative vitality to the devotee), or by the devotee's perfect bestowal of attention. A religious appeal realizes in the highest degree the possible force of being-appeal (distinctively, the promise of actual flourishing) and of call-appeal (distinctively, the promise of loyalty).

Like any other appeal, a religious appeal will be compelling by virtue of (a) the motivation it furnishes, of which the supreme degree is devotion; (b) the benign effectiveness of the relation it arranges between appellant and subject of appeal, of which the supreme degree is salvation; and (c) the objective impressiveness that is apprehended in the appellant, of which the supreme degree is divinity. These are three distinct lines of inquiry into religious meaning formation. One can develop an account of the true nature and essential forms and implications of devotion *or* of salvation *or* of divinity. But these three realms of religious meaning are united, and their mutual involvement is indicated, by the form of appeal.

An appeal can become the sole compelling appeal in one or both of two ways. It can be supremely powerful *intensively*, its immediately presented quality being such as to overshadow the qualities of any other sort of appellant, as according to Rudolf Otto's portrayal of "the holy" as a focal *mysterium tremendum et fascinans*.[2] (The awe specific to the apprehension of the holy in Otto's account has a cousin in the uncanniness Heidegger ascribes to the uniquely meaningful "call of conscience" in *Being and Time*.)[3] Another example of this approach is Franz Rosenzweig's idea of revelation as the amazingly intense active presence of God in all beings as the summoning lover of humanity.[4] In discursive religious thinking, the concept of holiness or omnipotence or eternity is typically used to saturate all possibilities of ontological and axiological appeal and so could be called intensively dominant; at least, it is a placeholder for whatever really is intensively dominant, and a question to pose to any claimant to that status.[5] An appeal can also be supreme *extensively*, all-inclusively; it can identify itself with all other valid appeals and appropriate their power for its own, or (and this is another side of Rosenzweig's idea) it can establish an absolute orientation in life that decides the meaning of all other orientations.[6] In this respect too, a supreme appeal is amazing and strange, for although an absolute orientation provides a kind of perfect security, it is also capable of conflicting with various specific orientations that are generally accepted and useful in everyday life. To commit oneself totally to response to a supreme appeal is to hold oneself exhilaratingly and dangerously free of all other appeals.

An appeal could excel either intensively or extensively without being the sole compelling appeal. For example, I might acknowledge that "the universe" has a directly manifest impressiveness superior to that of any other being whenever comparison is drawn, or I might find a universe appeal mingled with the appeals of all beings, and yet I might decline for the most part to concentrate on it. Or I might date my existence in relation to a remembered divine initiative in time (like the birth of Christ or the Muslim Emigration), accepting far-reaching implications for my identity in locating myself in this way, and yet fail to take any actions determined by that orientation. In these cases my understanding of the situation seems to qualify as a religious view, while my lack of devotion is a reason to deny that I am under religious appeal. My non-devout view is only potentially or schematically religious.

A person is often said to be "devoted" to another person in love. Cases like this of a single dominant appeal are commonly recognized to resemble or overlap with the situation of being under religious appeal. Yet we still have reason to deny that being in love is full-fledged religiousness so long as we and the lover (if she or he is not literally mad) recognize that the beloved's appeal, though emotionally and practically dominant for the lover, is not really the only one that could ultimately matter. (The same would hold for "devotion" to a charismatic leader.) Critics of religious passion might claim that a sane person should be able to recognize also that the appeal of God or heaven or nirvana is likewise not really the sole compelling appeal. But a fully worked-out religious perspective neutralizes this objection (to its own satisfaction) by interpreting non-sacred appeals as negligible or by showing how the whole range of rightly heeded appeals actually belongs within the compelling religious appeal.

We noted that a cultural ideal mediates the appeals of many beings and persons. A religious appeal, if durable and widely shared, will be installed as a cultural ideal and will take advantage of this appeal-representing structure to make itself pervasive and inescapable. Indeed, it will position itself as the principle of culture and of all appeals, as something like the very nervous system of a society, so that all appeals acknowledged in a society express and reinforce the religious appeal—as, for example, in a wedding service in a Christian society the loyalty of spouses to each other may be characterized as implementations of their loyalty to God—and anyone who fails to heed the religious appeal is liable to be deemed thoroughly untrustworthy. To accomplish this, the religious appeal will impose its own organizing form, like the sacred/profane duality featured in Durkheim's and Eliade's accounts of religion, on all other forms of life, and this organizing form will be as important as the distinctively impressive content of any phenomenal manifestation in sustaining the appeal's commanding position.[7] The form makes everyday religious sense of people's lives. It actually generates experiential content through ritual, such as in the distinctively felt obligations and joys of holy days, which are based on calendrical repetition.

The classic modern theories of religion to which I have alluded treat religion for the most part as a dimension of the life of a culture with a unified religious ideology. Under these circumstances the appeal character of religion does contribute essentially to the socialization of culture members and the negotiation of appeal conflicts between religious and nonreligious appellants. But this scenario lacks an element that is of the highest importance in appreciating the implications of the appeal character of the sort of religion most of us most often deal with, the world religion sort. The world religions received their canonical formulations in milieux of highly articulated religious disagreement. For the purposes of a contemporary Hindu, Buddhist, Daoist, Confucian, Zoroastrian, Jew, Christian, Muslim, or Sikh, the decisive appeal of religious tradition was established (as attested by scriptures) in a marketplace of competing religious appeals and continues to be sustained in such a marketplace—which is to say that it relies on devices of competition like polemical critique and co-opting of rival claims and that it depends for its success on consciously free choices by individuals. The concept of *revelation* has, accordingly, a distinctive sense and use in the world religions.[8]

In small-scale, nonliterate societies, grounding occurrences of religious appeal or "hierophanies" can contribute excitement and gravity to a great proportion of the culture's norms. In early forms of the state, hierophanies take on the increasingly important function of supporting the authority of priests and kings in relation to their consociates and other states. Religious appeal can be quite closely tailored to the peculiar circumstances of the society in which it is entertained in either of these situations, and it seems reasonable to suppose that the more closely the appeal corresponds to a society's circumstances, without sacrificing its cosmic amplitude, the stronger it will be. In this situation the conditions of impressiveness and inclusiveness can be heavily skewed: many of the features that presumably helped to make the religion of pharaonic Egypt compelling for ancient Egyptians, for example, make it difficult for most other people to respond to it devoutly.

The hierophany of a marketplace religion must differ from this model. A marketplace religion cannot be sustained merely by the practices of a particular culture since its prospective adherents are divided, inquiring, and disagreeing. So it must have a portfolio that can travel. It must be plausibly universal in any setting. It must motivate and reward its individual devotees as independent, in some measure, rather than strictly as members of a culture. It will, to be sure, draw strength from ethnic and cultural rooting however possible. But it will never abandon its original marketplace advantage of offering a discursive, scripturally anchored body of information and principles that is ideally compelling *for anyone* for the twin reasons of its inherent persuasiveness (intelligible and communicable, comprehensively accurate, practically helpful, liberating) and its real connection with supreme goodness or holiness (as in having been delivered by a prophet or sage). The concept of revelation, however it is deployed ("Thus says the Lord," "Thus have I heard," "It is written," etc.), is central in the marketplace religions because it unites the more exoteric claim of a universal sense-making that can be studied by anyone, thanks to texts and text-normed practices, with the more esoteric "unveiling" claim of a grounding real connection with a transworldly holiness that all followers are challenged to seek to realize for themselves.

There are considerable differences in how the sages, seers, prophets, and messiahs of the world religions formulate their ultimate appeals. In one revelation, the linguistic event of speaking and hearing is irreducibly dominant, while in another, language is instrumental and dispensable. Holiness is touched in the very reception of one, while in another, holiness remains a distant point of reference. One revelation retains strong ethnic and cultural associations, while another throws its weight into universal outreach; one positions itself in an ongoing historical enterprise, while another offers liberation from historical concern; one relies on philosophical reasoning, while another repudiates it. Spanning all these differences, however, is the common appeal form of the *sacred teaching* as an individually and collectively appropriable commodity. Through the crucial mediation of literacy (though not only for the benefit of the literate), this religious appeal accredits itself as illimitably valid in a culturally heterogeneous world.

Revelation is not always taken directly and purely as an appeal. Depending on the context of discussion, revelation may be understood, for the most part, as consisting of a disclosure of specially valuable information, an illumination or ordering of experience, or a motivational infusion. Or the beneficial consequences of making contact with the "unveiled" appellant may be seized on as the point of the unveiling. The modern Christian theologian Rudolf Bultmann found it necessary to make an explicit argument for the appeal character of revelation against the background of a general pre-understanding of revelation as having to do just with the communication of information or the formation of belief.[9] Knowledge and belief cannot be pursued in a complete appeal vacuum, of course, any more than an appeal can fully register without the support and amplification of knowledge and belief; but knowledge and belief can very well be pursued outside of any conscious response to an invitation, simply in avid perception or intellection.

Even defined as an appeal, revelation is not the only religious appeal possibility. The devout may find themselves under supreme appeal in relation to one or more beings other than a scriptural teaching, or subject to a supreme set of appeals in a configuration quite different from that prescribed by their normative teaching. Nor is revelation a form of appeal that is necessarily decisive for religious meaning in practice, since it can be affirmed in a non-dominant, flexible, and even inessential role in a system of devotion. Nor is revelation the *only* potentially decisive form of religious appeal, since spirit-possession, ritualization, fear of death, and perhaps other kinds of event or practice or feeling can be decisive as well.

In spite of these caveats, the thought immediately occurs to us that revelation *asks* to be taken as the paradigm of all authentic religious appeal because in principle it is not merely personal, not merely prejudicial, and not merely emotional or sensuous (though it *is* capable of striking a subject at any given moment with unparalleled force). And it asks to be considered the supreme norm of the religious life because it is unconditionally exigent, not merely interesting or valuable. We have this conception of revelation because we live in the empire of the sacred teachings.

The argument for the religious supremacy of revelation has a specifically appellative logic of which we can now name the principal elements: (1) In its discursive aspect, a revelation partakes of the superordinate force of call-appeals in relation to being-appeals. Revelation's audience is not merely told about a religious appeal by a teacher or text; the hearing or the study of the discursive presentation is an encounter with the appeal and a subjection to it. (2) As a proposed universally feasible program for living, a revelation registers as a cultural *and* transcultural ideal, raising to hitherto unequalled heights the appeal-pull of our social affiliation. (Some traditions tell a poignant story about difficult early times when the actual communal base of the ideal was small, vulnerable, and composed partly of people whom many would consider unfit for successful fellowship. This magnifies the power exerted purely by the ideally possible solidarity of all subjects in the religion while adding relish to the contemporary experience of an extensive real community.) Revelation's pragmatic advantage in the marketplace of religious ideas is understood to derive from spiritual superiority: the community led by a genuinely "holy spirit" or the "true dharma" is limited by no other appeal. (3) A revelation centralizes religious appeal both theoretically, in providing a unified teaching able to answer all questions, and procedurally, in establishing a scriptural canon within which all essential teachings are guaranteed to be found. Thus, revelation qualifies as the supreme appeal by fitting itself to be the sole appeal.

In the regime of revelation, idolatry and distraction can become grave spiritual issues, and heresy and religious pluralism can be serious challenges to legitimacy. The sole appeal calls its devotees down a uniquely necessary and sufficient path, not merely a good path. The pneumatological gain in the religion's ideal of perfect inclusion is threatened by problems of exclusion—problems that are more difficult to handle responsibly, the more one knows about rival revelations—which motivate careful rethinking of the form and content of revelation.

I have claimed that appealing to appeal in the interpretation of meaningfulness is different from appealing to desire, need, or function. Even if it is true that appealing cannot be psychologically or culturally consequential if it lacks the support of those other vectors, still its distinctive interest lies in its supervening on and interrupting them. Because I try here to hold a focus on this purely appellative side of appeal experience, I say only a minimum about the relation of appeals to needs, desires, and functions. Thus, at this juncture I do not propose to make much of the fact that people were threatened by social disintegration and cultural alienation in the Axial Age and that the world religions promised a uniquely effective rescue from such troubles. The appeals of revelation did and still do respond to a passionate appeal *being made by* the audience of revelation, reflecting back upon them the urgency of human beings' own appeal together with the beneficent beauty of divinity—their panic over fault, suffering, lostness, and death shaping their perception and heightening their appreciation of a divine perfection of wholeness and vitality. (This circuit of appealing is represented within the immediate encounter with the "holy," according to the standard phenomenological description, by the chasm that is felt to open up between the unworthy self and the superworthy or transworthy Other.)[10] Thus, the divine appeal of revelation in the experience of religious subjects can be seen as a fusion of appealing and being appealed to, a maximum energy package of appealing.

The ideal of revelation is a pinnacle in appeal thinking. A world religion reckons revelation generically supreme among all appeals, even if perfect consistency is not attained in following specific revelations. It has always been possible to observe disagreements between revelation appeals and to conclude that they discredit each other, but it has also been possible to conclude that multiple revelation-appeals must be interpreted as fragmentary representatives or as diversely positive and negative witnesses of one true universal revelation. The ideal has been powerful enough to sustain the presumption of one true revelation even where (as in "Hindu" India) devotional practices strongly imply revelational pluralism.[11]

The ideal of revelation confirms the position of humanity as addressed by a divine Other. But the notion of supreme appeal is also pointed in a different direction, away from the normative primacy of a supreme Other, by the maieutic model of illumination used in the Axial Age teachings we categorize as philosophical—most explicitly in the Upanishads and in Socratic dialogues—for which normative primacy belongs to the self-possession of *Self* once it becomes fully vibrant in freedom from all distraction. This Self-aiming has been set forth as a basic alternative to the Other-devoted stance of "religion." Whether philosophy or religion, so understood, can maintain its proper stance is made a problem by this opposition. Religion, from philosophy's point of view, is irresponsibility to self, while philosophy, from religion's point of view, is irresponsibility to the divine. Is a combination of responsibilities attainable?

With this possibly very Kantian question I will move next to direct consideration of Kant and the modern Western reconstruction of religious appeal and theology. But first I will indicate the understanding on which I use the term *theology*. Like "revelation," theology is a category with specific Western affiliations; in fact, the modern religious thinkers I will discuss are all Christian or Jewish. However, just as there is a cross-culturally shared premise of ultimate religious appeal that can not-too-misleadingly be designated by the single word *revelation*, so there is a correlated approach to normative religious thinking, and I propose to study practitioners of "theology" primarily as examples of this broadly sharable approach rather than as exponents of Christianity or Judaism. For these purposes, *theos* is construed simply as whatever is divine, and *logos* as whatever constitutes appropriate teaching in response thereto. If the customary associations of the term *theology* impose a certain pull toward the premises of a divine being and a properly logical interpretation thereof, I do not wish to hide or negate that pull; we should consider to what extent it arises from our basic communicative situation and can, accordingly, affect religious thinking even in non-theistic and non-rationalistic settings.

Kantian Revelation and Neo-Kantian Theology

Kant's conception of reason follows appellative logic in several notable ways: (1) Reason is a lawgiver that confronts us by issuing the categorical imperative of fair practice in every applicable form; we are subjected to call-appeal, overriding all mere being-appeal, manifesting inescapable interintentional relationship. Thus, practical reason establishes our ultimate orientation.[12] (2) Reason speaks for all subjects under any conditions, and it speaks precisely about assuring the basic conditions of their coexistence; thus, reason presents us with a compellingly pure, disinterested ideal. (3) Uniquely free from conditioning by experience in its practical exercise, and master of the interpretation of experience in its theoretical exercise, reason speaks as our sole unconditional authority.

But the appeal of Kantian pure practical reason is vulnerable on all these points. (1) The supposed "call" of reason is questionable: Does it really proceed from a *person*? Is it really from an *other*? Is practical reason perhaps just what ethical irrationalists take it to be, a formal device that acquires moral and personal significance only when it is made the instrument of prosocial passions? (2) The "pure" ideal of perfect practical consistency or fairness is less inclusive of good and therefore less compelling than the ideal of full flourishing, of righteousness and happiness combined, which Kant can recognize only as a postulate of faith.[13] (3) The transcendental apriority of reason can be challenged as well: perhaps the intellectual strategies of reason always depend for their form and power on their emplacement in a contingent cultural process.

Yet these three aspects of the Kantian appeal—its communicative reasonableness, its formal purity, and its apriority—are mutually supportive. The purity and apriority of the demand of conscience warrant its reasoning against any mere rationalizing of my inclinations. The reasonableness and apriority of the moral law reconcile me to the subordination of my quest for happiness to the rigorous formal rule of righteousness. The reasonableness and purity of the moral law together give it a status as good as a priori even if the basic Kantian argument to apriority—the "transcendental deduction" of necessary formal conditions for the possibility of experiences we actually have—cannot be sustained.

Whatever be the force of these considerations, Kant recognizes an existential fragility in pure moral reasoning and looks to religion as the *appellative fulfillment* of morality. (Note that an ideal's "appellative fulfillment" is not the same as its "logical foundation"; it is a matter of finding a maximum of meaningfulness rather than of establishing constraints of formal compossibility.) Religious concepts apply in all three dimensions of that supreme appeal: (1) In reasonable call-appeal: Religion may be defined as the acknowledgment of our moral duties as the Divine Being's commands.[14] (Rational autonomy is not impaired, for we obey divine commands only because they agree with our inner sense of moral necessity.[15] In fact, our moral ideas have "*brought about* the concept of the Divine Being that we now hold to be correct.")[16] (2) In purity: Kant traces the peculiar rigor of the "dialectic of pure practical reason" wherein belief in God is demanded by the subjective practical necessity of filling out the ideal of righteousness to include a hoped-for happiness for all who have made themselves worthy of it.[17] If there is not a divine administration of the world, this hope is in vain. (3) In apriority: God is the supreme reality (*ens realissimum*) that ultimately grounds the unconditionally applicable a priori forms of our experience, though again only as the postulated fulfillment of a subjective theoretical necessity.[18]

Kant's claim, then, is that the appeal of pure practical reason is revealed by the critique of reason to be more rationally compelling than any other philosophical appeal could be, and that when it is religiously amplified (in a rationally lawful way) it is more humanly compelling than any other appeal could be. Kant's interpretation of religion is overwhelmingly attractive at this juncture in religious history for a bundle of reasons. For rationalists, it tames religious meaning without dismissing it. Pro-religious rationalists have a means of putting religious ideas to good use and entering into constructive dialogue with confessional religionists, while the latter are offered a powerful strategy for apologetics or critical fundamental theology. The Enlightenment clash of faith and reason is mitigated. More fundamentally, the power of the Kantian religious paradigm proceeds from the basic structure of appealing, and in doing so, it recalls the formation of the seminal revelations of the world religions. In an open marketplace of competing appeals (where for Kant and his primary audience the featured alternatives are Christianity and "natural religion," Judaism and Islam being entertained peripherally as foils), the Kantian appeal solicits each individual on the premise of a radically personal, discursively presentable motivation, perfectly universal grounds of assent and scope of application, a perfectly inclusive community (though only of rational beings), and an intimately friendly relationship with an existing religious tradition that can amplify and operationalize it so fully that no susceptibility is left over in us for a real rival appeal.

Kantian revelation was not universally accepted on its own terms. Schleiermacher centered religion in feeling rather than practical reason. Hegel tried to overcome the empty formalism of Kantian duty and Kant's strictures on the cognitive possession of divine reality by staging a dialectical self-production of reality. Kierkegaard developed a new version of the Pauline appeal of paradox, affirming the divine appeal as a scandal for the intellect. Feuerbach shifted the controlling a priori from abstractly consistent reason to loving I-You relation. But these alternative proposals (to mention just a few of the most influential) were all broadly of Kantian form and fell within the parameters of a Kantian discussion insofar as they placed before the individual a philosophically constituted a priori standard at the doorway of religion as the critical key to the interpretation of traditional religious claims, and also insofar as they projected a universally inclusive and uniquely authoritative appeal-from-which-there-could-be-no-appeal.

Kantian revelation as an evolving theme of late-modern Western theology can be understood as a radiation of neo-Kantian and post-Kantian alternatives analogous to those we have already examined in philosophy. A number of widely read theologians of the late nineteenth and early twentieth centuries—primarily German, Protestant, and university-based—reacted to the cultural malaise in general, and to the skeptical implications of scientific analyses of religious phenomena in particular, by working out a more precise characterization of religious appeal. They sought to retrieve the concept of divine revelation from two understandings they believed to have become untenable: a traditional, pre-Enlightenment view of revelation as a historically real, contingent, inexplicable, and overpowering event; and an idealist transmuting of revelation into the rational self-realization of Absolute Mind.

The pioneer and prototype of neo-Kantian theology in the late nineteenth century was Albrecht Ritschl, who, under Lotze's influence, explicitly gave Kant credit for accurately formulating the core Christian ideals of a spiritual lordship of humanity over material nature and a supreme goal of universal moral fellowship, that is, the "Kingdom of God."[19] Ritschl traded on the Kantian division of the realms of theoretical and practical reason by characterizing religious propositions as "value judgments" in contrast to neutral judgments of fact. "Value judgments" became his vehicle for restating the Lutheran thesis that genuine religious knowledge belongs only to those who confide in God as their savior.

> But if Christ by what He has done and suffered for my salvation is my Lord, and if, by trusting for my salvation to the power of what He has done for me, I honor Him as my God, then that is a value-judgment of a direct kind. It is not a judgment which belongs to the sphere of disinterested scientific knowledge, like the [Christological] formula of Chalcedon. When, therefore, my opponents demand in this connection a judgment of the latter sort, they reveal their own inability to distinguish scientific from religious knowl-

edge, which means that they are not really at home in the sphere of religion. Every cognition of a religious sort is a direct judgment of value. The nature of God and the Divine we can only know in its essence by determining its value for our salvation.[20]

The source of these value judgments and the sense of our salvation will be found in the immanent appeal of our practical freedom as compellingly aroused in encounter with Christ. But our value judgments, like Christ's revelation, Ritschl asserts, express the *reality* of spiritual life; consequently, Kant was wrong to deny religious *knowledge*.[21] Living a divinely forgiven and reconciled and thus empowered life of striving to bring about the highest good, the kingdom of God, produces ultimately valid knowledge of the world.[22] Thus, Christian theology is not cognitively isolationist, even though it should protect its insights by maintaining its difference from other means of producing knowledge claims that are not rooted in the value-directed Christian life. The lordship of the real world is one of its great themes.

Following one of Ritschl's emphases, Adolf Harnack argued in his celebrated lectures on the essence of Christianity that the "kernel" of Christian revelation is its affirmation of the transcendental values of the "infinite value of the human soul" and the solidarity of all humans in love, while every incredible or irrelevant claim in scripture may be set aside as revelation's "husk."[23] This became the classic statement of so-called liberal theology's commitment to conscientious valuing and of its freedom from the threats posed to religion by historical research. In his answer-piece *The Essence of Judaism*, the Jewish modernist Leo Baeck disputed the status of Jewish tradition in Harnack's historical perspective but roundly agreed that the essence of true revelation is a universally applicable (and quite Kantian) "ethical monotheism."[24]

Along another neo-Kantian line, Wilhelm Herrmann accepted the unconditional obligation of Kantian conscience without any assurance of success or happiness and argued that the despair of the moral subject must be overcome by an actually experienced intervention of divine forgiveness revealed in Jesus: "Jesus . . . assumed that humans know the one eternal law, but try to hide from it. He wanted to help human beings not to a new law, but to a better righteousness."[25] For Herrmann, the meaning of the specifically religious appeal of divine grace is "brought about" by the ethical appeal (to use Kant's phrase) in the sense that its relevance is established by the ethical appeal. But in another sense it is independent, for in each case it inheres in a contingent individual experience of an actuality.[26]

Immediately following the First World War, a revolt against neo-Kantian theology generated major new options in twentieth-century theology. The appeal motif in the new "dialectical theology," as it was called in the 1920s, and the disagreements that broke the movement apart warrant our attention. Before turning to dialectical theology, however, I would like to make a general comment on the appellative position of neo-Kantian value theology—I give it that title to highlight the conceptual parallel with neo-Kantian value philoso-phy—in consideration of the important role this approach continues to play in religious discussion.

A strength of value theology as regards the issues of the spiritual breadth and sole sufficiency of religious appeal is that its basic presumption of a cen-tered and structured universe of appeals allows it to engage, reconcile, and dominate all manner of appeals and ideals. As I noted in reviewing value philosophy, values are flexible in their definition and freely negotiable in their application. (Values may indeed just as well be called "meanings," depending on how broadly or deeply human volition is to be featured in the concept of meaning.) An actual appeal or proposition concerning goodness can always be interpreted, according to the concept of value, as (a) *irreal* (Ritschl would prefer to say "spiritual") in its definitive nature and thus detachable from the worldly conditions that limit the relevance and compossibility of beings and happenings, and (b) necessarily *organized* by a logic of valuation—as governed abstractly by a philosopher's principles of full-fillment (Rickert) or concretely by a theologian's re-proclamation of grace and the kingdom of God (Ritschl). Value theology can implement its religious appeal through the various subor-dinate values of politics, economics, art, and science and can decisively inter-pret all lesser values in light of the value or values it holds supreme. This harmonious relationship with the general culture is also its great weakness in the eyes of theologians who understand revelation as more radically critical of culture than a Kantian position could be and for whom a "culture-religion," even a sober neo-Kantian one, can only be a false substitute for authentic devotion. But the value orientation continues to be strongly represented in academic theology and religious leadership (we will see evidence of this later) because value theologians are very well positioned to sift, assess, refigure, and combine all the appeals that register in a given cultural setting. The principle of human meaning-making serves as their conducting thread.

* * *

The theological approach developed by Ritschl, Harnack, and Herrmann came to a point of crisis. The external side of the crisis was the scandalous First World War, which many representatives of this theology had supported. Internally, neo-Kantian theology had a problem in its understanding of re-ligious appeal.

A basic question we have raised for Kantianism is whether the appeal of practical reason is really only a self-discovery and whether, if it is rightly interpreted in that way, it can be considered a genuine appeal. It is useful to keep the sharper appeal question, "*With* which beings and callers is a good life lived?" from melting into the general question, "What does good life consist of?" The superordination of appeals to other kinds of apprehension depends on the preeminence of the *with* issue.

Now, one would expect theistic religious thinkers who accept the ethical appeal of Kant's categorical imperative to subordinate that ideal, as Kant would not, to an appeal of God. Their religious position would be centrally committed to satisfying the *with* requirement of appeal-experience in this way, since that position is distinctive and putatively commanding in the marketplace of value proposals precisely by virtue of its relation to a personal Divine Revealer. A standard devout objection to value theology is that its commitment to humanly judged values precludes this relation, so that humanity remains alone, vainly relying on itself for salvation. While Ritschl, Harnack, and Herrmann did invoke the Divine Revealer, they did not highlight an actual calling of humans by God. Instead, they followed Schleiermacher's lead and placed their emphasis on the *life* of the Christian believer as affected by acquaintance with an established spiritual message of Christianity. Their aim was to make the Kantian moral life more concrete, fully individuated, and fully engaged with each individual's fallibility and sociality. Herrmann could say that the religious life itself is the religious revelation.[27] What enables and initiates this life is not a call heard from outside but a discovery of a hidden inner resource of spiritual power.[28] In moving inward into religious experience—and staying away from the contested ground of the Bible as a discursive appeal in its own right or as representing a historically actual appeal—value theology's appellative force was weakened.

There are, however, other aspects of Herrmann's position that anticipate the appeal revival to come. He repeatedly says that our knowledge of God is contingent on God's self-revelation, and he does not identify God with humanity. The God that can save us is necessarily a God beyond our capacities, a God who (he says in one place) always remains unsearchable.[29] The divinely graced life is no natural outgrowth of the desperate life of human conscientiousness; it is a real interruption. Nevertheless, salvation for Herrmann really is fully intelligible in rational Kantian terms. If there has been a psychological interruption in the life of the Christian, still there has not been an interruption of rational sense—at least, not enough of an interruption to satisfy someone who conceives of theology or devotion as essentially based on a uniquely exigent appeal from beyond the humanly intelligible world.

Revelation in Dialectical Theology:
Barth, Gogarten, Bultmann, and Brunner

The value theology of Ritschl and Harnack understood religious experience as ethical experience (at an inspirational pitch) and the religious community or ideal state of the world as an ethical society of fully appreciative collaboration. Herrmann tended to lay more stress on actual encounter with revelation (presented by Jesus as God's concrete gracious word) and with one's fellow human beings as partners in an ongoing real history.[30] His appeal to the supreme *actuality* of the religious life brought him into conflict with neo-

Kantian philosophers for whom the actual is always judged by the ideal, its givenness (*Gegebenheit*) always taken up in an assignment (*Aufgabe*) given by reason.[31] The next major theological development, therefore, seemed quite improbable: one of Herrmann's students, Karl Barth, combined, in the 1922 edition of his commentary on *The Epistle to the Romans*, a heightened appeal to actual God-encounter with a hypercritical Kantian stricture against "religious experience" claims.[32] His argument was inspired in part by Friedrich Gogarten, who had begun to work out a similar position in which the exteriority of the human You and of God as absolute You is central, and was substantially approved by another of Herrmann's students, Rudolf Bultmann.[33] Barth, Gogarten, Bultmann, and their sometime ally Emil Brunner would enact on this new ground their own version of the drama of post-Kantian appeal thinking.

The controlling principle in Barth's *Romans* commentary is the exteriority of the authentic appellant, exterior even to "religious experience" and transcendent of "value."[34] The point of the supreme appeal of revelation is not to find a capstone or anchor for everything in one's existence but to call everything in one's existence into question—to pose a more radical problem of justification for our existence than we ever could pose for ourselves. The most apt paradigm for this "crisis" of an unlimited calling-into-question is precisely the *call*, the interruptive summons of a Word emanating from one who cannot be contemplated, not even honorifically as a value or an immanently respected imperative of reason—a Wholly Other.[35] "For a definition of *revelation* [I go] to a sentence of Luther, 'I do not know it and do not understand it, but sounding from above and ringing in my ears I hear what is beyond the thought of man.'"[36] This accosting word puts us in a different position than we take in forming world-"views," for "it is possible to turn our eyes in different directions or shut them, but not our ears."[37] Strange as the divine call is, it is a personal address and has wholly different implications than the "ineffable" music-like experience of a soul that imagines itself united with the divine.[38] A confessional but critically circumspect "dialectical theology" holds that the subject reached by the supreme appeal is bound to respond with an affirmation of the Other's advent together with a concession that concepts, images, and feelings cannot contain or adequately indicate the Other.

> Obedience is the sense for the specific peculiarity of the Divine and for the Wholly-Other-ness of God . . . a readiness to retreat from every concrete position which we have occupied . . . from every method of thought or manner of behavior [*Denk- und Arbeitsgewohnheiten*] . . . This is the obedience congruous to the Gospel of Salvation. But who is competent for such obedience? Speaking soberly and very obscurely, we answer—*not all* [that is, *no one* we know].[39]

The obedient dialectic of Yes and No—the accosting specificity of revelation affirmed by theology, and the otherness of God acknowledged by theology's critical reservations—recalls the polarity of fascination and awe in the religious experience of the "Wholly Other" as described by Otto; but unlike an "experience" as such, it is fundamentally active and communicative. Indeed, it must be active beyond normal measure, with more-than-human effectiveness: Barth compared the Yes and No of dialectical theology to the two watery walls of the Israelites' path through the Red Sea by which the floods of "unqualified words about God" are held back.[40]

In a public controversy with Harnack in 1923, Barth criticized the pretension of neo-Kantian modern theology to participate in forming a fully responsible culture-consciousness by means of "historical knowledge and critical reflection" and "a high regard for morality":

> [Harnack:] Is there . . . really any other theology than that which has a firm connection and blood relationship to science? And if there be such a one, what power to convince and what value does it have?

> [Barth:] If theology regained the courage . . . to become a witness of the *word* of revelation, of judgment, and of the love of *God*, then it could also be that "science" in general would have to look out for its "firm connection and blood relationship" to theology rather than the other way around. For it would perhaps also be better for the jurists, physicians, and philosophers if they knew what the theologians should know. Or should today's accidental *opinio communis* of the others really be the norm from which we must gain the "power to convince" and the "value" in our activity?[41]

Barth is suggesting that revelation not only trumps but swallows the ideal of truth. In another part of the exchange, he shows that he is primarily concerned to respond to what he holds to be the *one* revelation of God, a uniquely supreme *source* of meaning:

> [Harnack:] If the liberating exhortation is still valid, "Whatever is true, whatever is honorable, whatever is just . . . whatever is gracious, if there is any excellence, if there is anything worthy of praise, think about these things," how is it permissible to erect a dividing wall between experience of God and the good, true, and beautiful, instead of uniting them with the experience of God through historical knowledge and critical reflection?

> [Barth:] [Consider] ". . . the peace of God, which passes all understanding" (Philippians 4:7). The "dividing wall" indicated by this "passes" is basic and insurmountable. If "the peace of God . . . will keep your hearts and your minds in Christ Jesus" and make the exhortation in Philippians 4.8 ("whatever is true") *possible*, then it is peace of a kind that *passes* all understanding. There *is* a connection between it and that which *we* call good, true, and beautiful, but the connection is precisely the dividing wall, the divine *crisis*, which is the only basis on which it is possible to speak seriously of the good, true, and beautiful.[42]

Barth would later try consistently to make Jesus Christ central rather than the more abstract concept of "the divine *crisis*," but his point about "the only basis" will remain structurally the same. Later Barth-influenced interpretation of religion will see the lines of religious intelligibility and religiously motivated practice deriving entirely from revelation in a distinctive grammar of faith.[43]

* * *

"Encounter" can be thematized in various ways, even as an interesting or moving "experience," but *speech*-encounter has distinctive implications of responsibility in practical partnership. Dialectical theologies are powered by this sense of responsibility, which is a good reason to include them in the larger movement of dialogical thinking. The appellative strength of this theological approach is that besides centering on a superlatively commanding type of appeal it cultivates a continuous, active engagement with the appellant and with each other in our shared relation to the appellant. Here God's revelation is not a riddle in the dark but a concretely performed communicative action that invites further communicative actions from all its hearers. The "crisis"-flaunting self-critical moves of the dialectical theology of the 1920s are meant to guard the proclamation of a sole and sufficient supreme appeal against the bigotry and tyranny of dogmatism and to keep the lines of devout communication as open and active as they can be. Nevertheless, the dialectical approach exacerbates the supreme appeal's problem of worldly representativeness insofar as it resists fixing any concrete content in the divine Word and so resists letting any concrete data have directive significance. The wrestling between Barth, Gogarten, and Brunner over revelation's terms of inclusiveness forms a classic debate-complex for this position—a controversy over true appeal and true heeding that was superheated by the 1930s division between the "German Christians," who affirmed what they saw as a renewal of the German state under Hitler, and adherents of the Barth-led "Confessing Church," who dissociated themselves from the state in the name of a free gospel. The controversy brought into sharp focus rival theological priorities paralleling those we have considered in appeal-oriented philosophy.

In Barth and Brunner's 1934 debate on the possibility of a Christian "natural theology," Brunner's main points are (1) that the biblical appeal itself acknowledges (as in Romans 1.18–21) that the Creator's appeal is apprehensible apart from Christ, in a "general revelation" in the created world, even if sinful humanity has lost the ability to hear it; and (2) that the human constitution, though marred by sin, still retains, thanks to "preserving grace," a capacity to sense the relevance of the divine appeal, a "point of contact" without which God would be heard by no one. Barth responds by attacking the "abstraction" of formulating principles of revelation and grace separately from the essential Christian responsibility of directly heeding the revelation of Jesus Christ and trusting that gift of grace alone. He asks, quite evocatively in the circumstances of the German church conflict, "*Where* is all this going to lead us?"[44] "Abstraction" in this context is less an intellectual issue of content than a spiritual issue of bonding and fidelity. Brunner's "general revelation" only serves to distract us from the sole properly compelling appeal. For one who holds faithfully to the sole sufficient appeal in its own concrete character, there can be no validity that is not drawn from it—that is, from God's own actual accomplishment—directly. A question about how it is *possible* for us to be related to God "cannot be raised and answered except as a peripheral question, invalid and ever to be invalidated again."[45] Asking possibility questions presumes detachment from the appeal. Brunner thinks that in taking this line Barth is abdicating from the rhetorical challenge of making people aware of the need they actually have for God—the need to activate their own appealing as part of the event of revelation; moreover, Barth's refusal to base any claims on a divinely instituted order in creation must lead to chaos in religious ethics and pedagogy, reducing Christian discourse to disconnected outbursts of proclamation and completely individualistic responses.[46] For Barth, though, Brunner's assertion of a revelation and grace in creation is a way of defining human need and justifying human thought and action apart from the sole true determination of humanity in Christ, opening the door to the most willful and destructive self-determinations.

Barth disagrees similarly with Gogarten's claim that to understand God requires a correlative understanding of humanity.[47] Not that Gogarten's plea for attention to anthropology is dictated by an apologetic program of reconciling religious with nonreligious insights or appeals; rather, it stems from his sense of the urgency and relevance of the divine appeal in every moment and every connection of life. For "it is just through the temporal, visible world and its specific visible, temporal character [*So-sein*] that God speaks to us."[48] Like Buber, Gogarten argues that the I only encounters *actuality* and only actually lives when it encounters and answers a You; a life of I-development not yet fissured by You-encounter is a sub-actual life of illusions.[49] Less like Buber and more like the Christian I-You thinker Ferdinand Ebner, Gogarten restricts the sense of actuality to interpersonal encounter—all merely "natural" experience must be considered instrumental to interpersonal relationships—and urges the further restriction that God alone is the absolute You, the You who can never be reduced to an other-I and thus evaded.[50] (Christ consummates the relation with the absolute You by breaking the self's bondage to all rival claims; in that sense, Christian revelation is decisive.)[51]

According to Barth's way of hearing the divine appeal, however, the appeal is not pervasive *in* worldly human relations (even if it is universally capable and applicable), but rather its epicenter is in its mysterious source *in* God and—not to think about God abstractly—in its controlling point of formation in Christ.[52] Gogarten binds Christology to anthropology, claiming that the revelation of God occurs wherever people deal with people with full seriousness—which is to say, in Christian awareness of one's radical need for forgiveness. And he expands his anthropology into a social ethic of "orders of creation" that are given by God and apprehended by faith.[53] Gogarten is resisted on this front not only by the liberals whose idealism he directly attacks (such as Ernst Troeltsch) but also by critics who worry about the "system" that his claims make. These include, on the one hand, theological critics who fault him for being too restricted in his appellate subjectivity, too little disposed or able to hear the divine appeal with the scriptural and classical Christian witnesses to it; and on the other hand, his philosophical friend Eberhard Grisebach, who thinks that he is asserting a dogmatic construct and thereby departing from actual life, that is, defecting from responsibility to his uncontrolled fellow humans.[54] Barth's specific worry with Gogarten, as with Brunner, is that he is in effect setting up a separate revelation from the one true and sufficient revelation in Christ.

The split between Barth and Gogarten came to a head in 1933 when Gogarten felt obliged to align himself with the German Christians (briefly) for the sake of opposing anarchic modern individualism.[55] At this point Gogarten does not adopt the German Christian assertion that "the law of the *Volk* is the law of God" but proposes rather that "the law of God is met [not without ambiguity] *in* the law of the *Volk*."[56] He believes that Barth's Confessing Church alternative represents a religiously irresponsible separation of the inner life of the church from the historical life of the people.[57] (Although Gogarten was a political conservative, in this respect he showed a way that liberation theologians would take later in requiring that the interpretation of divine revelation be linked to a socially well-informed, ideologically critical, and practically engaged grasp of the situation in which it is promulgated.)[58]

For Barth, the freedom of the church in relation to worldly appeals reflects the power of divine grace over the power of sin. It is important for the church to engage the world, but only on the divine appeal's own terms. Nor can the divine appeal be identified with that of any present being, even if it be a Christianly interpreted historical situation: Barth maintained, against Gogarten's Lutheran preference for finding God in the "concrete," a traditional Calvinist emphasis on the incapacity of any creation to contain the Creator.[59]

* * *

Barth's theology turns out to have stronger analogies to the Heideggerian philosophical option of ontology than to the Buberian dialogical option insofar as its exclusive priority is the heeding of a single supreme, logically unique appeal. Already in the bombshell appeal of *Romans*, Barth borrows from the Marburg neo-Kantian philosopher Hermann Cohen the theme of the essentially non-given "Origin" of all reality, which, as the idealist prototype for the realist Being of beings in Heidegger's thought, encompasses all beings with an uncanny ultimate horizon of infinite tasks of interpretation: "The true God, Himself removed from all concretion [*Gegenständlichkeit*], is the Origin of the KRISIS [a New Testament word for "judgment"] of every concrete thing [*aller Gegenständlichkeit*], the Judge, the negation [*Nicht-Sein*] of this world."[60] Here Barth is even willing to model divine revelation on Platonic recollection—understanding the ground and norm of recollection in neo-Kantian fashion, that is, anti-ontologically. After the 1920s, however, he stops explicitly borrowing from philosophers and claims to have stepped free from the eggshells of philosophy.[61] In his *Church Dogmatics* he concentrates on the concretely given revelation of Christ as scripturally attested and classically interpreted in Western orthodoxy. Fidelity to this supreme and richly articulate (though still mysterious) appeal requires the theologian, first, not to be blocked from making Christian affirmations by the abstract considerations of God's otherness that dominated *Epistle to the Romans,* and second, not to grant authority to any other appeal and not to let any other appeal of significance pass without subjecting it to God's command in Christ.[62] With this practical commitment comes a cognitive orientation to God's uniquely unconditional (if mysterious) reality and truth. All beings are what they really are just in relation to God.[63] Thus, a fellow human being, for example, *is* the exigently appealing fellow-human-reality *only as* presented as the "neighbor" of Christian revelation.[64]

So rises the "Chinese wall" of Barth's "revelation-positivism," according to critics who worry about a disconnection and insensitivity of theology in relation to the actual world.[65] The Chinese wall allusion may be inversely apt: Barth can be seen as trying to prevent the interpretation of revelation from following the classic Chinese supreme appeal trajectory by which an imposing great ancestor (Shangdi) is ultimately replaced by an impersonal structure of reality (Tian, "Heaven").

* * *

At this time Bultmann shares Brunner and Gogarten's concern with the status of worldly beings in relation to God, especially the psychological and historical situation of hearers of Christian proclamation. But the emphases of Bultmann's theology show him to be, of all the dialectical theologians, relatively closest to neo-Kantian value thinking. One such feature is the critique of "objectifying thinking" that powers his project of demythologizing the historic sources of Christian faith. The goal of demythologizing is to free Christianity from the misguided demand that people believe factual propositions (especially historically irrelevant ones—the Harnackian "husk"), instead letting faith focus directly on issues of spiritual truth and well-being. The divine appeal is conveyed by a meaning that is independent of its actual origin, a church proclamation free of the historical Jesus.[66] In contrast to Barth's concern to read the divine appeal *from* the *given* revelation of Jesus Christ, Bultmann's main concern is to read the appeal as calling for a *decision* from each person respecting the *future* of that person's existence. "God is for Jesus the Power who constrains man to decision, who confronts him in the demand for good, who determines his future," he wrote in *Jesus and the Word* (1926).[67] The priority of the future, and with it the neo-Kantian commitment to the

sovereignty of human valuation with respect to worldly actualities, is under-
lined again in Bultmann's 1955 Gifford lectures:

> The genuine life of man is always before him; it is always to be appre-
> hended, to be realized . . . But the fact that man can either gain his genuine
> life or miss it, includes the fact that this very thing which he is really aiming
> at, genuineness of life, is at the same time demanded from him. His gen-
> uine willing is at the same time his being obliged . . . Historicism is perfectly
> right in seeing that every present situation grows out of the past; but it
> misunderstands the determination by the past as purely causal determina-
> tion and fails to see it as leading into a situation of questions . . .[68]

> To be historical means to live from the future. The believer too lives from
> the future; first because his faith and his freedom can never be possession;
> as belonging to the eschatological event [of Christ] they can never become
> facts of past time but are reality only over and over again as event; secondly
> because the believer remains within history. In principle, the future al-
> ways offers to man the gift of freedom; Christian faith is the power to grasp
> this gift.[69]

Bultmann rejects the idealistic discourse of "values" and the presumption that
humans can master their lives, but insofar as his center of interest is human
practical reason taking stock of its own possibilities in a state of heightened
lucidity about itself and confronting the *quaestio iuris*, he takes the basic neo-
Kantian stance. His "decisions" are the equivalent of "values." (Rickert's view,
by the way, is historically and existentially sensitive enough to allow a closing
from his side of the apparent gap between what he means by "values" and what
Bultmann means by "decisions.")

Barth protests what he sees as Bultmann's characteristically modern shift
of theological interest from God's action to the human experience of "faith."[70]
Even more than Brunner, Bultmann has given priority to the general conditions of intelligibility of the divine appeal for the sake of arousing human
response to it. In taking this approach, Barth thinks, Bultmann fails to acknowledge the independent determining power of revelation. Barth does not
appreciate the future-directedness of the divine appeal's power as Bultmann
understands it.

Borrowing Marion's term, we could say that Barth, Gogarten, and Bultmann specify three fundamentally different anamorphoses of revelation corresponding to three ontologically basic dimensions of our existence: the constituted, the constituting, and the to-be-constituted. This basic complexity in
our appellate situation continues to be expressed in dramatic relations among
confessionally, politically, and existentially oriented theologies, each warning
against and trying to correct for the deficiencies of the others.

* * *

Dialectical theology, whether keyed to existential valuing as in Bultmann, to the encounter with the actually present Thou as in Gogarten, or to the divine ground of all meaning as in Barth, shares with other popular monotheistic theologies a strong anthropocentrism. Although the status of nonhuman beings becomes a question of high importance in Buber's version of theism, no other leading thinkers of his generation take that question seriously. Starting in the 1960s, however, ethical thinking in general is significantly affected by the perceived degradation of the planetary ecosystem and of human-nonhuman relations in Western industrial civilization. Appeal issues come to the fore again in contemporary work in ecological theology, where supreme appeal thinking is subjected to searching new tests.

Appeals in Ecological Theologies: Ruether and McFague

I objected earlier that Rickert's value philosophy screens off the appeals of actual beings with artifacts of human volition. Ritschl's theology comes under the same objection in exalting the domination of the "natural" by the "spiritual"—that is, the domination of such things as bodily entities by such things as "value-judgments"—to a degree that now, in a post-Cartesian and ecologically sensitive climate, seems grotesque.[71] So it is by a noteworthy twist of intellectual history that some of the most powerful contemporary pleas for ecological concern are made by theologians whose fundamental position on religious appeal has more in common with the neo-Kantian liberal theology of a hundred years ago than with its main rival types. One sees, of course, how liberals are of all theologians freest to adopt such a cause and most likely to be interested in it; they are the ones most geared to dialogue with contemporary science and politics and to a fully "responsible," critical, and constructive appropriation of religious traditions. Yet the instrument of liberal theology's freedom and responsibility, human reason, is so deeply implicated in ecological ills that it must actually be appealed *against*. The error and danger in the worldview so baldly expressed by Ritschl must be exposed and corrected.

A serious problem for an ecological theology, then, is how it can shift from the older neo-Kantian appeal of reason-as-revelation to another appeal that will preserve its revelational orientation along with its critical freedom with respect to tradition. If the essential revelation of monotheism is not to be identified with pure practical reason, with what may it be identified? If revelation is in the natural world—if "the heavens declare the glory of God, the sky proclaims His handiwork" (Psalm 19.2)—then how are natural beings to be interpreted otherwise than as tools and signs used by a humanoid super-Subject?

One possibility is to abandon revelations of the Axial Age type altogether and instead hearken devotedly to the tremendous and fascinating appeals of the natural world, following the lead of Henry David Thoreau ("The most alive is the wildest") or Annie Dillard ("God used to rage at the Israelites for frequenting sacred groves. I wish I could find one").[72] But really doing that would involve departing from the communicative mainstream of our civilization. That radical pluralism of appeals is effectively barred in any case by ideals governing discussion of the sort we are having right now—ideals that inevitably force the vision of a Thoreau or Dillard into the mold of a single supreme appeal of "Nature."

Three possibilities that can be projected from our survey of major options in appeal philosophy after Kant are these:

(1) Adapt the neo-Kantian approach so that values and principles of "fulfillment" retain their position of a priori authority but nonhuman beings are allowed a determining role in the constitution of value and fulfillment. Ecological discourses of "intrinsic value" and nonhuman "rights" take this line. In theology it is possible to derive nonhuman value from the creation principle, as for example, Jews and Christians can appeal to the Genesis claim that God, monarch of valuation and being alike, explicitly affirms the goodness of the physical world and all its constituents.[73] The values in all beings would then represent a cosmically inclusive harmony principle rather than the anthropocentric harmony principle of pure practical reason.

The core problem with value appeals, however, as we have seen, is that values objectify the subjective, imposing on the other being the face of the subject's appreciation of it and imposing on the free subject an improper quasi-objective constraint. This process is least distorting, and even necessary up to a point, to the extent that we are working toward consensus in our valuations. Value talk may be inevitable, for example, in a negotiation between loggers and environmentalists, who look for different kinds of goodness in a relationship with a tract of land. The color-coding of sharable values was a spectacular device for changing the meaning of color in post-apartheid South Africa.[74] Still, value thinking is systematically misleading as a way of thematizing the actual appeals of beings, especially of nonhuman and transhuman beings.

(2) Another possibility is to follow the Heideggerian shift of focus to a mysterious enabling ground of all beings, tracing revelation to that ground but (as was necessary also with the neo-Kantian approach) correcting the anthropocentrism in Heidegger's hearing of the call of Being by attending more to meaning clues associated with nonhuman beings. The popular theological option that best approximates this type may be Thomas Berry's "universe story," which marshals all possible pieces of evidence and scientific inference to evoke wonder at the existence, pervasive interdependency, and creative-and-destructive character of the universe as a "single, multiform, sequential, celebratory event."[75] But this understanding of revelation runs, with Heidegger, the risk of de-realizing individual entities and events. Even when the appeal of the universe is built up by impressive specific cases, the specifics are logically auxiliary to the universe. They illustrate universal theses; the meaning of their appeals is molded by the Great Appeal.

> The evocation of the Ecozoic era requires an entrancement within the world of nature in its awesome presence: *whether in* the Himalaya mountains or the Maine seacoast, the Pacific islands, the Sahara desert, the Greenland glacier, the Amazon rainforests, the Arctic snowfields, the prairies of mid-America, *or any of the other* fantastic presentations that nature makes of itself wherever we look [emphasis added].[76]

Here monotheism becomes a way of neutralizing nature, as in the sacramental symbolism of the medieval Christian outlook.

(3) Or we might follow Buber in refracting the ultimate appeal of an eternal You through the momentarily supreme appeals of particular beings, extending You-status to nonhumans. We noted the danger of the subject's receptivity to individual beings being overridden by the subject's all-fulfilling relationship with one eternal appellant, but some form of that supreme relationship will be essential in any monotheist use of Buber's approach.

A main finding in our earlier discussion of value thinking, dialogical thinking, and phenomenological ontology was the relatively greater appellative strength of Buber's position. In two of the best examples of ecological theology, a move toward Buber emerges as the most convincing solution of the problem of affirming natural appeals under the aegis of a supreme religious appeal.

The ecological theology of the Christian writers Rosemary Ruether and Sallie McFague does not represent a romantic swerve away from the appeals of civilization toward the direct appeal of nature. Rather, it seeks to provide rational justification for valuing physical nature in the context of accepting the fullest possible human responsibility. Using Ritschl's terms, one could say that Ruether and McFague argue for a spiritual adoption of nature. But a pneumatologically crucial shift has taken place: "nature" for them is not the *instrument* of the ideal fellowship but rather is admitted as a *partner* in an expanded fellowship. Nonhuman beings are seen as producing their own values, values that are sufficiently commensurable with the values of anthropomorphic freedom and order that our recognition of them draws us into a larger universe of interests. One of two things has happened here: either the theologian has reformulated the control of actualities by values on a more generous value program, or the theologian's conception of the unit of meaningful experience has developed into something fundamentally different from a posit of human free will, something more in the nature of a call-relationship between beings. I submit that Ruether best illustrates the first alternative, McFague the second.

Neither Ruether nor McFague takes anything like a confessional position of obedient hearkening to a determinate divine appeal. Both are candidly autonomous evaluators and selective users of the intellectual and spiritual "resources" of religious tradition. The primary criterion of their evaluation is clearly ethical. The materials of religious revelation figure for them as possible means to the end of responding adequately to existing fellow beings, guided by an ideal of fairness. As ecofeminists, however, they cannot answer the question

"What is orientation in thinking?" just by pointing to a formally pure practical reason as Kant did. They are obliged to take account of historical patriarchy's distortions of fair, healthy relationship between men and women and between humanity and nonhuman beings. Consequently, much of their work consists of cultural assessment, and one of their chief objects of attack is a masculinist spirit-nature dualism that dominates modern philosophy and science, including Kantianism.

Ruether finds important the value-idea of "Gaia," a female-affiliated immanent world-divinity, as a corrective against heedless despoliation of the natural world, but she also wants to preserve a world-transcending ethical sense of ultimate value: "We need a vision of a source of life that is 'yet more' than what presently exists, continually bringing forth both new life and new visions of how life should be more just and more caring" (5).[77] Like Rickert's ideal of *Wertwirklichkeit*, Ruether's ideal spans the division between value and actuality, but it does this in such a way as to rectify the false separation of humanity from the larger natural order. She recognizes exigent appeals that are appeals of the larger world, not merely of human freedom (31). Human freedom has indeed a crucial role in expressing and serving the world's appeals, but it has also shown an unhappy tendency to cling to itself, claiming purity and permanence for itself. "We are called to affirm the integrity of our personal center of being, in mutuality with the personal centers of all other beings across species and, at the same time, accept the transience of these personal selves" (251). Release from the illusion of my own permanence *enables* me to value the "personal centers" of other beings. She brings this last point to ground by mentioning that her eye is caught by the eye of a bird and by the flashing red fur of her dog (252). If we ask what exactly Ruether claims we are "called" by in the above passage—the supreme "call" to which Ruether's exercise is devoted in its character as theology—the answer would be "the great Thou, the personal center of the universal process, with which all the small centers of personal being dialogue in the conversation that continually creates and recreates the world" (253).

The Buber echo here is loud.[78] But Ruether's work as a whole is not really in the same spiritual location as Buber's. The eye of the bird does not carry the weight of her argument as the presence of the tree does in *I and Thou*. Instead, the main force of the appeal she presents lies in the ideal program of fairness and interdependency that she works out in her cultural evaluation, above all in her balancing of "Gaia," the valuable actuality of the world, with "God," the valuable possibility of a greater world. She operates as a value gardener, nurturing some of our affirming tendencies and checking others.[79]

One can react to Ruether from Buber's perspective in opposite ways, either rejoicing in ideas that affirm the independent appeals of beings in the world or sadly confirming that in this case as well, as Buber put it, "a world of ideas and values . . . cannot become present for us . . . All the prescriptions that have been excogitated and invented in the ages of the human spirit . . . have nothing to do with the primally simple fact of encounter."[80] Of course, *I and Thou* itself is not free of this ambiguity. The discourse of You-saying can be essentially equivalent to the neo-Kantian discourse of values so long as it is taken as a representation of the subject's comportment under appeal rather than as an indexical attestation of beings' appeals. But Ruether makes this sort of gesture only in a fleeting and auxiliary manner, whereas it is clearly a main concern of Buber's.

Sallie McFague develops her ecological theology from a modern ethical monotheist starting point similar to Ruether's—distinguished mainly by her interest in analyzing how biblical metaphors and parables mediate the ideal of unconditional love—but she makes a more serious and explicit move toward Buber while appealing for authentic perception of the appeals of beings. She employs the ideal of Christian "incarnationalism," that is, an orientation to finding the divine in bodily beings, to motivate Christians "to love the natural world for its intrinsic worth . . . by obeying a very simple rule: *pay attention to it*" (27).[81]

> "When you think about it, we almost never pay absolute attention. The minute we do, something happens. We see whatever we're looking at with such attention, and something else is given—a sort of revelation. I looked at the heart of a daffodil in this way the other day—deep down. It was a pale yellow one, but deep down, at the center, it was emerald green—like a green light. It was amazing" [May Sarton]. By paying attention to some fragment, some piece of matter in the world, we are in fact praying. (29)

Christians are commanded or inspired to love everything, not as do-gooders merely but in full amazement, and cannot love amazedly what they do not know. But love's knowledge requires an affirming openness to the known being's own appeal, a discovery of delight in a being on new terms set by the being itself. On the pivot of "loving seeing," then, the balance between one's own desires and assumed constraints, on the one side, and the appeals of beings, on the other side, must be righted. McFague calls a being a "subject" insofar as it can be allowed to make its own appeal, and in that sense of the term, she proposes a "subject-subjects" model of experience (36–39). This model, constructed and consciously chosen, is justified primarily insofar as it supports experiences richer in intimacy and in recognition of differences (95–97). It has appeal-force insofar as it effectively represents the appeals of many beings. In principle, the subject-subjects model supports the appeals of *all* beings, discomfiting critics who insist on discriminating between different levels of practical importance in the appeals of different sorts of beings.[82]

McFague finds a strong version of the subject-subjects model in *I and Thou* but faults Buber for being too much interested in looking through particular Yous to the Eternal You, causing him to be effectively alone with God. One protection against this looking-through, she says, is to accredit touch as our primary sense, on a continuum with the loving kind of seeing (91–95).

A model of being and knowing that begins with touch will . . . insist on being bonded to skin, fur, and feathers, to the smells and sounds of the earth, to the intricate and detailed differences in people and other life-forms . . . [for] God is found in the depth and detail of life and the earth, not apart from it or in spite of it . . . An ecological model . . . suggests cosmology, not just a psychology, a way of being in the world rather than a way for an individual to find God. (102–103)

Another, more schematic protection of the appeals of beings lies in what McFague calls a "new sacramentalism": "The focus of this Christian loving eye is not vertical but horizontal; not on 'God in this tree,' but *'this tree* in God'" (172). This orientation will support a more adequate appreciation of God, richer in content than the heavily anthropomorphic theological tradition has hitherto allowed.

So may a value theologian cross over to the dialogical position—by the force of the *this*.

* * *

Another spiritual trend of importance in the later twentieth century, thanks to an accelerated development of global culture, has been seriousness about interreligious conversation—another relative blind spot of the dialectical theologians and in the Kantian lineage generally. Here, though, lies an obvious application of dialogical thinking. We will now examine the most intentionally inclusive and communicative of contemporary theological options.

Theology of Full Openness: McDaniel

Religion can arise only with the will to truth, which puts all other considerations on one side.

—Wilhelm Herrmann [before 1922][83]

We who have come from a background of liberal theology could never have become theologians nor remained such had we not encountered in that liberal theology the earnest search for radical truth . . . We can never forget our debt of gratitude to G. Krüger [who] saw [in 1900] the task of theology to be to imperil souls, to lead men into doubt, to shatter all naive credulity. Here, we felt, was the atmosphere of truth in which alone we could breathe.

—Rudolf Bultmann [1924][84]

Man as man cries for God. He cries not for a truth, but for truth; not for answers but for the answer—the one that is identical with its own question.

—Karl Barth [1922][85]

> *We understand our lives as open-ended journeys in which we seek, not*
> *certainty or an end to ambiguity, but rather depth, breadth, and meaning.*
> *We realize that the pilgrimage is ongoing, that in matters of ultimate*
> *importance absolute certainty is unattainable and perhaps undesirable,*
> *and that change is to be expected . . . [The] spirituality we seek takes the*
> *fact of our connectedness with the entire range of existence, and with God,*
> *as the heart of Christian spirituality. It is a worldly spirituality, one that*
> *finds God in the enjoyment of rich relations to the entire range of existence.*

—Jay McDaniel [1990][86]

The search for truth that Herrmann, Bultmann, and Barth cite is pointed toward a *core* of truth, a central or essential or deepest truth. Truth is figured as a singular appeal, a supreme command. The spirituality associated with this truth can never be so contingently responsive to a variety of beings as to be "worldly" in any very straightforward sense, even if it decides to ground truth in something it calls the world. In the relentlessly centering conversation that dialectical theology carries forward, the dominant questions have to do with *how exactly* and *where exactly* God is met, and *what crucially* God says.

For a theologian of full openness, in contrast, the priority is to assure breadth and inclusiveness—accommodating the widest manifold of appeals. McDaniel's standard of "rich relations to the entirety of existence" assumes a teeming plurality of appeals, all of which at least potentially express a divine appeal. He conceives the divine appeal more as enabling than as constraining, more as a limitless lure, like an ocean's horizon, than as a summons that draws the meanings of a situation to a point. For him, Christian affiliation means being inspired by Christ to hear everything diverse appeals might reveal, rather than being obliged by Christ to filter all appeals through a single decisive appeal. Like the dialectical theologians, McDaniel inherits from liberal theology the project of freeing the Christian position from authoritarianism and dogmatic belief, but he differs in his view of what true Christian freedom is *for*. "Christianity frees us to say 'yes' to life in its fullness . . . [It is] a way that excludes no ways, at least those that can enrich our own capacities for love and compassion" (3). Theology should be open to many things that God says in many places and in many more ways even than the rationalist Harnack was prepared to take seriously in his plea for all things "good, true, and beautiful."

In McDaniel's view, theology should be fully open, not merely for the sake of a rich experiencing by the religious subject, but to promote the fullest feasible *real harmony* among beings—a state of affairs designated by biblical devotion as shalom. The appeals of beings often register with us as appeals against restrictions or distortions of their terms of coexistence with us. A supremely compelling ideal, then, is that of a "sacred ground" on which a fuller harmony is possible (22). (The Kantian hope of happiness realized in proportion to moral worthiness among agents is a more limited sacred ground of the same type, an ideal of projected fulfillment, as distinct from a *holy* ground on which one trembles before a numinous actual appellant.) The ideal of shalom is the criterion by which religious persons distinguish which gods or goddesses to heed (159). McDaniel's title, *Earth, Sky, Gods and Mortals*, indicates four major directions in which the most meaningful heeding can occur.

McDaniel does share with neo-Kantianism a fundamental orientation to values—for his supreme criterion of shalom is certainly a value, and his earthly, celestial, divine, and mortal realms of sensitivity are like neo-Kantianism's value-spheres insofar as each is defined by a distinctive kind of subjective response. But he shares with dialogical thought an orientation toward maximized reciprocity with actual beings, and this leads him to propose two major new ground rules for the constitution of experience that neo-Kantian epistemology has little affinity for.

(1) An adequately inclusive experience must be alert to the appeal not only of each individual being, according to the ordinary understanding of an individual being as a spontaneously resolved unity for sense perception, but also of larger existing wholes and communities of beings. Beings are in truth "internally related" to each other insofar as their relations to each other are mutually constitutive, as for instance in prey-predator relations (27). "An inclusive appreciation of the web of life leads to a reverence for life. To revere life is to appreciate the value of living beings for themselves, for one another, and for God" (28). Despite his use of value language at this juncture, McDaniel intends an ontic affirmation; it is a matter of recognizing the appeal of "the web of life" as an actual being, not of projecting a rational ideal of systematic interconnection onto really separate individual beings. If the larger whole were not an actual being to take account of, if it were not (in value talk) an "intrinsic value" "in its own right," then the sufficiently expansive human self-realization that ecological spirituality requires would not obtain (176). For the sake of the largest experiential realization of all, McDaniel argues that the world may be seen as the body of God (102–106). Seeing the world this way will encourage us to enjoy everything in the world as God putatively does, to be disposed to work for healing throughout the world, and "to accept our own finitude and our dependence on something that ultimately eludes our cognitive grasp . . . We are never spectators of this totality. Instead, we are within it" (105–106). If there is an important difference between McDaniel's perspective and that of Berry's "universe story," it lies here, in McDaniel's more limited and incremental apprehension of a greatest appellant.

(2) Actualities are continuously subject to transformation. A Whiteheadian metaphysical perspective enables McDaniel to embrace the Buddhist view that "reality is a dynamic no-thing-ness, an emptiness in which all beings are becomings" (48). God, as an appellant, is not emptiness itself but a becoming like ourselves. To recognize any being adequately, then, I must participate fully in the transformations that I and the other being respectively and in some ways jointly belong to. My basic standards for interpreting experience cannot be exempted from transformability; that is one of the reasons why it would be

wrongheaded to close myself off in one religious tradition without being open to learning from others. On this point, McDaniel goes beyond the "critical" neo-Kantian doctrine of revisable experience in the direction of Heidegger's radical questioning. He also differs from the neo-Kantian orientation to value judgments and the ideal of actual value fulfillment, for these assume known or knowable values.

One might object, in the spirit of Harnack's objections to Barth, that *responsible* participation in transformation requires reference to ascertainable, generally valid values. But a theologian of openness could reply, in a hyper-critical maneuver akin to that of the early Barth, that taking a fully responsible stance requires that it be possible to *appeal against* any constituted value whatsoever. Ultimately, it is important to say what makes this possibility count for so much. McDaniel would make more lucid contact with supreme exigency if he shifted from a metaphysical argument for becoming over being—an argument that makes openness an attribute of the theoretical object, "reality"—to a pneumatological argument for an openness of responsible response to other beings as they present themselves.

* * *

The theology of openness could be interpreted as a departure from the Kantian problematic of modern ethical monotheism, and even from the Axial Age "world religion" problematic of revelation, if its primary commitment were to richness of experience as such. The theologian of openness would then be more like an aesthete than a prophet—a sort of tourist, looking curiously into all the appeals the world offers, loyal only to the thrill of appeal-facing, rather than the devotee of a world-traveling universal appeal of revelation. On the aesthete's terms, the focused exigency of each appeal is so thoroughly subordinated to the subject's freedom in experience that one could say the exigency is more feigned than received. But McDaniel's theology of openness is not free and random in that way. It turns *from* an identified center of responsibility (Christian), and not to *whatever other* appeal there might be, but to *that* and *that* appeal actually confronting the appellate subject, accepting the discipline imposed by each of many; and it coordinates these disciplines within a unifying discipline of response to a central superappellant (God) and an ideal of a real active togetherness of all things (shalom). It is subject to the revelation norm of universal validity while accepting fully the challenge of composing the meaning of that revelation from actual appeals. It carries a considerable burden of awareness, for global communication and academic religious studies now confront a theologian with a cornucopia of appeals, all of which deserve dedicated response. It is an embarrassment of riches: the plausibility and feasibility of a theology of openness would obviously be in jeopardy if it could not follow a convincingly nonarbitrary regimen in heeding appeals. McDaniel's discipline is to combine an adherence to shared standards of discussion in devotional and academic communities with scrupulous acknowledgment of the contingencies, limitations, and particular revelations of the theologian's individual path through life.

We have now reached a maximum of appellative appeal in theology, as far as I can see. The requirements of a theology of openness push us to the outer limits of possible human responsiveness and tact. If the appeal of openness to appeals were the only potentially dominant appeal in theology, McDaniel's type of theology would be the most persuasive. In fact, there are many other potentially dominant theological appeals, ranging from the blazing face of an adored god to a blessed rage for order in the universe. But it is useful (and, I would add, encouraging) to know that among the centers of greatest theological persuasiveness there is one that so impressively minimizes the risks of repression of appeals and oppression of beings.

Transition to the Issue of Attitude

Is it simply at the discretion of the conscious subject whether a being *will appeal*, initiating meaningful encounter, rather than registering merely as material for possible intentions, a "thing," "information"? Philosophers will always tend to give this impression inasmuch as philosophical reasoning caters to the freedom of the individual mind. But obviously the subject is not the sole determiner of the occurrence of appeal. I confess: I am not the author of most of my bodily and mental powers of reception. I am part of a larger biotic and social system. As a religious subject, I am a creature of divine determinations. Nevertheless, the difference between encountering actual appeal and encountering mere perceptibility or information is a difference for the subject and so necessarily appears somehow in the subject. What is it in or about the subject that differs in these two kinds of case? What accomplishes the disposing of the subject that Marion calls *anamorphosis*? It is at least a basic aiming or orientation, perhaps sustained to the extent of constituting a comportment. In terms of ordinary psychology, we may point to it with the appropriately vague, flexible term *attitude*. It seems that a lucid communicated appeal must target this variable and be concerned with measuring it before, during, and after the appeal; a lucid assessment of appeals must take full account of it.

Has not a certain attitude been assumed all along in construing phenomena as appeals? Could someone change from seeing phenomena as a *spectacle* without abandoning the fundamental attitude of a surveyor (or voyeur), with all its gratifications, and adopting instead the attitude of one who heeds? Would not a subject see phenomena more as impositions than as happy expansions of existence if he or she were fundamentally averse to them? Suppose that the appeal of the appeals account of experience can be conveyed strongly enough to awaken in its audience the appreciative attitude needed—

how can this attitude be stabilized against experiences (including, we must say from the perspective we have taken here, differently pointed appeals) that would undermine it?

Our study of appeal proposals since Kant has shown some deep differences in the construal of appeal that can occur *within* a philosophical or religious attitude that is centrally responsive to appeals. We have been alerted to a key variable in the appellate subject. Taking up basic attitude issues is a necessary next step in pursuit of the best intellectual and spiritual security that the responsive attitude can have.

Attitudes

The Question of Attitude

You are attending to my words. Your attitude is good. We can work together.

Actually, I know almost nothing about your attitude—or very little, at least, in relation to many of the possible motives and tendencies that could affect real dealings between us. You are only a pale gleam somewhere in the darkness of the virtual theater in which I form this discourse. Yet I am almost sure that dealings between us are possible. I trust (how could a communicator not trust?) that you have a basically prosocial and pro-intellectual attitude; in other words, your susceptibility to meaningful experience has a structure that lets me and my thoughts into your life; my discourse's appeal to you is not a drastic, desperate interruption. I can begin to take stock of the possibilities of our relationship by reckoning on this attitude of yours as a relatively constant, central, comprehensively determining principle of your feeling, acting, and thinking, a sort of rudder-propeller combination that is basically fixed but also amenable to some adjustment. The spiritual quality of our life together will depend crucially on this setting. Our joint flourishing is, I hope, well framed, braced, balanced, and borne along by it. But *is* there such a thing in you? If so, how is it formed? It is hard to be clear about this observationally. We can draw from a long list of terms to discriminate among kinds of qualification of feeling, acting, and thinking—attitude, orientation, outlook, disposition, conviction, comportment, character, temperament, attunement, mood, feeling-tone, life-stance, and so forth. It is not certain that observation will be able to establish a definite warrant for any of these categories in any given instance; nevertheless, it seems that we *want* and *need* to reckon on a main person-principle for the sake of dealing with each other effectively. The attitude that I appeal to in you is therefore an a priori principle of intentional complementarity. What a supposed attitude actually amounts to, in this sort of usage, is not grasped but is only prospectively definite.

In modern social science, *attitude* is a stipulated "evaluative disposition" that is ordinarily formative for a subject's thought, action, and feeling but is not necessarily expressed in behavior in a given situation—for discrepancies between actions and attitudes is a significant topic of inquiry—and can be changed under the right conditions.[1] Attitude can even be quantified and empirically measured as degree of agreement with evaluative propositions.[2] But attitude has no timeless guarantee of relevance as a working concept of science. One can reasonably argue from an empirical point of view that attitudology is a systematically misleading way to construe thought and behavior because it leads us to exaggerate the regularity in our behavior and gives a notional psychic center too much credit as the cause of our real or imagined regularity. The theory of attitudes might conceivably go the way of the theory of "humors." Meanwhile, though, attitudes answer to the requirement that we be able to track tendencies of thought and behavior by means of locatable, characterizable, and correlatable factors of significant practical import. And there seems to be an inescapable relationship between the observational requirement that there be something to keep track of in human phenomena and the social, practical requirement that we be able to maintain an interintentional focus.[3]

The modern term *attitude* has been taken over from art analysis, where it refers to the dispositions of the figures in a picture.[4] Such figures are deployed, fixed, yet charged with a history and a future of action in relation with each other and their world. This is an important clue. The idea that we *can* perceive, assess, compare, and draw implications from agents' states of intention vis-à-vis the world—an ordinary idea that pictures vivify and tend to validate, though without conclusively confirming it—is very powerful. It seems that we could scarcely get along without it. On the other hand, we tend nowadays to be deeply suspicious of the confining implications or the possible abuse of power in imputing or prescribing a definite attitude to someone.[5] Attitude claims are often manipulative and misrepresentative.

To get the clearest view of how the concept of attitude is able to exercise these problematic powers, I propose to build up the concept experimentally from what appear to be its elements.

The Elements of Attitude

At the bottom of a river lies a sunken boat. Its attitude is bottom-up. To know this is to know which part of the boat would be presented first if one dove down to work on it and where other parts would be in relation. As long as the attitude holds, the boat will be in a kind of equilibrium in relation to us, and there will be a certain continuity in our dealings with it.

On the surface of the river, meanwhile, a minnow is holding a position in the current, tail waggling. Its bodily attitude is that it faces upstream. To know this is to be able to better anticipate its actions. The animal, unlike the inanimate object, is centered not only for the observer but for itself; it can make its own use of the practical continuities of the situation.

In neither of these cases would we speak of a being's attitude if we did not contemplate dealings with it. Our practical interest brings a kind of polarity into the system of relations, counter-centering the attitude-holder and ourselves. (It has been claimed that holding a psychological "attitude" implies regarding *something* as somehow *important*; I am suggesting that another normally necessary condition for our ascribing an attitude to a being is that its interaction *with us* is somehow important.)[6]

An inanimate object, as such, can have an attitude only in a weak sense. A synonym for attitude in this sense is *orientation*. Anything has an orientation just insofar as it can be found on some sort of map. Because a boat is a vessel of purpose, however, we think of it as a quasi-living agent journeying in the world; in operation, it faces upstream or downstream much as a fish does, and in its sunken state there is a pathos in its belly-up position. We have to forget all that to view it on a map just as we would view a big rock. Still, that thinnest map-sense of attitude is fundamental. Attitude issues always concern *how a being stands in relation to other beings*. For this reason, besides any other reasons that might apply, attitude is a factor of *realizing*: that is, to ask about a being's attitude is to ask how everything relating to it *does* stand, and to have an attitude is to address the world as one takes it really to be (even if one is negating it). This implies that to impute a certain attitude to an individual is to specify a whole world-budget of interactions in a certain way, and that making a new ascertainment of how things stand calls for a new ascertainment of attitude. It also implies that to be aware of oneself as possessing an attitude is to have all the issues one faces qualified by the issue of attitude—to have to decide what is real or desirable based on acceptance or rejection of a certain centering of oneself by a system of relations (as, for example, a self-consciously responsible spouse continually chooses a marriage-centered agenda of fulfillment, but outside of that relationship might see happiness, even "salvation," quite differently). Thus, attitude gives generality to the meaningfulness of appeals, rightness on top of goodness.

The minnow, meanwhile, is more than an operating boat. Understanding that it is a *self*-operating being, we judge that its body is upstream-facing *because* it wants to watch for food in that way. Usually when we speak of an agent's attitude we are more directly concerned with its desires and beliefs than with its bodily position. But there is a kind of stationariness even in the psychological meaning of attitude. This stationariness in a mobile being is united with an implied movement that led to it and movements that are likeliest to come from it.[7] Attitude, then, is neither an actual reaching for this or that, nor a neutrally open state of affairs in which no reaching is more likely than any other, but a disposition (in the sense of deployment) to reach. This disposition is the more complex kind of orientation that an actively self-centering being has. It is oriented not merely on a map but in the system of agents and in its own system of motivations.

To possess an attitude is to *be aimed* in a certain way. Being aimed is not aiming; having an attitude is not intending. The minnow aims to maintain its upstream-facing attitude, we may suppose, but that aiming is neither its bodily attitude nor its mental attitude (if it has one) toward such activities as maintaining certain bodily attitudes. Its attitudes are aspects of the total position in which or from which its aiming is produced. There is swimming and there is wanting, but there is no "attituding." I admit that we can speak of sailors "attituding" a ship (short for "setting the attitude") if they are taking actions to change or maintain the ship's position. Stretching the same model, we might even speak of sailors "attituding" their own minds and bodies in taverns on shore. But subjects in this scenario do not perform or accomplish the attitude, call it Attitude A, from which they work on prospective Attitude B. Attitude A is always already given. The subject of an attitude is emplaced, its self-centering centered *by* the relationship it has with a larger system. We may look upon attitude in its involuntary aspect mistrustfully, as a pose maintained at some distance from a subject's true intention and spontaneity, even "put on"; or we may welcome the implication that various practical developments are likely to turn on and around an attitude by virtue of its *pivotal* role in the system of interaction (just as a salvage strategy revolves around a sunken ship's attitude).[8]

Nothing in having an attitude resists a change of attitude. It would probably take a lot of hauling to change the attitude of the sunken boat, but that is because the boat is heavy and stuck in the mud, not because it has an attitude. The minnow can instantly reverse itself with a flick of its tail. After a quick bite, it might cease to be aggressively food-seeking and become lazily current-avoiding. Religious salvations hinge on the possibility of a lost soul's turn-around, and religious narratives track changes of attitude that can be severe and sudden. I might stop feeling guilty or start feeling guilty for a past action, and thus in an important sense might stop or start being the person who led a certain life.[9] Such changes are limited by the capacities of things, to be sure—I know I will never see a ship balanced upright on the point of its prow, and I know with equal certainty that I will never take perfectly full responsibility for my past actions—but they occur in a range of possibility wide enough to make attitude hypotheses interesting.

As thus changeable, an attitude may not be equated with a state of intentional momentum, like an emotionally intense "passion" or a disposition to act in certain ways carried forward from past habituation (an Aristotelian *hexis*). The difference between attitude and states of intentional momentum makes it possible to ask vicious or passion-crazed persons to act responsibly. It may be as hard to get them turned toward right actions as it is to pull a sunken boat out of river muck; it may be beyond our powers. Supposing they do take the right attitude at a given moment, there may be no real prospect of their holding it. But their taking the right attitude is always thinkable; we have room to hope. Once they take a good attitude, we expect whatever depends on their intentions to go relatively well, just as a top-up attitude makes everything go better in operating a ship.

We have found important implications already in the simplest model of agent attitude. Now, to make the minnow model more fully relevant to human situations in which the concept of attitude plays an important role, let us imagine a whole population of minnows who feed, rest, and reproduce in common waters, sometimes hindering and sometimes helping each other, and who have a spatially and temporally extended awareness of what is going on and what can go on in this respect. Imagine further that part of their activity is on an illuminated side of the river, perceptible by some or all parties, but part of it is in the other, completely dark side of the river, and that their experience of this situation motivates them to draw conclusions about the relation between what they and their fellows do in the light and what seems to be happening in the dark, from which they derive plans of conduct. These beings will have a use for a very interesting concept of attitude. Their hypotheses about why visible actions start as they do will rest on the possibility of attributing positions and changes of position to agents embedded in *two* streams of circumstance, one visible and one invisible, the relation between the two streams contingently but somewhat legibly patterned.

For example, Minnow A comes out of the dark side of the river many times each day, never from a predictable point but always hurrying and angling upstream, looking for food; the other minnows know that they are liable to get smacked aside by A if they loiter near the light/dark border. They express the probability of dealing with A on these terms by asserting that A gets aimed that way in the dark. Bringing this sort of focus to their observation of A serves to bring their own aims into the sharper focus of an adopted practical policy ("Well, since *that's* A's attitude—"). They can contemplate A's agency as a distilled essence independent of particular actions ("A *is* keen to find food"). Admirers of A can place trust and hope in A's being-aimed, thinking of it as a wellspring of desirable actions. They can excuse A for straying from the pattern now and then ("A is generally keen to find food, but that time there must have been a distraction"). They can try to follow the model themselves, even in novel situations ("What would A do?"). They can elaborate on A-ism, contrasting it with a more relaxed B-ism.[10] They can argue that A's being A-ish, or A-ism generally, is or is not compatible with some good. Or they might observe that as a matter of fact, A's A-ism is part of a widely shared pattern, a "social attitude" that is or is not desirable and that does or does not fit well with A's more idiosyncratic tendencies. The minnows might have no thought of A having *desires* or "drives," and still have reason to conceive of A's attitude; but even if they do think something like "A is hungry," that idea does not apply squarely to the events that concern them, since A's forays in the light could be preceded by any sort of preparation in the dark whatsoever. (From our vantage point, of course, we can see that the motivation of desire might and very probably does determine an animal's attitude.)

At this stage, the minnows' concept has almost as much structural complexity as our concept of intention, which links the inward frame of reference in which desires and choices are experienced or supposed to exist with the outward frame of reference in which practical consistencies can be observed. Thoughtful minnows can debate whether the concept of an enduring "disposition" is empirically warranted and whether it should be regarded as causally explanatory. They have logical room in which to adopt either a more strongly explanatory and ontologically committed concept of attitude or a weaker view of attitude as a contingently useful term of convenience for behavioral predictions. Some will argue that A spontaneously turns in the dark, others that A is distinctively affected by darkness, and still others that A is affected in the dark only by some ordinary river-causes that could be disclosed by an infrared light, if they had one.

To bring the minnows farther into our thinking, we must place them in a river that is generally murky and twinkling, rather than all dark on one side and all light on the other, and have them think of themselves and each other as *essentially* both mysterious and knowable, so that a seen minnow is always in a way unseen and yet, even as invisible, visible in a way. In this situation the minnows construe each other's dispositions boldly, thinking they have a key to predicting and interpreting actions with unobservable antecedents, but circumspectly too, because in regarding themselves and each other as free, they consciously wait to see how each minnow will define herself or himself in emerging into the light. But the overwhelmingly evident and important result of this complication of minnow life is that attitude itself becomes in a new way an *issue* of continuing acute interest to the minnows. Intentional orientations affect what will happen at every moment in the vitally interesting class of social events.

Now the minnows' practical system is ripe for enrichment in one last momentous way: the minnows will *communicate* with regard to attitudes and so will participate in each other's attitude formation, producing concepts of attitude *as* communicatively in play ("mood," "temper") and concepts of specifically communicative attitudes ("sincere," "responsive," "overbearing"). The question of the *justification* of attitudes will be added to the question of the accuracy of perceptions and beliefs regarding attitudes. Minnows will attribute attitudes to themselves and to each other as a reckoning with darkness-in-light (inasmuch as attitudes are vague, only loosely predictive, freedom-respecting constructs) and light-in-darkness (inasmuch as attitude awareness enables anticipation and coordination). The attitudes they perceive or infer in each other, or impute to each other, will be storm clouds or encouraging beacons in cooperative living. They will be able to feel an exalted trans-individual unity in jointly realizing prosocial attitudes.[11] Claims about attitude will be persuasive when related to the dark-in-light aspect, descriptive when related to the light-in-dark. As targets of persuasion, the crucial underpinnings of attitudes will turn out to be the original upwelling of the subject's self-aiming in "desire" or "preference." In this aspect, attitudes will be "good" or "bad" and only ambiguously actual. (To what extent are they the products or pure posits of attribution? To what extent are they symbols of a larger ethical or political order?) Descriptions of attitudes will hinge on factual or logical pre-suppositions that might or might not be correct and accordingly will or will not make relevant contributions to the map of practice. The concept of attitude now *mediates* between everyone's desires, choices, and actions, and as a device for seeking the most important successes and solutions, the concept can be abused and cause no end of confusion. But it is a mandatory concept. You cannot be a minnow and not have an attitude. The minnows are us.

***

We have so far discovered two main ingredients in the concept of attitude:

1. Deployment in relation to other beings in a world, gauged according to possibilities of interaction; a *pose*, that is, a position established in a history of interaction; by implication, a specification of a whole world-system of interactions.

2. A most comprehensively determining yet alterable principle of intentions and actions, which can be the object either of prescription or description; a *poise*, that is, a tenable equilibrium an agent possesses through some range of situations, a condition under which an agent has relative freedom in determining how to interact with other beings; by implication, a specification of an agent's whole budget of aims and investments of energy.

Poses and poises are identified as generic, sharable, classifiable, and yet also as individuating ("If *that's* his attitude . . ."). As an ideal of knowledge of the being to which it is ascribed, attitude stands for a definite potentiality and a potentiated actuality: to envision a being as holding an attitude is to envision it as pregnant with the main lines of interaction with it. To describe or praise an attitude is to cite an actual interaction between the attitude-holder and other beings as it takes place along recognizable lines. To the degree that the relevant interactions hinge on incalculable causes and lead to incalculable effects, however, our supposed knowledge of a being's attitude must always be partial and vague. We know the most about it in the limit case of an inanimate object represented at a fixed time and place. At the opposite extreme, the attitude of a wholly invisible but hypothesized free agent (a transcendent God) is purely an *issue* for us, and a revelation may address this issue otherwise than by furnishing concrete data for knowledge (as, for example, in the humbling of Job).

Both the positional and intentional issues of attitude revolve around profound *how* questions—most profoundly as they imply and run into each other. "How" means "In what way?," and "In what way?" implies an agent taking a way. A way is determined by what is encountered and done in a certain setting and sequence. It takes place in a world and implements a practical manner. Objectively, a way is an order of occurrences; subjectively, it is an order of experiences and choices. Ascription of an attitude assumes and extends a way being taken by us in which an agent is found and a way being taken by an agent in which we find ourselves. The world implied by both ways must be shared: if a ship is swallowed by the river bottom and disappears from the salvage frame of reference, a diver can no longer determine its attitude, and the same thing happens to my sense of you to the extent that I find that you live in a different world. (Insofar as you do have a presence in my world, I can consider you "unworldly" or "nonchalant," for example; but if your position is really enigmatic, the meaningfulness of such characterizations will be in doubt.) We recognize, on the other hand, that the choices involved in the taking of ways may vary between subjects and between sections of one subject's life. That is why principles that organize choice are of great practical significance.

So arises an array of practical *how* questions. They evoke philosophical *how* questions: How are the poses and poises of intentional beings constituted? What makes for vibrancy, sustainability, and superordinacy in them? What determines an attitude's context of relevance, its scope of application? How can we most justifiably participate in or relate to the most important attitudes in our very asking of these questions?

Besides essential ingredients of attitude, we have seen various clues to an important negative feature. Attitude is necessarily indeterminate in a strong way. The concept of attitude is for seeking as much as it is for describing, for anticipating unexpected instantiations as much as expected ones—for living in play. We use the general idea of a unity of intentions and relations with other beings to designate provisionally a reality that we impute, or hope for, but that we may never experience contact with and that, indeed, can never conclusively be established. The content of any representation of attitude must be elusive—first, because it refers to the free inwardness of an agent; and second, because the supposed unity of intentions and relations with other beings is inherently dynamic. You can have good reason, at a given moment, to pronounce that "Sam has a reasonable attitude," but you can never entirely predetermine the relations among the various streams of Sam's existence and between Sam and the world that future events will bring. (Even after Sam dies, changes in social attitudes can necessitate a changed understanding of his attitudes. Sam might once have been a "benevolent slave owner," for example.)

Or perhaps it would be better to say that attitude is multideterminate. It is often not clear whether a description or prescription of attitude applies more properly to an emotional state, an intentional capacity, a practical orientation, or an experience, or to one mixture and balance of these ingredients more than another, for there is no general necessity why any one of these variables should carry decisive directive weight but always a possibility that it will. (In a given situation, the application can be specified: "If you really loved me, you would do your share of the housework"—but also can usually be disputed: "How can you say I don't love you just because I grew up not having to clean up after myself?") Conversely, we can rarely be sure whether a claim about emotion, intentional capacity, practical orientation, or experience better fits the more structurally domineering category of attitude. A prime criterion in resolving what we think must be the ethical charge involved: if, for instance, we mean to treat love as a fundamental ethical principle, then we have a compelling reason not to conceive love merely as emotion, as intentional capacity, as practical orientation, or as experience, but rather to tie it essentially via the category of attitude to the rectifying of relationships and from that starting point trace its implications in emotion, intentional capacity, practical orientation, and experience.

The relations among these categories call for more explanation.

Attitude and emotion. Emotion manifests how a subject feels its relation to other beings with regard to their shared prospects for flourishing. Emotion may be very much absorbed in its object, as in hatred, or very self-absorbed, as in joy, but it is always both objectively and subjectively informed: hatred without a self-feeling of being combatively roused would reduce to simple disapproval, and joy without an appreciative other-feeling would reduce to euphoria. Since emotion's essential theme is the state of a relationship, an emotion is a spiritual bellwether—a psychological fact, to be sure, but a directive claim as well, insofar as it proposes a rectification of relationship between beings. Hatred proposes that shared life is being deeply threatened by something that ought to be destroyed. Joy proposes that shared life is being powerfully fostered by something that ought to be celebrated.

Emotions express the dynamism of life in relationship and so of attitude. Emotion would be irrelevant only in a worldless existence, such as in the existence implied practically by the ideal of perfect detachment and explained theoretically by nondualist metaphysics. (Even so, emotional events might be held to be of great importance in the worldly journey toward transworldly liberation, as in Indian theories of *rasa*.)[12] It has been difficult for philosophy to recognize the import of emotions because of philosophy's dual commitment to the ideal of a regular, stable world-order and the correspondingly stabilized ideal attitude of reasonableness. With regard to the issue of rectifying relations among beings, philosophical rationalism is a completism—it posits a presently achievable resolution. (That resolution may be an open scheme for forming beliefs, as in pragmatism, but still we are given our principle to hold on to.) Emotional dynamism must intrude upon the rationally specified rectification of relations among beings as a disturbance, and this disturbance is more threatening than some incidental weakening of the philosopher's powers of attention. It is a challenge to the feasibility and even the pertinence of what the philosopher most basically hopes to accomplish.

Philosophers sometimes do credit emotions with cognitive or a quasi-cognitive valuational content in consideration of their potentially great directive relevance.[13] It is crucial, however, to distinguish the directive relevance an emotion possesses by virtue of its relation to attitude from the directive relevance it possesses by virtue of its informativeness about the prospects of right action or its practical utility in energizing right action. Joy, for instance, is a notably good emotion because it involves appreciative perception of other beings and encourages affirming treatment of other beings, but it is even more importantly good because it supports a sustainable intentional centering of the subject in affirming relationship with other beings.

Attitude and intentional capacity. I observed above that the changeableness of attitude implies a difference between an attitude and an intentional tendency or acquired nature like an Aristotelian *hexis.* The point is worth developing further.

I take it that our *ultimate* moral and practical concern is with *how things go* among beings rather than with any being or quality abstracted from that larger event. It follows that the moral and practical value of possessing a state of intentional momentum or capacity like a "virtue"-disposition, or a whole complex of good dispositions amounting to a good "character," must ultimately depend on the virtuous state's efficacy in sustaining the right attitude. Virtue and character are powers the agent brings to relationships with other beings; they make an agent morally promising and may even notionally justify the agent (that is, they may satisfy us as we contemplate fitting the agent into situations); but the agent's own attributes cannot of themselves actually set an agent right. The attitude issue concerns how agents are actually set right, and to observe or call for a good attitude is to engage this issue more directly and fully than the concepts of virtue or character are capable of (except when they are enlarged to borrow the meaning of attitude).

Let the attitude of responsibility illustrate this point. Responsibility appears often in contemporary moral discourse as a root principle or necessary condition of moral worth. It is predicated primarily of agents, though also of institutions and policies. To praise Jane as a responsible person is to commend her fundamentally. To this extent, responsibility seems to play the role of a virtue. But nothing much like responsibility is found in an Aristotelian list of virtues. It is true that many of the virtues are relevant to it: a person who is courageous, generous, patient, and just is much more likely to act responsibly than a person who is cowardly, stingy, impatient, and unjust. We could specifically craft a definition of "the virtue of responsibility" as a disposition to be attentive and responsive to the just claims of others, including also the requisite cognitive virtue of perceptiveness.[14] In doing so, however, we would miss a key point. Jane is so profoundly approvable in being responsible precisely because she is *actually* interacting rightly with other beings—she has a track record of this, and she is in the midst of this. If we redesign responsibility as a virtue, we abstract her from this superordinately important consideration.[15]

A complementary way to reveal the categorical gap between virtue and attitude is to observe how a whole battery of virtues could fail to set an agent right in the absence of a right attitude. Jane could possess courage, generosity, patience, and justice and still have a fundamentally frivolous or bitter orientation that would make us hope for a "turnaround." I grant for the sake of argument that it is possibly true that the possessor of *all* Aristotelian virtues in full measure would have no psychological room left for taking a bad attitude—could not be so reckless as to be frivolous, so ungenerous as to be bitter, and so forth. In that way Aristotelian moral psychology would track the pivotal moral power and relevance of attitude, though without having directly thematized it. Even granting so much significance to the virtues, however, we cannot guarantee on the basis of virtues the agent's actual taking of a good attitude, which involves the agent's actually being set right in relation to other beings, which assumes the impingement of actual appeals on Jane's life and actual deployments of Jane's powers—as Jane is actually being careful with the claims of her job, of friends, and so forth.

Often when we call a person responsible we mean to say simply that she or he will function as expected. The agent is then seen as an objective vector in our practical calculations. But attitude-holding subjects are more than objective *pragmata;* they are experiencing worlds unto themselves and responsible fellow-agents. To envision a strong or well-informed person as a holder of an attitude, then, is to allow her or him a commanding place in our world of subjective pluralism and cooperation *as* strong or well-informed—that is, to respond from our own centers to her or his centering as bearing with those qualities on the rectification of relationships—and to respond similarly to any additional social or political force that arises from our intentional synergy in this relationship. Strength and knowledge have directive force in this aspect that they do not have as objects of an essentially manipulative calculation of agents' intentional capacities. In consideration of this, a community may call for certain capacities or beliefs in its members. Although we should be critical of any effort to manipulate what cannot properly be an object of manipulation —namely, a person's defining limits of capacity or a subject's rational autonomy in believing—we should not forget the depth of communal concern with members' qualifications.

Certain affective capacities bear particular weight in accounts of moral and religious meaningfulness. For Hume, a sympathetic constitution and a generally benevolent disposition are prime requisites of morality: without this susceptibility and motivation, our standards of moral obligation either would never be conceived or would not have genuinely moral (as opposed to expedient or tyrannical) force.[16] The early Schleiermacher argues by an implicitly similar logic that the key to authentic religion is possession of a "sense and taste for the Infinite."[17] Following in that vein, Georg Simmel, one of the earliest explicit attitude theorists of religion, at times makes religiosity sound like a temperament or sensibility analogous to musicality: "What makes a person religious is the particular way in which he reacts to life in all its aspects, how he perceives a certain kind of unity in all the theoretical and practical details of life—just as the artist gives *his* own particular response to existence as a whole and fashions *his* own world from it."[18]

These claims are well warranted as descriptions of moral and religious experience. But once a moral attitude is deemed uniquely decisive for moral meaningfulness, like Kant's respect for the moral law, it is possible to find examples of sympathy and benevolence without it and to disqualify them as moral. Once a religious attitude is held to be decisive for religious meaningfulness, as for example, faith on Luther's view (or piety on Schleiermacher's mature view), it is possible to find examples of Infinity-tasting without it and to disqualify them as religious.

Attitude and experience. Experience is often appealed to as the concrete terminus of a question about whether or not a certain fact or meaning obtains. The presumption is that any valid claim about a fact or meaning must ultimately be anchored in a subject's realizing of it. In this aspect, experience is minimally necessary. In its maximal, optimal aspect, experience is invoked as the most inclusive phase of subjective realizing; experience is the "best teacher" —especially when it is lifelong or communal or historical. But experience tends to be normatively overrated in both of these aspects for at least two reasons: (1) More than subjective realizing is needed to validate a claim, even if subjective realizing is a necessary condition of the kind of validation that we consider most felicitous; what is unconditionally necessary is the functional success of a claim in rectifying relations among beings. (2) No extension or summing up of experience can suffice by itself to rectify relations among beings, even if experience is an indispensable teacher of spiritual agents. If, however, experience is understood not merely as subjective grasping and concrete determinacy but as an achievement or history of basic orientation, or as a trace left by relating, then it is properly regarded as loaded with directive import. On this understanding there can even be a sort of spiritual positivism, as when we allow precedents in law to control justice decisions in the present. But we should be clear about the difference between this spiritual positivism and a flat-footed positivism that respects only subjective possession or objective determinacy. Spiritual positivism can go flat-footed under the cloak of the appeal to experience. Holding the categories of attitude and experience distinct is a defense against this.

*** *** ***

You are attending to my words. I would like to write: You are *still* attending to my words and your attitude is manifestly *very* good—but I cannot, because I do not know that you first read the beginning of this chapter. Let me suppose that you did read the whole chapter. Have I any basis besides gratified vanity if I declare that your attitude is, just insofar as you stuck with the chapter and all else being equal, better than if you had merely glanced at the first page? That would be an extremely vulnerable claim, but at least we know how it *can* make sense. We can fill in presumptions about curiosity, diligence, respect, loyalty, and so forth, all variations on the theme that you, noble reader, are oriented to flourishing coexistence with other beings.

The ease with which we can define good attitudes and the goodness of attitudes (even faddish paradoxical ones like "irreverence" and "punk") is revealing. "Attitude," unlike "act" or "perception," is usually understood from the ground up as good or bad since it has to do directly with more extensive or more restrictive prospects for relations among beings. As we noted at the start, the great difficulty in principle with attitude is not in seeing how and why a good one is a good one but in observing or assuring that an attitude is real. This difficulty is overcome only by stipulation: thinking of you as a free agent who does act in regular ways, I am licensed to hope that you are a sapient, responsible force in the world, geared to doing just such things as carefully following my discourse, and to count patterns in your behavior as evidence that you are geared this way and that your behavior is good conduct.

The next greatest difficulty in thinking about attitude may also demand a solution by pure stipulation. Supposing that we are going to live by regulating our attitudes, how best can we cultivate and compose attitudes in relation to each other—so as to be appropriately passionate *and* steady, or serious *and* playful, or loving *and* critical, or reverent *and* ambitious, or all of these together? I took the minnows to the brink of this question but held it back, since I did not want to crush them with too much to think about at once. Let them think about it now; having adopted the concept of attitude by which to steer themselves, let them take up the advanced navigational challenge of formulating ideals of attitude for the sake of maximizing all the good in life that depends on attitude. When they reach their Axial Age and address each other with world-traveling, individual-empowering teachings of sufficient insight, they will undoubtedly propose ideals of *one* sovereign attitude, the attitudinal complement to the appellative ideal of one supreme appeal. From then on, their philosophical and religious history, like ours, will revolve in large part around attempts to live with such ideals.

Attitude in the Axial Age

We worship the Good Mind of the Lord . . . and the Good Faith, the good law, and Piety the ready mind within your people!

—Zarathushtra[1]

The Axial Age Initiative of Attitude Thinking

We have already used Jaspers's conception of a mid-first-millennium BCE "Axial Age" to frame an account of appeal thinking. The same approach is needed to enter understandingly into attitude thinking, its close companion, since another of the compellingly relevant novelties of Axial Age teaching is the project of explicitly defining a right attitude of the subject responsive to supreme appeal. Axial Age teachers show that the most promising orientational strategies for relating effectively to great appellants are great appeals in their own right.

But we must proceed under a warning flag. Although attitude engineering is manifestly a central Axial Age concern, there is no Axial Age word that can accurately be translated "attitude." Like *value* and *appeal, attitude* is a modern concept that presupposes, among other things, the modern state of historical, psychological, and sociological interest in a pluralism of norms. Ancient people certainly were concerned about changes of mood, differences of temperament and character, alternate basic states of motivation, and deep issues in the justification of intentions, and they did regularly use terms corresponding to terms we use for specific attitudes. They did not, however, set about surveying and correlating these things with an emphasis on the variable *as variable*. That is our modern emphasis. About a hundred years ago, we rather suddenly began to ask the term *attitude* to carry a large part of the psychological and normative load of our effort to think through pluralism, and we have been speaking of attitude remarkably often ever since.

A good example of the oldest documented attitude thinking will be found in the "Sumerian Variation of the 'Job' Motif." One modern translator assures us it was "composed, no doubt, for the purpose of *prescribing the proper attitude* and conduct for a victim of cruel and seemingly undeserved misfortune."[2] Clearly there is a righteousness motif in the text. Significantly, though, the text's primary focus is a prosperous relationship with a god rather than a good attitude for its own sake:

> Let a man utter constantly the exaltedness of his god . . .
> Let his lament soothe the heart of his god,
> (For) a man without a god would not obtain food . . .
> "I am a young man, a discerning one, (yet) who *respects* me *prospers* not,
> My righteous word has been turned into a lie . . .
> You have doled out to me suffering ever anew,
> I entered the house, heavy is the spirit,
> I, the young man, went out to the street, oppressed in the heart,
> With me, the *valiant*, my righteous shepherd has become angry, has
>   looked upon me inimically . . .
> My god, you who are the father who begot me, [*lift up*] my face,
> Like an innocent cow, in *pity* . . .
> They say—the sages—a word righteous (and) straightforward:
> 'Never has a sinless child been born to its mother' . . ."
> The righteous words, the artless words uttered by [the young man], his
>   god accepted,
> The words which the young *man* prayerfully confessed,
> *Pleased* the . . . *flesh* of his god, (and) his god withdrew his hand from the
>   evil word,
> . . . which oppresses the heart . . .
> The encompassing sickness-demon, which had spread wide its wings, he
>   *swept away* . . .
> He turned the young man's suffering into joy,
> Set by him the . . . *good* . . . spirit (as a) watch (and) guardian,
> Gave him . . . the tutelary genii of friendly mien.

To us it seems obvious that by praying the young man adjusts his balance and perspective so that he can live more happily in a morally challenging world. The final provision of a "good spirit" of "friendly mien" fits this interpretation perfectly. But what the speaker explicitly worries about is whether he is on friendly or inimical terms with a powerful god. He avows his sinfulness not to modify his sense of himself but to "please his god." We might suppose that the "good spirit" that will help him is a figure for his own attunement, but he himself—as far as we can tell—thinks of it as a real, separate being. Even as the translation nudges the speaker's understanding nearer to our own at key points, we can readily see, once we watch for it, a great difference between the way the young Sumerian sizes up his life and the way we typically do. To be sure, it is a fair hypothesis on our part that attitude formation is on the agenda of this ancient discourse. But it should be recognized that something has happened in conceptual history that enables us to state and trust a much stronger attitude claim (that the prayer's point is "to prescribe the proper attitude") than an ancient Sumerian would have found plausible or even intelligible.

The most important part of the shift between Bronze Age attitude thinking and our own occurred through the middle of the first millennium BCE and flashes out in expressions like this: "He does not boast of what he will do, therefore he succeeds . . . He does not contend, and for that very reason no one under heaven can contend with him" (*Daodejing*).[3] Here an attitude is asserted, not merely as a requirement in a specific context of practice or worship, but as lying in the very grain of reality and so as a universal desideratum for human agency. The eighth-century Hebrew prophet Micah *might* be making a very similar assertion: "[Yahweh] has told you, O man, what is good . . . to walk modestly with your God; then will your name achieve wisdom"; whether we are justified in interpreting this particular text in this way, we can scarcely doubt the trend of foregrounding attitude by the time we read "Humility precedes honor" in Proverbs, and "Blessed are the meek" in the Christian New Testament.[4]

By what logic does this change occur? I have already remarked the historical development of a newly individual-centered communicative situation in the Axial Age civilizations (chapter 2). Here it will be useful to identify the anthropological and cosmological assumptions about how human life *can* be centered that become available to Axial Age thinkers and that fundamentally shape their proposals.

The idea of a personal center, expressed by words that we usually translate as "heart" or "mind" or "soul," plays an important role already in the "Theology of Memphis" (early third millennium BCE):

> Ptah the Great, that is, the heart and tongue of [the gods] . . . gave birth to the gods . . .
>
> There came into being as the heart and there came into being as the tongue (something) in the form of Atum. The mighty Great One is Ptah, who transmitted [*life* to all gods], as well as (to) their *ka*'s, through this heart, by which Horus became Ptah, and through this tongue, by which Thoth became Ptah.
>
> (Thus) it happened that the heart and tongue gained control over [every] (other) member of the body, by teaching that he is in every body and in every mouth of . . . (everything) that lives, by thinking and commanding everything that he wishes . . .

The sight of the eyes, the hearing of the ears, and the smelling the air by the nose, they report to the heart. It is this which causes every completed (concept) to come forth, and it is the tongue which announces what the heart thinks.

. . . Thus life was given to him who has peace and death was given to him who has sin. Thus were made all work and all crafts, the action of the arms, the movement of the legs, and the activity of every member, in conformance with (this) command which the heart thought, which came forth through the tongue, and which gives [the dignity of] everything.[5]

This text reflects not only the heady discovery that one can think of all reality as proceeding from the centralized command of personal agency in its royal aspect but also the pre–Axial Age tendency to multiply such centers—in large rosters of gods, on the cosmic scale, and in specialized centers within the individual human being corresponding to different issues, like the *ka* for traveling or being imparted. (Homeric Greek psychology is interested in the distinct dynamics of the *thumos* in which an agent is emboldened or intimidated, the *noos* of perception, and the *psuche*, or life-breath that departs upon death.)[6] The persuasive model of the living human body suggests a concrete diversity of organ functions and manifoldness of expression at the same time that it shows a certain unification by intent.

Axial Age thinking, in contrast, plunges into the depths of the principle of unity, taking the heart, mind, and soul concepts with it. The *Brihadaranyaka Upanishad* prepares for this plunge with a litany on the centrality of the heart:

Who is the god of the southern quarter?—Yama.—On what is Yama founded?—On the sacrifice . . .—On what is the sacrificial gift founded?—On faith, for a man gives a sacrificial gift only when he has faith . . .—On what is faith founded?—On the heart, for one recognizes faith with the heart . . .—You're absolutely right, Yajnavalkya!

Who is the god of the western quarter?—Varuna.—On what is Varuna founded?—On water.—On what is water founded?—On semen.—On what is semen founded?—On the heart. For that very reason, when someone has a son who is a picture of him, people say: "He's dropped right out of his heart!" . . .—You're absolutely right, Vajnavalkya![7]

Then comes the move to *atman*:

On what is this heart founded?   —What an imbecile you are to think that it could be founded anywhere other than ourselves! If it were anywhere other than ourselves, dogs would eat it . . .—On what are you and your self (*atman*) founded? [Various breaths are mentioned, then:]—About this self, one can only say "not _____, not _____." He is ungraspable . . . undecaying . . . has nothing sticking to him . . . neither trembles in fear nor suffers injury.[8]

This self is indescribable because it is conceived as *centering as such*—not a material nature at all, but a function. In the cosmologically oriented counterpart to this idea offered by the Greek philosopher Anaxagoras, the centering principle is still understood materialistically, yet in sharp distinction from all other matter:

> All other things have a portion of everything, but Mind is infinite and self-ruled, and is mixed with nothing but is all alone by itself. For if it was not by itself . . . the things that were mingled with it would hinder it so that it could control nothing in the same way as it does now being alone by itself. For it is the finest of all things and the purest, it has all knowledge about everything and the greatest power.[9]

This is an intellectual adaptation of the royal version of the centering principle. Adapting Anaxagoras in turn, Plato proposes a correspondence between the inner rule of reason in each of us and the world-rule of a cosmic intelligence; these powers are conjointly enabled by the primal possibility he calls the Good.[10] Then Stoicism takes additional cues from Heraclitus's idea of *logos* and Anaximenes' idea of a breathlike world-uniting *pneuma* to argue for a living world-soul and rational world-intelligence of which each individual person's life and reason is a microcosmic token.[11]

That is but one illustration of how the problem of a fully valid centering of human life can be worked out. Collectively, Axial Age texts suggest three quite different (but not necessarily incompatible) models for attitude centering:

1. *Monadic agency.* The how of a monadically conceived centering, like that of "self" or "mind," is basically person-like: if it brings order, that is conceived (as by Anaxagoras) on the model of a ruler's administration; if it contains peace, that is conceived (as in the Upanishads) as a subject's bliss. Attitude ideals based on such a conception tend toward the idealization of either one supreme agent or a fellowship of agents in the world. To appeal to a great mind or self is to place one's hearer in an inwardly strengthened position to the degree that he or she does identify with the ideal—even though he or she may be decentered in being located at some distance from it or placed in a role complementary to it.

2. *The Way.* Rather than build right attitude into a single ideal personality, one can take one's bearings by attending to a way that is found in the world and that can be predicated of the world or the world's root causes. The Way does imply an agent, since it is a sort of thing that is taken by an agent, but it is not itself an agentic capacity. To the extent that the Way determines attitude, the how of attitude-centering is externally guided by patterns of possibility or occurrence rather than internally generated by a personality. Way appeal decenters a subject permanently, placing him or her in the essentially complementary position of a performer in an ensemble; one could say that the Way appeal creates through its distinctive summons a more profoundly sociable subject. In classical Greece, the conception of *moira* as an ultimately unchallengeable apportioning of opportunities and goods is fundamental for thinking about justice and virtue. Plato's Form of the Good can be understood

as a non-agentic Way, although in the whole scheme of Plato's thought, this Way is dominated by the imperious operations of reason. (The Hindu dharma can be similarly overshadowed by the soul's quest for blissful freedom from attachments.) The profound Greek trust in the way of conflict, *agon*, so richly expressed in sports and drama, was influentially articulated by Hesiod, who praised competitive emulation, and Heraclitus, who proclaimed strife the father of all things.[12] The Pythagoreans may have been devoted to a way of harmony.[13] The best-developed examples of explicit Way thinking, however, are Confucian and Daoist claims about an unchanging and unchangeable, effortless, supremely effectual Way of Heaven.

3. *Inspiration.* Whereas a Way appeal addresses the problem of plural intentional centers by drawing agents into a sort of dance, an inspirational appeal short-circuits the division between agents by means of a visitation of one by another. Whereas the strongest aspects of a Way are its stability and sustainability—the true Way being independent of the chances and flaws of actual occasions—an inspirational appeal banks on the power of a specific actual connection to establish the best orientation. Thus the frightening or violent aspects of an inspiration are secondary to the impressively reassuring sense it gives of direct connection to the first cause of right order. Inspirational appeals thrive in a personalized cosmos like that of the Hebrew prophets, but even Kongzi could make one: "Heaven begat the power that is in me. What have I to fear from such a one as Huan T'ui?"[14]

Combinations of these models can be very powerful. In the Christian New Testament, for example, inspiration becomes a steady Way and a great agency all at once in the conception of a divine Spirit that will constantly, actively guide the members of the Christian community after the earthly departure of Christ.[15] Paul writes: "If you are led by the Spirit, you are not subject to the law . . . the fruit of the Spirit is love, joy, peace, patience, kindness, generosity, faithfulness, gentleness, and self-control . . . If we live by the Spirit, let us be guided by the Spirit" (Galatians 5.16–25). Christians propose to take on in-spiration as something like an acquired second nature when they speak of being "born" in the spirit and, on this basis, living in the world "from God."[16] This is an ideal of maximum intimacy and solidarity between a supreme intentional center and imperfect worldly selves, conserving at the same time the real distance and difference between a divine self and a worldly self.

The Featured Attitudes of Axial Age Teaching: An Overview

Supplication of the ancestor, god, or lord is a very old kind of discourse in which certain pressures shape the selection of attitudes to emphasize. When an agent has power that might fatefully impinge on us, we have a vital inter-est in understanding and influencing that agent's intentional state. A benign disposition is desired. When the agent is outside our everyday sphere of di-rect communication or operates even when present in a larger frame of reference than we can oversee or hope to exert influence in, we will want to be able to appeal to the construct of a firmly established, always-and-everywhere-effective favorable attitude. So a powerful, sublime agent is customarily addressed as gracious and merciful.

The appeal *to* the powerful agent is most intensely formulated as the appeal *of* a complementary sort of agent—for instance, a lowly appellant whose humility or fallibility serves as a foil to the greatness of the one appealed to. In this way, the appeal posits an order not merely advantageous to the appellant but inclusively wholesome. An Egyptian prayer of the thirteenth century BCE does this shrewdly: "Though it may be that the servant is normal in doing wrong, still the Lord is normal in being merciful."[17] In the prologue and epilogue of his seventeenth-century BCE law code, Hammurabi projects a powerful combination of righteous majesty (for he is the officer of the gods) and careful humility in his dealings with the gods, which his subjects are called upon to emulate.[18]

In earlier appeals for relationship with a superior, the attitude of one party typically corresponds not with the attitude but with the factual capacity of the other—that is, mercy corresponds not with humility but with fallibility, humility not with mercy but with superior power. The explicit tone is prudential. Later, though, with increasing confidence in the intrinsic power of the attitude appeal, attitude typically pairs up with attitude: "At scoffers He scoffs, but to the lowly He shows grace" (Proverbs 3.34). Now a certain tenor of relationship is posited as an end in itself, offering a type of solution that no longer depends directly on the motivation of practical-empirical problems: a consciously spiritual *justification*. The prescribed attitudes are taken out of their original practical location in ruler-subject relations and universalized in scope.

There is a priestly version of this situation wherein universalizing attitude prescription is fostered by and ambiguously related to an essentially esoteric cult of communion between initiates and divinity. But for our purposes it is the exoteric outcome that is most important: the figure of the Israelite priest who is able to enjoy an ideal heart-to-heart relationship with Yahweh within the temple, for example, is changed, when published through scripture, into the figure of the wise or righteous person who all adherents of the scriptural faith are called to be.[19]

The most celebrated religious attitudes all have a strong rhetorical rationale as complements to the imputed greatness of a sublime power-holder: the *reverence* in which appellants avowedly hold the great agent, showing that they fear to lose what the relationship provides; the *fidelity* with which appellants attend upon the great agent, insisting that they will allow no higher priority or distraction to upset the relationship; the *hopefulness* with which appellants address the future while staying in the great agent's good graces.

But the relationship with the great agent, compelling as it is, does not exhaust the significance of such attitudes. For *peers* in a society can reasonably suppose that their life together will go better if all are disposed to be careful not to give offense, to be serious about keeping promises, and to work cheerfully and energetically. Indeed, they can legitimately worry that the absence of any of these attitudes would cause a social problem; an irreverent society would be plagued by insult and injury, a disloyal society by betrayal and confusion, a hopeless society by depression and sloth. From an administrative point of view, the utility of these attitudes is great—so great, in fact, that a lord has as much prudential reason to maintain the ideal imperiousness, steadfastness, and graciousness of the appellate lord as the lord's appellants have to be reverent, faithful, and hopeful. The lord is well-advised, both as administrator and as spiritual leader, to appeal to subordinates to maintain those attitudes, construing the attitudes themselves as great insofar as they are essential to their society's greatness.[20] Ordinary people can recognize the same benefit in the idea of a great appellate ruler, not necessarily one with whom they have actual dealings: "Muses . . . tell of Zeus your father and chant his praise . . . For easily he humbles the proud" (Hesiod).[21] Such considerations contribute to the universalizing of attitude prescriptions in which attitudes attain their normatively strongest form. (Notice that the logic here differs from the Feuerbachian logic of constituting divinity by projecting our own human strengths, maximized, into its image.)

Excessive self-assertion is a predictable problem for good public order whether in pragmatic or spiritual perspective. Labeling the problem "pride" covers it morning, noon, and night in all agents and also invites humbling comparison with a Great Agent supremely powerful by virtue of his or her place in the practical system, as in the case of a king, or by stipulation, as in the case of an idealized god. Like Zeus, Yahweh and Indra are portrayed from early on as mighty foes of human hauteur.[22] It follows that *humility* deserves praise, some of which we have seen above. During the Axial Age, humility progresses from being seen as the human complement of divine power to being seen as peculiarly beautiful and powerful by its own spiritual and metaphysical virtue. Even God and Nature become humble in stories of divine condescension (as in creaturely incarnations) or self-emptying. Complementariness becomes an end in itself rather than an auxiliary of hierarchical order.

Before the sense of a universalized humility can be seen, however, the ideal of *righteousness* offers a robust solution of the problem of excessive self-assertion in that it can be applied in all situations to all agents, human and divine alike. A righteous person is one whose own ordering principle is the same as the ordering principle in all other ideal members of a greater order. This subjective principle is essentially universal, like its objective counterpart, justice; in Greek and Hebrew the words for righteousness and justice are the same (*dikaios/dike, sedeq/sedaqa*). The social order in which righteous persons live is not necessarily egalitarian as regards who is allowed to perform which worldly action. The point of righteousness is to play a somehow justified role consistently—whether in fierce partisan loyalty, which is the tenor of the righteous Israelite's covenant responsibility, or out of deep personal resources of insight and fortitude, as in the case of the righteous Greek philosopher Socrates. Demonstrations of a sense of propriety may be all the more pungently demonstrated when social rankings and roles are sharply divided as in this Confucian anecdote told by Mengzi (Mencius):

> [Mengzi:] "Duke Ching of Ch'i went hunting and summoned his gamekeeper with a pennon. The gamekeeper did not come, and the Duke was going to have him put to death . . . What did Kongzi find praiseworthy in the gamekeeper? His refusal to answer to a form of summons to which he was not entitled."
> "May I ask with what should a gamekeeper be summoned?"
> "With a leather cap. A Commoner should be summoned with a bent flag, a Gentleman with a flag with bells and a Counsellor with a pennon. When the gamekeeper was summoned with what was appropriate only to a Counsellor, he would rather die than answer the summons . . . Rightness is the road and the rites are the door."[23]

Although the story celebrates and justifies class division, its more important point is the gamekeeper's equal social entitlement. The righteousness ideal posits that each person is intellectually and practically capable of doing what is necessary to sustain the greater order.

A specifically intellectual or communicative version of righteousness is the *reasonableness* to which Heraclitus summons his audience: "Although the Logos is common the many live as though they had a private understanding . . . Listening not to me but to the Logos it is wise to agree that all things are one."[24] "All things are one" can be read as applying both to the perceiving of a unity of being, for which a sober attitude is requisite, and to the project of forming a common understanding with one's fellow subjects, for which a collegial attitude is requisite. Indeed, it is characteristic of appeals to "wisdom" to be concerned as much with building a community that will see things the same as with perception of how things occur in the same ways, because the ideal of agreement of perceptions and the ideal of perceived regularity essentially imply and so involve each other.

Righteousness is a personally sustainable attitude, in principle, because one can feel that one is flourishing in it; there is a distinctive satisfaction in living uprightly, irreproachably, responsibly in one's role. But righteousness by itself does not answer for the composition of the greater order it serves beyond the abstract form of justice, which means that its motivation can be undermined by appearances of undeserved inequality; neither does it answer for the complete, highest well-being one would hope to reach within its constraints. Thus it seems advisable to buttress righteousness with a *reverent* fear of offending (an ideal motivation that is distinct from the rhetorical construction of the reverent appellant discussed earlier) and with a *benevolent* inclination toward others that will foster personally and socially happy outcomes even where the systemic conditions for righteousness are imperfectly met. Reverence and benevolence can function as auxiliary cooling and warming influences that help keep the precarious balance of righteous other-regard from being lost. More importantly, they are attitudinal reasons *for* righteousness; righteousness can take a wrong direction in the absence of either, as is shown incisively in Confucian texts:

> The "Duke" of She addressed Kongzi saying, In my country there was a man called Upright Kung. His father appropriated a sheep, and Kung bore witness against him. Kongzi said, In my country the upright men are of quite another sort. A father will screen his son, and a son his father—which incidentally does involve a sort of uprightness. (*Analects* 13.18)[25]

> An Emperor cannot keep the Empire within the Four Seas unless he is benevolent; a feudal lord cannot preserve the altars to the gods of earth and grain unless he is benevolent; a Minister or a Counsellor cannot preserve his ancestral temple unless he is benevolent; a Gentleman or a Commoner cannot preserve his four limbs unless he is benevolent. To dislike death yet revel in cruelty is no different from drinking beyond your capacity despite your dislike of drunkenness. (*Mengzi* 4.A.3)[26]

Although reverence and benevolence are motivationally stronger than righteousness, neither is guaranteed fulfillment. Experience can give me the impression that my own disposition has no significant relation to other agents' exercise of power or access to well-being; why then should I be respectful or benevolent toward anyone? In intellectual life, experience can mock my commitment to reasonable interpretation; why then should I be reasonable? So the question of motivation has a further depth. The search for a fully sufficient determination of an attitude or way of life can only end with the adoption of a kind of attitude that by definition fully mobilizes and commits the subject. *Faith* and *devotion-love* are such attitudes. They are heavily featured, not in the first wave of Axial Age texts, but in subsequent texts that exploit and respond to the attitude openings of the Axial Age—most influentially in the New Testament, *Bhagavad Gita*, and Mahayana Buddhist scriptures. To lack reverence, benevolence, or righteousness is to be defective as a member of society, but to lack faith or devotion-love is, in the later perspectives, to miss contact with reality altogether.

Faith and devotion-love presuppose a relationship with a person or truth— a person who figures as a truth, or a truth treated as a person—and propose that salvation comes in an utterly unreserved, energetic confiding of oneself to just the good that is available in and through that relationship. The emphasis in faith (Hebrew *emuna*, Greek *pistis*, Sanskrit *shraddha*) is on the firmness of attachment to the other; faith is the opposite of doubt. The emphasis in devotion-love (Hebrew *ahaba*, Greek *agape*, Sanskrit *bhakti*) is on the fervent seeking of togetherness with the other; it is the opposite of indifference. Both faith and devotion-love preclude going one's own way, which they qualify respectively as failure and betrayal. Faith and devotion-love are more obviously impossible to realize perfectly than reverence, benevolence, or righteousness because the claim they make on the person's will is explicitly infinite. (Religious subjects do not normally pray or otherwise take special measures to increase their reverence, benevolence, or righteousness.) A classic bundled prescription of devotion-love and faith is: "For God so loved the world that he gave his only Son, so that everyone who believes in him may not perish but may have eternal life" (John 3:16). "Believing in" the Son-figure means adhering unreservedly to the supreme benevolence of divine love that is embodied in the sending of the supremely dear one. Adherence to that principle is stipulated either as the one valid way toward eventually receiving eternal life from God or else as constituting eternal life in itself.[27] Either way, a motivational maximum of impeccable orientation and perfect fulfillment is indicated.

Devotion-love involves passionate attachment and is quite different from benevolence, which, as Kongzi notes, flourishes with sympathy: "You want to turn your own merits to account; then help others to turn theirs to account . . . the ability to take one's own feelings as a guide—that is the sort of thing that lies in the direction of ren [benevolence]" (Analects 6.28). One can most readily be benevolent toward colleagues or inferiors; devotion-love all but negates the distance and difference inherent in those relations. Classic Chinese ethics has little in common attitudinally with the Hebrew drama of love between Yahweh and Israel, with its fierce avowals of election and reproaches for Israel's infidelity; even the Mohist program of universal love is in a coolly rationalist, utilitarian mold. Where passionate attachment does appear in the Chinese teachings is in the love of wisdom that sages exhibit. Kongzi says: "There may well be those who can do without knowledge; but I for my part am certainly not one of them" (Analects 7.27). "I have been faithful to and loved the Ancients" (7.1). "Only those who burst with eagerness do I instruct; only one who bubbles with excitement, do I enlighten" (7.8).

In Indian scriptures, faith is most often taken for granted as the basic religious posture—paradigmatically, that of reaching toward the invisible gods by sacrifice, not doubting that such gestures are meaningful—or treated as a virtue instrumental to the best life. Faith is not glorified in the Christian manner as the centrally interesting issue in life. Christianity maximizes the interest of faith by seeing it not merely as an enabler of the highest love but as the very warp or woof of the highest loving—loving the universal God in spite of God's invisibility, loving neighbors in spite of their unattractiveness or enmity, loving colleagues in spite of their fallibility. Such love cannot reach a supremely satisfying togetherness if it is not joined with perfect trust. In the Upanishads, however, knowledge of the character of reality is seen as the key to salvation, and so faith is characteristically bundled with knowledge rather than love, a pattern that holds also in the Bhagavad Gita: "Faithful, intent, his senses subdued, [the man of discipline] gains knowledge; gaining knowledge, he soon finds perfect peace."[28] The Gita then adds devotion-love to this bundle as part of its theistic amplification of Upanishadic wisdom: "Focus your mind on *me* [says Krishna], let your understanding enter me; then you will dwell in me without doubt . . . the man of devotion is dear to me."[29]

The *Gita*'s praise of devotion-love, bringing the energy and enjoyment of passionate love to the faith-relation, reflects a momentous new turn in Indian thought and a new tension and divergence in religious perspectives. The theme of "perfect peace" had emerged in the Upanishads as the leading classical Indian attitude motif. This ideal proceeds from a recognition that passion upsets an individual's inner order much as self-assertion upsets public order. Indeed, the two problems are linked insofar as excessive self-assertion is driven by passion. But the disruption of inner order is the more serious problem intellectually in that it blocks apprehension of the supremely appealing Brahman. Passion's antidote is detachment; the state of maintaining detachment, a state that is its own blissful reward, is *tranquility*. The pursuit of tranquility is encouraged by comparing ordinary life with a supremely calm agent-state, like a Buddha's bliss. Dominant appeals to detachment and tranquility arise in Hinduism and Buddhism in India, in Chinese Daoism, and in Hellenistic philosophy. In all of these teachings, the counsel of detachment is logically linked to a perception of a general impersonal order in the cosmos that reveals attachment to be inherently painful and futile. But now the theistic approach of the *Gita* puts a personal twist on cosmic order and so reinstates the kind of intentness that confirms the distinct existence of lover and beloved for the sake of relating them. An emphasis on love relation henceforth marks major currents in Hinduism and Mahayana Buddhism.

Ancient Hebrew culture is distinctive in never developing the idea either of an impersonal cosmic order or of a corresponding subjective autonomy. The book of Ecclesiastes, a controversial inclusion in the Hebrew Bible, looks like the exception that proves the rule: "All is futile! What real value is there for a man in all the gains he makes beneath the sun? . . . There is nothing better for man than to enjoy his possessions, since that is his portion. For who can enable him to see what will happen afterward?" (1.2–3; 3.22). But Ecclesiastes does not point to a power by which an individual can get the better of this frustrating world. Its ideal is enjoyment of what one happens to possess, a moment-by-moment freedom from contingencies of consequence, not *tranquility* in freedom from the very principle of contingency (the principle of world-illusion or attachment, in Indian thought). In the Hebraic context it is not possible to be so completely separated from a god's will (like a Skeptic, an Epicurean, or a Buddhist) or so merged with it (like an Advaitan Hindu or a Stoic) as to claim that degree of independence.

Thus is composed a very full menu of prescriptively irresistible attitudes, the fruit of a tremendous Axial Age optimism (to use a modern attitude category) about the possibility and utility of specifying such things. It is challenging for us that the classic attitudes are not simply harmonious. Any given pair of them can be either combined or driven apart, depending on context and motivation. Detachment and devotion-love form an especially difficult, seemingly antithetical pair, but no less popular a teaching than the *Bhagavad Gita* shows us how they might belong together.

* * *

We can improve our grip on the issues raised by the classic attitude conceptions by probing more deeply into each of the great Axial Age literatures. Each of them brings to light a distinctive set of basic concepts and questions. These realms extensively overlap, as I have been indicating, yet each has its own integrity, its own intellectual and spiritual and historical stubbornness. By examining each more on its own terms (though still quite selectively and summarily), I hope to make more evident how the real quality of our attitude thinking today depends on our partnership with these sources—which is why they are properly called classic and why we properly think of ourselves, even as thinkers, as historical.

Attitude in Classic Chinese Thought: The Power of a Way

A passage from the *Book of Odes* cited earlier draws a sharp focus on the issue of right attitude in the ruler: "August was [Zhou founder] King Wen, continuously bright and reverent . . . Make King Wen your pattern and all the states will trust in you."[30] The king was a pivotal figure in the ancient Chinese spiritual economy. Ideally he would maintain reverence for heaven and benevolent concern for the welfare of his subjects; others would prosper in sharing in those attitudes; and whoever fell out of tune with them, ruler or subject, would come to grief. In ancient states generally, the king is typically seen as the fulcrum of the people's relationship with the divine—the subject-point at which the people's needs and appeals are focused, the agent-point from which divine power is directly applied to their affairs. In the Chinese version of this ideal, the "son of Heaven" governs not so much as the strong-armed officer of a higher paternal-royal authority (a court of ancestors or Supreme Ancestor), but more as the sagely exemplar of an impersonal pattern, a distillate of what makes persons worthy—and so not by the stormy force of divine intervention, but rather by the spiritual cogency of heavenly order, a cogency like that of musical harmony. The most obvious question this conception raises concerns the extent to which one person's maintaining of an attitude can be influential on others. To rule one's own life well simply in taking the right attitude, that is plausible—but to rule a country? Under what conditions does an agent's right orientation produce desirable consequences in the wider world?

It is not known how much help the early Zhou rulers actually got from the concept of the Mandate of Heaven. We do know that the Zhou social order was in serious disarray by the mid-first millennium BCE, and that Kongzi could address the crisis by modifying the ideas of a Son of Heaven and the Way of Heaven to apply more directly to everyone, so that in principle there can be as many decisive points of contact with goodness as there are individuals. Laozi (Lao-Tzu) could speak of a ruler sharing the greatness of the Heavenly Way and be understood to refer to anyone at all who understands that greatness.[31] "By being inwardly direct, I can be the companion of Heaven. Being a companion of Heaven, I know that the Son of Heaven [the emperor] and I are equally the sons of Heaven"—by the time of the *Zhuangzi* (Chuang-Tzu) this was a familiar proposition that could be poked at.[32]

Kongzi is an expert on traditional ritual forms—that is his marketable skill—and the *Analects* make it clear that he finds scrupulous observance of customary forms of propriety to be essential to a life worth living.[33] But the *Analects* also show that Kongzi is keenly interested in the centering of propriety in basic right attitudes. He appeals repeatedly to *ren*, an ideal of being a true noble among nobles that he helps to transform into the broader norm of humaneness.[34] "He whose heart is in the smallest degree set upon Goodness (*ren*) will dislike no one" (*Analects* 4.4). Implementing the master orientation of *ren* in a younger passage in the *Analects* are the more specific attitudes of courtesy, magnanimity, faithfulness, diligence, and kindness, all of which have manifest good consequences.[35] A personal partnership with Heaven grounds, frames, and protects the cultivation of *ren* (*Analects* 7.22).

Two other principles that may be regarded as "one thread running through" Kongzi's teaching are "loyalty" (*zhong*) and "consideration" or "likening-[others-]to-oneself (*shu*)."[36] The idea of *zhong*, broadened beyond its primary meaning of loyalty to one's superior, is to apply oneself wholeheartedly to the right. This has an attitudinal root in sincerity. *Zhong* becomes one of the official Confucian virtues.[37] The implication of *shu* is that one will not do to others what one does not wish done to oneself; it is affiliated with the attitude of sympathy.[38]

For Kongzi, *ren* is a natural human potentiality, but he does not think of it as a spontaneously budding power to the degree that Mengzi does.[39] Nor is *ren* inherently stable once acquired. Instead, it is a difficult target for mind and will to hold on to:

> I for my part have never yet seen one who really cared for Goodness . . . One who really cared for Goodness would never let any other consideration come first . . . Has anyone ever managed to do Good with his whole might even as long as the space of a single day? I think not. Yet I for my part have never seen anyone give up such an attempt because he had not the *strength* to go on. (*Analects* 4.6)

The habit of being considerate of others is helpful in the pursuit or construction of *ren*:

> As for Goodness—you yourself desire rank and standing; then help others to get rank and standing. You want to turn your own merits to account; then help others to turn theirs to account—in fact, the ability to take one's own feelings as a guide—that is the sort of thing that lies in the direction of Goodness.[40]

A. C. Graham suggests that *ren* be conceived as "an orientation which makes right action effortless, following attainment of just the right balance between self and others, a precarious balance which hardly anyone is able to sustain."[41] Why then, one wonders, is the balance of goodness so hard to maintain?[42] It is noteworthy that in *Analects* 7.33 Kongzi denies that he *is* a man of *ren*, though he takes credit for putting forth unsurpassed moral effort and claims elsewhere, in 2.4, that "at seventy, I could follow the dictates of my own heart; for what I desired no longer overstepped the boundaries of right." Perhaps it is the great intrinsic value that Kongzi sees in learning and in eagerness to learn that makes him unwilling to cap off the pursuit of *ren*; a disciple of *ren* would no more claim to embody *ren* than a true scholar would claim to be the master of all knowledge (7.21, 15.30). Or *ren*-fellowship is conceived more fundamentally as an open, ideally inclusive community of seekers than as a distinction of attainers from non-attainers. Alternatively, Kongzi's thought in 7.33 may be related to his complaint that he has never been placed in the right social position "to show what I could do" (7.32). The implication would be that the full attainment of *ren* requires active reciprocal relations, not merely an individual's subjective readiness for them. That fits the well-recognized way in which Kongzi's ethics and spirituality are oriented to a social scheme—a scheme crucially supported by individual dispositions—rather than to individuals' qualities or experiences considered in separation from practice.

We should not think of *ren* as difficult in the manner of a brilliant technique, like juggling swords, for a favored image of right orientation is the actionless action of the sage-king Shun. "What action did he take? He merely placed himself gravely and reverently with his face due south; that was all" (15.4). It is more like tightrope walking. The point is to center life properly, a practice that will appear outwardly simple or delightfully harmonious even though meeting its inward preconditions poses a great challenge.

Kongzi set great store also by the attitude of filial piety, which became the chief theme of one of the Confucian Classics.[43] "Surely proper behavior towards parents and elder brothers is the trunk of Goodness?" (1.2).[44] We saw that Kongzi disapproved of a man who wanted to uphold his reputation for righteousness by testifying in court against his father. Each of us should be deeply mindful of our debt to our parents, as appropriately ritualized in three years' mourning for a parent's death; on the other hand, a younger *Analects* passage limits attention to dead ancestors with an assertion that service of the living is more important.[45]

The external referent of right attitude in Confucianism is the Way of

Heaven. It is ultimately the appeal of Heaven's "greatness" that inspires and then radiates from the sage: "Greatest [as sage-king] was Yao . . . 'There is no greatness like the greatness of Heaven,' yet Yao could copy it" (*Analects* 8.19). It came to be said about Kongzi that "only the most sagacious in the world . . . are expansive like Heaven . . . thus they are said to be the complement of Heaven."[46] In Mengzi's view of the sage's goodness, however, the relationship-distance between Heaven and humanity might seem to be superseded:

> The desirable is called "good." To have it in oneself is called "true." To possess it fully in oneself is called "beautiful," but to shine forth with this full possession is called "great." To be great and to be transformed by this greatness is called "sage"; to be sage and to transcend the understanding is called "divine."[47]

But Mengzi also praised King Wen in these terms: "[He] gazed at the Way as if he had never seen it before."[48] So the commanding appeal and the most-responsive attitude remain key reference points for him as well.

***

The philosophical Daoism of the *Daodejing* and the *Zhuangzi* wears the appearance partly of an ancient indigenous wisdom—perhaps as old as the Upanishadic wisdom in India, to which it is similar in content—and partly of a riposte to Confucianism and other leading Chinese philosophies of the later first millennium BCE. Whereas Confucians value human culture, custom, and deference, Daoists value the "natural," the spontaneous, and the idiosyncratic. Whereas Confucians trust reasonable discourse, Daoists are fond of paradoxes, riddles, and dreams. Whereas Confucians are content within the ordinary limits of mortal life, the imagination and desire of Daoists run beyond these limits. But Daoists share with Confucians the premise that an identifiable right attitude, accessible to any individual, is the sovereign justifier and ultimate benefit and that this attitude can helpfully be conceived as participation in the Way of Heaven (or as a state of being "mated to heaven").[49]

Daoism proposes to form a perception of Heaven's Way more radical than the observation of natural regularity, already a commonplace of Chinese think-ing. What is the ultimate ground of existents, occurrences, patterns, and dis-tinctions generally? It cannot itself be an existent, occurrence, or pattern of the ordinary sort; it must precede distinctions; and yet it must somehow be essen-tially related to the world of which it is the ground. "The Way is like an empty vessel that yet may be drawn from without ever needing to be filled. It is bottomless; the very progenitor of all things in the world . . . a deep pool that never dries. Was it too the child of something else? We cannot tell" (*Daodejing* 4). "Because the eye gazes but can catch no glimpse of it, it is called elusive" (14). "It was from the Nameless that Heaven and Earth sprang" (1). The *appeal* of the Way is universal and implicit: "Dao gave them birth . . . perfected them, giving to each its strength. Therefore of the ten thousand things there is not one that does not [in essence] worship Dao and do homage to its 'power.' No mandate ever went forth that accorded to Dao the right to be worshipped" (51).

How is Heaven's Way related to our practical choices? It can be stipulated as an a priori truth that the most practically estimable way in which we can imagine things being done cannot diverge from the most-basic Way by which everything in our universe *has* happened and *does* happen, the Way that has made and does make everything possible. This Way alone is necessarily successful. But such a principle of sure success holds self-evidently only from an ideally unlimited perspective and might have no implications for human practice, or very dangerous ones (even assuming one can genuinely perceive a cosmic Way as opposed to projecting one wishfully). It might lead to immoral power-worship, paralyzing fatalism, or wild fantasticality. Thus it must be shown how a human agent in fact achieves the best pose and poise by replicating the cosmic Way. The *Daodejing* sketches this demonstration by relating empirical observations of practical futility to its analysis of the derived and alienated state of ordinary existents and intentions. "Those that would gain what is under heaven by tampering with it—I have seen that they do not succeed . . . Those that tamper with it, harm it. Those that grab at it, lose it"— the basic cause of this situation being that "among the creatures of the world some go in front, some follow; some blow hot when others would be blowing cold. Some are feeling vigorous just when others are worn out" (*Daodejing* 29). The way of the world is a jostling and straying of things in their individual, limited forms, with their limited and errant forces. The ideal agent, however, "has all the time a power that never errs [because] he returns to the Limitless"; he is the non-tamperer, "the greatest carver [who] does the least cutting," the one who cuts no special figure in the world (28).[50]

Seen outwardly, the hallmark of effective action is that it does not interfere or destroy. It is yielding and permissive, like the source of all things. The ideal of the great carver who does the least cutting is fascinating and could be of great practical-hermeneutical power. But one cannot actually set about carving things without cutting or ruling the land while remaining unknown (*Daodejing* 10). This side of Daoist prescription floats before us as a vague practical utopia. Where Daoist prescription directly touches us is in the realm of attitude, and the strongest appeal in philosophical Daoism is inherent in the attitudes it recommends—especially in the appeal of peacefulness.

The ideal Daoist attitude-complex comprises desirelessness ("Only he that rids himself of desire can see the Secret Essences; he that has never rid himself of desire can see only the outcomes"),[51] undemandingness, moderation, humility, submissiveness ("the female by quiescence conquers the male"),[52] calmness, and openness (*Daodejing* 34, 9, 22, 45, 16). The Daoist sage is truly helpful, though not in the obtrusively learned and "humane" manner of the Confucians (27). The key to the authentic Daoist attitude implied by all these descriptions is, paradoxically, not to take an "attitude" at all, for to pose or be poised as one being among others is to give oneself over to strife. Thus Daoist attitudes are best understood as the worldly facets of an inward transcendence of the world:

> Of old those that were the best officers of Court
> Had inner natures subtle, abstruse, mysterious, penetrating,
> Too deep to be understood.
> And because such men could not be understood
> I can but tell of them as they appeared to the world:
> Circumspect they seemed, like one who in winter crosses a stream,
> Watchful, as one who must meet danger on every side.
> Ceremonious, as one who pays a visit;
> Yet yielding, as ice when it begins to melt.
> Blank, as a piece of uncarved wood;
> Yet receptive as a hollow in the hills.
> Murky, as a troubled stream—
> Which of you can assume such murkiness, to become in the end still and
>   clear? (15)

Certain appropriate attitudes and actions clearly have a place in the Daoist life. What is proposed is not a complete negation of psychology and practice but a *turn* from the world *toward* the Nameless lurking *within* the world-constituting relations between the Nameless and inferior levels and domains of goodness. The *Daodejing* lays out the order of dependence in its description of the world's degeneration:

> After the Dao was lost, then came the "power" [*de*, innate "virtue"];
> After the "power" was lost, then came human kindness [*ren*].
> After human kindness was lost, then came morality.
> After morality was lost, then came ritual.
> Now ritual is the mere husk of loyalty and promise-keeping
> And is indeed the first step toward brawling. (38)

Confucians would endorse the notion that meaningful ritual must be grounded in morality, morality in kindness, and kindness in the Way. They think that all these elements of goodness can be in force concurrently. The Daoists differ by warning against giving *any* credence to supposed forms of goodness other than the Way itself. To do so is to be alienated from the Way and so fated to err. Therefore the "right Daoist attitude" may be appreciated as such only out of the corner of one's eye, so to speak, as one turns toward the Nameless. It would perhaps be equivalent to say that Daoism prescribes *one* perfect attitude of flexible receptivity and responsiveness, an attitude that never stiffens into a pose.

With this important qualification of Daoist attitudes noted, then, we find that Axial Age China produced not merely one classic set of attitude conceptions and claims, but a classic opposition of attitude-complexes: Daoism revolving around stillness and acceptance, Confucianism revolving around exertion and discriminating regard. The opposition itself became ingrained in Chinese culture as the ideals of Confucianism were applied especially to public life, while Daoist ideals were applied to private life. As the two teachings matured in what Waley calls the "moralistic period" and Graham calls "the [period of the] discovery of subjectivity," both granted an ever more central and powerful role to the individual human agent.[53] "For a man to give full realization to his heart is for him to understand his own nature, and a man who knows his own nature will know Heaven . . . All the ten thousand things are there in me," says Mengzi.[54] Xunzi (Hsün Tzu) disagrees with Mengzi's claim that goodness is humanly innate but agrees on the structuring premise that the Way is known by the "heart."[55] To aid in the full realization of the heart, Chinese literature by the third century BCE abounds in general attitude prescriptions.[56] The argument that a basic orientation makes all the difference to a person's meaning-world gets more elaborately developed than in the earlier summary praises of sincerity or quiescence (but still lacking a term for "attitude"):

> Most listeners of the age are penned in somewhere, so when they listen they are sure to get things the wrong way round. There are many reasons for being penned in, but the crucial ones are sure to result from what a man is pleased with and what he dislikes . . . There was a man who lost an axe, and suspected his neighbor's son. He watched the way he walked—he's stolen the axe. The way he looked—he's stolen the axe. The way he talked— he's stolen the axe . . . When digging in his own yard he found the axe. Afterwards when he saw his neighbor's son again, there was nothing in gesture or posture to suggest a man who steals axes. It was not that his neighbor's son had altered, it was himself that had altered. The alteration was from no other reason than being penned in somewhere. (*Lü Spring and Autumn* 13.3)[57]

The fable of the axe implies that attitude, understood as a conjunction of perception, knowledge, and desire, is what fundamentally rectifies one position and makes another wrong. It also shows a recognition that attitude is liable to be suddenly changed according to what is perceived, known, or wanted.

* * *

The Chinese Axial Age produces a complex understanding of the power of a right Way. Heaven's Way, which we are able to observe on the large scale and in the long run, is unconditionally superior and omnipotent. There are durably relevant opposed (or, from a later perspective, complementary) ways to participate in Heaven's way: the Yang-aggressive way of Confucianism, and the Yin-recessive way of Daoism. Taking the Daoist way leads to a transcendence of ordinary human agency, a sort of immersion in primal nature. In this orientation, all goes well simply because all fundamentally does go well. Taking the Confucian way leads toward the perfection of ordinary human agency in its distinctively high, socially constructive position within the natural order. In the ideal Confucian order, all goes well because we all mean well. (Mengzi combines these suppositions from a Confucian point of view: "The people turn to the benevolent as water flows downwards or as animals head for the wilds.")[58] That all does not in fact go well does not count more against one of these views than the other; instead, painful experience continually gives each view grounds for appealing against the other and so jointly bolsters them. A thoughtful person is called from quiescence to earnestness, from earnestness to quiescence, each attitude functioning more credibly as a sovereign attitude in the situations to which it is better suited. (Here too Mengzi proposes a synthesis, seemingly more verbal than substantive: "Benevolence is man's peaceful abode.")[59]

We can state in summary thesis form several major points of attitude thinking that emerge in the work of the Chinese sages:

(1) Attitude is the most crucial normative issue because one's basic attitude is one's most fundamentally determinative relation to a cosmically real, indestructible, and inescapable Way, harmony with which is a necessary condition for the flourishing of all beings.

(2) A sovereign (fundamentally and comprehensively life-rectifying) attitude is accessible to all hearers of the right teaching.

(3) The sovereign attitude or Way is elusive, however, and endlessly calls on all a subject's powers to attain it or participate in it; it may not, strictly speaking, be humanly attainable, but only divinely so.

(4) The sovereign attitude or Way is implemented in worldly life by more specific attitudes, "virtues," among which filial piety can be seen as most important.

Attitude in Classic Indian Thought:
The Power of Detachment and Attachment

The best-known Axial Age Indian thought centers on a strategic insight into the oneness of reality that implies the ultimate *un*reality of formed, diverse beings. Much as Confucianism and Daoism bring the Mandate of Heaven from the actual king to Any-Individual, the Upanishadic teachers offer any hearer access to an actual yogin's realization of oneness. The way to this position is prepared by the Brahmanical literature of the early first millennium BCE in which the prayer-word *brahman* becomes (like Hebrew *ruach* and Greek *pneuma*) a principle of cosmic communion and the rectification of relationships, a principle that is already praised in its own right in the *Rig Veda*.[60] Then the transitional Aranyaka literature shows increasing interest in the symbolic meaning of priestly ritual, making the knowledge of that meaning an end in itself.[61] Finally, in the Upanishads, the knowledge of an ultimate essence of this meaning is proclaimed to be sovereign and salvific: "When a man rightly sees, he sees all, he wins all, completely."[62] But on what understanding of "seeing" could seeing or knowing just in itself, an inward formation of an individual, constitute winning, the rectification of interactions with other beings? What exactly makes for seeing "rightly"?

Assuming that we are disturbed by our experiences and prospects of loss and that conventional prayer and sacrifice cannot really cure this problem, Upanishadic reflection leads our attention to the unchanging, indestructible source of all things on two tracks: (1) the cosmological or ontological order of dependence in which a pervasive invisible essence of all things is prior to all concrete existents, even gods; and (2) a psychological or intentional order in which, according to one discussion in the *Chandogya*, the power of naming depends on the power of speech, speech on mind, mind on intention, intention on thought, thought on deep reflection, deep reflection on perception, and perception on strength.[63] The summary claim repeated throughout the Upanishads that ultimate reality, *brahman*, is the same as the true self, *atman*, encourages a combined sorting out of these two orders of dependence. Radical independence in being must turn out to be the same as radical independence in knowing, since the restrictions that *brahman* and *atman* surpass in their respective orders are the very characteristics by which the outwardness of existence differs from the inwardness of knowing and vice versa. The pure being of *brahman* comprehends and centers everything as only mind can, and the pure mind of *atman* participates in the extension of everything as only pure being can. In the pure mind we discover our "real desires" that cannot be frustrated.[64] If we perfect our identification with the common essence of all—dissolving our private subjectivity by surrendering words to the mind, the mind to the knowing self, the knowing self to the great self, and the great self to the peaceful self (according to the *Katha Upanishad*)—we enjoy the informing and powering of all things and no longer suffer from attachment to forms of being that we do not possess.[65] Thus we transcend the common religious scenario of appealing to a god's generosity or mercy.[66] What is truly pivotal for a human subject's well-being is its own disposition, not a contingent relation with an external being.[67] The "veneration" of a religious object in the sense of "worship" *of* it can now be interiorized as "meditation" *on* it.[68]

The *Mundaka Upanishad* mocks the limited otherworldly-yet-worldly salvation achieved by priestly practices: "Deeming sacrifices and gifts as the best, the imbeciles know nothing better. When they have enjoyed their good work, atop the firmament, they return again to this abject world" (1.2.10). This sets up a characterization of the superior way:

> But those in the wilderness, calm and wise,
>   who live a life of penance and faith . . .
> Through the sun's door they go, spotless,
>   to where that immortal Person is, that immutable self.
> When he perceives the worlds as built with rites,
> A Brahmin should acquire a sense of disgust—
>   "What's made can't make what is unmade!"

To understand it he must go, firewood in hand,
  to a teacher well versed in the Vedas, and focused on *brāhman.*
To that student of tranquil mind and calm disposition,
  who had come to him in the right manner, that learned man faithfully
    imparted
The knowledge of *brahman,*
  by which he understood that Person—the true, the imperishable.
    (1.2.11–13)

In this text a number of attitude qualifications (calm, tranquil, penitent, faithful) prepare for a climactic "knowledge of *brahman.*" A natural reading is: One must be calm in order to receive the knowledge; the desirable attitude is a means to obtaining the desirable apprehension. But the relation between attitude and knowledge appears to be even closer than that, for we are told presently that knowledge of *brahman* involves perfect calm: "The seers, sated with knowledge . . . become free from passion and tranquil, and their selves are made perfect" (3.2.5). (The same claim is made for the knowledge of the Four Noble Truths in Buddhism.)[69] And we have been told that to understand the rites is to be disgusted by them. One cannot be in tune with the rites if one sees that they cannot produce the highest benefit; on the other hand, one cannot be brought to see the incapacity of the rites to produce the highest benefit as long as one is entirely in tune with them—hence the preliminary kicking at "the imbeciles [who] know nothing better" and the praise of renunciation.

It might seem preferable to interpret detached tranquility as an "experience" rather than as an "orientation" when it is a question of the very substance of salvation. For the knowledge and self-perfection cited here are a fulfillment, not a scheme for fulfillment. In this context, however, it is not clear how to draw a line between experience and orientation. To be sure, the "sated" knower is not to be conceived as merely "well-oriented" or rightly aimed toward other beings—for in an important sense other beings as such are no longer in the picture—but neither is he or she to be conceived as merely "having" a flawless mental representation of a world or "taking" pleasure in a world, for the self that would draw such things out of a world to have for itself has been undone.[70] The great point is that all has come right. Insofar as a private self and a plurality of beings *are* still in the picture, the perfect state does necessarily involve a right orientation of the self in relation to those beings. Insofar as private self and plurality of beings have been transcended, the perfect state transcends both orientation and experience in their ordinary senses. Certainly the bliss that is promised in the perfect state may not be identified with any sort of pleasant experience that would be the object of passionate attachment.[71]

In comparison with the Buddhists and the Greek Skeptics and Epicureans, who quite provocatively subordinate the pursuit of knowledge to the maintenance of a desirable attitude—advising us to choose what and how to believe according to the effect of beliefs on our tranquility—the Upanishadic teachers do not baldly present their reasoning as tranquility-technique. But it is an open question whether the Upanishads are really different in this respect, since their reality descriptions seem for the most part to be rigorously constrained by the value of tranquility. To make out a difference, we might distinguish between tranquility (1) in its character as freedom from all bias, as a condition *for* true perception of reality; and (2) in its character as an ultimately desirable state, as a condition *on* what can be believed or registered fully of true reality—interpreting the Upanishadic ideal along the lines of (1) rather than (2). But (1) and (2) can run together, as our passage has shown: one is freed from the illusion of believing in the independent reality of dependent beings by one's disgust with them, which is grounded in one's desire for perfect happiness and stabilized in the attitude of detachment. Upanishadic philosophy differs from Buddhist and Greek cognitive instrumentalisms, then, not by abjuring perspective (2) but by affirming (1) together with (2); that is, by granting a determining power to perception as such as well as to desire and disposition. Thus it supposes that progress can be made with purely logical arguments like "What's made can't make what is unmade!" whereas the strategy that is standard in Skepticism and popular in Buddhism is to neutralize all arguments with counterarguments of potentially equal validity.

The Upanishads do not single out and revolve around an attitude ideal in the way that Skepticism and Epicureanism revolve around tranquility (*ataraxia*), or even in the way that the *Bhagavad Gita* highlights detachment and devotion-love. Nevertheless, there are clear Upanishadic signals of the practical primacy of attitude.

> Man is undoubtedly made of resolve. What a man becomes on departing from here after death is in accordance with his resolve in this world. So he should make this resolve: . . . "This self (*atman*) of mine that lies deep within my heart—it contains all actions, all desires, all smells, and all tastes; it has captured this whole world . . . It is *brahman*. On departing from here after death, I will become that."[72]

The theistic *Shvetashvatara Upanishad* dramatizes the relationship between the speaker and a personalized Ultimate Reality: "Finer than the finest, larger than the largest, is the self that lies here hidden in the heart of a living being. A man who, by the creator's grace, sees that desireless one as the majesty and as the Lord will be free from sorrow" (3.20). "There is no likeness of him, whose name is Immense Glory. His appearance is beyond the range of sight . . . Those who know him thus with their hearts—him, who abides in their hearts—and with insight become immortal" (4.19–20). Responding to the "grace" perceived in the "creator" together with the epistemological requirement of apprehension by the "heart," the attitude of devotion-love (bhakti) appears in the *Shvetashvatara*'s formula for connecting insight and attitude in mortals: "One should never disclose [this supreme secret] to a person who is not of a tranquil disposition . . . Only in a man who has the deepest love for God, and who shows the same love towards his teacher as towards God, do these points declared by the Noble One shine forth" (6.23).

Just here we arrive at a significant midpoint in the Axial Age shift to a focus on inwardness. Devotion-love and detachment are each conceived at this stage as a balance of relational comportment and inward formation. Devotion-love is perfect commitment, both in the sense of dedication to the service of another and of concentration of one's forces. Detachment is perfect freedom from external bondage and perfect peace within. The *Bhagavad Gita* amplifies this compound ideal by weaving together many variations of benign attitude:

> One who bears hate for no creature is friendly, compassionate, unselfish, free of individuality, patient, the same in suffering and joy. Content always, disciplined, self-controlled, firm in his resolve, his mind and understanding dedicated to me, devoted to me, he is dear to me . . . Disinterested, pure, skilled, indifferent, untroubled, relinquishing all involvements, devoted to me, he is dear to me. (12.13–16)

⁂

Talk about attitudes becomes proportionally much more conspicuous in the *Bhagavad Gita* than in the Upanishads. The *Gita*'s teaching resembles Buddhism in this respect, whether due to the influence of Buddhism upon it or simply due to the larger Axial Age trend.

Early Buddhism shares with Upanishadic thought the general project of publishing the yogin's key to liberation from entanglement in an essentially dissatisfying world. It is like Upanishadic thought also in conceiving salvation as tranquility and in putting more faith in the attitudes of detachment and tranquility than in cultic practice or the observance of worldly dharma duties. This makes sense, again, because of the link between tranquility and a completely general perception of the ultimate unreality of worldly beings (or, we could perhaps equivalently say, a general detachment from all worldly beings). Buddhism's most important difference lies in its emphasis on compassion.[73] The dominant Upanishadic perspective on salvation is a challenging one: the seeker must be wholly committed to discovering the truth, rightly aimed, and fortunate enough to find a qualified teacher. What reason is there to think that a worldly individual could ever become truly well-aimed? This difficult question was addressed in a new way by the *Shvetashvatara Upanishad*'s hint of divine "grace." The appeal to grace in personal relationship that just peeks out in one of the latest of the principal Upanishads comes to full flower in Buddhism, which announces that the world-savior came with his teaching "for the happiness of the multitudes, out of sympathy for the world."[74]

Buddhist scriptures grant an important role to sympathy in the sense of a general resonance with the sufferings of others (*anukampa*), as Buddhism initially depends on that attitude for its appeal.[75] A more definite systematic role in Buddhist practice is accorded to the four "sublime attitudes" (*brahma-vihara*, "godlike ways of living") of benevolence, compassion in the sense of being concerned with (though not saddened by) the unhappiness of others, sympathetic joy or being happy with the happiness of others, and equanimity.[76] These attitudes are thought to be fundamental for progress toward enlightenment, yet not of the very substance of enlightenment; cultivated as ends in themselves, they lead to rebirth in a divine world rather than to liberation from all worlds.[77] (An attitude is relevant and finds fulfillment only in some sort of world.)

The attitude of equanimity must not be confused with the equanimity that is a "limb of enlightenment" itself.[78] This second equanimity is a norm for the meditating mind. Sympathetic relations with worldly beings form a supportive platform for the direct cultivation, in meditation, of the equal-mindedness of radical release from all attachment to beings (as distinct from the attitude of nondiscriminatory regard for all beings). Subsequently, in the worldly comportment that follows meditation, the sublime attitudes again come into play, drawing support in their turn from enlightenment—as, for example, threats to sympathy and practical equanimity can be repelled by the full realization of the unreality of all beings.

Benevolence and the varieties of sympathy are thus essential to the Theravada Buddhist *life*, though not to the Theravada conception of the ultimate goal. Mahayana Buddhism, in contrast, asserts that benevolence and sympathy must belong to the substance of enlightenment, since solidarity with all worldly beings is the ultimate expression of nondiscrimination:

> When the Bodhisattvas [at the highest stage] face and perceive the happiness of the samadhi of perfect tranquilization, they are moved with the feeling of love and sympathy owing to their original vows . . . made for all beings, saying, "So long as they do not attain Nirvana I will not attain it myself." Thus they keep themselves away from Nirvana. But the fact is that they are already in Nirvana because in them there is no rising of discrimination.[79]

The perfect bodhisattva, Mahayana's ideal, is "selfless" in a different sense than Theravada recommends. This is a "selflessness" that is an attitude and belongs in a world; without a world, there could not be nondiscrimination.

* * *

Axial Age Indian thought is rivaled only by parallel developments in Greek philosophy (and to a lesser extent by Chinese Daoism) in its commitment to analysis of the structure of reality as the high road to the rectification of human existence. On the strength of an intellectually penetrating analysis of the general character of experienced reality, the Upanishadic or Buddhist mind sees through all worldly beings to a non-concrete ground of all. From this extraordinary vantage point, worldly beings can no longer figure as objects of attachment. In the absence of attachment it is possible to maintain an attitude of perfect tranquility. From this tranquility flows a personal (yet not merely personal) experience of bliss and a peaceful, compassionate mode of participation in worldly life.

The decisive insight into the illusory and impermanent nature of all concrete beings, which is finally validated by the achievement of calm, is originally accessible only by means of a thorough calming; indeed, there may be no meaningful distinction between "knowledge" of *brahman* or *atman*, on the one hand, and the "attitude" of tranquility, on the other, when both knowledge and attitude are fully realized. In the midst of the classical Indian pursuit of detachment, however, there leaps up the flame of *bhakti*, an idealized wholehearted attachment to the divine. Henceforth, there is an ambiguous relationship between the intentness of the calm sage and the passion of the devotee (and correspondingly between non-theistic and theistic versions of Hinduism and Buddhism). Polemicists can claim that one attitude or the other is inauthentic and dangerous; irenicists can argue• that the object of both attitudes must ultimately be identical and that the two attitudes must converge in their full rounding out.

These are some distinctively Indian attitude theses:

(1) The ideal attitude can (in the case of tranquility, at least) contain the very substance of life-rectifying knowledge and experience. Without it, knowledge and experience will be incorrigibly distorted by our passions.

(2) Ideals of perfect detachment and perfect attachment can be harmonized—when detachment is from worldly beings and attachment is to a transworldly divine being.

(3) A sovereign attitude can support but also override social pieties—as Arjuna's world-detached attachment to Krishna overrides his pious reservations against attacking his relatives in the *Bhagavad Gita*.[80]

(4) The attitudes that make for a well-lived life, such as benevolence and equanimity, remain distinct from the sovereign attitude, just as worldly life remains distinct from full enlightenment.

Attitude in Classic Greek Thought: The Power of the Rational Soul

According to intellectual historian Bruno Snell, Heraclitus (ca. 500 BCE) is the first Greek thinker to make a theme of "soul" in the sense of a power of self-centering and inwardness, but the concept is already brewing in the archaic lyric poets. Archilocus of the early seventh century explicitly considers how human beings are oriented, in each case modifying a thought in Homer:[81]

> [But those things, I suppose, were dear to me which a god put in my heart;]
> For different men take delight in different actions. (*Odyssey* 14.228)[82]

Each man has his heart cheered in his own way. (Archilocus 41)

For the spirit of men on the earth is as the day
that comes upon them from the father of gods and men.
    (*Odyssey* 18.136)

Such a mind . . . do mortal men have
as Zeus may usher in each day, and they think their
thoughts in accord with their daily transactions. (Archilocus 68)[83]

Homer records changes of human attitude as relatively simple effects, like the darkening of the ground when a cloud passes before the sun. The newer view opens up human inwardness as a problem to explore; the mind is seen as subject to multiple determinations, including self-determinations. Heraclitus sights an endless territory and at the same time announces an infinite responsibility when he says, "You would not find out the boundaries of soul, even by travelling along every path: so deep a measure does it have."[84] How can a thing of such immeasurable "depth" be rightly attuned and aimed?

Heraclitus stands in the sixth-century tradition of Ionian speculation on the constitution of "nature" that stems from Thales, but he dramatically changes focus from the objects of experience to the manner of its interpretation: "Although the Logos is common the many live as though they had a private understanding" (195). The concept of an eminent "word" that is common by definition, a principle of unity in understanding, is implied by the whole Ionian project of ascertaining, through an ideally open discussion, what must be true of reality. Given a grounding of its own, this *logos* becomes the guarantee of the meaningfulness of that enterprise and its results. At the same time, *logos* is an appeal and a principle of attitude. "Listening not to me but to the Logos it is wise to agree that all things are one" (196). For Axial Age minds enjoying a new degree of freedom from the constraints of mythic narration and custom-bound value judgments, the idea of a "logical" orientation toward general articulability, commensurability, and systematic unity is a powerfully relevant new proposal because it promises a more intelligent and collegial community. A *logos*-word is not someone's dictatorial pronouncement but a "measure," a "reckoning," a "proportion" expressing publicly ascertainable forms and relations. *Logos* could, of course, betray freedom rather than strengthen it, depending on how it is conceived and policed. It could be a diamond cage imprisoning our minds. But the effective openness of discussion under the sign of *logos* will be its redeeming feature, however limited or limiting its deliverances at a given juncture might be.

It is very late-modern of me to place so much emphasis on discussion in the operation of *logos*. Heraclitus, in contrast, thought of *logos* objectively as the "steering of all things through all" and of its subjective aspect more in terms of a sense-mediated actual communion with the world (227). It is the most inclusive perception, wakeful and sober, best attuned to the working-together of the world-system. According to Sextus Empiricus, Heraclitus taught that "in the waking state [our mind] again peeps out through the channels of perception as though through a kind of window, and meeting with the surrounding it puts on its power of reason" (234). (The arch-rationalist Parmenides, Heraclitus's near contemporary, sought to "put on the power of reason" in a pure reflection on the conditions of thinkableness that yielded an uncompromising conception of pure Being—Being as such—as the only reality. Parmenides was as intent as Heraclitus on orienting the mind toward reality as a whole.)[85] But even if Heraclitus did not particularly tout philosophical discussion, he did prescribe "reliance on what is common to all" in political activity and warned that individual insolence (*hubris*) is more dangerous than a conflagration (250, 248).

Hubris, a famous preoccupation of classical Greek tragedy, figures as a great threat precisely because the human mind's own resources are now seen in a fascinating new light as extraordinarily powerful. If all goes well, human powers will be managed in such a way that the human city-state will itself embody and guarantee holiness; there will be a time "when Athens is extolled with peerless praise for reverence, and for mercy!" (Sophocles), having been established by the humane god who appeals to "that spirit in reverence which hears Persuasion and which thinks again" (Aeschylus).[86] But the city-state has a tough row to hoe. The Athenian persecution of the philosophers Anaxagoras and Socrates in the later fifth century reflects, among other things, a felt upset of the balance of orienting powers in the Greek ethos: free inquiry into matters of heaven as well as earth is seen as hubristic or, to state it the other way, as *asebes*, "impious," insufficiently disposed to credit the ancestral gods and ways. Impressive as they are to us, the efforts of the Ionians, Pythagoreans, and Eleatics to stabilize an understanding of ultimate reality and worth under the auspices of *logos* were not at all confidence-building at the time; the results of philosophical inquiry were difficult to grasp, often wildly counterintuitive (as in Zeno's disproofs of plurality and motion in support of Parmenides' exclusive affirmation of Being), and impractical-seeming. The mischievous *logos*-merchants known as sophists seemed to excel only in "making the weaker argument [appear the] stronger," a scandal animating Socrates' accusers.[87]

The charges against Anaxagoras and Socrates tellingly represent the Axial Age turn in the history of Greek attitude thinking because they make their foremost appeal, not to a law or to the will of the gods, but to an attitude, *eusebeia*. The issues raised by these charges are laid out in Plato's dialogues that deal with the prosecution and punishment of Socrates, the *Euthyphro*, *Apology*, and *Crito*. These dialogues could be called the Piety Cycle, since their main concern is to explore what is at stake in appeals to piety, what in principle justifies the trumping claim that an action is pious or impious, and how the rational reconstruction of piety by the philosopher breaks from traditional or popular forms of piety. On his way to court, Socrates questions the self-appointed religious expert, Euthyphro—a man whose piety is highly suspect, since he has chosen (like his Chinese counterpart "upright Kung") to prosecute his own father for an ambiguous offense—and finds that no consistent formula for "holiness" (*to osion*), that is, no consistent norm for piety can be deduced from facts about what pleases the gods.[88] Although holiness continues to elude definition in this dialogue, the important suggestions emerge that it has to do with rightness in the human relationship with the divine and that it serves the purpose of preserving the family and the state.[89]

Next, in the *Apology*, Socrates' peculiar relationship with the divine is disclosed—it involves heeding a command from the oracle at Delphi to test all claims of wisdom and, more generally, heeding a personal *daimon*, a sort of gyroscopic implant of goodness that keeps him from taking unjustified steps— and this relationship is vindicated against an incoherent traditionalist piety invoked by his opponents. The dialogue argues that Socrates' kind of piety could not lead him to corrupt the youth, contrary to what is charged; that it makes him take his civic responsibility more seriously than others do; and that it enables him to face death undaunted.[90] The most telling application of true piety comes at last in the *Crito*, where, in order to ground the claim that his escape would unjustly harm the state, Socrates adduces a no-harm principle in these terms:

> Socrates: Is it right to requite evil (*kakos*) with evil, as the world says it is, or not right?
>
> Crito: Not right, certainly . . .
>
> Socrates: For doing evil to people is the same thing as wronging them (*adikein*).
>
> Crito: That is true.
>
> Socrates: Then we ought neither to requite wrong with wrong nor to do evil to anyone, no matter what he may have done to us. And be careful, Crito, that you do not, in agreeing to this, agree to something you do not believe; for I know that there are few who believe or ever will believe this. Now those who believe this, and those who do not, have no common ground of discussion, but they must necessarily, in view of their opinions, despise one another . . . therefore consider very carefully whether you agree and share in this opinion, and let us take as the starting point of our discussion the assumption that it is never right to do wrong or . . . to defend ourselves by doing evil in return.[91]

Socrates calls an "opinion" (*doxa*) what obviously must be more deeply rooted and encompassing in scope than any ordinary opinion. The orientation never to do wrong or evil is a "starting point" (*arche*) and "assumption" of ethical argument, he indicates; it is not subject to logical examination in the way that ordinary opinions are. (Compare Aristotle's assertion in the *Rhetoric* that a speaker's *eunoia*, "goodwill," is a basic condition of credibility.)[92] It is not a personal "virtue" of, say, sensitivity, although sensitivity and other virtues might be necessary for its full psychological and practical implementation; nor, on the other hand, is it an impersonal sort of "principle," since people will despise each other in not sharing it and will not be able fairly to discuss its merit. It is a centering of a person (the sustaining of a poise, virtue-like) *by* the center of a larger manifold (a posing, principle-like). It is a basic attitude. Plato wants us to see that the righteous basic attitude taken by Socrates does not accord with the way of the world, the popular attitude. Like Heraclitus's orientation to the *logos*, it is a counter-attitude.

Plato's dialogues everywhere show keen interest in human character qualities—not only their distinguishing features but their natural variation, the conditions of their formation, and their relation to wisdom and right ordering on the large scale. The *Republic* lays out a plan for cultivating in each soul a good disposition or manner of life (*euetheia*)—the inward counterpart to the *eunomia* of good government that Solon classically praised two centuries earlier[93]—with attention to good rhythm (*euruthmia*), good diction (*eulogia*), and good deportment (*euschemosune*).[94] The stability of this ideal culture depends on the good orientation of its philosopher-guides, those whose cognitive quest for excellence has led them to postulate and so far as possible embrace the unchanging essences of things and who are led in this quest finally to the Essence of essences, the Good, which is to reality and rational understanding what light is to visual experience.[95] Plato's approach to the Good is quiveringly attitudinal:

> Socrates: It is right to consider [knowledge and truth] as being like the good or boniform, but to think that either of them is the good is not right. Still higher honor belongs to the possession and habit [*hexis*] of the good.
> Glaucon: An inconceivable beauty you speak of, if it is the source of knowledge and truth, and yet itself surpasses them in beauty. For you surely cannot mean that it is pleasure.
> Socrates: Hush . . .[96]

Socrates' "hush" is *euphemei*, "speak well," a religious caution against blasphemy. It expresses most immediately the difference between the orientation to the ultimate good and an orientation to near-term private consummations. (Plato presents his optimistic theology in *Laws* and *Timaeus* as a warranted and consistent "speaking well" of the gods.)[97] To be centered by the all-enabling center of all essences, the Good, the individual soul must *turn* to seeking that center in the light of the illumination it gives from beyond. But Plato tells a parable of prisoners in a cave to suggest that the soul must *be turned*, released somehow from its fetters, like an exceptional prisoner (representing the philosopher) who is allowed to turn away from the deceptive fire-shadows on the cave wall toward the sunlight at the cave mouth (*Republic* 514–18). At this juncture the claims of the *Republic* all hinge on the main practical premise and rhetorical emphasis of right worship in the sacred cult: the soul's chance of salvation lies in "conversion" (*metastrepho*, "turning around," and *periagoge*, "leading around of a way of life"), a turning like that from the transiency of the world to the mysteries of resurrection or from false gods to the true God (518e). Such conversion depends crucially on the appeal of the Good in its aspect as

Beauty. It will not come about simply as the result of the soul's having a good idea. But it presupposes also an attunement of the soul to the Good, indeed an "indwelling power in the soul" (518c).

One more twist of attitude engineering is needed before Plato can end this phase of his discussion. It resembles the compassionate Mahayana twist on the classical Buddhist conception of enlightenment, although its root attitude is different. The Good-loving philosophers must be induced to apply their wisdom for the benefit of their fellow human beings rather than enjoying it peacefully on their own, as they would selfishly prefer. They will be tempted to scorn political work as the relatively dismal occupation it is, but in civic piety of the Socratic type, they will shoulder it—since, after all, the state raised them, and their civic debt must be respected (*Republic* 519–21).

* * *

Socrates' contemporary Democritus is credited with a treatise on "good spirits," *Peri Euthemies*, one surviving passage of which suggests that he saw an ethical application of his atomistic physics:

> Good spirits come to men through temperate enjoyment and a life com-
> mensurate (*biou symmetrie*). Deficiencies and excesses tend to turn into
> their opposites and to make large motions in the soul. And such souls as are
> in large-scale motion are neither in good balance nor in good spirits.[98]

This dynamic empiricist approach to setting the soul in right order stands in stark contrast to the rationalist Socratic-Platonic strategy of conforming to the one transcendent Good. Seen together, the two approaches prefigure the great opposition of Epicureanism and Stoicism that dominated ethical discussion in the Hellenistic period and long after in the West.

Plato's student Aristotle stands in the middle of all these developments, and his ethics is in many ways the most mature Greek expression of the Axial Age. He makes articulate, rigorous use of concepts of the practical good of happiness, practical intelligence, emotion, "state" or "disposition" (*hexis*), character, and virtue understood as a functional excellence of the soul adhering to rational principle. He provides a systematic guide to specific virtues and vices with their associated feelings; he rationally reconstructs divinity as a blessed self-thinking of pure Mind and optimistically affirms our intellectual kinship with perfect, imperturbable Mind despite the necessity of dealing with "things that could be otherwise" in our world. Most importantly, his ethics has the great appeal that it promises to enable any mature and nonvicious individual to steer himself (or herself, we would add) toward the best life. Aristotle cautions that practical intelligence is concerned with good order not only in the individual's life but in the community as well, and his method of inquiry, quite different from the oracular procedure of a Heraclitus, involves a communal sifting of opinions on the best life.[99] Nevertheless, it is impossible to miss in

Aristotle the basic theme that philosophy is the path of individual *mastery* of the good life through rational self-exertion. Aristotle never worries how, in Plato's terms, a cave prisoner might come to be unfettered and so brought into the basic right order. He is already sufficiently knowing and calm in his contact with Mind. He admits that the happy person needs some luck—for circumstances outside one's control can hinder or advance one's fulfillment—but sees no call for grace. Aristotelian discourse retains only the mildest religious gestures. Rather than concern himself with reforming piety as Socrates and Plato did, Aristotle operates post-piously. In this regard he is a harbinger for the attitudinal plausibility of Skepticism and Epicureanism, and perhaps also a trigger for the pious backlash of the more devotional side of Stoicism.

* * *

Aristotle's younger contemporary Pyrrho, the founder of Skepticism, breaks fundamentally with the Platonic and Aristotelian orientation to theoretical insight. The conclusions he draws from the impressive yet interminably clashing appeals of dialectical argumentation are: (a) that no knowledge claim can be conclusively sustained; (b) that since no belief can be secure, no belief can be salvific; and (c) that the salvation of perfect tranquility *is* available through a methodical suspension of belief.[100] Thus Pyrrho offers his followers not a new theory but a new *agoge*, a happy way of life.

Epicurus, of the same generation, boldly makes belief a function of desire. "We do everything for the sake of being neither in pain nor in terror."[101] While the Skeptics seek a blessed state through the complete avoidance of believing, the Epicureans seek peace through the adoption of congenial metaphysical and theological doctrines. The atomic theory of Democritus suits them very well metaphysically since it implies that death is the simple disassembly and end of an individual's existence—a most calming view. Nothing prevents them from introducing an indeterministic swerve in the motion of the Democritean atom in order to relieve the mind of worry about fate.[102] Belief in blissfully indifferent gods makes for a less anxious view of worldly affairs.[103]

The classic opposition of Stoicism and Epicureanism—a Roman analogue to the relationship between Confucianism and Taoism in imperial China—makes an important subject in the conceptual history of attitude. Here too, the opposition is founded on a deep agreement. To be sure, the Epicurean view of reasoning as strictly a means to the attainment of the pleasant life does have importantly different implications than the Stoic idea that in reasoning we realize the goodness of "nature," cosmic reason, and the world-soul, for Epicureans place their orientational confidence just in the individual pursuer of the happy life, whose body is the seat of pleasure, and find a transindividual center only in the contingently useful philosophical constructions of friends comparing notes, whereas Stoics look to a single great cosmic center and satisfaction and think of themselves as responsible citizens of a cosmopolis. And Epicureans decenter time (to free us from gloom about our impending nonexistence) and causation (to give us personal freedom to pursue accessible goods), whereas Stoics center time and causation in "the substance of god" and the sympathetically interconnected "condition of nature" and Fate (to which we can gladly be resigned).[104] The Stoic strategy is to strengthen the very kind of appeal that Epicureanism is dedicated to neutralizing. Nevertheless, both schools agree that reasoning is central in human life *because* it frees the individual from mental bondage to the variable external circumstances of life, thus assuring tranquility (*ataraxia*), the condition most congenial to the soul and most godlike. Both schools adopt what Martha Nussbaum calls the "medical model" of philosophy, directly addressing causes of disturbance in the individual.[105] The late Stoic Marcus Aurelius repeatedly thinks, "Either providence or atoms," reminding himself of his rational ability to sift and master the implications of different worldviews, as one might take a daily pill.[106]

Although the discourse of virtue superficially connects Epicureanism with classical Greek philosophy, the Epicurean derivation of virtue from the self-regarding orientation to tranquility is conceptually foreign to Plato and Aristotle, for whom intellectual grasp of the good is the supreme soul-fulfillment and the basic condition of human excellence. Despite the resemblance between Stoicism's interest in harmonizing individuals with divine providence and Plato's approach to the Good, Stoicism is involved in the same subjectivist shift that we find in Epicureanism, for Stoic harmony is guaranteed by the principle that "thinking makes it so."[107] Stoicism construes the content of thought to fit its agenda, and its agenda is control:

> Make it, therefore, your study at the very outset to say to every harsh external impression, "You are an external impression and not at all what you appear to be." After that examine it and test it by these rules which you have, the first and most important of which is this: Whether the impression has to do with the things which are under our control, or with those which are not under our control; and, if it has to do with some one of the things not under our control, have ready to hand the answer, "It is nothing to me." (Epictetus)[108]

Stoics offer many arguments for divine providence from the order in the world, but the clincher, in which the fundamental commitment to rational control becomes apparent, is: "Since [the world] embraces all things and since nothing exists which is not within it, [it] is entirely perfect; how then can it fail to possess that which is the best? but there is nothing better than intelligence and reason; the world therefore cannot fail to possess them."[109] The greater Center that Stoicism appeals to is deliberately projected from the individual human center, specifically my rational "leading part," and not an independent reality, function, or appeal—unless I choose to think of it as one—this in spite of the preservation of the *form* of establishing an independent appeal through sheer recognition of reality ("And contemplating the heavenly bodies the mind arrives at a knowledge of the gods, from which arises piety, with its comrades justice and the rest of the virtues, the sources of a life of happiness").[110] The really good news is that my "unconquerable" reason can be satisfied "with its own righteous dealing and the peace which that brings."[111]

It can be argued that the Stoics, like Heraclitus earlier and Kant later, transcend subjectivism when they submit to an autonomous supra-individual force of reasoning.[112] From another point of view, however, Stoicism's most significant strength lies precisely in the enlightened subjectivist posture it shares with Epicureanism. The two schools together form a classic touchstone in Western culture because, in sharing the premise that our fear- and hope-prone basic orientation provides the ultimate warrant of our beliefs, they can plausibly claim to exhibit the most difficult global issues of life most honestly.

An alternate interpretation of Epicureanism and Stoicism would pull them back from the extreme subjectivist ground that Skepticism occupies and locate their interest and strength rather in their *balancing* of subjective and objective warrants. On this view, the physics and logic developed by Epicureanism and Stoicism are to be taken just as seriously as their characterizations of the good life inasmuch as both schools make a sustained attempt to coordinate immediately felt issues of subjective orientation with empirical and logical data. "He that knoweth not what the Universe is knoweth not where he is."[113] (Yet "the study of physics is not to be taken up for any other reason than to distinguish good from bad.")[114] Such an interpretation seems to fit Stoicism better than Epicureanism because of Stoicism's distinctive attitude of reverence for the greater whole—although an Epicurean's prudential curiosity might not be inferior to Stoic reverence in motivating objective inquiry.

* * *

Classical Greek attitude thinking gives distinctively strong support to these theses:

(1) We can find within our own power of reason—not simply as a perceptual or intuitive faculty but as a manageable procedure—the means of most fundamentally rectifying our lives. (According to an important minority view held by Plato, a divine inspiration and "conversion" are necessary to right reason.)

(2) In being rational we are consubstantial with cosmic goodness—either because our rationality *is* that goodness in us, as Plato thinks, or because we best exercise our rationality in managing our beliefs such that we live in a congenial world, as Hellenistic philosophers tend to think.

(3) Civic piety can be a decisively important element of the rectified life. (The position Socrates takes in the *Crito* resonates with much else that is *polis*-affirming in Plato and Aristotle, and then with the cosmopolitanism of the Stoics.)

Attitude in Classic Hebrew Thought:
The Power of Personal Responsibility

Psalms and Proverbs in the Hebrew Bible are treasuries of attitude prescription. The spiritual summarizing and codifying process at work in these texts continues in the Christian New Testament as well. To understand the force of the now-clichéd formulas that fill these books, we must consider how specific conceptions of right attitude were forged in the context of Israelite Yahwism under the ideological leadership of a distinctive class of Axial Age teachers, the classic Hebrew prophets. Again under a warning flag, I offer "personal responsibility" as a rubric for these conceptions without a corresponding Hebraic term, and perhaps with too much contemporary resonance; but no other rubric seems to accommodate as well the implications of the Hebraic way of stressing relationship issues.

Broadly speaking, "prophets" are designated communicators with divine beings, and they were common in ancient societies. They certainly were abundant in the ancient Israelite kingdoms. We are told that in Elijah's time, at the height of a persecution of Yahwism, *only* 100 prophets loyal to Yahweh were saved in Israel as against 850 prophets of Baal and Asherah (1 Kings 18). It is apparent also that even within the land of Canaan there were significantly varying conceptions and styles of prophecy, depending on individuals, institutions, and circumstances. But a normative mold of prophecy is formed by a certain succession of biblical writers who collectively develop a powerful rhetoric of religious appeal keyed to attitude terms such as righteousness (*sedaqa*) and love (*hesed*). Like Zarathushtra, they think good attitudes belong originally to the divine being and prescribe them to humans on the assumption that humans can and should share in the divine orientation. Enabling and framing this sharing is a definite partnership, a covenant worked out historically between Israel and its god Yahweh.

Generally, the job of prophets is to inquire how a god will react to human actions; the target of wonderment is the freedom of the god, human motives and prospects being treated as relatively straightforward. The needy people appeal to the god via the prophet and hope the prophet can obtain a useful answer. For the classic Hebrew prophets, in contrast, the deep question is not about what Yahweh will do—for Yahweh's justice and mercy are utterly assured, his rewards and punishments predictable. The question is about human unholiness. The classic Hebrew prophet poses as a conduit, like any prophet, but functions more as a mirror, like a moralist. The prophet embodies Yahweh's concern for the people as an appeal *to* the people. Yahweh's anger or grief or creative resilience in response to the people's missteps is a more important theme than the neediness of the people. It characteristically comes out as an exclamation to *turn* from sinning and *turn back* to Yahweh, the return getting its direction from a historic covenant made between Yahweh and

Israel, a covenant like that made between a king and vassals. Because Yahweh holds so preponderant a power in his relationship with Israel, a prophet can exploit the most startling implication of the concept of attitude as distinct from character or motivation by offering the prospect of a sudden, momentous turnaround: "Be your sins like crimson, they can turn snow-white . . . If then, you agree and give heed" (Isaiah 1.18–19); "Cast away all the transgressions by which you have offended, and get yourselves a new heart and a new spirit, that you may not die, O House of Israel" (Ezekiel 18.31).

The most important attitude key words in prophetic discourse are *righteousness* and *mercy*. Conceptions of humility, reverence, and faithfulness also play a significant role.

1. *Righteousness* (sedaqa). The common meaning-element in *sdq*-words in the Hebrew Bible is right order. The idea of being in right order evokes questions about the basic nature, the particular facet, the cause, the site, the appearance, the internal dynamics, and the fruits of right order. There are ordinary moral expectations of right order, such as for sincerity and equity. Fallible humans could expect to be set in right order through regular procedures of worship at a sanctuary, for example, or simply by trusting God as Abraham did: "And because he put his trust in the Lord, He reckoned it to [him as] *sedaqa*" (Genesis 15.6).[115]

Amos (mid-eighth century BCE), the earliest writing prophet, issues an oft-quoted call for righteousness: "Let me not hear the music of your lutes. But let justice (*mishpat*) well up like water, righteousness (*sedaqa*) like an unfailing stream" (Amos 5.23–24). *Sedaqa* for Amos is not simply an umbrella term for right actions. Although he does condemn unjust actions taken by the Israelites, notably abuses of the poor, he seldom refers directly to rules of right action.[116] He speaks frequently of "the Lord," but not as of a giver of commands that must be obeyed; rather, he counterposes a general word of promise, "Seek the Lord and live," with references to Israelite communities that seek death, in effect, by choosing evil (5.4–15). He is interested in a general principle of intentional order, in right*ness*. The cause of evil, he thinks, is a comprehensive perversion of will, a turning away from divine justice and mercy. "You have turned justice into wormwood" (5.7). In turning away from God, Israel has adopted an evil *source* for its life; accordingly, God "loathes the Pride of Jacob" and turns away from the melody of Israel's worship (6.8). "Righteousness," however, would be the immanent source of goodness in life. Thus Amos's best hope is that righteousness will flow as beneficently and reliably as a permanent river, due ultimately to the spring-like beneficence of the divine moral orientation. Righteousness is a principle of human choices but not the product of this or that particular choice. Taking human freedom in relation to God as the central problem, the prophet's examination of the overall orientation of human freedom leads to affirmation of a divine function: the true principle of human righteousness is divine righteousness.

The prophetic discourse of righteousness is especially intense in the book of Isaiah, where *sedeq* or *sedaqa* appears at least 59 times.[117] The book develops Amos's hope of a flow of righteousness from God to humanity: "Till a spirit from on high is poured out on us . . . then justice shall abide in the wilderness and righteousness shall dwell on the farm land" (Isaiah 32.15–16). Isaiah of Jerusalem associates righteousness with an ideal sense grounded in or closely related to the attitude of reverence: "[The Messiah] shall sense the truth by his reverence for the LORD: he shall not judge by what his eyes behold, nor decide by what his ears perceive. Thus he shall judge the poor with *sedeq*" (11.3–4).

In a summation of Isaiah's view in chapter 26, two models of God's relationship to righteousness coexist ambiguously: (1) an extrinsic relationship whereby God desires, commands, and rewards righteousness in humans; and (2) an intrinsic relationship according to which righteousness is conceived as God's own good way of being, immediately and sufficiently beneficial to humans who share in it.

> The path is level for the righteous man;
> O Just One, You make smooth the course of the righteous.
> For Your just ways, O LORD, we look to You;
> We long for the name by which You are called.
> At night I yearn for You with all my being.
> I seek you with all the spirit within me.
> For when Your judgments are wrought on earth,
> The inhabitants of the world learn righteousness.
> But when the scoundrel is spared, he learns not righteousness;
> In a place of integrity, he does wrong—
> He ignores the majesty of the LORD. (Isaiah 26.7–10)

Similarly, we can understand the threatened blinding of the people both as retribution for disobedience and as an immediately necessary effect of its failure to share in the divine attitude:

> Because that people has approached [Me] with its mouth
> And honored Me with its lips,
> But has kept its heart far from Me,
> And its worship of Me has been
> A commandment of men, learned by rote—
> Truly, I shall further baffle that people
> With bafflement upon bafflement;
> And the wisdom of its wise shall fail,
> And the prudence of its prudent shall vanish. (29.13–14).

A counsel of attitude rather than action holds the most promise: "'You shall triumph by stillness and quiet; your victory shall come about through calm and confidence.' But you refused. 'No,' you declared. 'We shall flee on steeds' —therefore shall you flee! 'We shall ride on swift mounts'—therefore your pursuers shall prove swift!" (30.15–16).

For Second Isaiah, writing after the fall of the kingdom of Judah, the promised salvation of God seems to have the same nature:

> Listen to me, you who pursue justice [sedeq],
> You who seek the LORD . . .
> teaching shall go forth from Me,
> My way for the light of peoples.
> In a moment I will bring it:
> The triumph I grant is near . . .
> Listen to Me, you who care for the right [sedeq],
> O people who lay My instruction to heart!
> Fear not the insults of men . . .
> For the moth shall eat them up like a garment . . .
> But My triumph shall endure forever,
> My salvation through all the ages. (Isaiah 51.1–8)

2. *Mercy* (hesed). "For I desire *hesed*, not sacrifice" (Hosea 6.6). Whereas Amos had pleaded for righteousness instead of worship, his near successor Hosea pleads in a similar formula for *hesed*, variously translated as steadfast love, kindness, goodness, or mercy. Hosea heightens the role of love in the Yahwist imagination by taking up the model of adultery for Israel's disobedience of Yahweh, bringing an intense pathos to their reciprocal orientation. The prophet is able to look beyond Israel's failure to a glorious conclusion made possible by the perfect faithfulness of love (more fundamentally, by the adjustability of attitude): "I will heal their affliction, generously will I take them back in love; for my anger has turned away from them" (14.5). "I will espouse you forever," Yahweh promises: "I will espouse you with righteousness and justice, and with goodness and mercy (*hesed*), and I will espouse you in faithfulness" (2.21–22). Second Isaiah returns to this theme in the Babylonian exile: "In slight anger, for a moment, I hid My face from you; but with *hesed* everlasting I will take you back in love" (Isaiah 54.7–8). Can a spouse so perverse be taken back into a meaningful marriage? In Jeremiah's version of the prophecy, Yahweh will write a wholly new covenant in the "hearts" of the people so that "no longer will they need to teach one another and say to one another, 'heed the LORD' . . . for all of them shall heed Me" (Jeremiah 31.34). The attitude problem will be solved forever.

The Hebrew Bible gives much attention to Yahweh's *hesed* but relatively little to human *hesed*—as though *hesed* is too great for humans or is the prerogative of Yahweh in his king-like role of supreme power.[118] (*Ahaba*-love, predicated freely of Yahweh and humans alike, centers on the fact of personal attachment rather than on a principle.) Considering the holy asymmetry between the divine and the human, humans might more properly hope to act "for goodness' sake" rather than *in* that extraordinary goodness. Still centuries away is the Pharisaic idea, adopted also by Christianity, of the direct imitation of God in love, *being* loving *as* God is loving.[119] We read in Micah 6.8 that *hesed* ought to be *loved:* "[The LORD] has told you, O man, what is good, and what the LORD requires of you: Only to do justice and to love *hesed*, and to walk modestly with your God." This formula of loving love can be read as calling attention to the permanent issue of basic attitude—the difference between the current intention one *has* and the attitude one is *called* to take—and also (perhaps equivalently) as preserving a respectful distance between human and divine agency.

3. *Humility and reverence.* There is no one frequently repeated key word for humility or reverence in the Hebrew Bible, but these attitudes are often commended in one way or another. Human pride is a chronic problem. Isaiah of Jerusalem speaks especially often of bringing low the haughty, so that "none but the LORD shall be exalted" (Isaiah 2.11). He also attacks the false greatness of idols: "Men shall turn to their Maker [and] not turn to the altars that their own hands made" (17.7–8). Second Isaiah steps up the synthesis of the cognitive critique of idolatry with the call to right orientation:

> To whom, then, can you liken God, what form compare to Him?
> The idol? A woodworker shaped it, and a smith overlaid it with gold . . .
> Do you not know? Have you not heard? . . .
> Have you not discerned how the earth was founded? . . .
> [The] Creator of the earth from end to end . . . never grows faint or
> weary . . .
> They who trust in the LORD shall renew their strength.[120]

Meanwhile, Second Isaiah's songs of the Servant exemplify humility most powerfully.[121] This bruised Servant is the extreme antitype to the popular ancient ideal of the unruffled sage.

The fear-words *yare* and *yira* occur very frequently, but usually as verbs, and often in commands to "fear not." They mean "reverence" in propositions like "You shall each *yare* his mother and father" and "*Yira* for the LORD—that was [Zion's] treasure."[122] While Proverbs makes a mantra of "*yira* of the LORD," neither here nor elsewhere in the Hebrew Bible can we find a free-standing noun "reverence" or the adjective "reverent" comparable to the Greek *eusebeia* and *eusebes*.[123] The absence is significant, because words like "fidelity," "wickedness," "upright," and "loyal" do very frequently appear. Furthermore, the book of Job features a paragon of reverence as memorable in his own way as the knight of faith, Abraham. We can say at least that the linguistic restriction, whatever its causes, fits with a general Israelite mistrust of being dispositionally available to revere anything other than Yahweh. Fear of the Lord explicitly overrides ordinary regard for fellow human beings: an Israelite is commanded to kill (almost) *anyone* who proposes worship of false gods, even a sibling, spouse, or child.[124]

In the Hellenizing Greek Septuagint, it is another story. To "The fear of the LORD is the beginning of wisdom" (Proverbs 1.7), for example, the Septuagint adds "and *eusebeia* toward God is the beginning of discernment."[125]

The New Testament is generally more cautious, referring by *eusebeia* to a general pagan reverence that is at worst an impotent alternative to faith, at best a desirable predisposition for hearing the gospel, but never, except in the more Hellenized Pastoral Epistles, the main tenor of the Christian life itself.[126] *Eusebeia*'s essential affinity is with an encompassing order of things, not with one personal God.[127]

4. *Faith.* Faithfulness-in-relationship (*aman, emuna*) is an important orientational ideal in the Hebrew Bible, but it has importantly different meanings depending on whether the divine party to relationship and the relationship's objective are considered to be present or absent. Thus, Israel as the recipient of a yet-unfulfilled promise "has faith" that God *will* do something, as for example Abraham (a type for the imperiled people later) has faith that God will enable him to have many descendants. Israel as the recipient of an address or command, on the other hand, is expected to be "faithful" in actual situations and subject to known requirements, much as spouses should be attentive and loyal to one another. Either way, Israel should hold its Godward aim. Yahweh's own *emuna*, his "truth," is his comprehensive steadiness. It guarantees that Israel's faithfulness will be meaningful. Characteristically, Yahweh's *emuna* is cited, not as a sort of philosophical principle, but as a dimension of a personal act: "[The LORD] was mindful of His *hesed* and *emuna* toward the house of Israel; all the ends of the earth beheld the victory of our God" (Psalm 98.3).

Later, the theme of faith (*pistis*) dominates Christianity in quite a new way. Faith is seen in the New Testament as the requisite less of an already-functioning partnership (as between Yahweh and Israel) and more of a bold new initiative by which humans can participate in the inbreaking rule of heaven (according to Jesus) or in the mystical body of Christ (according to Paul). Faith for Jesus is a variable power, and life goes well as a function of one's faith; he admonishes those of "little faith" and admires those of "great faith."[128] ("Great faith" works much like the "extraordinary spirit" ascribed to Daniel in the second-century BCE book of Daniel; thanks to this spirit, Daniel was elevated to power by the Persian emperor and kept safe when unjustly thrown into a lions' den.)[129] The Gospel of John's Jesus promises eternal life just in aiming oneself trustfully and obediently toward the "Son," who already stands in this relation to the divine "Father."[130] For Paul, faith is the crux of a momentous decision to enter into a saving relationship with God. Paul evokes the figure of Abraham, in whom the venture of Israel began, as the prototype of the new venture of the Christian church, a community formed by God's right ordering of human lives through the death and resurrection of Jesus:

> We say, "Faith was reckoned to Abraham as righteousness" [Genesis 15:6] ...
> He received the sign of circumcision as a seal of the righteousness that he
> had by faith while he was still uncircumcised. The purpose was to make
> him the ancestor of all who believe without being circumcised and who

thus have righteousness reckoned to them, and likewise the ancestor of the circumcised who are not only circumcised but who also follow the example of the faith that our ancestor Abraham had before he was circumcised. (Romans 4.9–12)

Faith in the sense of "believing that" salvation is available on certain terms is different from faith in the sense of "trusting in" a God with whom one lives. Although the two aspects of faith are not ultimately separable, the dominance of the first makes for a markedly different spiritual climate than the dominance of the second. It fits with an attitude of estrangement from the world.[131] It is liable to become a self-absorbing fetish, as the Letter of James warns: "Do you want to be shown, you senseless person, that faith apart from works is barren? Was not our ancestor Abraham justified by works when he offered his son Isaac on the altar?" (James 2.20–21). Faith can separate the believer from the world either in the relatively benign manner of a quietist attitude of detachment or in the malignant form of world-hating—the latter possibility conspicuously risked by the Johannine literature as it plays up the theme of the world's enmity toward God.[132]

* * *

The Hebraic heart. Its reliance on the model of intense personal relationship with a god makes the Hebraic way of describing or prescribing attitudes especially volatile. The question of how human "return" to rectify this relationship will come about is of dominant interest, like the question of how true lovers will get together in a romantic plot. God's lover-appeal is the biblical plot's motive force. Only in the Platonic-Aristotelian philosophy of an appealing divine Beauty and in the love and lovableness of Krishna and bodhisattvas in the bhakti strain of Indian religion are there close parallels to the Hebrew view in other classical literatures.

One way to express this distinctive Hebraic understanding of attitude is to say that the Hebraic "heart" is often presented as *in motion*, not stable as in a firm ruler or tranquil sage. In the Hebrew Bible as elsewhere in Axial Age literature, "heart" is a ubiquitous invocation of an agent's intentional center, moral force, and susceptibility to appeal. To ground the description of an agent in the agent's heart is to claim full confidence in the description; thus, one cannot fully "believe in" someone's love or justice without conceiving of a heart in which love or justice is rooted. (Nor, for that matter, can one fully believe in anyone or anything except "with all one's heart.") Heart talk is centering; heart *drama*, therefore, is wrenching. The passionate, oft-disappointed quest for love and justice in the history of Israel makes a roller-coaster ride for the Hebraic heart. Even Yahweh's promise to uphold the Davidic dynasty turns on the fact that David was dear to Yahweh's heart (1 Samuel 13.14). This is to say, in effect, that David was an event, a turning point, for Yahweh. The heart always *is* the responsibility of its possessor, that is, the agent's power of response. That Yahweh can harden Pharaoh's heart against the Israelites' plea for freedom, or give Saul another heart to become a prophet (1 Samuel 10.9), or give all Israel a new heart under the new covenant envisioned by Jeremiah underlines the way in which personal responsibility always crystallizes afresh at a certain juncture in a history. Even a generalizable prescription like "True sacrifice to God is a contrite spirit; God, You will not despise a contrite and crushed heart" (Psalm 51.19) is naturally more occasion-specific, more responsive to the latest turn in a relationship story, than is the case with a prescription to attain tranquility.

Israel's experience in governing its heart, as biblically attested, is not encouraging. According to Martin Buber, the "unformulated insight" derived from this experience by rabbinical Judaism is that the human heart lacks a stable orientation of its own, and its confusion is continually worsened by worldly experience; it requires divine direction as granted in the Torah.[133] A rather Chinese-sounding Talmudic saying is, "One does much, the other little, if one only directs the heart to heaven!"[134] On this view God is more like a lodestar, less like a passionate partner. The New Testament moves in the same direction insofar as it almost never ascribes a heart to God.[135]

In general, one goes into an agent's "heart" to see or to show actual and possible changes in the personal center, but the New Testament writers are sure not only that God's intentions are immutable (as Hebrew prophets would have agreed) but that the divine-human relationship is a settled thing. Divine desire, grief, or anger of a personal sort (as opposed to the impersonal "wrath of God" of which Paul speaks) have disappeared. Nevertheless, this more thoroughly eternalized God is still intimately related to human hearts. God is described twice as *kardiognostes*, "heart knowing," and is said by Paul to "test" and "direct" hearts.[136] Jesus claims that God gave the inadequate divorce law of Deuteronomy in consideration of the hardness of the people's hearts.[137] The intense pathos realized in the prophets' expressions of God's angry or grieving heart reappears in Jesus' emotional disturbances, Paul's groaning with creation, and the horror-scenes of John's Apocalypse.[138] Compensating for the loss of drama in the divine heart is a new excitement in the human heart; expressions in Luke, "How *slow* of heart [you are] to believe all that the prophets have declared!" and "Were not our hearts *burning* within us ... while he was opening the scriptures to us?" (Luke 24.25, 32, emphasis added), reflect a time-sensitive urgency in the prospect of participating in the heavenly kingdom. This usage hints at the important contrast between the Christian ideal of conversion as a great turning point that ought to be the axis of every individual's life, and the Jewish ideal of a continuously appropriate return (*teshuva*) to God mediated by the already-given spirit of the covenant. But it is affirmed in both perspectives that God gives the good heart.

* * *

In summary, the preeminent theses of Hebraic attitude thinking are:

(1) The condition of right orientation is *turning* to God, which can happen at any time, even against heavy odds. (The *Bhagavad Gita* endorses the *possibility*, though not the Platonic or Hebraic *necessity*, of a divinely empowered turn.)[139]

(2) Humans are properly exhorted to attend and adhere to a rectifying attitude rather than to embody it—to judge with righteousness rather than to be righteous, for example, or to love mercy rather than to be merciful. This way of speaking preserves a distance between actual and ideal psychology and between the human and the divine.

(3) The notion of a free-standing sovereign attitude—that is, the possibility of regarding anything like "piety" or "faith" or "love" as an absolutely good thing in itself—is avoided, perhaps even actively distrusted. Perfectly rectifying orientation must be actively relational and God-directed. In comparison with the mandated orientation to God, filial and civic piety are planted in relatively shallow soil.

Classic Attitude Issues

We can trace a general development of attitude thinking in the first millennium BCE from (1) an essentializing of the agency of masterful and servile figures to (2) universal prescriptions of attitude, followed by (3) taxonomies of dispositional components of better and worse lives (the virtues and vices). At the hinge of this development, the high Axial Age literature is keenly interested in what is meaningfully and helpfully prescribable with regard to the centering of feeling, thought, and action in individual agents in the best possible relation with a greater center. Among the themes of Axial Age attitude thinking that deserve to be cited as essentially enabling or troubling of our normative thinking today are these:

1. *The sovereign attitude and the problem of the preemption of rectification.* The Axial Age texts move toward formulating an attitude that can plausibly be identified very closely with complete rectification of a life, whether as the substance of that rectification or as a uniquely powerful cause of it. Often the sovereign attitude is presented not as one distinct attitude but as a composite, like Hosea's bundle of righteousness, mercy, and faithfulness or the faith-tranquility pairing in the Upanishads. Not rarely, however, a single attitude conception exerts a hegemonic fascination such that every other consideration is pulled into alignment with it, as tranquility does in the Upanishads (along with classical Buddhism and Hellenistic philosophy), benevolence does in classical Confucianism, and love begins to do in the *Bhagavad Gita*.

The appeal of attitudes as manners and sites of rectifying life and the appeal of the idea that there are recognizable and attainable attitudes in which one's life is rectified merge with the appeal of the view that there is a single such attitude that one can be wholly intent on recognizing and attaining. As for which attitudes are best able to carry such a normative load, we have seen three ways of deepening and broadening the right poise: one that plunges into the heart to enlist all possible energies there, as in the appeal for devotion-love; one that clears out all troublemaking tendencies in the heart, as in the appeal for tranquility; and one that features and fine-tunes the balance between the subject and other beings, as in the appeal for piety or benevolence.

Ultimately, we will have to face the implications of the diverse and divergent Axial Age sovereign attitude proposals as posing a live issue for our own normative thinking. If, as seems likely, it will be desirable to find a way to reconcile the different orientations, not letting any one entirely eclipse the others—supposing that each corresponds to a durably relevant aspect of meaningful life—then some qualification of sovereignty claims will be required. But even before we take up that issue, a problem that stares out at us in this first reconnaissance is that the idea of a sovereign attitude is dangerously close to being self-contradictory: the sovereignty of an all-rectifying attitude must have its seat in the larger situation and not within the subject whose life needs to be rectified; but the appeal of being able to enjoy the benefits of the exercise of that sovereignty is hard to separate from the appeal of acquiring that power for oneself.

The problem is deeply inscribed in the discourse of virtue. An "excellence" (Greek *arete*) or "essential power" (Latin *virtus*, Chinese *de*) of an individual agent belongs to that agent in quite a strong sense. The agent may have gained a virtue only through cultivation and may be able to lose it, as a knife may lose its sharpness, but still the virtue is a characteristic of the agent so long as it obtains. But virtue is also defined as a generally approvable disposition, and in that sense it must be a function of the agent's justification in relation to other beings. One could think of the virtuous disposition quasi-physically as a shaped responsiveness to stimuli, like a metal needle's responsiveness to a magnetic field. On this model, a virtuous person always points to the good as a compass needle points north. The project of virtue is to fashion such persons. On the most optimistic ancient view, an attainable virtue or set of virtues is sufficient to rectify one's life. But this view is in tension with the insight that rectification depends on attitude; for even granting that a person can become so constituted as to choose and act reliably in generally approvable ways, the possession of that constitution is not the same as the possession of a right attitude, since attitude is a variable in an open system of relations (which is why it can always change in a twinkling). To say that a being has a characteristic is to say something about what that being foreseeably brings to actual occasions, not to determine comprehensively how it stands in actual occasions. No being can have the characteristic of being rightly oriented in relation to all other beings. A compass can have the characteristic of always lining up in a certain way in a magnetic field, but it cannot have the characteristic of always pointing in the right direction—unless it is conceived as miraculously divinatory. A key can have the characteristic of always fitting a lock, but it cannot have the characteristic of always opening the right door—unless it is a "lucky key." Similarly, only a "lucky virtue" could be guaranteed to produce fully approvable results or to rectify an agent's life.

Augustine challenged the implicit "lucky virtue" conception of popular virtue ethics—the basic idea shared by the Hellenistic schools that rational self-cultivation produces *eudaimonia*, "happiness," a state of full flourishing—by asserting that pagan virtues are really vices: aiming to acquire a sufficient power to rectify their lives, or claiming to possess such power, agents remain sunk in the spiritual coma of selfishness.[140] An Augustinian formula for the true situation is that "will is to grace as the horse is to the rider": regardless of how an agent is accustomed to choose and act, how the agent is in the world is an open question that the agent can address at any moment proudly or humbly, passionately or detachedly, but never conclusively.[141] "Free will" is Augustine's anthropological conception of the inherent openness of the question on the human individual's side; "grace" is his theistic conception of how the question is ultimately capable of being resolved, necessarily outside the human agent's power. The concept of sovereign attitude threatens to annul both free will and grace.

2. *The problem of attitude's relation to cognition, action, and feeling.* Although Axial Age teachers do not see the relation of basic orientation to cognition, action, and feeling in one standard way, they explore and strengthen the linkages among these variables—to show true knowledge and true peace as identical, for example, or to make idolatry or insensitivity to divine "signs" a function of faithlessness and vice versa, or to weld faith to works or the Four Noble Truths to the Eightfold Path, or to show that the higher pleasures are necessarily virtuous or that the virtues must be pleasant. Since the basic challenge accepted by attitude thinking is to think through the centering of life, all of these dimensions must be integrated in an adequate representation of rectified life. The cognitive and volitional linkages tend to give each subject more control over his or her attitude, and expanding individual control is generally an Axial Age priority. The linkages with will and feeling, on the other hand, involve intimate discovery of the actuality of rectified life, whether in horrified estrangement from righteousness and love or in reassuring virtuous pleasure.

There is an obvious difficulty here with finding an adequate justification for one normative psychology against others, since such accounts are profoundly stipulative and the grounding of one can never preclude the grounding of others in principle but will prevail only practically, tactically, and rhetorically, according to the concrete exigencies of a communicative situation. But another, often subtler problem in the background of attitude discourse is that the full exploitation of possible linkages between these dimensions of subjective existence threatens to make all such reference points indeterminate. An attitude becomes the psychological night in which all cows are black, and a spiritually disastrous practical anesthetic, if it leaves no relatively independent roles for cognition, will, and feeling to play in the subject's life. The attitude ideal of tranquility effectively preempts our receiving any cognitive notification of appellants, for example, if it stipulates that nothing upsetting can ever be learned or stated. The ideal of piety preempts all freedom of initiative if it makes one's will radically compliant. The ideal of love preempts feeling access to appellants if it homogenizes the texture of all contact with beings (what then does it mean to love an enemy?). Strong claims for an attitude ideal will risk one or more of these semantic and practical collapses caused by the attitude solution overwhelming the elements of life it is called upon to rule.

3. *The problem of temporal bias.* A main thread in Axial Age philosophy and religious teaching is the critique of customary observance, especially of sacrificing. Traditionalism is under attitudinal attack in every movement we have touched on, even in Confucianism, which demands that tradition be resuscitated, reconstructed, and validated by the reasoning of diligent "learners." There is a shift of religious interest in the Axial Age and its aftermath away from a past-oriented pious deference to ancestral ways and toward a hopeful, future-oriented faith in a messianic worldly salvation or a release into an otherworldly or nonworldly salvation. The felt irrelevance of pious deference in light of a manifest inadequacy of customary good order opens attitudinal space for hopeful faith, as is especially evident in post-exilic Judaism, Christianity, the Hellenistic mystery cults, and Mahayana Buddhism. In India, however, where a future-oriented hope of obtaining earthly and heavenly goods was already a prominent Vedic theme and strongly endorsed as a rationale of priestly practice, some Axial Age critics saw the future as no less distracting and useless than the past. Thus, the Upanishads transposed the Brahmanical faith in the possibility of a heavenly reward for merit into a faith in the possibility of release from all worldliness. This release could most helpfully be conceived as a *present* possibility, ideally a present actuality. To know Brahman is to be radically tranquil; to be radically tranquil is to know Brahman; knowledge of Brahman can be actualized at any moment, under the tutelage of Upanishadic revelation. In this respect, Upanishadic thought is the earliest on a trail taken by all the classic Axial Age movements. The right attitude *is* happiness. A good man cannot really be harmed, say Socrates and Kongzi.[142] Heaven's way is at hand, say the Confucians and Daoists from their different angles (and Jesus later) Submit to the divine order, says Stoicism (and later Islam). Awaken, says Buddhism.

The bias toward the present will come in for profound questioning later, as we shall see in our review of attitude-sensitive modern Western thought. A structurally basic problem worth noting here in brief is that the determinacy of a basic attitude prescription depends on an ontological determinacy in that to which subjects are to be oriented, and the minimally requisite ontological focus in the target of a great attitude always implicitly picks out one time-phase over others—the zone of the already-constituted (past), of the to-be-constituted (future), or of constituting as such (present). In taking an attitude, one turns toward one aspect of reality, preferring it to others. Being grateful, for example, involves turning appreciatively to something in the realm of what has been done. One cannot be grateful with regard to future possibilities any more than one can be hopeful about past accomplishments. But a fully inclusive supreme appeal or a fully competent sovereign attitude could not fail to have regard for all dimensions of reality. Can an omni-attachment be conceived that simultaneously plunges into past, present, and future? Can a perfect detachment achieve comprehensiveness except at the price of disregarding everything, in which case the whole problematic of rectification is elided?

* * *

The Axial Age legacy of attitude thinking consists partly of a web of classic disagreements. The most obvious of these we have seen in the specifying of rival sovereign attitudes and in basic underlying divergences between strategies of attachment and detachment. But there are metaphysical disagreements to consider here as well: a basic orientation must be deployed in some system of space, time, substance, and causality, all variables that may be apprehended in various ways. Thus, Axial Age teachings take different positions with regard to the *plurality of beings*, ranging from ideals of benevolence, piety, and righteousness that presuppose and affirm an apportionment of living opportunities among beings to ideals of faith, tranquility, and ardent love that imply a transcendence of inter-being division and thus of the *world* in the ordinary sense. There are also differences regarding the *dynamism* of human agency along a spectrum ranging from the maximum of self-exertion in Confucian self-cultivation, to the tenacity of filial piety or messianic faith, to "non-action" and contemplative quietism; and these are related to the different appreciations of *time* that inform an optimistic self-application to the Way, or a fervent eschatological hope, or a serene eternalism or nonchalance.

Living commonsensically, one supposes that one's attitudes will continually adjust according to "how life is treating you," either helpfully or hinderingly, through ever-changing circumstances; but Axial Age teachers begin to assert that those who adopt a certain basic attitude live in a different reality than those who do not. To what extent and with what importance do metaphysical commitments really depend on attitude-taking? That remains to be argued out in two great waves—first, in deriving civilization from institutionally sustained religious commitments, as in the medieval "Christendom" and "house of Islam" projects; and second, in reassessing and reconstructing civilization after religious traditions lose their preeminent authority, as in the modern European Enlightenment. Since we ourselves are enmeshed in the Enlightenment problematic—less, I think, for the negative reason that traditional religion is weakened than for the positive reason that the Enlightenment renews the radical directive scene-setting that makes our Axial Age classics classic—we can move the present inquiry more directly forward by picking up the thread of attitude thinking in Kant and his successors than by examining the religious attitude deepenings of a Bonaventure, an Ibn al-'Arabi, a Kabir, a Wang Yangming, or other great contributors to premodern segments of our spiritual history.

Attitude Issues in
Modern Philosophy

Modern European philosophy renews the Axial Age probe into basic attitudes as determinative of meaningfulness, extending the initiatives of Hebrew and Greek thought. I find the basic attitude issues to be engaged most directly and with the most interesting conceptual specifications along a certain predominantly German line, thanks in large part to a starting point furnished by Leibniz. The story in brief is that Leibniz's optimistic monadology inspires rival orientational priorities of intentional activity (Kant, Fichte) and receptivity (Schleiermacher); the challenge of validating, amplifying, and coordinating the claims of these attitude programs is taken up with increasing articulateness by Kierkegaard, Nietzsche, and Dilthey. Jaspers and Heidegger renew, at an advanced level, the rivalry between Kant's and Schleiermacher's programs, while Buber strikes a noteworthy balance between them. Most recently, powerful implications of the discussion continue to be developed as Levinas and Derrida explore a limit ideal of responsible openness.[1] Staging this discussion is an advantageous way to bring into view issues of attitude thinking that are worth taking most seriously.

A current in modern philosophy that mainly gets left out of my account is the primarily British and British-inspired discourse on "sentiments" and "affections," an approach that often does address basic attitude issues but in doing so characteristically tends to construe attitudes simply as positive psychological facts rather than as live issues of interintentional self-determination. This orientation leaves the heart of the directive question untouched. What it means directively to adopt the empiricist bias and how philosophy of this sort affects the larger discussion are matters worth careful study, but for the most part I will not get into them.

The Primacy of Freedom: The Road to
"Ethical Idealism" from Leibniz to Fichte

A clear early sign that attitude issues would become a central concern of modern philosophy was the reputation Leibniz gained for "optimism," a stance he deliberately set against Spinoza's resignation to purposeless natural determinism.[2] Spinoza and Leibniz both wrote for a public suspicious of traditional formulations of faith in the wake of the terrible schisms and wars of religion in early modern Europe and the inspiring rise of a new scientific ethos. Both faced the challenge of regaining human poise in the larger, stranger world disclosed by telescopes and microscopes. Whereas Descartes had sought to balance himself in this new situation with a cautious mixture of skepticism, traditional Christian theism, and Platonic mind-matter dualism, Spinoza and Leibniz boldly pinned sanity and virtue to a new analysis of the fundamental causation of the world. The world for Spinoza is a realization of all that can be simply because it cannot be prevented from being. For Leibniz, it is a realization of the best that can be according to the action of a first cause for "sufficient reason," that is, with perfect motivation: "And this is the cause of the existence of the best: that his [necessarily unlimited] wisdom makes it known to God, his [necessarily unlimited] goodness makes him choose it, and his [necessarily unlimited] power makes him produce it."[3] The Leibnizian optimism consists of aligning with this divine orientation, counting on the adaptation of things and events to the best world-harmony even when one's own power to advance or enjoy this harmony is painfully limited:

> The love of God also fulfills our hopes, and leads us down the road of supreme happiness, because by virtue of the perfect order established in the universe, everything is done in the best possible way, both for the general good and for the greatest individual good of those who are convinced of this, and who are content with divine government, which cannot fail to be found in those who know how to love the source of all good . . . since God is infinite, he can never be entirely known. Thus our happiness will never consist, and must never consist, in complete joy, in which nothing is left to desire, and which would dull our mind, but must consist in a perpetual progress to new pleasures and new perfections.[4]

This is a dynamic, future-oriented new edition of the Platonic "euphemism" that gathers and refines the best things that can be said about the best being or cause.

Leibniz and Spinoza both deduce all causes and effects from the principle that the first condition of all beings is an illimitable being. They are both determinists, although Leibniz argues that only a wise and benevolent choice causes the actual world to exist rather than any of innumerable other possible worlds, whereas for Spinoza these notions of choice and possibility are illusions nourished by ignorance and passion.[5] Their dissimilar moods of optimism and resignation could be chalked up to personal temperament, or, more objectively, to the rhetorical exigencies of appeal—the one appeal keyed to a maximum of enthusiasm, the other to a maximum of respect for how things are, apart from our interests. But there is also an important difference of metaphysical structure in the two positions.

Answering a correspondent who has dared to suggest that his preestablished cosmic harmony comes to the same thing as Spinozan determinism, Leibniz invokes his *pluralism* of substances: "It is precisely by the monads that Spinozism is destroyed. For there are as many veritable substances, and so to speak living mirrors of the universe always subsisting, or concentrations of the Universe, as there are monads; whereas in Spinoza there is but one sole substance. He would be right, if it weren't for the monads."[6] Several lines of thought lead Leibniz to his monad-substances. Logically, there must be subjects of predication, since everything that can truly be said must be said of something, in "S is P" form—that is, there must be *homes* or *owners* of objective sense.[7] Physically, there must be qualitatively distinct origins of motion, since otherwise distinct motions would not obtain; motion, we can say, is always an *expression* of something, that is, it proceeds from a distinctly identifiable nature.[8] Metaphysically, there must be "simple," indivisible, imperishable substances, since otherwise we would be faced with the absurdity of existing things being founded in one way or another upon nothing; what is essentially indivisible cannot be matter, of course, but it can be the centeredness of a diversity as such, which Leibniz calls *perception* (§§2–3, 12–14). As we live in time, we know that this perception is a coherent life, unfolding according to what Leibniz calls its internal principle of *appetition* (§15).

Now, taking these points, why not draw Spinoza's conclusion that there is just one ultimate logical home, one expression, and one perception-appetition of which all other phenomena and experiences are modifications, since to assert otherwise is to limit what is intrinsically illimitable? Leibniz believes that a fundamentally homogeneous one-substance world would fail to be a world at all. It would be God without creation—a comatose sort of God. Instead, the illimitable power of primal being is properly expressed in the generation of an infinitely great ensemble of actualized perspectives on the diverse possibilities of being, constrained only by compossibility and the rule of choosing the best. Each monad is conceived, accordingly, as a perception of the universe (the totality of compatible possibilities of being) from a unique point of view (§57). Monads coexist diversely without disrupting the real wholeness of the universe because each monad centers the whole in its own complementary way, just as the original constitution of each monad proceeds from the cosmic centering of primal being. Since only monads are ultimately real, the ultimate object of a monad's perception is just monads, which is to say that *what* each monad centers is ultimately a combination of the monad's own powers of impression and expression with the powers of all other monads rounding out the best possible world.

Perhaps the strongest warrant for Leibniz's metaphysical view will be found by using the interior access each of us has to the being that each of us is (§16). Contrary to materialisms old and new, it is evident that the mental life at the core of our sense of our own reality is not the sort of thing that can be directly handled in the realm of extension.

> One is obliged to admit that *perception* and what depends upon it is *inexplicable on mechanical principles,* that is, by figures and motions. In imagining that there is a machine whose construction would enable it to think, to sense, and to have perception, one could conceive it enlarged while retaining the same proportions, so that one could enter into it, just like into a windmill. Supposing this, one should, when visiting within it, find only parts pushing one another, and never anything by which to explain a perception. Thus it is in the simple substance, and not in the composite or in the machine, that one must look for perception. Moreover, there is nothing besides this—besides perceptions and their changes—that one could possibly find in a simple substance. (§17)

The self that receives impressions of a larger world and expresses itself by acting in the world, insofar as it is conceived as a center point—the experiential subject or the responsible agent—must really *consist of* centering. Primal being can center all centerings without absorbing all finite beings into itself on the Spinozan plan. The best example of how this can work is in reasoning. To center rationally is to center one's individual field of living by means of conscious cognizance of necessary truths, the same truths God realizes—especially the truth that we necessarily are members of the best of all possible worlds (§29).

> Souls in general are living mirrors or images of the universe of created beings. But the spirits are also images of divinity itself—of the very Author of nature. They are capable of knowing the system of the universe, and of imitating it to some extent through constructive samples, each spirit being like a minute divinity within its own sphere. (§83)

> All must result for the benefit of the good, that is, of those who are nowise malcontents in this great state, who trust in providence after having done their duty, and who love and imitate, as is proper, the author of all good, taking pleasure in the consideration of his perfections according to the nature of a genuine *pure love.* (§90)

Thus, the basic normative principle governing the thought and conduct of finite subjects, "reason," represents our sharing in a divine orientation toward good-maximizing. Although Leibniz does not employ a term like "attitude," "disposition," or "orientation," he finds the identity of substance itself in a manner of centering, that is, "soul," and the perfection of substance in love. So it is fitting that the first new attitude label of modern philosophy, "optimism," should be applied to him.

***

The contrast that emerged in modern philosophy between the Continental rationalism of Spinoza and Leibniz, on the one hand, and British empiricism, on the other, especially from Hume forward, repeats an opposition between ancient Stoicism and Epicureanism.[9] The rationalist side is committed to a necessary world Centering from which individual centerings properly derive their principle. The empiricist side wants to acknowledge contingency at two levels: meaningfulness is seen to occur as psychologically contingent centerings of meaning and value supervene on physically contingent centerings of actual beings. Important attitude positions are taken on the empiricist side, notably in Hume's ethics of sympathy and benevolence and in utilitarian hedonism. But the most profound exploration of the attitude principle is destined to unfold from the Leibnizian starting point. We can now see why this would be. Leibniz resolved the awkward Cartesian problem of mind-matter relation with a distinctive conception of substance as perception-appetition. The *what* of reality is identified with *how* possibilities of being are seen, addressed, and inhabited; this *how* is treated essentially as an *issue*, given that monads are infinitely many and diverse; and the issues raised by different manners of existence-in-relation are found to be amenable to discussion, given that the self-conscious monads share a universe of rational discourse. Thus, Leibniz's monadology is that version of the modern subject-centered mode of philosophizing the very axis of which is the relationship of the centering of the finite being with other centerings rather than the problem of finding adequate grounds for knowledge or an adequate elucidation of cause and effect.

Spinoza's *Ethics* is a formidable effort of attitude engineering as well. As Spinoza lacks the Leibnizian concept of perception, however, the Spinozan subject lacks the qualified ontological and axiological independence of the Leibnizian subject and so does not pose as deeply interesting an attitude issue. The ideal Spinozan subject adapts intelligently to the particularities of its life situation, but one couldn't say it is thrilled with its distinct perspective on the universe or its distinct position in an adventure of optimizing; instead, its overriding aim is to minimize suffering by attaining constant awareness of the necessity in all occurrence. Leibniz too appeals to universal necessity to reconcile all rational beings to the actual world. Leibniz's determinism can be *taken* as equivalent in attitudinal implication to Spinoza's. But Leibniz appeals to the *self*-determination of monads—based on God's *choice* of the best among alternative worlds, which involves each finite monad's programming with the best compossible *appetition of its own* by which it will comport itself in one way rather than another among worldly alternatives—according to an intelligent principle of final causation cooperating in preestablished harmony with the mechanical principle of efficient causation.[10] Having rejected belief in freedom and final causation as an asylum of ignorance, Spinoza cannot have an orientation to the "best" in the sense that is crucial for Leibniz; he can aspire only to the supreme "good" of certainty about divine determination as such.[11]

In the estimation of most later philosophical critics, Leibniz and Spinoza share a grave limitation in their dogmatic metaphysical rationalism: their appeal to universal necessity, whether efficient or final, cannot be made convincing. Their views become more plausible and applicable if their determinism is dropped or reformulated as open rather than closed. Spinoza then is a naturalist, perhaps of all major philosophers the most powerful patron of neuroscience. Leibniz's model of a harmonized maximum of diversity of lives, taken as heuristic rather than necessitarian, offers valuable stimulation and guidance in ethics, aesthetics, and theology. Spinoza and Leibniz themselves would claim that their attitude agendas cannot be fulfilled without their necessitarian metaphysics. For them it is the cognitive achievement of discerning that the world must possess a certain character that relieves the subject of avoidable suffering and ineptitude and so gives the subject the most tenable orientation. Nevertheless, we can conclude that what Spinoza and Leibniz hope to establish as knowledge is more authentically understood and sustained as a cognitive orientation. For the true backbone of dogmatic rationalism is not ontological necessity as such, which after all is indemonstrable, but the optimism in it that pushes toward a congenial ontological framework. Leibniz is friendliest to this shift by virtue of his emphasis on the free "autarchy" of each monad.[12] The Leibnizian philosopher embraces the metaphysics of the best possible world just because it is the most choice-worthy view, that is, because it stands in the happiest relation to the philosopher's intellectual freedom. Seen from Leibniz's perspective, Spinozan philosophy lives from optimism, too, but of a sadly constricted sort.

* * *

It is customary to portray Kant as a skeptically chastened Leibnizian who, abandoning dogmatic metaphysics, found alternate grounds in practical reason for affirming God, freedom, and immortality. To appreciate the full strength of the Leibniz-Kant connection, however, it is important to recognize, on the one side, how Leibniz is already working on a basis in practical reason (that is the upshot of our review of the Leibnizian optimism) and on the other, how Kant depends on the Leibnizian monadology for his critique of metaphysics even before he develops his account of pure practical reason.

Kant takes up the Cartesian quest for the foundations of knowledge in a new and more powerful way with the tacit aid of the Leibnizian concept of perception. Kant seeks the conditions of rational knowledge in *rules of synthesis* because he already understands experience as essentially a *complicatio*, a diversity in unity, rather than the interior picture show contemplated by Locke and Hume. Consequently, the central questions for Kant's theoretical philosophy are (1) which rules of synthesis are necessary if there is to be any coherent experience at all, (2) which rules of synthesis are necessary for a rationally optimized experience, and (3) what relations hold between rules of synthesis, beings, and appearances. Rules of the first sort are deemed constitutive of phenomena (so that anything we perceive must be related to other things as "cause" and "effect," for example) and therefore objectively necessary; the second sort (for example, the principles of totality and unconditional ground) are unavoidably regulative of our thinking, though not constitutive of the objects we think about, and so are only subjectively necessary. The constitutive rules are interpreted as forms of knowledge *of* beings *as* phenomena (not as the beings are in themselves apart from our construal); the regulative rules are interpreted as forms by which we organize and find our way around in our experience and vis-à-vis supersensuous referents like beings-in-themselves. Although Kant treats the rules of synthesis primarily as logical forms, it is evident from the fact that experience is *actual* that the synthesis in question is a real *activity* and *action* of mind, a processing of sensory input combined with an expressive gesturing.

In his theoretical philosophy, Kant certainly does not take over Leibniz's view that each mind is an autarchic monad, its sequence of experience generated solely by an implanted principle of appetition, its relationships with other beings brought about solely by divine prearrangement. For Kant, the receptivity of the mind to other beings via the faculty of intuition is as fundamental as the spontaneity of the mind's powers of intellectual formation. However, the most basic initial figuring of intuitions is accomplished by the still more primordial "spontaneity" of what Kant calls the transcendental synthesis of imagination.[13] This is a point of deep resonance with Leibniz. Given the priority of the mind's spontaneity in world-experience, the great theme of Kant's theoretical philosophy must accordingly be *how* the rational finite mind comports itself in a larger world, partly graspable and partly not, under different kinds of constraint—or, to use the title of his 1786 paper, "What is Orientation in Thinking?"

A comparison with Hume on the issue of a priori rules of experience is instructive. Hume does not allow an a priori synthesis of experience at all, beyond purely logical relations among ideas.[14] Experience is as it is as a fact. But there are some very general consistencies in the fact. Thus we confidently expect like effects to follow like causes because actual experience of constant conjunction has habituated us to do so. What Kantians call a priori rules of synthesis, Humeans call regularities of nature. Kantians say that a priori rules of synthesis are transcendental not empirical, that is, conditions of the very possibility of "nature" rather than observed facts in nature, while Humeans say that Kantian a priori rules are, at best, regularities of nature announced in a loud idealist voice.

Considered strictly for their objective descriptive value, the Kantian rules and the Humean regularities could be equivalent: everything that can be observed and affirmed on Kantian premises can also be observed and affirmed on Humean premises. But the implications of the two views for the role of the subject in the constitution of experience are sharply different. The empiricist subject of Hume is a passive effect of experience, whereas the Kantian subject is the main engine of experience. The Humean subject finds itself with certain fateful attitudes, such as the expectation of causal regularity or benevolent attachment to the welfare of fellow subjects, without being able to derive these attitudes from its own autonomy; it is a centered seat of intention a posteriori but not a centering center a priori. Lacking a centering center within, the Humean subject lacks motivation to posit or acknowledge active relationship with a divine Centerer of the world. The Kantian subject, however, projects a world orientationally from its own manner of synthesis, and that world, though thoroughly constructed in its phenomenal aspect, includes an infinite ensemble of supersensuous beings-in-themselves, among them the ideal universal Centerer.

Kant argues that our true rules of orientation with regard to supersensuous beings and situations can be brought out most clearly in the philosophy of pure practical reason. Only in pure practical reason do our objectively unconstrained relations with the supersensuous come under true a priori constraint —the immanent constraint of rational freedom in moral obligation.

> We must assume the existence of God when we wish to judge concerning the first causes of all contingent things, particularly in the organization of ends actually present in the world. But far more important is the need of reason in its practical use, because here the need is unconditional; here we are compelled to presuppose the existence of God not just if we *wish* to judge but because we *must* judge, for the pure practical use of reason consists only in the prescription of moral laws [which] all lead to the idea of the highest good that is possible in the world so far as it is possible only through freedom, i.e., morality.[15]

Kant's conception of pure practical reasoning departs radically from the tradition of identifying the choice-worthy with the ontologically more perfect. It is geared instead to the procedural perfection of being able to universalize for all agents the policy implicit in any action one takes. The "supreme good" ideal of strict fairness dominates the "complete good" ideal of maximized happiness—for persons may rightly only hope for the happiness that virtue has made them worthy of.[16] Leibnizian optimism is given an austere turn:

> If we inquire into God's final end in creating the world, we must name not the happiness of rational beings in the world but the highest good, which adds a further condition to the wish of rational beings to be happy, viz., the condition of being worthy of happiness, which is the morality of these beings, for this alone contains the standard by which they can hope to participate in happiness at the hand of a *wise* creator . . . One cannot ascribe to a supreme independent wisdom an end based merely on benevolence. For we cannot conceive the action of this benevolence . . . except as conformable to the restrictive conditions of harmony with the holiness of His will as the highest original good . . . nothing glorifies God more than what is the most estimable thing in the world, namely, respect for His command, the observance of sacred duty which His law imposes on us, when there is added to this His glorious plan of crowning such an excellent order with corresponding happiness.[17]

The perfectly good will that interests Kant most is not the will of God but the pure scrupulousness of a morally principled human being. This will is truly sovereign, in the most important sense:

> Even if, by some special disfavor of destiny or by the niggardly endowment of step-motherly nature, this will is entirely lacking in power to carry out its intentions; if by its utmost effort it still accomplishes nothing, and only good will is left . . . even then it would still shine like a jewel for its own sake as something which has its full value in itself.[18]

Kant is consciously close here to the Hellenistic philosophers of sovereign attitude, especially the Stoics.[19] For Kant, too, the most important cosmological principle derives from the most stringently prescribed attitude, as the moral agent's unavoidable wish for perfected virtue and proportional happiness generates a virtual world of "rational faith" in which the existence of a holy and lovable God is a capstone postulate.[20] This rational faith-world is the defensible armature of religious imagining and hoping. We can give a definite sense to the proposition that the person of a certain faith lives in a different world than the person without it: the possessor of rational faith experiences as a necessary synthesis a world with meaningful features that do not belong to the world-synthesis of a person in whom pure practical reason is inadequately expressed. (Speaking from the vantage point of discovering his own radical freedom in a society of such freedoms, Fichte declares: "My world is the object and sphere of my duties and absolutely nothing else.")[21] Those features are appeals that resonate with a construal of rational agents as autonomous monads. Although the moral assumption of free action has no place in knowledge of nature, for which any phenomenon must have been necessitated by a phenomenal efficient cause, still it is fully cogent from the practical standpoint of acting "as if" free.[22] The moral ideal of "worthiness to be happy," which has no standing in an empiricist world outside the conventions of justice that people adopt at the prompting of their natural benevolence and insights into utility, has in the Kantian world an a priori majesty like that of heaven over earth.[23]

* * *

An assertion always puts a meaning into play and in some way addresses referents and interlocutors; it is also always in some way a self-assertion. Some assertions display this latter dimension more clearly than others. The Kantian appeal to the conditions of the possibility of *rational* experience is the self-declaration of a certain rational subjectivity that insists on rigorous explanatory oversight of phenomenal experience on the one hand, and on perfectly autonomous self-determination on the other. From a non-Kantian perspective, this argument can sound like a sort of bullying. For a Humean moralist, for example, Kant's moral theory involves a frightening dismissal of "natural" features of human psychology—including benevolent feeling, the real wellspring of moral value—in favor of a rule-making formalism that is liable to be turned willfully and heartlessly in whatever way a supposed universal rule can rationalize.[24] From Kant's perspective, however, any appeal to natural fact—be it the sweetest natural inclination to care for others—gives away freedom and with it the very possibility of true responsibility and unconditional worth. Such a move is actually a self-discounting or self-disguise of rational freedom, and so an abuse of it. Kantian argumentation, on this view, is properly, honestly, and responsibly a self-assertion of rational freedom. This rational freedom is fulfilled in the cognitive sphere in the fully regulated knowledge of natural objects, but it is supremely interpreted as the "good will," an orientation to universal law in practical rule-following and in the ultimate construal of the world as a theater of practical fulfillment. As a standing attitude, this will is a *Gesinnung*, a disposition that is a personal "determination."[25]

> The [moral] disposition [*Gesinnung*], i.e., the first subjective ground of the adoption of the [moral] maxims, can only be a single one, and it applies to the entire use of freedom universally. This disposition too, however, must be adopted through the free power of choice, for otherwise it could not be imputed. But there cannot be any further cognition of the subjective ground or the cause of this adoption (although we cannot avoid asking about it), for otherwise we would have to adduce still another maxim . . . Since we cannot derive this disposition, or rather its highest ground, from a first act of the power of choice in time, we call it a characteristic of the power of choice that pertains to it by nature (even though the disposition is in fact grounded in freedom).[26]

Although the moral disposition is *free* and so exposed to corruption, it is also *perfect*, always fully itself, inasmuch as it exists outside of phenomena; we can judge a person's character without depending on an endless induction of manifestations of the person's intentions. (But inasmuch as we *are* phenomenal beings, we are estranged from this perfection: "The disposition, which takes the place of the totality of the series of approximations carried on *in infinitum*, makes up only for the deficiency which is in principle inseparable from the existence of a temporal being, [namely] never to be able to become quite fully what he has in mind.")[27]

Kant brings modern philosophy to ground that was first occupied by the Axial Age thinkers. It shows a principle to a free subject by which the subject can rightly order its life in alignment with a world-centering. But the theme of subjective freedom is now expressed more strongly than ever before. (Compare, as doctrinal *assertion,* the fate-defying swerve attributed to the atoms of reality by the Epicureans, and as an *asserting* of freedom, the fierce calls to choose the way of righteousness in Zoroastrian and Hebrew prophetic texts.) The Kantian world-centerer is reason itself. The referent "God" is auxiliary to the featured appellant, the good will as we immediately actualize it. And this creates a serious problem, as we saw earlier, of relation between attitude and appeal. The Humean qualm I expressed above about the bullying potential in Kant's ethics is a tremor indicating that problem. If a moral agent should indeed be careful *to take the categorical imperative in the right way,* not willfully or heartlessly, then what *beyond* the categorical imperative is the supreme appeal that must be heeded, and what *beyond* rule-consistency is the proper basic moral attitude?

Let us probe the Kantian position a little further to see what answer it might generate to this question. Rule-consistency is appealing in a purely intellectual way because it involves formal perfection—more specifically, the virtue of clear intelligibility as regards its identity and firm certainty as regards its status in the larger scheme of experience. But formal perfection is not the same thing as moral worth. Another Kantian touchstone in the good will is its independence of contingent inclinations. This feature places it in a second world "higher" than the sensuous world.[28] But to value a will for its independence or aptitude for mastery might amount only to a sort of power worship. Not until we hit on the essential relation of the good will to *other subjects* have we found all the requisites of its moral qualification. For Kant, the reference to a plurality of rational subjects is implicit in his first "universal law" formulation of the categorical imperative and is then brought to the fore in his alternate formulation that all rational subjects must be treated as ends in themselves.[29] Kant takes it for granted that each of us acknowledges the fellow-rationality of other subjects. If we did not, the most important part of the practical reasoning game could never be played. Duties of fidelity and beneficence would lose their point. But Kant does not have an argument against moral solipsism. Moral solipsism is practically self-contradictory only if one has the basic disposition to comport oneself responsibly within a plurality of rational agents.

Only that disposition lying behind all argument provides the final answer to the question about basic moral meaningfulness.

Kant's disciple Fichte sees the rational undecidability of this issue for Kantianism and abruptly proclaims a call of "conscience":

> The voice of my conscience calls to me: whatever these beings may be in and for themselves, you ought to treat them as self-subsistent, free, autonomous beings completely independent of you . . . Respect their freedom. With love take up their purposes like your own. This is how I ought to act . . . I just said that I *think* of them as beings like myself. But strictly speaking it is not thought by which they are first presented to me as such. It is the voice of conscience, the commandment, "here limit your freedom, here suppose and respect other purposes," which is first translated into the thought, "here is certainly and truly a self-existent being like myself."[30]

Natural observation cannot establish the existence of radically free beings. "We know of each other only through our common spiritual source" and only in faith, that is, in good, free willing.[31]

How does such a commandment of conscience get generated, what authorizes it, and what expressions and entailments does it have *as a moral demand*? Traditional monotheism confronts these questions with the majestic superiority of a divine creator, judge, and redeemer. God is figured not simply as a potentate but as the ultimate enabler and sustainer of the best possible relationships among subjects, perfectly just and loving. This supreme Centerer is in a unique position to command and reward finite subjects in a specifically moral way, enforcing unconditional requirements of other-regard and collective flourishing. On the monotheist view, an authentically moral attitude in a finite subject differs from merely willful adherence to a personal code, on the one hand, or ad hoc sentimentalism, on the other, by its essential reference to this supreme Centerer.

Kant still refers to God as the commander of the moral law and the realizer of the highest good, but the Kantian God is not a real centerer independent of the reason that speaks in each finite subject's mind. There can be no substantially appealing divine revelation distinct from the deliverances of reason. That is why secularist Kantians and religious enemies of Kantianism can treat the atheist implications of Kant's position as an open secret. Fichte, a progressive Kantian accused of atheism, vividly stakes out a position on this issue by making theistic affirmations in the third part of *The Vocation of Man*.[32] The key for Fichte is the ideal of pure will, a "sublime" will not limited by our sensuous entanglements, absolutely free, active, and necessarily consequential (on its own terms, in its own sphere). This sounds at first like the Platonic Form of Kantian will, indeed like Kant's own idea of the holy will.[33] But Fichte opens up a more dramatic relationship between the finite will and the sublime will than a purely ideal conformation: "Between [the sublime will] and all finite rational beings there is a spiritual bond, and it itself is this spiritual bond of the world of reason. I purely and resolutely will my duty, and It then wills that I succeed, at least in the spiritual world."[34] The human being differs from the sublime will by virtue of its emplacement in a particular worldly existence among similar but different existents.

> I neither survey nor see through that spiritual order, and do not need to. I am only a link in its chain, and can judge the whole just as little as a single tone of a song can judge the harmony of the whole. But I must know what I myself ought to be in this harmony of spirits; for only I can make myself into that, and it is directly revealed to me by a voice which comes to me from that world. In this way I am connected with the One *which is there*, and take part in its being. There is nothing truly real, lasting, imperishable in me except these two parts: the voice of my conscience and my free obedience. Through the first the spiritual world bends down to me and embraces me as one of its members; through the second I raise myself into this world, grasp it, and act in it. That infinite will, however, is the mediator between it and me; for it is itself the original source of it and of me.[35]

This language could serve as a somewhat warmer expression of Kant's picture of the moral situation. Kant too can dramatize the relationship between a human will subject to duty and the perfectly free holy will. But Kant stresses an entirely standard dignity of the subject, always separate from the needs and desires that individuate subjects, while in Fichte's more genuinely Leibnizian vision, rational subjects are really and importantly different from each other as unique possibility-realizing perspectives on being.[36] The "spiritual world plan" in which Fichte locates his own distinctive and complementary personal existence is treated by his faith as an *actuality* rather than as a long-run projection of hope.[37] The individual agent's subjection to this larger reality warrants Fichte's appeal to the directive force of "vocation," *Bestimmung*, going beyond the mere self-determination of "disposition," *Gesinnung*.

On a less Leibnizian note, Fichte moves farther than Kant in a democratic direction pointed by the French Revolution: rational subjects are not merely pawns of a monarchic God but construct the sense of rational personhood in their interactions. Kant could project a Kingdom of Ends in which all rational subjects are co-legislators only by abstracting from personal differences.[38]

To interpret these Fichtean affirmations as religious window dressing on Kantian rationalism is to miss the work Fichte is doing on the concept of basic attitude. By clearly marking out three different kinds of intentional centering in the theater of freedom—mine, that of other finite subjects, and that of the sublime will as the source and mediator of finite wills—Fichte tries to save the Kantian position from the justificational crisis to which its emphasis on autonomy leads. The point of discriminating and adopting attitudes is to attain a right orientation in a larger order, to be centered as a centerer by a greater centering. Fichte's God is conceived as fulfilling the recipe for a sovereign attitude referent—a Centerer of centerers among centerers. Moreover, Fichte's God is positioned to make a distinct compelling appeal to each finite subject, not merely by virtue of being perfect as each finite subject is not, but also concretely by relating each subject to the rights and duties of other subjects. That belongs to the sublime will's character as "spiritual bond." (In later writing Fichte calls the sublime will "love.")[39]

To his peremptory insistence on an ultimate free decision of the will in "faith," Fichte adds the consideration that freedom is made a serious matter by my inner compulsion to act, by the rights and predicaments of other subjects, and by the prospect that action can produce a better world.[40] In Fichte's interpretation of the Kantian concept of the highest good (the union of virtuous intent and happy outcome), we hear Leibnizian optimism singing in the key of pure freedom:

> Whatever it is in me that compels me to think that I ought so to act compels me to believe that something will result from this act. It opens the prospect of . . . a *different and better* world than the one that exists for my sense of sight. It makes me desire this better world, to embrace and long for it with my whole being, to live only in it and be satisfied only with it. That commandment is itself my guarantee for the sure attainment of this purpose . . . As I live in obedience, I at the same time live in the intuition of its purpose, live in the better world which it promises me.[41]

Note that this appealing better world is entirely a construction of reason; reason itself, not an improved actual environment or fellowship of beings, is the supreme appeal. "I am not hungry because there is food available to me, but rather something becomes food for me because I am hungry. Just so, I do not act as I act because something is my purpose, but rather something becomes my purpose because I ought so to act."[42]

The Primacy of Receptivity: Schleiermacher

In his life of Schleiermacher, Dilthey refers to the great tendency of the German intellect to start with the whole.[43] This tendency promotes a unified conversation. But it can also take dramatically different expressions, as Fichte and Schleiermacher show.

Fichte infers from the frustrating difficulty of his debate with non-idealists that when genuine first principles are irreconcilable, the choice between them is unconstrained by any principle and "what sort of philosophy one chooses depends, therefore, on what sort of man one is; for a philosophical system is not a dead piece of furniture that we can reject or accept as we wish; it is rather a thing animated by the soul of the person who holds it."[44] Fichte goes on to characterize dogmatists as indolent, unscrupulous persons, and he plays up his own boldly self-confident attitude tending (as he himself admits) to arrogance, an attitude that well fits his project of constructing the whole world from the initiative and with the energy of an ego. The ego radiates the wholeness of the whole.

Schleiermacher, on the other hand, is the thinker of the generation after Kant most dedicated to the centripetal aspect of the Leibnizian-Kantian conception of reality-centering; he is like a Yin to the German Idealists' Yang, driving toward the realization of any and all meaningful connections as inward. "I must think the deepest speculative thoughts, and they are fully one with the inmost religious feeling," he writes in a letter; and the satisfaction he expresses is not the idealist one of articulation and rational appropriation but rather one of achieved unity, a unity as much of contact as of form.[45] The idealists make the most of the Kantian principle of the productive spontaneity of reason and arrive at a religious position in which the absorption of the divine appeal by human reason is brazenly announced. "Spirit," writes Hegel, "has its center within itself [and] is self-sufficient being, which is the same thing as freedom."[46] By "spirit" Hegel means human rationality; spirit and freedom are realized in the productions of human culture. Schleiermacher, more oriented to the receptivity of human consciousness than to its spontaneity, makes the antithetical claim that the basic human reality is dependence on infinite Being. He makes this claim in and on behalf of an attitude, piety, that is conspicuously absent in Hegel. Schleiermacher takes this attitude to be the essence of religion. Thus he proposes to orient religion on a basis of deference and circumspection and thereby rescue it from falsification just at the heady moment at which German Idealism proposes to consummate the Enlightenment by swallowing religion whole in the triumphant self-possession of reason.

Our primary concern in this phase of our inquiry is with Schleiermacher's contribution to the concept of attitude rather than to his particular attitude prescription. The key to his thinking is an anthropological premise he shares with Kant: human existence is a synthesis of receptivity and spontaneity, and the very middle of this synthesis—the "how" of the synthesizing—is the Archimedean point of meaning-making, the point at which a change changes everything: "The immediate self-consciousness is always the mediating link in the transition between moments in which Knowing predominates and those in which Doing predominates, so that a different Doing may proceed from the same Knowing in different people according as a different determination of self-consciousness enters in."[47] The capital question, then, is: How is the "how" or "immediate self-consciousness" determined, what makes it make the meaning it makes? For the idealists, the answer must be that rational freedom determines itself. But this answer is unacceptable to Schleiermacher for at least two reasons. First, a self-determining freedom is estranged from the natural world, which figures for it only as a foil. Its causal relations with and affections by the natural world are reduced to expressions of itself, and this view impoverishes our understanding of life. Second, a self-determining freedom can rectify itself on its own terms but cannot encompass the larger issue of its rectification vis-à-vis the whole of reality. Thus, Schleiermacher will argue that the religious attitude of cleaving humbly to the whole of reality is something more than a possibly attractive or useful way of conducting oneself; it is the adequate realization of the transepistemological truth and transethical justice of being centered in one's "immediate self-consciousness" by the intrinsically supreme Centerer, the All or the Infinite.

Schleiermacher's attack on idealism in the first edition of *On Religion* (1799) draws on a "higher realism" inspired by Spinoza: "Religion breathes there where freedom itself has once more become nature; it apprehends man beyond the play of his particular powers and his personality, and views him from the vantage point where he must be what he is, whether he likes it or not."[48] Not that Schleiermacher wants to insist on the mechanistic determinism of Spinoza. But the point of the relationship between the individual and the universe, he thinks, is for the individual to reflect the actual universe rather than project abstract universalizations upon it. He writes in his *Soliloquies:*

> The sense of freedom alone did not content me; it gave no meaning to my personality, nor to the peculiar stream of consciousness flowing within me, which urged me to seek something of higher ethical value of which it was the sign. I was not satisfied to view humanity in rough unshapen masses, inwardly altogether alike [i.e., in rationality] . . . Thus there dawned upon me what is now my highest intuition. I saw clearly that each man is meant to represent humanity in his own way, combining its elements uniquely, so that it may reveal itself in every mode, and all that can issue from its womb be made actual in the fullness of unending space and time.[49]

The core idea here is Leibnizian insofar as it contemplates a generation of beings for the sufficient reason of realizing the richest diversity. It leans more toward Spinoza, however, in asserting an actual communion of beings against the functional autarchy of the Leibnizian monads. It implies that our basic interpretive and practical challenge is to form a community among diverse beings rather than to standardize them. (From this point extend Schleiermacher's trailblazing inquiries in hermeneutics, characteristically combining a dramatic view of the separation between individual minds with a divinatory optimism.)[50]

The Leibnizian scenario of plenitude is also the most charged scenario of attitude formation. Since each being has a vocation of distinctness along with an essential fulfillment in its relation to the whole, the relation of each being's principle to the principle of Being is properly the first question about the meaning of each being's existence and the first concern for each being. Schleiermacher acknowledges that the disciplines of metaphysics and morals are defined by their concern with the relation of humanity to the universe, as religion is, but holds that a positive orientation to this relationship in its infinite amplitude is essentially religious; thus, metaphysics and morals alike depend on a grounding in religious attitude to be fully serious and relevant— for "religion is the only sworn enemy of all pedantry and one-sidedness."[51]

The function by which the religious or perfectly rectifying orientation is achieved in the 1799 *On Religion* is "intuition," *Anschauung,* in an intimate relationship with "feeling," *Gefühl*. *Gefühl* is a popular term in the Age of Goethe for personal realizing of the meaningfulness of life; we shall see presently how it serves the later Schleiermacher as his main attitude category.[52] But first we should note the force of "intuition" in the earlier Schleiermacher. *Anschauung* refers in Kant and Schleiermacher alike to the givenness of a being to a knowing subject. But Schleiermacher departs strikingly from Kant in speaking of an intuition of the universe (Kant regards "the universe" as a thing-of-principle that cannot be the actually given content of any concrete experience).[53] And Schleiermacher seems to open the door for a really exterior appeal of divinity by claiming that "every original and new intuition of the universe is [a revelation]."[54] Whereas intuition in Kantian epistemology is only a "blind" perceptual quantum until it is interpreted through concepts, for Schleiermacher it is already an understanding of a thing that proceeds sensibly from a formative real relationship between the subject and the object. In the "natal hour" of an experience of the highest meaningfulness, Schleiermacher writes,

> I lie on the bosom of the infinite world. At this moment I am its soul, for I feel all its powers and its infinite life as my own; at this moment it is my body, for I penetrate its muscles and limbs as my own . . . With the slightest trembling the holy embrace is dispersed, and now for the first time the intuition stands before me as a separate form; I survey it, and it mirrors itself in my open soul like the image of the vanishing beloved in the awakened eye of a youth.[55]

What exactly are the respective roles of feeling and cognitive form in meaningful experience? *On Religion* speaks to this crucial Axial Age question ambiguously; in later work, Schleiermacher associates religion more strictly with feeling and moves toward more clearly noncognitivist formulations.[56] *The Christian Faith* asserts as phenomenologically self-evident that self-consciousness has the two "elements" of moving itself and being affected and that affection by an Other is the "primary" element inasmuch as activity without receptivity would be "an indefinite 'agility.'" "Even the self-consciousness which accompanies an action (acts of knowing included), while it predominantly expresses spontaneous movement and activity, is always related . . . to a prior moment of affective receptivity, through which its original 'agility' received its direction."[57]

Why, we may ask, should priority be shifted from activity to receptivity? Why should we view an intuition nostalgically as the trace of an original union from which it is falling away, rather than teleologically as the potentially apt constituent of a meaningful synthesis? Or why should we be impressed more by the dependence of thoughts and actions on a prior affection by an Other than by the dependence of affections for their meaningfulness on the rational subject whose thoughts interpret them and whose actions express them? Why should the feeling of dependence be religiously decisive rather than the feeling of freedom? Part of Schleiermacher's answer is that a feeling of absolute dependence is possible and a feeling of absolute freedom is not. This asymmetry simply expresses the ontological finitude of the human subject, never entirely self-creating or alone. Thus, there is a chance of finding a sovereign attitude in the zone of dependence, but not in the zone of freedom. Another part of the answer is that what enables any cognitive or practical item to participate in the most thoroughly rectified life is its anchorage in a bond between subject and universe that is predominantly formed by the universe. This is how Schleiermacher assures a centering of human centering by a greatest, necessarily transhuman Centerer. Remember that to have an intuition is to be positioned in a certain way, not merely to be notified about something. (Compare the sense of the parallel English word *insight*: we often understand an insight to be strategically fortunate.) To have an intuition of an object as essentially representing and belonging to the universe is to be positioned, ultimately by the universe, in an unrestricted appreciative deference toward the universe.

But on what basis can one justifiably hold that the universe positions a subject, or indeed does anything? In a note to a later edition of *On Religion*, Schleiermacher accepts the Kantian point that "we cannot be conscious of [the Infinite] immediately and through itself. It can only be through a finite object, by means of which our tendency to postulate and seek a world, leads us from detail and part to the All and the Whole. Hence sense for the Infinite and the immediate life of the finite in us as it is in the Infinite, are one and the same."[58] Here he identifies the religious attitude with a "taste" or "liking" for seeking the Whole. Then:

> We cannot really have this feeling except it is occasioned by the action of single things. But if the single things are in their action only single, the sole result is definiteness of the sensuous self-consciousness . . . our single life reacts against it, and there can be no feeling of dependence except fortuitously in so far as the reaction is not equal to the action. If, however, the single thing does not work upon us as a single thing, but as part of the Whole, it will be, in acting upon us, an opening for the Whole. This result will depend entirely on the mood and attitude of the mind [*Stimmung und Richtung unseres Gemüthes*]. But then our reaction will appear to us determined by the same cause and in the same way as the action, and being over against the Universe, our state must be the feeling of entire dependence.[59]

The word that marks the hinge of this argument is "as," the phenomenal correlate of the "how" of synthesis: religious experience involves experiencing oneself and other beings *as* members together of an inclusive whole.[60] The "mood or attitude" on which this "experiencing as" depends, however, is precisely not a "subjective" state in the sense of any sort of whim; it essentially bears the sense of "originality" and non-arbitrariness because it is the solidarity of the subject with the All, the "stirring" of the All for the surrendered subject that constitutes the divine "revelation."[61] The subject feels "absolutely dependent" on the All.[62] That feeling is what resolves the question of the perception's justification and indeed of the ultimate rectification of any other perception or action that it "harmonizes."[63] In fully religious subjectivity, an internally unlimited *complicatio*, all modes of consciousness and all ingredients of experience are lucidly interelated.[64]

The identification of religious attitude with feeling reflects a certain subjectivism in the sense of an orientation to individual actualizations of meaningfulness, but also realism in the sense of a determination to be subjected to reality. Schleiermacher blends the imperatives of inwardness and contact together in addressing the theme of vocation: "That I speak does not originate from a rational decision or from hope or fear, nor does it happen in accord with some final purpose or for some arbitrary or accidental reason. It is the inner irresistible necessity of my nature; it is a divine calling; it is that which determines my place in the universe and makes me the being I am."[65] He wants to speak for the supremely grounded attitude of humble participation in the universe without giving the impression that he has "taken an attitude."

Schleiermacher means to improve on an abstract Kantian view of subjective freedom and dependence by understanding the life of the individual subject as *essentially* in community with similarly situated fellows. One of his moves is metaphysically idealist, appealing to the principle that "everything inward becomes, at a certain point of its strength or maturity, an outward too, and, as such, perceptible to others."[66]

> The proper object of this desire for communication is unquestionably that where man originally feels himself to be passive, his intuitions and feelings; there he has to ask whether it might not be an alien and unworthy power to which he must submit . . . How should he keep to himself the influences of the universe that appear to him as greatest and most irresistible? How should he wish to retain within himself that which most strongly forces him out of himself and which, like nothing else, impresses him with the fact that he cannot know himself in and of himself alone?[67]

The feeling of absolute dependence is seen as a priori, ready to blossom in any subject's life. But its expression must always be individual and particular, in accordance with the naturally and culturally specified position occupied by a subject; and along this line Schleiermacher prompts us to consider a more radically social and historical constitution of directive meaning without himself moving into that terrain.[68] We saw an analogous nudging by the idealist Fichte. Their common inspiration is the pluralistic plenitude ideal of Leibniz.

* * *

For future reference I want to call attention here to three significant issues posed by Schleiermacher's attitude conception. (I am proceeding on the assumption that Schleiermacher's claims about "feeling" and "immediate self-consciousness" speak directly to our questions about attitude, as I think his lines of argument bear out.)

1. *Attitude and cognition.* Like Kant and Fichte, Schleiermacher claims that attitude differs from knowledge, but he firmly ties the feeling of absolute dependence to a certain *apprehension*, that of having a sense of oneself and the beings with which one is dealing as members of the universe or the Infinite. There is a circularity in this, for he seeks to establish an apprehension of solidarity with the All as the cognitive aspect of piety just because he is already committed to the distinctive religious attitude of humbly acknowledging an actual dependence. (He could have taken the quite different way of attending to the rigorous formulation of an ideal, like Kant's ideal of pure practical reason, to fit an attitude of zealously pursuing the purest good possible.) Thus, he gives a misleading impression in suggesting that one will be motivated by intuitions of the greatness of the universe to adopt an attitude of humility, for such intuitions presuppose an attitude of that sort.[69] Admitting that an attitude needs cognitive support to be stable, the question remains, What most fundamentally motivates and grounds an attitude? For ethical idealism, the answer is freedom's self-determination. We have seen why Schleiermacher rejects this answer. But even if it is true that the subject's freedom is always already inflected by the subject's actual dependence, as he argues, how could any given realization of the subject's actual dependence not already be inflected by the subject's freedom? Granted that a pure feeling of absolute freedom is impossible, what compels us to think that an authentic pure feeling of absolute dependence is possible?

It seems that the only alternative to a stalemate between the Schleiermacherian and Kantian approaches, apart from a complete reformulation of the question, would be a combination of the two, keyed to an active symmetrical reciprocity between free willing and dependent feeling. Schleiermacher approaches such a position in his late notes to *On Religion*, as we have seen, and also applies something like it to worldly experience in *The Christian Faith*.[70] To sustain a conception of the feeling of dependence as noncognitive yet distinct from freedom, however, it will be necessary to interpret the feeling of dependence as a realization, not of *what* exists merely, but rather of *how* things are, in a transcognitive sense of "how." The feeling of dependence must become a response to other beings as free also, more tact than grasp.

2. *Attitude as experience.* A related problem is that by approaching the anthropological midpoint from the side of actuality and affection, Schleiermacher slides from the category of attitude into the category of experience. This is the opposite of the Kantian tendency to construe attitude as an intentional determination of practical reason. Each position must learn to warn against the other's distortion without confirming its own. Attitude can neither be a congealed actuality like an experience nor a freely assumed initiative like an intentional act. It is to be noted from Kant's side that Schleiermacher's "piety" could not have its supreme directive force if it were merely a content in

the experience of one or more persons; it must enlist a self-responsible freedom to have that force. Schleiermacher will maintain, on the other hand, that Kantian righteousness cannot be supremely rectifying of a person's life in the absence of a harmonization of the person with the *real* Whole *by* the supreme Centerer of that Whole.

The disentangling of attitude and experience might seem to be hindered by Schleiermacher's exalted talk in *On Religion* of something that looks like an experience of exceptional significance, the ineffable original unity of the conscious subject with Being, which he treats as decisive for religious feeling. There is an intimate relation here between the sensed *actuality* of unity with Being and the *orientational aspect* of the subject's existence in this situation. Schleiermacher thinks of the event as radical reception and radical receptivity at once. But it is important to distinguish between the event's experiential aspect as an accomplished reception and its performative aspect as a receptive potentiality.

3. *Basic attitude and religion.* Notwithstanding their opposed emphases, Schleiermacher and Kant together bring about a remarkable convergence between the very idea of a basic attitude and the ideal of religion. On the Kantian view, a subject can have a truly centered orientation, a *Gesinnung* as opposed to a stew of sensuous inclinations, only by willing freely, that is, rationally. Morality is identified with the radical disposition to will freely; religiousness is identified with the humanly whole disposition to make oneself worthy of happiness in consideration of one's subjectively necessary interest in the greatest possible gratification. For Schleiermacher, the key to orientation is adequate awareness of the environment in which one takes one's position. Thus, quality of orientation improves as one is aware of more that is other than oneself, and the highest-grade orientation turns out to be the same as the essence of religiousness, namely, the feeling of the Infinite.

Schleiermacher wants to make a case for a distinct "sphere" of religion alongside science and morality in the economy of human experience and valuation and for a distinct anthropological seat of feeling alongside knowing and doing.[71] He points to virtuosi of feeling, authentic priests, as the religious counterparts of scientists and moralists.[72] But another, possibly more important aspect of feeling's difference from knowing and doing is its unique depth and comprehensiveness of effect. Insofar as the feeling of the Infinite is the same thing as being really oriented, Schleiermacher can represent piety as the fundamental condition for sound knowledge and practice in general.

> Without religion, how can praxis rise above the common circle of adventurous and customary forms? How can speculation become anything better than a stiff and barren skeleton? Or why, in all its action directed outwardly and toward the universe, does your praxis actually always forget to cultivate humanity itself? It is because you place humanity in opposition to the universe and do not receive it from the hand of religion as a part of the universe and as something holy. How does praxis arrive at an impoverished

uniformity that knows only a single ideal and lays this as the basis everywhere? It is because you lack the basic feeling for the infinite, whose symbol
is multiplicity and individuality . . . Why, for so long, did speculation give
you deceptions instead of a system, and words instead of real thoughts? . . .
Because it lacked religion, because the feeling for the infinite did not
animate it . . . Those who lack the desire to intuit the infinite have no
touchstone.[73]

Piety can affect the quality of all human knowing and doing because, as a
determination of feeling, it belongs to the *formative* midpoint of our living
synthesis of receptions and actions. But it also exerts a special power because
its *content*, relationship with the Infinite, gets expressed in beliefs about divinity and immortality and in practices of devotion—that is, in the "sphere" of
religion.

Conceiving religion as the most adequate basic attitude yields for both
Kant and Schleiermacher a dogma-free theory of the true reference of purportedly religious beliefs and practices—what distinctively religion is about and
what could validate it. On this basis they are able to criticize any and all specific
beliefs and practices that purport to be religious (their actual execution of this
criticism, not surprisingly, confirms Protestant Christianity as supreme among
the religions.)[74] But Schleiermacher differs sharply from Kant in his endorse-
ment of psychologically and culturally determinate expressions of religion
under the Leibnizian sign of "multiplicity and individuality." To the extent that
religion has a "sphere" of its own, it is *not* undogmatic, as Schleiermacher
himself acknowledges in writing a Christian dogmatics. Even if dogmatic
propositions are interpreted "as having arisen solely out of logically ordered
reflection upon the immediate utterances of the religious self-consciousness,"
the fact that the religious self-consciousness always manifests an individual
perspective—for instance, the perspective of one to whom a particular historic
savior-figure has brought a sense of reconciliation with the universe, on a
certain understanding of the universe—implies that what counts for one person
or community as fully adequate orientation can and indeed will differ from
what counts that way for others.[75] If that is so, does Schleiermacher occupy a
bogus "universal" religious position when he tells us what the essence of
religion is? He claims to articulate a fundamental piety that is shared by all the
religious, a commonality in which they themselves tolerantly and curiously
rejoice, despite inevitable differences in the content of their religious visions.[76]
It is evident, though, that only the relatively tolerant and curious among the
religious—the liberals, as we would say—will agree to defining true piety so
broadly. Conservative religionists will contest the open conception of the
infinite, affirming instead a fully determinate divinity that commands all religious interest. So long as this sort of disagreement resists any mediation, the
general principle of orientation to all-reality cannot serve as the evaluative
anchor Schleiermacher wants it to be—though it undoubtedly helps us see into
the depths of religious position-taking.

The Freedom Fighting of Kierkegaard and Nietzsche

Kierkegaard and Nietzsche, whose ideas do not affect the larger philosophical conversation until the twentieth century, are important pioneers in articulating transrational attitude issues.

Kierkegaard intensifies the Kantian concentration on the free initiative and practical possibility of the subject. His theme is the actual challenge each individual faces in living freely and responsibly as an existential "synthesis of the infinite and the finite."[77] To rise to this infinitely demanding synthesis requires "passionate" thinking.[78] We saw how for Schleiermacher the category of feeling provides for the crucial relationship between the subject and actuality, one of contact (even if contact with the Infinite is achieved only in the subject's relating to finite Others as tokens of the Infinite). An analogously important category in Kierkegaard is mood (*stemning*, Danish cousin to German *Stimmung*, "attunement") which, like passion, pertains to the all-important relationship the subject has with itself in its project of existing. The category of mood offers a relatively calm, settled perspective on issues that Kierkegaard more often addresses in the energized register of passion or in the directively supreme category of spirit. (Schleiermacher had used *Stimmung* in his aesthetics to express a permanency of *Gefühl*.)[79]

In the Introduction to *The Concept of Anxiety*, Kierkegaard notes a danger of mistaking the mood that is proper to an inquiry into sin:

> That science, just as much as poetry and art, presupposes a mood in the creator as well as in the observer, and that an error in the modulation is just as disturbing as an error in the development of thought, has been entirely forgotten in our time, when inwardness has been completely forgotten, and also the category of appropriation . . . Outside of itself, the error of thought has dialectics as its enemy, and outside of itself, the absence or falsification of mood has the comical as its enemy.[80]

This could pass as a basically aesthetic observation on rhetoric if one missed Kierkegaard's ethically and religiously focused *way* of taking up the issue of inwardness and appropriation, concerned more with the self-definition of the subject than with the felt quality of experience. Kierkegaard's way is earnestness, which differs from the disinterested mood of science; it is the mood of person-to-person address about how matters stand most fundamentally with an actual person's life.[81] (Kierkegaard's corpus is deeply interesting to us as a communicative problem and comedy by virtue of his provocative overlaying of limited, possibly feigned moods of aesthetic relish and rational disinterestedness upon ethico-religious earnestness. There are moods within moods and moods behind moods.)

The moods of anxiety and despair show us possibility as impossible to deal with. Unrestricted possibility, the awareness that anything might happen, weighs on us more heavily than actuality does. In this aspect, the future is our worst enemy. "Whoever is educated by anxiety is educated by possibility, and only he who is educated by possibility is educated according to his infinitude."[82] The positive resolution of this predicament is "faith." In one of his direct discourses, Kierkegaard identifies faith with an expectancy of victory that refers to eternity rather than to any particular outcome in time.[83] The sovereign attitude of faith so understood is a common human property that no individual can cause another to gain or lose, which makes it an appropriate centerpiece of spiritual anthropology.

Kierkegaard likes to call faith and other attitudes "passions" to indicate that a basic orientation is a general human possibility of realizing inwardness—alternatively, a "movement" in an eternally meaningful "moment," or a "concentration" of all upon a single "point"—and that it is not a calculable product of thinking or willing but must be sustained by real relation with an unassimilated and so only paradoxically apprehended Infinite. This relation is "spirit."[84] Lest the language of passion lead to an embrace of a merely sensuous intensity or idiosyncratic kind of immediacy, he attaches to Karl Rosenkranz's discussion of the concept of *Gemüt*, "heart" or "disposition," his own claim that "earnestness is a higher as well as the deepest expression for what disposition is . . . the acquired originality of disposition, its originality preserved in the responsibility of freedom and . . . affirmed in the enjoyment of blessedness."[85] Kierkegaard's position now sounds very Kantian. One's "originality" is one's intentional grounding in authentic selfhood.

> One may be born with a disposition, but no one is born with earnestness. The phrase "What has made him earnest in life" must of course be understood, in a pregnant sense, as that from which the individuality in the deepest sense dates his earnestness. Having become truly earnest about that which is the object of earnestness, a person may very well, if he so wishes, treat various things earnestly, but the question is whether he first became earnest about the object of earnestness. This object every human being has, because it is *himself* . . .[86]

To be surely oneself is to realize eternity, and conversely "whenever inwardness is lacking, the spirit is finitized."[87] Put differently, being aimed rightly in relation to oneself involves being aimed rightly in relation to the ultimate rectifier. The attitude of maximal concern for the concrete exercise of one's freedom is the inner face of the movement whose outer face is the attitude of radical optimism or faith. But this attitude is impossible in either its inward or outward reference if it is not enabled by the infinite, for the finite self's own resources cannot be equal to the challenge. Once the "deeper self" that recognizes this situation is awakened, the alternative basic attitudes available to the self are despair, "a misrelation in a relation that relates itself to itself and has been established by another," and faith, in which "the self rests transparently in the power that established it."[88]

Kierkegaard contributes two major theses to modern attitude thinking.

The first is a more radical statement of the Kantian primacy of the practical: he argues that an attitude decisive for the rectification of human life must be grounded in its own purely orientational movement, contingent most fundamentally on another such movement from beyond all reckoning (for a Christian, the love of God) rather than on rational ideality. (Given his characteristic appeal to absurdity, as in believing "by virtue of the absurd," it is not hard to misread Kierkegaard as *deriving* faith from the self-wounding of reason in addressing the infinite and the impossible; but although the passion of inwardness involves holding fast to the absurdity of divine grace as the extreme of objective uncertainty, the *fueling* of this passion in the cognitive faculty is not its *grounding*.)[89] This pneumatological thesis synthesizes a claim about the determining power in a human life of pure poise and pose, understood dynamically, with a claim that the point of reference for the ultimate rectification of a human life is necessarily *exterior* to the human being. Without this exteriority, the self simply manages itself, for better or worse; the category of the spiritual is not attained.

Kierkegaard's second major thesis concerns the relevance of temporality to eternity. The eternal in an individual's life is the unrestricted validation of the meaningfulness and worth of every present actuality in that life. Unlike Platonic recollection, which realizes a "fullness of time" in the present through rational mastery of nontemporal forms of worldly experience, eliminating all uncertainty, Kierkegaardian faith redeems the present with expectancy of victory in the inherently uncertain future.[90] I suggest that Leibniz's metaphysical optimism can be seen as a design for the concretely arduous and adventurous campaign of living in the greatest expectancy, although whenever Leibniz's view is expressed as a proved, deterministic system, it clearly is antithetical to the faith Kierkegaard is talking about.

***

Friedrich Nietzsche is a thinker of radical intentional freedom for whom the ideal of a divine Centerer is decisive, as it was for Kierkegaard, but who resolves the status of theism in the opposite way. Perhaps the pithiest of all cognitive framings of a basic attitude is "If God is dead, all things are permitted," a somber warning from Dostoevksy, but a principle of awed joy for Nietzsche.[91] In Nietzschean perspective, the atheist orientation dissolves the last and most dangerous bonds of valuational objectivism, bonds that still cramp Kierkegaard's spirit; in Kierkegaardian perspective, the exterior provoker and partner of Nietzschean subjectivity remains obscure, so that the category of the spiritual is somewhat suppressed. Either thinker, however, offers a hard-won unconditional optimism of self-realization that mocks all objectively justified optimisms. As little as they sympathize with Leibniz's metaphysical approach, Kierkegaard and Nietzsche both stand in Leibniz's lineage insofar as they enact another great revolt of pluralism against totalizing programs of idealism and scientific materialism. Their frighteningly dynamic view of self-realization can claim the "appetition" of the Leibnizian monad for an ancestor.

Nietzsche's optimism is formulated in reaction to Schopenhauer's pessimism. Schopenhauer had argued on a combination of transcendental and empirical grounds that life is essentially miserable because it consists of the phenomenal projection of an infinitely striving, never-ultimately-satisfiable noumenal will. Attitudinally, Schopenhauer set himself up as an anti-Leibniz, opposing the best-of-all-possible-worlds argument with an argument (borrowed from Hume) that our world is necessarily the worst of all possible worlds since a world any less harmonious could not be sustained.[92] Nietzsche took seriously the descriptive side of Schopenhauer's pessimism but sought a way of rejecting its sour directive conclusion:[93] "Is there a pessimism of *strength*? An intellectual predilection for the hard, gruesome, evil, problematic aspect of existence, prompted by well-being, by overflowing health, by the *fullness* of existence?"[94]

Nietzsche's first major formulation of basic orientation arrives in *The Birth of Tragedy* in the form of a distinction between fundamental ways of feeling life and dealing with life that he finds modeled in classical Greek culture, the formation-oriented "Apollinian" and the transformation-oriented "Dionysian."[95] Nietzsche's Apollinian-Dionysian duality seems in many ways an extension of the duality of the "beautiful" and the "sublime" that Burke and Kant made a great topic in the previous century, a topic that was already deeply intriguing insofar as the purely "aesthetic" appeal of things in each category to our "feelings" could be seen to be entangled with moral and cosmological issues.[96] But whereas the Enlightenment's "beautiful" and "sublime" are defined in terms of attraction and repulsion in a well-ordered economy of interactions, Nietzsche roots the Apollinian and Dionysian artistic impulses in an inescapable and unbearable problem of existence, the "wound in existence" of suffering, and assesses cultures according to their more or less honest and more or less desperate ways of dealing with that wound.[97] The strength and ultimate weakness of the heavily Apollinian culture of the modern West, Nietzsche asserts, is the self-congratulatory optimism it maintains in denial of the wound. The Hellenic culture that Nietzsche admires, in contrast, is able to "justify" existence by evolving a tragic myth that accepts "even the ugly and disharmonic [as] part of an artistic game that the will in the eternal amplitude of its pleasure plays with itself."[98] The subordination of the Apollinian to the Dionysian attitude becomes Nietzsche's ideal.[99] This implies that the mission of reason, whether in reflection or in discussion, is to recognize and foster the surging of power—a difficult mission, since power is pluralist, differentiating, and not shy of conflict and confusion!

Nietzsche's other great contribution in this context is his genealogical critique of values. That a cultural stance or set of valuations can have its hidden causes analyzed and attacked based on a revolutionary insight into the true character and the whole history of human motivation—this, as Nietzsche acknowledges, is an old Jewish and Christian idea (perhaps the most imposing argument of this sort being Augustine's *City of God*), but Nietzsche proposes now to apply it to the guiding Jewish-Christian spirit of European culture. The valuations of this culture express the poisonous resentment of the strong by the weak. Christian love, for example, loves only a human being that is wretched or humbled, and cruelly fixes humans in this position.[100] The "revaluation of all values" in the Jewish-Christian God's championing of the lowly over the noble, and of otherworldly over worldly fulfillment, now must be revalued in turn, as its own nihilistic consequences become unmistakable (not least in theories and inventories of "value").

> Christianity was from the beginning, essentially and fundamentally, life's nausea and disgust with life, merely concealed behind, masked by, dressed up as, faith in "another" or "better" life. Hatred of "the world," condemnations of the passions, fear of beauty and sensuality, a beyond invented the better to slander this life, at bottom a craving for the nothing, for the end, for respite, for the "sabbath of sabbaths"—all this always struck me, no less than the unconditional will of Christianity to recognize *only* moral values, as the most dangerous and uncanny form of all possible forms of a "will to decline" . . . Morality itself—how now? might not morality be "a will to negate life," a secret instinct of annihilation . . . the danger of dangers?[101]

In the oracular *Thus Spoke Zarathustra*, Nietzsche offers a prophet of new valuations, a man who celebrates the fully generous power represented by the sun.[102] He warns, however, that the revaluation project cannot terminate in a new set of "values," least of all in a new optimism about humanity or the universe; sun-worshiping Zarathustra must not be taken seriously and *followed*. What authentically expresses the freest and most powerful engagement with life, rather than "values," is the overcoming of all values in untrammeled life-affirmation.[103] This is the meaning of the teaching of Eternal Recurrence, which Nietzsche claims to be his supreme idea: it is the cognitive framing that fits, not the "gloomy," "self-hardening" Stoic love of fate, but the free adventurer's zest for everything that actually happens.[104]

> Have you ever said Yes to a single joy? O my friends, then you said Yes too to *all* woe. All things are entangled, ensnared, enamored; if ever you wanted one thing twice, if ever you said, "You please me, happiness! Abide, moment!" then you wanted *all* back. All anew, all eternally, all entangled, ensnared, enamored—oh, then you *loved* the world. Eternal ones, love it eternally and evermore; and to woe, too, you say: go, but return! *For all joy wants—eternity!*[105]

Nietzsche's "eternity" of recurrence is the peculiar being and truth of *becoming* that endlessly recurs, not because it is metaphysically constrained (say, by Platonic form), but because it can never be stopped from gushing.[106] This strange conception of a wound-eternity overcomes the ideal of eternity as a fixed, full being; it is impressed on us that the good that can be named is never the real good, and the centering that can be codified cannot be the one thing needful. The reformed time-sense that accompanies this valuation differs from any selective devotion to past or present or future; the boundaries of any nostalgia or reveling or expectancy are overrun as "eternal recurrence" synthesizes all possible appreciations.

The dancing *lightness* of the Nietzschean sovereign attitude is deliberately contrasted with the Kantian seriousness of gloom and cruelty.[107] The Nietzschean "immoralist" characteristically enters moral discussion by *interrupting* those who insist that intention must be constrained by a specific form. The maintenance of any such "must" is theoretically unwarrantable (for no supposed necessity or obligation can be proved not to be the creation of a free will to power) and practically disingenuous, a free feigning of unfreedom. A Nietzschean intervention demonstrates this. It is a self-vindicating trickster move of mischief, but it can also be considered a constructive move insofar as it helps to overcome repressions and flush out poisons that have been built up by seriousness. Clearly Nietzsche *is* serious about the project of living more fully, that is, in all possible individual and transindividual amplitude. But precisely this seriousness comes to itself in a free lightness. Thus, to declare oneself "serious" as a Nietzschean philosopher is, on the one hand, necessarily to solicit the respect of others with some positive regard for accepted standards of sharable orientation (rationalistic, democratic, humanitarian), but also, on the other hand, to be committed—or nerved, rather—to defy such standards insofar as they function only as weaker reactive forces in relation to greater potentialities of life.

Nietzsche is critical of "spirit" talk, yet capable also of resorting to it warmly and lightly—unlike his follower Ludwig Klages, for example, who makes a categorical opposition between the vital "soul" (*Seele*) and life-denying "spirit" (*Geist*).[108] Nietzschean pneumatology is above all a pragmatics of invitational provocation. Its point is to enliven comportment in relationship rather than to prescribe form to relationship.

Dilthey on Historical Life-Attunement

For Wilhelm Dilthey, the important philosophical issues are defined primarily by the German idealists and Schleiermacher. Dilthey's own theoretical initiatives add dramatically to the vocabulary and analytical depth of attitude discourse.

Dilthey tackles two great problems. First, he wants to elucidate the basic orientation of humanistic thinking toward the free, purposeful actions and interactions of agents in its deep difference from the orientation toward inert objectivity that prevails in the positivist sciences. This leads him to draw a programmatic distinction between the cognitive ideals of empathetic understanding (*Verstehen*) and objectifying explanation (*Erklärung*).[109] Second, he recognizes that while rational humanistic inquiry requires some degree of objectivity and some practicable methods of validation, it has to reckon with considerable individual and social variation in the formation and redemption of claims of understanding. That variation is driven by non-rational psychological and historical factors.

"Although I found myself frequently in agreement with the epistemological school of Locke, Hume, and Kant, I nevertheless found it necessary to conceive differently the nexus [*Zusammenhang*] of the facts of consciousness which we together recognize as the basis of philosophy," Dilthey writes in his preface to *Introduction to the Human Sciences*.[110] *Zusammenhang* is always Dilthey's key word, often qualified as "living." It suggests a continuing coexistence of things (it can also be translated "connectedness" or "context") and so brings multiplicity deeper into the core of experience or reality than does the Kantian "synthesis of a manifold," which typically treats multiplicity as resolved into unity. Much of Dilthey's earlier work revolves around a concept of the "psychological *Zusammenhang*" of lived experience. He argues that a description of psychic life as we actually experience it is necessary preparation for any humanistic inquiry that would neither fly from the actuality of the natural conditioning of our life, in the manner of idealism, nor reduce human experiences and acts to natural facts, in the manner of positivism.[111] Analysis of a specific cultural system of economics, law, art, or religion must be led back to the psychological nexus that forms its ultimate context. The nexus has two primary, reciprocally conditioning constituents: a structural "breadth" of perceptions, impulses, and so forth; and a developmental "length" of purposive self-realization in time.[112] Dilthey advocates an interdisciplinary *Zusammenhang* of perspectives commensurate with the richness of the psychological nexus: "We must begin with culturally developed man . . . having recourse to all the resources of artistic representation . . . Throughout we will appeal to comparative psychology, the history of evolution, experimentation, the analysis of historical products."[113]

Dilthey honors the metaphysical attempt to grasp reality as a unity but demurs from metaphysical knowledge claims. We must study life as a unified nexus, but the ultimate identity or purpose of life must be reckoned an enigma:

> The term "life" expresses what is to everyone the most familiar and intimate, but at the same time the darkest and even most inscrutable. What life is, is an insoluble enigma. All reflection, inquiry, and thought arise from this most inscrutable of things. All knowledge is rooted in this never wholly knowable thing . . . One can, as it were, pursue its tone, rhythm, and stirring melody. But one cannot dissect life into its constituent parts.[114]

The life-enigma does not lie only at the end of long inquiry: we are concretely confronted with it by procreation, birth, chance, the antagonism of natural forces, corruption, and death.[115] Religion, philosophy, and art, all trying to rise above their social-historical contexts to deal with the enigma directly, produce interpretive representations that Dilthey, adapting an ideal of Schleiermacher's, calls "world-intuitions" (*Weltanschauungen*). To understand religious, philosophical, and artistic visions most profoundly, one must be aware of the attitudes that motivate *Weltanschauungen*. There are two levels of attitude, one that can be called a *Verhaltensweise* (a manner of comporting oneself) geared into a certain purposive system—as, for example, an attitude of scientific rationality gears into scientific work—and another, more basic level, which motivates our entry into the various purposive systems of our cultural repertoire, giving us our most general teleology.[116]

Dilthey agrees with Fichte that one's basic attitude depends on what kind of person one is. It is somewhat attributable to the creative freedom of the person, somewhat explicable also in terms of the proportions of generic human tendencies that each individual embodies.[117] But he follows Schleiermacher in emphasizing that a basic attitude is grounded in actual experience involving contact with other beings and the historical mediation of a culture. Dilthey's term for the most basic attitude is "life-attunement" (*Lebensstimmung*). Life-attunements, he says, "form countless nuances of [our] position on the world at the bottommost level of the development of world-intuitions."[118] He tells an audience, "I have no solution of the life-enigma; but the life attunement that has grown in me by reflecting on the implications of historical consciousness, this I would like to share with you."[119] The implied structure of *Stimmung* is more capacious than that of Schleiermacher's *Gefühl*: it does not require a primal scene of contact ("lying on the bosom of the Infinite") but rather allows for a substantial reciprocal influence among really separate beings of any number, on any scale, and in any mode.[120]

In his main work on "Types of World-Intuition," Dilthey does not claim objective necessity for his principles of *Weltanschauung* classification; they are to be validated by their usefulness in promoting a deeper insight for each interpreter (46–47).[121] In general, religious world-intuitions are those that relate to a supremely powerful invisible reality accepted as such. Artistic world-intuitions are those that amplify the significance of actual life-experiences; metaphysical world-intuitions are those that aim to establish a single, universally valid system of knowledge of the whole (chap. 2). Dilthey identifies three main types of metaphysical world-intuition (chaps. 3–5). *Naturalism*, represented by Democritus, Epicurus, Hobbes, Hume, and the positivists, grows out of an immediate consciousness of the human being's subjection to the forces of life in nature. *The idealism of freedom*, from Socrates to Cicero to Kant to Bergson, is motivated by an immediate "heroic" consciousness of discontinuity between human will and nature. *Objective idealism*, as seen in Heraclitus and Parmenides, the Stoics, Spinoza and Leibniz, Schleiermacher, and Hegel, expresses an expanded sympathetic regard for the world as a whole. In each case it is possible to show how characteristically recurring doctrines are rooted in the basic orientation of the world-intuition—as, for example, materialist ontology, sensationalist epistemology, and a cosmology of empirical uniformity articulate the sense of naturalism. Thus, each attitude is operationalized as an *approach*. The central principle of variation among the metaphysical attitudes can be expressed in terms of spatial relationship, the three options representing determination of the inner by the outer, of the outer by the inner, and of balanced codetermination of inner and outer. No one view can overcome the others because no such view is provably true. No one of the basic orientations is compulsory. Yet a world-intuition can be compelling, according to Dilthey, if it clearly expresses "a typical condition of a human soul" (49). It survives in the struggle for influence among constantly proliferating intuitions (28).

The first appeal to which the philosophical (or religious or artistic) attitude responds, then, is that of the *life-enigma*. Compelling interpretations of the life-enigma become chief appeals in turn, promising the most effective response to the first appeal. Dilthey notes that the later adherents of a world-intuition type can be acutely conscious of their affinity with predecessors and of their shared rivalry with adherents of other types (a point made especially about the idealists of freedom, 61–62). Each approach can be adopted by colleagues, by long-term movements, or by whole cultures as part of the fabric of what Dilthey, following Hegel, conceives as living "objective spirit," a larger appellant being in its own right. For Dilthey himself—and, he thinks, for his generation, living at the end of metaphysics—the supreme intellectual appeal and sovereign approach is "historical consciousness," thanks to which he is able to appreciate the force of all human intuitions in their largest *Zusammenhang*. Historical consciousness is the higher realization that the conflicts of world-intuitions are grounded in life itself (44).[122] Experimentally interpreted cultural history provides the most basic mise-en-scène for critical directive thinking.

Jaspers on Types of Subject–Object Relation

Karl Jaspers achieves a new synthesis and explicitness in attitude thinking in *Psychologie der Weltanschauungen* (1919), where he expands, refines, and attempts to ground Dilthey's classification scheme for world-intuitions by elucidating further the structure and dynamics of subjective existence along Kantian and Kierkegaardian lines, emphasizing subjective freedom. He proceeds with existential wariness, for Kierkegaard especially has made him sensitive to the attitude issues raised by theorizing about attitude. He claims to offer only an "observational" contribution, not a "prophetic" one—to see the possible movements of the human spirit, not to make any (v, 2–7).[123] (Is this an authentic and feasible scruple? Kierkegaard avows such restraint often, but always with some degree of irony.)

Jaspers asserts that the fundamental variable from which different world-intuitions proceed is subject-object relation (21). The "Ur-phenomenon" of subject-object division can be regarded as a primal question to which realized subject-object relations are answers (42). There are "sphere-forming" a priori formats of subject-object relation such as the rational and the aesthetic, in themselves neither subjective nor objective (25–26). On the subject side of the relation we find possibilities of "attitude" (*Einstellung*—a "placing-in" of or by the subject), while on the object side are correlated possibilities of "world-picture" (*Weltbild*) (41). (Dilthey had said that a world-intuition must contain an "inner relation" between "life-experience" and "world-picture.")[124] Jaspers credits Kant with the basic insight that an unknown life moves behind the forms of subject and object, becoming comprehensible through them though unaccountable in itself (13, 27). "The fundamental thought of our . . . inquiry is that of a variety of relations between subject and object, of many meanings that subject and object, in their lack of fixity, can take on" (21).

In the realizing of subject-object relation there are evolutions, hierarchies, and mixtures of *Einstellungen* and *Weltbilder* alike. How then do we know whether a certain attitude or world-picture is actually in force? What is decisive in determining the presence of an attitude is whether we reach or fail to reach understanding.

> People reach reciprocal understanding with each other only by communicating within the same attitude. When they proceed in different attitudes they live, speak, think and act past each other. Insofar as attitudes stand next to each other as different spheres of experience, a world-intuition can affirm an individual attitude, isolating and absolutizing it, and on that basis negate others . . . [but] insofar as attitudes can be built on each other in a vital and hierarchical way, one subordinated to another and maintained only in relative independence, a reciprocal understanding . . . can come from different attitudes that are similarly directed to the same point on a pyramid. An example of the first relation is the conflict of active and contemplative, of rational and aesthetic, of epicurean and ascetic; examples of the second relation are the reciprocal understandings [accessible to those oriented to] the rational and the aesthetic within [the orientation to] the mystical or the ideational, of [those oriented to] enjoyment and ascesis within the orientation to self-formation, of [those oriented to] activity and contemplation within enthusiasm. (51)

We can picture the relation between attitude and reciprocal understanding on the basis of a literal translation of *Einstellung* as "placing-in": subjects who place-in in the same way are subjects who can be in, or be headed toward, the same place. Our attitude discernments reflect our extensive experience of finding ourselves placed together and not together.

Another kind of attitude discernment concerns the degree to which an attitude has the full effect proper to its kind. All actual attitudes are somewhat "inauthentic," somewhat lacking in the depth and force they ideally should have: we think and say things without fully possessing the relevant experience, feeling, or insight, for example (36). At best we can discriminate relatively authentic embodiments of an attitude from relatively inauthentic embodiments. A common pathology of attitude is *formalization*, in which for the sake of definiteness and completeness the general form of an attitude is affirmed at the expense of engagement with the concrete contents of the life it forms—the particularity of the stirrings of motivation, the individuality of the beings encountered. Thus, for example, "humanitarian love" might replace love of actual human beings (39).

Jaspers does not wish to argue that there is a single sovereign *Einstellung*—as we will see presently, the larger structure of his attitude conception leads him to make a claim of this sort for "faith" at what he regards as a more fundamental level—but he does note that the *Einstellung* of enthusiasm superordinates itself to others inasmuch as it moves toward overcoming all subject-object opposition. "In the enthusiastic attitude, people feel in their innermost substance, in their essential being, supported or—what is the same—grasped by the totality, the substantial, the essential of the world" (117–18). Clearly, enthusiasm is closely related to mysticism, but an important difference is that enthusiasm still moves within subject-object relation and features longing, restlessness, and the stress of momentary conditions. In contrast to reflexively rational and aesthetic attitudes, the enthusiastic attitude opens up to infinite being in such a way that all past, present, and future aspects of experience become the content of a lively present (114). Jaspers identifies enthusiasm with love, which between persons achieves "perfect understanding" in depth (124).

Attitudes and world-pictures are merely formal possibilities. They only become real when they are activated in the life of spirit (*Geist*). If an attitude can be taken or abandoned, can be turned in one direction or another in hierarchical relations with other attitudes, what then most fundamentally motivates the taking of an attitude? Jaspers identifies the most basic expression of our existence as our *valuing*. Intuitively familiar spiritual types like pessimism, individualism, rationalism, and skepticism represent ways in which we value (219–21). (Jasper's "spiritual type" corresponds schematically to Dilthey's *Lebensstimmung*, though Jaspers conceives spiritual type more as Kant would, as a function of spontaneity, while Dilthey conceives *Lebensstimmung* more as Schleiermacher would, as a fruit of experience.)[125] The original upsurge of valuing cannot be objectified or grounded, although values are (like attitudes and world-pictures) abstracted from our concrete valuing, and ideal rank-orderings of value are formed into a prescribed way of life (220–22). Valuing is the spontaneous adhesion or repulsion of the center of intending, *Geist*, in relation to all its possibilities; it is the most basic qualification of the "how" of subject-object relation so far as the subject's own powers are concerned. (On this point, Jaspers is closer to Nietzsche's view of subjective freedom than to Kierkegaard's.)[126]

It is important to distinguish the attitude descriptions and claims that pertain to *Einstellungen* from those that pertain to the spiritual types. Why, for example, does Jaspers treat enthusiasm as an *Einstellung* but pessimism as

a spiritual type? In what sense is pessimism more basic or subjectively ultimate? The answer lies in the essential reference of the spiritual types to what
Jaspers calls "limit-situations" (corresponding to the principal concrete facets
of Dilthey's "life-enigma"), problems that both shape and threaten finite existence. "The common feature [of limit-situations] is that—in this objective
world of subject-object separation—nothing is firm, there is no indubitable
absolute, no footing [*Halt*]" (229). We are subject to unresolvable contradic-
tions in our rational interpretation of the world (for example, in the Kantian
antinomy between the requirement to think of all causes as conditional and
the requirement to think of at least one cause as unconditional), in our practical deliberation (recognizing that the pursuit of any value generates disvalue,
as for instance my project of serving humanity as a writer requires me to exploit
people who can help me publish), and in our inner life in which desires are
bound to aversions and pleasures to pains (233–39). All our actual achievements and experiences are transitory, and death ends everything. And yet:

> Human beings are relatively seldom in despair. They have a place to stand,
> before they are liable to be thrown into despair . . . We ask what the
> conditions are for [attaining this] and thereby we come to the center of the
> spiritual types. Which footing they have, how they have it, seek it, find it,
> and keep it, that is the characteristic expression of their living powers. If we
> ask about spiritual types, we ask where people have their footing. (229)

The most basic of all questions is whether to say Yes or No to life as a whole
(285). Pessimism is a life-approach at this level.

An apparently suitable word for attitude with this most basic and (in the
Kierkegaardian sense) passionate qualification, referring to the *Halt* of existence, would be *Haltung*, which carries the sense of an inward formation of
comportment. Significantly, Jaspers does not use this word, although a number of philosophical anthropologists do later.[127] Jaspers does not want to falsify
human freedom by construing it as a "nature" or even by crediting it with a
settled "way" that would count as an "answer" to the deep questions of mental-
spiritual existence.

> By spiritual types we understand principles, ideas, powers. That is to say that
> they never become perfectly transparent, that we never know if we ulti-
> mately apprehend *one* power or many, or how many. And it follows that
> spiritual types are not to be placed beside each other in clear distinction like
> world-pictures . . . An attempt to characterize them must place *movement* in
> the foreground . . . What is important for us are processes. (285)

Jaspers's account of rationalism as a spiritual type should be compared
with Heraclitean rationalism, the basic disposition to heed the Logos that is
common. Whereas Heraclitus's rationalist affirmation responds to the problem of divergent private understandings, for Jaspers the great challenge lies in
the conflicted and ultimately ungrounded character of mental-spiritual life.[128]
Rationalism relative to this situation is the orientation to affirm against all

factors of indeterminacy that there is, at least in principle, a "place to stand" in life, a framework that can be lived in—or, in other words, that there is such a thing as validity, that there are "right" and teachable ways. This is "the *Halt* in the limited" (304). But Kant has taught us through his account of the antinomies of reason that rationalism overcomes itself, and Kierkegaard and Nietzsche have shown that the power and responsibility of the living subject in limit-situations cannot be settled on a firm footing or within a firm framework. "Philosophical doctrines do not coincide with the existence of human beings." "The intellectual world-intuition stands in various relations of tension with the actually lived world-intuition" (312).

Could there be anything like a "*Halt* in the Infinite," then? Jaspers finds a sort of footing for the ungrounded freedom of spirit in the basic attitude of faith. Spirit lives and develops through non-rational turning points, objectively unjustifiable resolutions in concrete situations, "conversions," metamorphoses; faith is acceptance of this situation, an affirmation of the power of the subject's freedom in opposition to impersonal certainty (334–37).

As becomes ever clearer in Jaspers's later work, from his perspective faith is the sovereign attitude, as the freedom of spirit is the supreme appeal. In an exchange with the Christian theologian Rudolf Bultmann, he figures authentic faith as a "liberal faith" that is "self-sustained, drawing its strength directly from transcendence . . . In liberalism everything is centered on the responsibility of man thrown back upon himself."[129] This commitment implies an endless project of attempting to comprehend reality and so a rejection of the orthodox conception of revelation.

> The belief that God . . . has revealed himself directly at one place and time and only there and then, makes God appear as a fixed thing, an object in the world. This objective entity is supposed not only to be revered on the basis of tradition, but also to possess the absoluteness of godhead . . . Liberal faith rejects this conception of revelation. It recognizes that the revelation of truth is a mystery, a series of sudden illuminations in the history of the mind; it recognizes that we are ignorant of how men arrived at this revelation, and that some of its elements have not been comprehended . . . It is not true that the liberal believer presumes to decide what is and what is not possible for God. But as a philosopher he is aware that objective knowledge is subject to conditions rooted in the structure of Being as it is given to us.[130]

This attitude toward the real character of human existence is linked to an attitude toward the potentially supreme appeal of an actual You (*Du*):

> You reproach me for ignoring the earnestness of the summons, of the encounter . . . all I can say is: The fact is, I know a You, I know a summons and encounter only among men. From the texts of the past only men speak to me, and these texts tell me something of their state of mind. I cannot deny that transcendence may be experienced as a You. For a finite being, which arrives at itself only in a dialogue with a You, the fiction of such a You as a cipher of transcendence at climactic moments of inward clarity

("and then one became two") is philosophically legitimate. Such an experience is marvelous indeed. But I believe that it also has its dangers. He who has found his God can so easily withdraw from communication in the world . . . If you question my thinking on the ground that I do not realize the seriousness of the encounter with the godhead, I question your thinking on the ground that you do not realize the seriousness of communication among men.[131]

In the later Jaspers, a passion for interhuman communication—a Heraclitean Logos-rationalism that can be called reasonableness, a commitment as much to sharing understanding as to rendering every theme appropriately determinate for cognition—becomes a dominant qualification of the sovereign attitude of faith.[132]

Heidegger on How We Are

Like Jaspers, Heidegger too aims at a critical synthesis of the major insights of the great German (plus Kierkegaard) conversation about fundamental orientation. Insofar as that conversation is a debate between claims of priority for a determination of life's meaningfulness by the subject (in *Gesinnung* and by a priori form-giving) and claims of priority for a determination of life's meaningfulness by reality as a whole (through *Stimmung* and *Zusammenhang*), Heidegger comes down with Schleiermacher and Dilthey on the side of a connectedness of subjects with reality that is given from reality—the Infinite for Schleiermacher, "life" for Dilthey, Being for Heidegger, the Whole or the Center of centers in any case. *Gesinnung* in the guise of "resoluteness" does have an important role to play in Heidegger's *Being and Time*, but only as related essentially to disclosures of "mood" (*Stimmung*) and "attunement" or "state-of-mind" (*Befindlichkeit*). Failure to recognize the subordination of *Gesinnung* to *Stimmung* in Heidegger's larger argument led to a common reading of *Being and Time* as an "existentialist" appeal to subjective freedom.[133] But Heidegger meant very early to be working on a radical corrective to idealism. He opposed the neo-Kantians much in the spirit in which Schleiermacher opposed Fichte.[134]

Heidegger proclaims himself dissatisfied with Dilthey's work as with "every tendency toward a philosophical anthropology" that piles together various considerations affecting the definition and meaningfulness of human existence without a perspicuous derivation of concepts.[135] And he thinks that Jaspers cannot justify his supposedly observational method in *Psychologie der Weltanschauungen*.[136] But he credits Dilthey with the decisive turn away from metaphysical construction toward the wholeness of the actual, under the rubric of "life," and sees in Jaspers's book a potentially pivotal inquiry into "the original motivational situations in which the fundamental experiences of philosophy have arisen."[137] Let us consider now how these two main concerns of Heidegger, the wholeness of the actual and the radical derivation of meaning from "original situations," are worked out in *Being and Time*'s distinctive attitude theses.

The most radical question about our being that can be formulated in the manner of Kantian transcendental inquiry is, How is it possible to inquire into the meaning of being? What most basic structure or event enables the realization or pursuit of meaning at all, the presence or promise of being at all? This question can never have a *known* infinitely radical sense because it must always be formulated on a ground the deeper ground of which remains obscure. For example, it can be pursued as the question of *What really exists?* on the basis of assumptions about the nature of entities and the role of entitativeness in reality that remain obscure. Or it can be pursued as the question of *What can we meaningfully think?* on the strength of assumptions about the nature and place of subjecthood in reality. We can never straightforwardly ask and answer the *ultimate* ultimate question. But Heidegger thinks we can *be oriented* to the infinite depth of philosophical questioning; indeed, we can adjust our concept of Being to make it a function of this depth and our active, fundamentally problematic relationship to it. As we saw earlier in Heidegger's appeal conception, the very idea of "phenomenon" as any sort of showing, giving, or obtaining can be radicalized so that it converges with the movement of questioning; and Being is then thought neither as an ultimate quasi-material potentiality nor as an ultimately stabilizing Form or Forming of all things, but strictly as the ultimate phenomenon, ultimate *as* the concern of questioners. The wholeness of reality, therefore, is wrought as well as disclosed in the practice of fundamental ontology as Heidegger understands it—but wrought more fundamentally by a receptive asking than by an a priori formation, so that it is more appropriate to think in terms of a primal *situation* than of a metaphysically objective "reality."

Dilthey expressed the real belonging-together of subject and reality as *Zusammenhang*, a conception that is admirably flexible and yet ontologically provocative, if not debilitating, in that it assumes already-set-up, already-understood things that can be brought into togetherness.[138] Dilthey's view was restricted by his Cartesian assumption that the center of connection is the reflexively conscious subject. In order to displace the center of relatedness from the Cartesian subject to Being, Heidegger adopts the term *Bewandtnis*, "involvement," in his analysis of the worldhood of the world. *Bewandtnis* expresses the relatedness of a turning toward (*bewenden*) each other of beings (§18).[139] (Another aspect of the relatedness that is essential to worldly being is an everyday always-already-being-concerned-with-things [*Besorgen*] that is presupposed by any specific intention [p. 57].) Conceiving the centering of beings as *Bewandtnis* allows inclusion of the turnings of beings in relation to each other—their always already being situated in relation to each other in some way, and their being on the way toward a certain relatedness with each other—in our conception of the beings themselves.[140] (Although a *Bewandtnis*-world is in one obvious way totally opposite to Leibniz's world of autarchic monads, we can see also that Heideggerian *Bewandtnis* is prepared by the Leibnizian idea that every monad is essentially referred to every other and to the whole according to the nature of perception in the regime of plenitude.)

Turning is the key to how *we* always already find ourselves thrown in a world as disclosed in the everyday phenomenon of moods (*Stimmungen, Gestimmtsein*) and state-of-mind (*Befindlichkeit*). "In this 'how one is,' having a mood brings Being to its 'there' " (134). "The way in which the mood discloses is not one in which we look at thrownness, but one in which we turn toward or turn away [*als An- und Abkehr*]" (135). "Ontologically . . . the *first* essential characteristic of states-of-mind is that *they disclose Dasein in its thrownness, and—proximally and for the most part—in the manner of an evasive turning-away*" from the difficulty of our being (136). That is, we are always "fallen" into the evasions of idle talk and idle curiosity. Yet we are attuned to the vexed profundity of this situation by certain ontologically revelatory moods. Anxiety, notably, discloses that the primordial character of our being—the binding in all its relationships and the moving of all its motions—is neither a form nor a matter that can be taken for granted, as would be implied by a definition of humanity as "rational animal," but rather *care* (182). "Self" and "will" are possible on the basis of care, not vice versa (194, 322). More in tune with Kierkegaard's passion than with Schleiermacher's peaceful repose on the bosom of the Infinite, Heidegger portrays the anthropological center as a bottomless being-troubled about a situation that cannot be resolved—freedom thrown into actual situations it cannot choose or control, projected toward open possibility and death, and always "falling" into estrangement from itself in the everyday life of the they-self (284).[141]

Insofar as Dasein accepts its own fundamental irresolution with suitable circumspection, it "wants to have a conscience" and is "resolute"; its resoluteness is its primordial authentic disclosure (296–97). Kantian *Gesinnung*, typically presented as sovereign by virtue of its independence of worldly contingencies, here has its authenticity conditions recast in "resoluteness," which is a function of *actual* situations and just for that reason essentially involves engagement with the *indefiniteness* of any situation for Dasein:

> One would completely misunderstand the phenomenon of resoluteness if one should want to suppose that this consists simply in taking up possibilities which have been proposed and recommended, and seizing hold of them. *The resolution is precisely the disclosive projection and determination of what is factically possible at the time.* To resoluteness, the *indefiniteness* characteristic of every potentiality-for-Being into which Dasein has been factically thrown, is something that necessarily *belongs.* (298)

The gold standard of Dasein's authentic address of existence is the "uttermost possibility which lies ahead of every factical potentiality-for-Being of Dasein": death, the possibility of the impossibility of any existence at all (262). "It is only in the anticipation of death that resoluteness . . . has reached the *authentic certainty* which *belongs* to it" (302). The privileged place given to "anticipation" (*Vorlaufen*) as Dasein's address of a possibility that can never be present indicates most sharply the essential inflection of care by temporality, and further, a privilege of the future in this inflection. "Primordial and authentic temporality temporalizes itself in terms of the authentic future and in such a way that in having been futurally, it first of all awakens the Present." "Only so far as it is futural can Dasein *be* authentically as having been. The character of 'having been' arises, in a certain way, from the future" (326). The past is produced from present moments, and the present is funded by the past only insofar as the past and present are already qualified by the future. A "historical" or "historic" happening is meaningful to us because it involves Dasein's futural address of possibility, and it is most meaningful when it does so in conscious anticipation of the end of every concrete set of human possibilities—heroically.[142] An effective historical testimony transmits this understanding and mood. "*Authentic Being-towards-death—that is to say, the finitude of temporality—is the hidden basis of Dasein's historicality*" (386).

Temporality is a phenomenon of care. It is orientational, and it makes a whole of Dasein's relations with actuality and possibility. It is not to be defined by the derivative idea of segments of an objectified time-line or even by the idea of a succession of events, either of which obscures the true unity and finitude of temporality. Future, past, and present are primordially the phenomena of the "towards-oneself," the "back-to," and the "letting-oneself-be-encountered-*by*" (328–29).[143] These are qualifications of basic attitude parameters.

* * *

In contrast to Kierkegaard's prescriptive move of dramatizing a divergence between authentic concern for personal existence and the evasions of sensibility and rationality, Heidegger makes the theoretical move of representing all our thoughts and practices, lucid and "fallen" alike, as founded on and derived from the most-basic phenomenon of care. The drama of Kierkegaard's existential alternative is worked into the fabric of this phenomenon. Heidegger intends to be an ontologist "educated by possibility" in the sense given this phrase in *The Concept of Anxiety*; presumably, he wishes not to be counted among the professorial blockheads whom Kierkegaard ridicules for abstracting from their own existence in their theories of existence.[144] But he also means to register the import of Kierkegaard's existential thinking more fully by reformulating it in the context of fundamental ontology. Heidegger's "theory" is not a world-picture but an attestation of *how* we find ourselves existing, entangled in the issue of the meaning of being. An adequate theoretical discourse at this level must be a lucid performance of this "how." The distinctive specification of the "how" of our existing that Heidegger offers in his theorizing is, as we have seen, "phenomenology" as most-radical questioning, an illimitable devotion to the meaning-constituting "how" of being right up to the limit of our capacity to participate in meaning-formation. For Kierkegaard, the choice to become a personal self is the change that makes all the difference to the meaning of existence; Heidegger elucidates the Kierkegaardian claim by showing that the "how" of care is *what* is changed to make all that difference, is *what* the difference is made *in*, is *what* Kierkegaardian passion is an infinitizing *of*— this "what" referring not to an objectified entity but rather to an always occurring, always presupposed meaning, the meaning figured as a "what" only in the sense provisionally required by the grammar of questioning.

Heideggerian questioning could be understood as a fundamentally aesthetic refinement of sensitivity if Heidegger were not concerned as much with an appeal as with an attitude. The "how" of Dasein's discovery of its thrown pose and anxious poise involves the "call of conscience," also termed the "call of care," which is Being's call.[145] As in Kierkegaard, the authentic disturbance of one's existence is predicated on relationship with an Other. The exteriority of Heidegger's calling Other, that is, the otherness of Being specifically in relation to the evasive everyday being of Dasein, is portrayed as an unnerving silence of nonparticipation in our concrete immersion—the education of possibility. For Kierkegaard, the confrontation with anxiety is preparatory to taking up the spiritual life of relation with a divine Other. The Other that Kierkegaard is living toward is not the Other that Heidegger is questioning toward, just as the attitude of faith to which Kierkegaard leads is not the ontological attitude to which Heidegger leads. (A religious attitude is part of a historically and psychologically concrete experience, Heidegger claims in his 1927 lecture on "Phenomenology and Theology,"[146] whereas a philosophical attitude belongs purely to the investigation of the meaning conditions of all experiences.)

* * *

After *Being and Time* Heidegger heightens the importance of attunement. In "What is Metaphysics?" (1929) he calls the disclosure of attunement the "ground-phenomenon" of our existence and claims that the meaning of the central metaphysical question posed by Leibniz, "Why is there something rather than nothing?" comes from a prior disclosure of Nothing in the mood of anxiety.[147] Herein lies the fundamental motivation for theoretical comportment in general.

> Only because Nothing is revealed in the very basis of our *Da-sein* is it possible for the utter strangeness of what-is to dawn on us. Only when the strangeness of what-is forces itself upon us does it awaken and invite our wonder. Only because of wonder, that is, the revelation of Nothing, does the "Why?" spring to our lips. Only because this "Why?" is possible as such can we seek for reasons and proofs in a definite way. Only because we can ask and prove are we fated to become enquirers in this life.[148]

Heidegger tries to make clear in "On the Essence of Truth" (1943) that attunement is a fundamental manner of disclosure, not to be confused with a factual "experience" that might or might not be credited with a disclosive effect. Truth itself is the "revelatory 'letting-be' of what-is" in a fundamental event of resonance (a further specification of *Being and Time*'s *Bewandtnis*):

> Every overt mode of behavior vibrates [*schwingt*] with this "letting-be" and relates itself to this or that actuality. In the sense that freedom means participation in the revealment of what-is-in-totality, freedom has attuned [*abgestimmt*] all behavior to this from the start. But this attunement or "mood" can never be understood as "experience" and "feeling" because, were it so understood, it would at once be deprived of its being and would only be interpreted in terms of, say, "life" and "soul"—which only *appear* to exist in their own right so long as they contain any distortion and misinterpretation of that attunement.[149]

In *Fundamental Concepts of Metaphysics* (1929/1930), Heidegger dwells on the problem of awakening the right fundamental attunement for philosophical inquiry. He believes the problem of the philosophical starting point is at the same time a problem of culture, for if we are to make the right start in philosophy, we must become alive to the attunement we are already embedded in.[150] Contemporary writing in philosophy of culture, typically noninvolving and sensationalistic, implies that profound boredom is our generally characteristic way of registering our alienation from Being.[151]

By the time of *Contributions to Philosophy* (1936–38), Heidegger is more concerned to speak to the dangerous human infatuation with technology, more willing to portray Being as an agent whose directive we are to heed, and more prone to speak of the mission of philosophy with devotional overtones. He plunges into the task of awakening right mindfulness in a more clearly prescriptive tone, proposing

> once again to give historical man a goal: namely, *to become the founder and preserver of the truth of be-ing*, to *be* the 't/here' [*Da*] as the ground that is used by be-ing's essential sway: to be *care*, not as a minor concern with some arbitrary thing, nor as denial of exultation and power, but more originarily than all that, because this care is always a care *"for the sake of be-ing"—not the be-ing of man, but the be-ing of beings in the whole.* (12)[152]

If the necessary fundamental attunement for this endeavor stays away, there will be only "a forced rattling of concepts and empty words" (16). This fundamental attunement can be named "in a distant way" as a trinity: startled dismay (*Erschrecken*), which tears familiar meanings apart to open us to Being's initiatives; reservedness (*Verhaltenheit*), the poised midpoint between moving away and moving toward Being and so "the ground of care"; and deep awe (*Scheu*), the manner in which one approaches and remains near to what is inherently most remote (11–12, 25). Though the coming of the fundamental attunement cannot be brought about as an intended happening, thought can prepare for the "crossing" to that other beginning (16–17). Not unlike a volcanic eruption, attunement is said to be "the *Versprühung* of the *Erzitterung* of be-ing as *Ereignis* in Da-sein"—which one might gloss as the flashing out of Being's own dynamic urgency in the event of a conscious being's existence. As a primal coordination principle, this is rather dissimilar to Leibniz's idea that we are united with God by the truths of reason; yet Heidegger would claim to witness in these terms to the underlying resonance and motivation of Leibniz's idea insofar as it is genuinely ontological.

One final observation relating to the "turn" of Heidegger's thinking after *Being and Time* will be important for our inquiry: Heidegger's basic orientation turns from the future, in treating Being-toward-death as the principle of Dasein's authenticity, to the past, in calling on Dasein to become involved in the *preservation* of Being's truth.[153] His style increasingly is one of a historical heeding. Heidegger does not develop a thematic of "faith" as Jaspers did and as he helped his theological colleague Bultmann to do. His orientation is signaled by a different devotion word: "For questioning is the piety of thought."[154] Can we hope to identify the fundamental motivation of a turn so fundamental? Perhaps not, but a basic point worth stating about the situation as regards the relative availability and force of possible basic attitudes in philosophy is that the alternative Heidegger intimates with his piety talk would otherwise go without witness. Heidegger's mission is to avert this orientational impoverishment.

* * *

Heidegger's attitude theses can, of course, be challenged in a variety of ways. One can agree with Michel Henry that Heidegger aligns mood and attunement too much with understanding and transcendence, missing affectivity's immanent revelation of being's self-sensing of power.[155] One can accept Heidegger's basic conception but disagree with the content or emphasis of his exemplifications: for example, one can choose to give more anthropological or ontological weight to happier moods, or assign the temporal dimensions of moods differently, or diagnose the general attunements of contemporary culture differently.[156] Or one can object that Heidegger's discussion of attunement is distorted in that it obscures possibly decisive valuational differences among moods by subordinating the distinctive "what" of each mood to the "how"-structure moods have in common.[157]

Still more basically, one can argue that attunements ought not to be held fundamental in the constitution of meaning but rather should be subordinated to cognition or practice or comportment-in-relationship understood differently. From a logical empiricist perspective, for example, the theme of attunement is largely a residue of psychological and linguistic confusion; the orientation to scientific observation, in contrast, consistently proves itself as practically effectual and rationally negotiable. From a Marxian perspective, Heidegger's concentration on mood reflects bourgeois society's fiction of an independent self-owning subject and forms no radical alternative to Cartesian subjectivism or German idealism; the best-warranted orientation is instead a teleological orientation toward working to eliminate the social-structural causes of oppression (including the false consciousness of subjectivist philosophies). (Ernst Bloch's philosophy of hope, which will be considered in the next chapter in its connection with developments in religious thought, is of this general form.)[158] The general Heideggerian reply to such challenges is that they fail to think with the greatest originality or radicalism. They exhibit relations with Being at particular junctures in the history of the thinking of Being, in particular folds of the fabric of that thinking, while remaining unconscious of their deepest motivation.

Still more radical are Nietzsche- and Freud-inspired critiques of the very principle of psychic, semantic, or semiological centering. These can all be called "play" arguments inasmuch as they seek ultimate disclosure and reward in release from the more confining constraints of centering. Seen from this angle, the important Nietzsche is not the one who, in the voice of Zarathustra, endorses a sun-like generous power and love of eternal return, but the one who ironizes all prophecy, even all univocal discourse, and agrees to believe only in an unseriously dancing god.[159] The important Freud is the one who unveils the indeterminately various "desiring machines" in the psyche rather than the one who organizes desire into a coherent "Oedipal" system.[160] (The important Heidegger, moreover, is not the heir of Schleiermacher, who obediently hearkens to the call of Being, but the heir of Nietzsche, who shows the impossibility of grasping a secure cognitive foundation.) Play takes over as a sovereign orientation toward turning to new things in new ways—an attitude that takes the subject more than it is taken by the subject, demolishing what Deleuze calls the cult of interiority.[161] The ideal of plenitude is understood as an ideal of ontological openness in accordance with a supreme appeal of possibility. There is a "Dionysian" self-abandonment to energy and transformation rather than an "Apollinian" trust in cognitively fixed forms and entities (to use Nietzsche's categories from *The Birth of Tragedy*).

It would be madness to contend for one universally valid way of adjudicating the claims of science, politics, play (least of all!), and fundamental ontology, but we can be clear at least about the ground Heidegger occupies within the rivalry of intellectual priorities. He too is an exponent of the attempt by modern philosophy to renew the Axial Age founding of the individual hearer-thinker as the holder and exemplifier of a sovereign attitude in essential relation with a supreme appeal. The force of this position is a function of the communicative situation philosophers are in, the communicative situation that makes philosophers (and gurus of all sorts) relevant at all: we find ourselves in a marketplace of ideas in which the meaning of everything is on offer to all and will be adjudicated subject by subject. I cannot fundamentally choose to leave this marketplace or seek *you* elsewhere. If there is a better mode of life than this, *I* cannot discuss it with *you*. The meanings of scientific, political, or playful agendas will be discussed in this mode if they are discussed at all. They will all be construed and will strive against each other as isms, basic orientations we are called upon to take.

Significant alternatives to Heidegger's view that deliberately remain within and extend the appeal-attitude project will be arguments that construe the preeminent appeal and attitude differently. The most important of these alternatives, I believe, and the one that brings the biggest change to the basic form of the project, is the philosophy of responsibility to the other being that is introduced by dialogical philosophers and subsequently developed by Levinas. This philosophy of responsibility is noteworthy also in deeply affecting the thinking of one of the most acute practitioners of the very differently motivated philosophy of play, Jacques Derrida.

The Philosophy of Responsibility from
Buber to Levinas and Derrida

An aspect of the *Lebenszusammenhang* that attracted Dilthey's attention is the problem of the experience of a being as "real," independent of the experiencer. He theorized that the basis of the experience of realness is the feeling that an object resists the subject's will.[162] Dilthey's student Buber likewise approaches the question of an exterior-to-the-subject reality on the basis of a prior confidence in a given connectedness of beings in "life" and "lived-experience" (*Erlebnis*).[163] But the answer Buber gives in *I and Thou* stresses opportunity and gift rather than obstacle and frustration. What makes this shift possible is the opening up of the question of realness to accommodate a fundamentally different mode of existence than that everyday sort of "experience" (*Erfährung*) in which we meet things as disposable and problematical. In "experience" it is always possible and appropriate to refer to things in the third person; Buber calls it the sphere of "I-It" relation. The Other *with* which I *am*, however, is not a content of "experience" at all but rather the fellow-being to whom I say You. In this mode of existence I am rescued from private arbitrariness, provided with a sufficiently exigent focus of attention—a centering—and drawn into a higher-energy intentional state of participating in reciprocity so that I am wholly actualized.[164] (As we saw in chapter 3, Buber's expansion of reality is formally similar to the heterothesis that leads Rickert to the realm of irreal values. The same move that opens the possibility of a superior appeal opens the possibility of a more adequate attitude.)

The I-You and I-It relations are *Haltungen*, "attitudes" of a sort intermediate between the receptive centering to which Schleiermacher and Dilthey were oriented and the active centering to which Kant and the German Idealists were oriented. One does not simply find oneself in a *Haltung* or have it come over one like a mood or a "religious experience"; one *enters* it *by* speaking. But it is not the product of a willful grasping or construction. To speak a basic word is to *be in* a relation *in* which the speaker is posed as fully (I-You) or only partially (I-It) realized, "destined" (I-You) or more at liberty to behave willfully (I-It). The I-You *Haltung* is specified as achieving the balance of "reciprocity" between the inner and outer centering of the subject so that it escapes the conflict between receptivity- and spontaneity-oriented attitude theses. "[The Other] does not stand outside you, it touches your ground; and if you say 'soul of my soul' you have not said too much. But beware of trying to transpose it into your soul—that way you destroy it."[165]

A complementary point about how appeal and response occur supports the plurality and balance of centerings. It is stated pneumatically: "Spirit is not in the I but between I and You. It is not like the blood that circulates in you but like the air in which you breathe. Man lives in the spirit when he able to respond to his You."[166] Airlike spirit, Buber says elsewhere, is not a *being*, not something that can be tracked continuously or expected, but a *happening*.[167] The locus of this happening and of directive culture generally is the "sphere of the between."[168] A spiritual being is one that is able to be oriented to the You in such a way as to live in the between. "Spirit," "the between," and "the life of encounter" become Buberian ideals.[169]

Buber's most important innovation in the appeal-attitude project is that he defines supreme appeal and sovereign attitude *both* in traditionally centering, stabilizing terms *and* in a decentering, irrealizing fashion. On the one side, he has much in common with the main line of modern (especially German) philosophy: a clear, directive a priori principle (You-saying) correlated with an authentic selfhood within (the I of relation) and an all-organizing referent without (the Eternal You in whom all lines of relation intersect).[170] These conceptions support a discourse of destiny (*Bestimmung*), a discourse that *answers* the questions raised by free individual existence.[171] But on the other, expressly pneumatological side, Buber's theme becomes the availability of the subject to recognize and interact with other beings in unforeseen ways; here the implied supreme ideal is "inspiration" for its own sake, involving new actualizations of the community of beings. These novelties pose or evoke fresh *questions* about the shape and direction of life-in-encounter. Buber means to hold the deepest orientative centering and the most radical dynamism of encounter together, the dynamism making for an orientation that goes under and imperiously commandeers all others, the centering making for a dynamism that always most matters.

Heidegger's project could be described formally in much the same terms. The crucial difference between the two approaches, as I pointed out in chapter 3, lies in Buber's refraction of all meaningfulness through actual Other beings.

* * *

The appeal-principle of exteriority in Buber is found in the Other Being, paradigmatically an actual presence, rather than in Being as Other. Levinas, who studied with Heidegger, follows Buber against Heidegger in this respect. He rejects the subordination of relations with beings to a relation with Being, seeing in this "ontologism" the expression of a tyrannical theoretical attitude of ideal self-confirmation that has dominated Western philosophy.[172] What Levinas considers to be the authentically metaphysical orientation to relation with the Absolutely Other is realized (in the extraordinary manner in which alone it *can* be realized) by appropriately addressing actual other persons. He endeavors to show this in a concretely phenomenological way, proceeding more in the zigzag manner of *Being and Time* than in the grandly typological neo-Kantian style used by Buber in *I and Thou*; but the question that leads him into the heart of the phenomenon is the same as Buber's question, namely, How do we realize the superordinate meaningfulness of *relationships* with Other *beings*?

Buber's I-You *Haltung* is a happy achievement of mutuality with Other Beings rather than resoluteness with respect to the daunting truth of one's finitude; a foray into the "between" is a success of communion (though not without demands and uncertainties attached).[173] On this point, Levinas is more Heideggerian, at least to the extent of emphasizing forensic associations and a constitutive difficulty in responsibility. The self of Levinasian responsibility is "ashamed" in relation to the Other, required to make apology, to repudiate its natural claim of self-sufficiency.[174] Exteriority sets up an infinite problem of justification. Against the symmetrical reciprocity of Buberian I-You relation, Levinas stresses the "curvature of intersubjective space" whereby the Other (primordially the more dignified *vous* rather than *tu*) commands me from "on high."[175] (More positively expressed, the meaning of all meanings is located in the self's *welcoming* the Other.)[176] In Levinas's later work, it seems that no expression is too extreme for the responsible orientation, which he claims consists of being "obsessed" by the Other and subject to the "persecution" or "hemorrhage" or "psychosis" of Other-concern, "traumatized," in "hostageship" (*la condition ou l'incondition d'otage*), and "substituting" for the Other to the extent even of being responsible for the Other's responsibility.[177]

Levinas has a split relation to the Kantian philosophy of attitude. On the one hand, he appears to be pushing to the extreme the receptivity-oriented attitudinal critique of idealism that we have traced from Schleiermacher to Heidegger. In portraying responsible subjectivity as "a passivity more passive than all passivity," a determination prior to any possible assumption of initiative or responsibility by a self, Levinas obviously sides with *Stimmung* against *Gesinnung*.[178] On the other hand, Levinas thinks that the sense of moral relationship requires a true pluralism of beings, which requires in turn that the intentional centers of individuals not be submerged in impersonal being or mystical participation in collective consciousness. There must be a "separation" of each subject from the whole, an ontological independence, both in the enjoyment of the world and in the formation of intentions; the responsible subject is a commanded *autonomy* whose response is not simply the effect of an outside cause.[179] Thus a place is preserved for the "accountability" sense of responsibility, the presumption of a certain subjective mastery. Making a move analogous to Heidegger's with the "call of conscience," Levinas wants to tie a knot of *Stimmung* and *Gesinnung* wherein a *Stimmung* gives the most fundamental (and rectifying) motivation to a fully alert *Gesinnung*. The difference is that Levinas gives a pluralist interpretation of the being that is called (an "atheist" self, more radically self-pertaining in being separated from Being) and of the being that calls (the Other being, more radically Other than Being).[180]

Levinas presents responsibility as an intellectual schema, like one of the fundamental existential categories of Heidegger's *Being and Time*—so that all actual experiences and intentions are to be interpreted as modes of it—but he also pronounces it "prophetically," that is, from his own center as primordially Other-concerned, as a practical either/or:[181]

> In opposition to the vision of thinkers . . . who require, among the conditions of the world, a freedom without responsibility, a freedom of play, we discern in obsession [with the Other] a responsibility that rests on no free commitment, a responsibility whose entry into being could be effected only without any choice. To be without a choice can seem to be violence only to an abusive or hasty and imprudent reflection, for it precedes the freedom non-freedom couple, but thereby sets up a vocation that goes beyond the limited and egoist fate of him who is only for-himself, and washes his hands of the faults and misfortunes that do not begin in his own freedom or in his present. It is the setting up of a being that is not for itself, but is for all, is both being and disinterestedness. The for itself signifies self-consciousness; the for all, responsibility for the others, support of the universe.[182]

God is located, not at the Buberian point of implied supreme presence where all lines of You-saying meet, but in the trace of an always-departed "immemorial" Otherness in which all Others' traces of Otherness are left.[183] A God who has always already passed by effects a supreme outer centering in a wholly inverted way, wholly as an *opening*, confirming the decisive responsibility of the human subject by pinning it to its centering burden of "support of the universe."[184] This means that Levinas departs from the modern philosophical initiative we have followed, as well as from most Axial Age teachings, in not providing for a centering of the human subject's centering by an objectively greatest, most inclusive Centering. God enters our thinking "an-archically"—perhaps as an integral part of a particular religious scaffolding that enables us to articulate responsibility in a telling way, but in any case not as a grounding principle.[185] God *must* enter somehow—this is Levinas's deepest difference from Nietzsche in understanding the structuring of goodness— because the life of the subject is infinitized as responsibility *for* others, that is, as a response to exterior *centerings*. This means that the interpretation of becoming, suffering, and the glory of self-discharge must all be subordinated to responsibility.

In his ongoing revision of Heidegger's temporal inflection of basic attitude issues, Levinas stresses, in *Totality and Infinity*, the futurity of life-with-the-Other, his emphasis falling on the open horizon of what-might-come-from-the-Other in the way of need or teaching or (in the phenomenon of paternity) simply in existing.[186] In his later publications, the dominant theme is the immemorial passed-ness of alterity implied by the prevoluntary election of the self to responsibility.[187] The supreme antiquity of the thought of the Infinite or the passing of God that registers the transcendence of Other-concern, Levinas says, is "the very diachrony of time . . . noncoincidence, dispossession itself," the distension of real occurrence beyond what can be established by the subject's own meaning-giving or by any standard meaning-giving.[188] All along, Levinas's most fundamental point about time is his disruption of the Buberian alignment of alterity with presence and reciprocity. "Alterity appears as a non-reciprocal relationship—that is, as contrasting strongly with contemporaneous-ness."[189] (Buber might reply that relationship with the Other qualifies temporality as an excess over a present of *graspable* contemporaneity just as it exceeds the past that can be recollected or the future that can be administered as a project, and that if an account of alterity were to bypass the present entirely—which Levinas clearly does not do, as we can see with his appeals to "the face" and sensible "proximity"—it would lose the point of contact with actuality that crucially distinguishes the otherness of responsibility from romantic exoticism.)[190]

Like Buber, Levinas uses pneumatic language to express an orientation governed neither by self-centering nor by objective centering.

> [The responsible self] is out of phase with itself, forgetful in biting in upon itself, in the reference to itself which is the gnawing away at oneself of remorse. These are not events that happen to an empirical ego, that is, to an ego already posited and fully identified, as a trial that would lead it to being more conscious of itself, and make it more apt to put itself in the place of others. What we are here calling oneself, or the other in the same, where inspiration arouses respiration, the very pneuma of the psyche, precedes this empirical order . . . Here we are trying to express the unconditionality of a subject . . . [as] *sub-jectum* . . .[191]

> In human breathing, in its everyday equality, perhaps we have to already hear the breathlessness of an inspiration that paralyzes [self-confirming] essence, that transpierces it with an inspiration by the other, an inspiration that is already expiration, that "rends the soul"! It is the longest breath there is, spirit. Is man not the living being capable of the longest breath in inspiration, without a stopping point, and in expiration, without return? To transcend oneself, to leave one's home to the point of leaving oneself, is to substitute oneself for another.[192]

Though Levinasian subjectivity is decentered, clearly Levinas's *proposal* has a center; the center that focuses the Levinasian pose and poise is the exigent issue and concrete dynamism of the rectification of relationships between persons. Probably the best expression for the unconditionally recommended orientation in this proposal is "responsibility," as for Buber, although Levinasian responsibility is more difficult; the unconditionally exigent appeal it posits is the claim of the actual Other being to be *served*, in contrast to the summons to mutuality that is primary for Buber. In view of Levinas's experiment with pneumatic language in *Otherwise than Being*, we might say that his proposal's ultimate ideal, or standard of experiential and intellectual evaluation, is best conceived as "spirit," again paralleling Buber—though Levinas is deeply wary of the entanglement of *esprit* and *Geist* with the unacceptable cognitive ambitions of idealism and ontologism and cannot speak of "spirit" with Buber's assurance.[193]

The responsibility of hospitality to the Other sounds surpassingly good to us; it gains entry to the heart, as unstoppable as a call for fair dealing but warmer in that it draws on the force of our most optimistic hopes for being received well by others; it becomes a catchphrase. If it is not the attitude that will rectify everything about your life, it is at least an attitude that can trump any other, even fair-mindedness, at any given juncture.

* * *

The most fundamental orientation represented and enacted by Jacques Derrida's philosophy of deconstruction is openness to new events of meaning. These arrive both as loss and gain—loss of the groundings and completions that our meaning-ventures always unfeasibly demand, gain of new possibilities in the "differance" of meanings from themselves. The challenge extended by Derrida, as earlier by Nietzsche, is wholly to affirm all this, to pursue our intentional flourishing in the most cognizant, least repressive way. But a question can always be raised about the orientation of this orientation, about how our responsiveness comes to be turned or is to be turned toward better responses, in an ineliminable spiritual sense of "better." The issue of responsibility, as Buber and Levinas understand it, demands to be taken up as the issue of the fundamental motivation of deconstructive responsiveness in meaning-interpretation and existential affirmation. Even if any particular representation of "fundamental motivation" can be unraveled by deconstructive interpretation, still the unraveling is haunted by the question of motivation. Levinas is the most significant asker of the question for Derrida because his formulation of responsibility is so profoundly deconstructive.[194]

Levinas's point of contact with postmodern play philosophies lies in what is commonly called his non- or anti-foundationalism, that is, his rejection of an intellectually accessible absolute centering of meaning. Levinas does not, of course, abjure the orientation to the Logos that is a precondition of rational discussion. He means to speak intelligibly and accountably as a philosopher. Can he push away his intellectual cake and eat it too? Derrida's first major writing on Levinas, "Violence and Metaphysics" (1964), questions Levinas's attempt to make philosophy host to the "prophetic" theme of the "absolutely

Other."[195] Adopting Heidegger's conception of philosophy as questional and as responsible for elucidating its own origins, Derrida portrays Levinas as speaking compellingly to this project. "Nothing can so profoundly *solicit* the Greek logos—philosophy—[as] this irruption of the totally-other; and nothing can to such an extent reawaken the logos to its origin as to its mortality" (152). Playing on the associations of Hebrew religiosity, Derrida pictures Levinas in a special location: "At the heart of the desert . . . this thought, which fundamentally no longer seeks to be a thought of Being and phenomenality, makes us dream of an inconceivable process of dismantling and dispossession" (83). But Levinas's thought seems doomed to self-contradiction as he purports to set aside conceptions by means of a conception, to indicate a non-object by a noun and an ostensive gesture, to express concern for an actually present being similar to myself as an absolutely mysterious Other, and to treat as possible what he must characterize as impossible.

For our purposes, these odd features of the discourse of relation with the Other can be treated as windows onto the problem of the cognitive stabilization of attitude. How can I serve the Other with no definite intuition or signification of what I am subjected to? Once I do "know what I am dealing with," am I not a master rather than a servant? Or consider the practical problems that make these intellectual questions serious: How can I practice peace in a world of strife? Can I act for any "constructive" result or for a more "open" future without falling in with the prevailing violence of general structure, of cause and effect? On the other hand, can I oppose the violence the world-system inflicts on beings without committing violence against the system in which beings are maintained and in *that* way violating beings? How does a responsible agent *locate* the one to whom she or he is responsible in a practical context?

Levinas responds in *Otherwise than Being* by presenting relation with the Other, not as a dilemma-generating disruption of experience and language but as an extraordinary fulfillment, not a problematic Unsayable simply but a sheer, unstoppable generosity of Saying that only equivocally congeals into something Said (namely, "Saying" as a philosophical theme, an intellectual quantum) in a strategic "indiscretion."[196] By adding layers of excessive emphasis and irony to its discourse on subject, object, being, and meaning, philosophy can be tilted to enact basic deference to the Other in an appropriately curved space-time of responsibility.

Meanwhile, Derrida, having assumed his own responsibility for sustaining the orientation of Logos, will defend phenomenology against any presumption of interrupting or superseding it:

> In phenomenology there is never a constitution of horizons, but horizons of constitution. That the infinity of the Husserlian horizon has the form of an indefinite opening . . . does this not certainly keep it from all totalization [that would repress Otherness]? . . . If a consciousness of infinite inadequa-

tion to the infinite (and even to the finite) distinguishes a body of thought careful to respect exteriority, it is difficult to see how Levinas can depart from Husserl, on this point at least. Is not intentionality respect itself? The eternal irreducibility of the other to the same, but of the other *appearing as* other for the same? For without the phenomenon of other as other no respect would be possible. (120–21)

Nevertheless, a commitment to questioning the fundamental motivations of philosophy's expressions requires us to explore the remotest frontiers of meaningfulness and grounding as these frontiers are drawn by philosophy's *actually* being linked, in Western civilization, with *its* Other, the Other of the Jewish "desert." So the discord between Levinas's claims and those of the great Logos marshals Hegel, Husserl, and Heidegger must be treated not only under the aspect of potential reconciliation but also, and more importantly, under the aspect of vexation. "Are we Jews? Are we Greeks? We live in the difference between the Jew and the Greek," Derrida proposes (153). His orientation is to construe the situation, within the limits of thematizability, as *most difficult*, or as he would prefer to say, most *open*. Why is openness his "unconditional" commitment, his categorical imperative?[197] Is it for the sake of being responsive to the issues that matter most to the most beings—a practically inclusive agency? Or is it for the sake of participating lucidly in the formally grandest problematic, necessarily inexhaustible—a theoretically inclusive consciousness? Or do these two programs go together?

We can see that Derrida maximizes practical concern for beings and intellectual difficulty at the same time in three thematic areas in which the issue of orientation comes to the fore: sexual difference, justice, and religion. (I bypass here another very germane Derridean theme, the gift, touched on earlier in discussing Marion's donology.)

1. *Sexual difference.* What a gender like "masculinity" or "femininity" is supposed to be in itself, as distinct from a set of physical sexual characteristics or behavioral sex roles, is a way of feeling, thinking, and acting humanly that is somehow grounded in physical sexedness and expressed in sex-linked practice. Each such way is conceived as an essence—one of the essential specifications of the human essence—and so as a possibility of authenticity or inauthenticity in any actual person's life. A gender scheme is an especially interesting site of basic attunement in everyday life because its sexual basis and expression imply that genders are continually, actively, consciously *attuning*—women bringing out masculinity in men in one kind of way, men enforcing masculinity in men in another kind of way, and so forth.[198] The idea of fixed general gender essences can be threatened by the dynamism of this process but has long been maintained as a stable framework for it, one that critics and victims of heterosexualism find oppressive.

Derrida affirms, against gender essentializing, that "desire for a sexuality without number can still protect us, like a dream, from an implacable destiny which immures everything for life in the number 2."[199] It is of course imperative to regard the meaning of sexuality, as of anything else, as open. But sexual difference is an especially important site of meaning-differance for Derrida because philosophers have had profound reason to deny that sexual difference is relevant to inquiries into truth and being.[200] There cannot be a final truth if truth differs sexually. Thus, Derrida plays the peculiarly elusive "feminine essence" against the supposedly unitary essence of truth so that the essence of truth becomes a casualty of the very idea of an essential difference, which is then undermined along with it as an essence (though not as a differance).[201] Even Levinas, he argues, has tried to neutralize the radical alterity of sexual difference by subordinating a feminine alterity of intimate relations and his own spontaneously disclosed masculine identity to his paramount truth of ethical alterity and identity. It is a dilemma of responsible openness: there is no Otherness or openness that does not have to be defended against some other Otherness or openness, but there can be no overriding of one openness by another without disrespectful contamination, violence, or ingratitude.[202]

2. *Justice.* Derrida distinguishes "justice" from all determinate "law" (rational as well as statutory) in such a way that justice can be identified as one of the undeconstructible fundamental motivations of deconstruction. Justice in this aspect is an *open ideal,* or another expression for an infinite quest for a fuller rectification of life, always still-to-come. The serious play of deconstruction "takes place in the interval that separates the undeconstructibility of justice from the deconstructibility of *droit* [law] (authority, legitimacy, and so on)."[203] But this is how justice itself works, for justice is realized, not in states of affairs or laws, but in concrete decisions and actions in which the relationship between the open ideal of full rectification, on the one hand, and rules, precedents, and given facts, on the other, is forged freshly. At no point can one say "I am just" or "This is just," for justice strictly is (here Derrida cites Levinas) the relation to the other.[204] Like the gift, justice can only be experienced as impossible, that is, as outside any fit we can make—but that does not mean that justice (or giving) never enters our experience.[205] "A certain interruptive unravelling is the condition of the 'social bond,' the very respiration of all 'community.' "[206]

One specific challenge of justice that Derrida takes account of in contemporary life is the victimization of persons who fall outside the protections of national "community" maintenance. He calls attention to Kant's cosmopolitan norm of a universal right to hospitality, which implies that each actual community must be perfectly hospitable. The ideal of the hospitable community is a good example of the "experience of the impossible," which could also be formulated as an impossible attitude: "we" must have scrupulous regard for ourselves *rather than* others, if we are to maintain ourselves as an actual community, while at the same time we must welcome all others.[207]

At this attitudinal frontier of the "experience of the impossible," Derrida seems to some critics to become practically irresponsible.[208] How can I perform concrete actions in the best public interest if I remain poised as a deconstructive questioner to unravel any political answer? Perhaps the best deconstructive answer to this challenge is to assert on the one hand (1) that we have always recognized a need for radical questioning of the order of our life (whether in the manner of an Amos or a Laozi or a Plato) to counter the brutality of the factual status quo, and on the other hand (2) that only deconstructive questioning can save us from jumping out of a realist frying pan into an idealist fire, an alternate brutality of insistence on a certain prescribed order. We will act in any case; there is little danger that contemplating the openness of the justice ideal will cause practical paralysis. But we should always try to act less insensitively and inflexibly.

3. *Religion* presents itself for deconstructive attention in various guises. Institutionalized religion is in many ways the ultimate foe and target of deconstruction because it marshals the greatest possible intellectual, emotional, and political forces in support of a permanently defined truth affirmed with perfect assurance and loyalty—characteristically a truth of "the holy, the sacred, the safe and sound, the unscathed, the immune."[209] The Kantian "religion of reason" provides an opening toward the critical reinterpretation of traditional religious ideals such as the supreme appeal and the sovereign attitude, and a philosopher concerned with religion is bound in some sense to join the Kantian enterprise—but a philosophy of religion, insofar as it takes the place of religion (even in claiming to displace it), is destined to reenact the repressions of traditional religion on the plane of a self-mystifying, arrogantly imperialistic pure reason. A Kierkegaardian religion of subjective passion locates appeal and attitude elsewhere than in the suspect jurisdiction of reason, but at the cost of running an excessive risk of irresponsibility: on the scary paradigm celebrated in *Fear and Trembling*, Abraham's religious passion is ready to play out over his innocent son's dead body. Levinas's version of the religion of reason, in which religion and reason are both defined as relation with the Other, offers a way of maintaining all loyalties at once: acceptance of the disruption of all comprehension and conative insistence by alterity, together with recognition that we depend on historic religious traditions as sustained by actual religious communities for our endowed capacity to pursue questions of and about ultimate meaningfulness. This way is impossible to practice, being fundamentally conflicted, but it is also impossible to refrain from practicing, since it is supremely appealing, as Derrida too is willing to allow (though without adhering to a religion to the extent that Levinas does). This most-appealing way is perversely located in the "desert" from which Derrida early heard Levinas speaking prophetically, "there where one neither can nor should see coming what ought or could—perhaps—be yet to come."[210] The incalculable origin of the supreme way is in "the desert of the desert" where there is no prefiguration whatsoever, but only the chance (in the most basic sense) of an adequate rationality and justice to come.[211]

Faith is to religion as justice is to law, for faith itself requires that religion be deconstructed.[212] This faith is identified as the aspect of relation to the

Other that pertains specifically to shared expectation and affirmation of the future that exceeds any designed future.

> You cannot address the other, speak to the other, without an act of faith . . . You address the other and ask, "believe me." Even if you are lying, even in a perjury, you are addressing the other and asking the other to trust you. This "trust me, I am speaking to you" is of the order of faith . . . So this faith is not religious, strictly speaking; at least it cannot be totally determined by a given religion. That is why this faith is absolutely universal . . . the messianic structure [also] is a universal structure. As soon as you address the other, as soon as you are open to the future, as soon as you have a temporal experience of waiting for the future, of waiting for someone to come: that is the opening of experience. Someone is to come, is *now* to come. Justice and peace will have to do with this coming of the other, with the promise . . . This universal structure of the promise, of the expectation for the future, for the coming, and the fact that this expectation of the coming has to do with justice—that is what I call the messianic structure. This messianic structure is not limited to what one calls messianisms, that is, Jewish, Christian, or Islamic messianism, to these determinate figures and forms of the Messiah.[213]

Derrida says he oscillates between regarding the historic religions as exemplifications of the more basic, universal structure of messianicity and acknowledging their revelations as absolute events in which messianicity has been most basically made available to us. He tries to hold both views (or attitudes) at the same time.[214]

On the matter of practical inclusion, a point that might seem peripheral to the intellectual content of Derrida's work but that reflects tellingly on his orientation is the attention he gives Islam in his recent writing on religion. Simply by treating Islam as a faith symmetrical with Judaism and Christianity, Derrida helps to rectify a long-running Western disallowance of Islam's Abrahamic credentials.[215] The compelling reason for Derrida to consider Islam is not conceptual; it is not that Islam presents a uniquely interesting form of religion; it is the fact that many human beings in this writer's practical world are involved in or affected by Islam.

* * *

The sovereign attitude of responsible openness—or, if the qualification "sovereign" becomes misleading in this context, the attitude that displaces any candidate for sovereign attitude by virtue of its unsurpassable degree of openness and the extreme degree to which it commits the resources of the subject-as-responsive—this attitude has the most strained relation possible with a cognitive stabilization. Asked where his work is leading, Derrida once replied:

> I don't know. Or rather I believe this is not on the order of knowledge, which does not mean one must give up on knowledge and resign oneself to obscurity. At stake are responsibilities that, if they are to give rise to decisions

> and events, must not follow knowledge, must not flow from knowledge like
> consequences or effects . . . These responsibilities . . . are heterogeneous to
> the formalizable order of knowledge.[216]

The cognitive framework for the attitude of greatest openness must be
defined by impotence and indeterminacy, as in the realization of "foundering"
of which Jaspers speaks, or the knowing non-knowing of "negative theology"
that Derrida often references.[217] What *is* clearly apprehended in this perspective is the lack of a straightforward connection between attitude and cognition.
It is impossible to derive the attitude of responsible openness from an insight
into the nature of reality. The ultimate insight in this frame of reference is just
"pluralism" or "anarchism," and from the bare metaphysical or ontological
thesis of pluralism or anarchism nothing follows except a general intellectual
provocation. Derived from actual engagement in relations with other beings,
however, and inflected by their appeals, such a thesis can become intellectually sovereign.[218] The attitude then enforces the appeals.

Besides this abstract cognitive menu "in principle," responsibility has a
definite history. Derrida claims that we could not respond if we did not inherit
and carry forward a certain repertoire of signs and gestures in which response
and faith—and, inescapably, religion—are embodied: "No responsibility without a given word, a sworn faith, without a pledge, without an oath, without
some *sacrament.*"[219] At a deeper level than the accretion of means of expression, the responsibility/religion complex has a *spiritual* history in which the
fundamental possibility and agenda of response may have been momentously
shaped; a religious revelation might be a supremely compelling juncture of
such a history. But Derrida will not adopt this view of revelation (though he
will entertain it), nor will he accept any certain accounting of a history of
responsibility (though he will entertain one). In *The Gift of Death*, he reviews
Jan Patočka's argument that Europe's defining responsibility descends from
two great conversions: (1) the Platonic conversion from orgiastic reveling in
group-consciousness to sober cognizance of the transcendent Good; and (2)
the Christian conversion from impersonal Platonic devotion to goodness to
relationship with a transcendent, awesomely mysterious Person who sees into
one's heart and to Whom one is therefore more radically responsible.[220] To
accept Patočka's argument would be to accept theism. Although Patočka wants
to define a purely reasonable, nonauthoritarian, nondogmatic spirituality of
responsibility, he cannot construct his orientational norm without drawing
from the well of Christian experience. Yet Derrida cannot simply dismiss
Patočka's view of responsibility on the grounds of its Christian contamination:

> For if it is true that the concept of responsibility has, in the most reli-
> able continuity of its history, always implied involvement in action, doing,
> a *praxis*, a *decision* that exceeds simple conscience or simple theoretical
> understanding, it is also true that the same concept requires a decision or
> responsible action to answer for itself *consciously*, that is, with knowledge of

a thematics of what is done, of what action signifies, its causes, ends, etc. In debates concerning responsibility one must always take into account this original and irreducible complexity that links theoretical consciousness (which must also be a thetic or thematic consciousness) to "practical" conscience (ethical, legal, political), if only to avoid the arrogance of so many "clean consciences."[221]

This point balances Derrida's more predictably subversive assertion that "there is no responsibility without a dissident and inventive rupture with respect to tradition, authority, orthodoxy, rule, or doctrine."[222] Derrida will not be maneuvered into embracing theism for the sake of responsibility, but he does not want to claim a clean atheist conscience either. His statement on the linkage between the theoretical and the practical shows that his responsibility ideal is not keyed strictly either to immersion in a supposed real entanglement of beings or to breathing the pure air of waiting on the Other. It must involve both.

The Frame of Modern Attitude Thinking

We have traced the entry of important terms into the philosophical attitude lexicon: *Gesinnung,* an actively self-determined intentional "disposition"; *Gefühl,* a receptive "feeling" determined by contact with an exterior reality; *Stimmung,* an "attunement" co-determined (distinctively in the manner of resonance) by a subject and an exterior reality; the "passion" of illimitable concern for the coming-right of existence, one's own or another's; *Haltung,* a "bearing" or "comportment" underlying and comprehending all specific manners of action. Any one of these categories can be made paramount in an account of the subjective aspect of the constitution of superordinate meaningfulness. All of them are transparently stipulative; one cannot establish their presence or power by psychological testing. They are founded on an ideally recognized need for a normatively best position for a subject to occupy together with a best understanding of that position. Their relevance in directive thinking is guaranteed by their structural roles in the basic problematic of orientation—a problematic entailed not only by what we believe to be the nature of subjective and objective existence but also by our communicative framework of individualized appealing. The new vocabulary of disposition, feeling, attunement, passion, and comportment is the heart of the modern contribution to attitude thinking, as the ideals of righteousness, reverence, tranquility, benevolence, and devotion-love were the heart of the Axial Age contribution. Whenever a general notion of attitude or orientation is invoked in directive discourse, we may surmise that the notion tacitly works in accord with certain of these specifications—for example, is asked to function as a relatively active, "dispositional" determination of a subject's freedom, with the powers, affinities, limitations, and polemical edges of that bias—or else still awaits that sort of specification.

In the Kant-Schleiermacher relationship, we find a powerfully articulated issue of basic attitude formation: idealist *Gesinnung* versus realist *Gefühl*, the priority of activity and possibility versus the priority of receptivity and actuality. Various possible forms of appeal to activity and receptivity have subsequently been realized by attitude-conscious philosophers at the opposed extremes and in mediating syntheses. Extreme positions like Jaspers's espousal of freedom and the Levinasian "passivity more passive than any passivity" owe their formation in part to a dramatic logic of contrast and antagonism. In synthesizing, on the other hand, at least two motives are important. The most obvious is the desire to enjoy all possible intellectual and practical advantages; one becomes dissatisfied with the limitations of sticking with one emphasis at the expense of the other. Another motive, more ambitious and only problematically reasonable, is to reach for an *amazing* combination of possibilities that are not readily seen as compossible. Dilthey well represents the first motive, Nietzsche and Buber the second.

The prominence of the concept of *Stimmung* in Dilthey's writing marks his move to a central position where it will be possible to affirm both the dependence and the independence of the subject in its basic orienting. The Diltheyan subject is fully historical, fully a constituent of objective spirit, and yet also autonomously dedicated to addressing the life-enigma in an ideally satisfactory way. "Attunement" gives the subject room to maintain his or her "world-intuition" responsibly, since more than one "world-intuition" can resonate with a subject's historical placement. Heidegger makes a move of similar structural interest in *Being and Time*, locating attunements in the broader category of how-one-finds-oneself (*Befindlichkeit*) and defining the principle of autonomous responsibility as resoluteness in anticipation of one's own death. Both Heidegger and Dilthey side with Schleiermacher insofar as they oppose idealism with claims that meaning-formation depends most fundamentally on the subject's membership in an inclusive actual whole. But Heidegger leans more heavily than Dilthey toward the priority of receptivity. It becomes increasingly clear in his work that he has no positive directive interest in a pluralism of "world-intuitions." He only concedes that we have to pick our way through the cultural junkyard of "world-intuitions" on our way to an authentic heeding of Being. The Heideggerian conception of attunement is strongly asymmetrical and *Gefühl*-ish: Being attunes us as the dog wags the tail. Dilthey, in contrast, accepts a necessity of ongoing negotiation among philosophical approaches.

Nietzsche's ambition is to be the ultimate *Gesinnung* thinker and the ultimate *Gefühl* thinker at the same time—or something even stronger than that. The apparently voluntary and involuntary aspects of his position are both overwhelming. On the one hand, he affirms the power of each individual subject to revalue all values; on the other, he veers toward Spinoza in holding that the consciousness of individual subjects is epiphenomenal in relation to events in bodies in an all-inclusive concatenation of forces.[223]

> What alone can be *our* doctrine? That no one *gives* man his qualities—neither God, nor society, nor his parents and ancestors, nor he himself. (The nonsense of the last idea was taught as "intelligible freedom" by Kant . . .) No one is responsible for man's being there at all, for his being such-and-such, or for his being in these circumstances or in this environment. The fatality of his essence is not to be disentangled from the fatality of all that has been and will be.[224]

Nietzsche's "fatality" is not conventional determinism, however, since for him the idea of causation, like the idea of intelligible freedom, is but a vain intellectual ploy to master existence. Thus, the reference points of the voluntary and the involuntary are destroyed. Nietzsche's alternative way to take bearings in reality is to affirm eternal recurrence. This affirmation is an individually distinctive, free event, the most free in the most robust sense (for it is not only contingent but most difficult); at the same time, its sense includes acknowledgment of one's actual solidarity with "all that has been and will be."

The tread of Buber's *Haltung* is heavier than the Dionysian dancing advocated by Nietzsche, but Buber attempts no less ambitious an overcoming of the disjunction of *Gesinnung* and *Gefühl*. Whereas Nietzsche aims to destroy the centers of ego and God, replacing them with an unlimited pluralism of power-realizing events, Buber's pluralism confirms centers and the significance of centering in every possible position. In I-You saying, the free initiative of the self comes into its own at the same time that the dependence of meaning-formation on the other being is at its height and is affirmed as being at its height. Buber's alternative to the sub-actual Apollinian mastery of experience, unlike the ecstatic Dionysian contact or merging with other beings that so strongly appeals to Nietzsche, is reciprocal *address* of beings, "spiritual" life in the "between."

Nietzsche and Buber establish a new philosophical baseline: later appeals to activity or receptivity presuppose one or both of their breakthrough syntheses. Thus the "hostageship" of an ontologically independent subject in Levinas, for example, is an acutely anti-Nietzschean heightening of Buberian responsibility, while Derrida's "serious play" is a neo-Nietzschean appropriation of that same responsibility. These later attitude appeals are theoretically precarious to the degree that they depend on Nietzschean or Buberian arrangements that deliberately court impossibility, claiming exceptions to rational requirements for experience. The greatest, most open attitude can be reconciled with rational subject-object relations only with the greatest difficulty.

One may wonder whether the rationality of reflexively self-possessed consciousness and fully determinate, graspable objectivity still ought to be accepted as the standard of cognitive stability. It is hard to see what could displace this standard, given that it has been formed precisely as the strongest possible satisfaction of our unavoidable interest in cognitive stability. Nietzsche would "revalue," Levinas would "call into question" this stability, which prompts the question: Are we in fact most fully realized as knowers when we know something as perfectly settled? No, we are not, if part of the essential aim of knowing is the widening or opening to exteriority of the conscious subject's relationship with reality.

* * *

The reader might protest that the great attitude debates in modern thought have mainly not been about the structural issues featured in this account but instead about the *character* or *content* and *prime objects* of basic attitudes—about things like love and death, and especially love and death. Should not a study of the issue of attitude in modern philosophy look, for instance, at the marginalization of love in Kant's account of the good will, at the central place of love in Hegel's early writings (determinative for his whole project of gathering reality into a fully cognizant unity), at Feuerbach's attack on religious faith in the name of love, at Kierkegaard's placement of subjective existence in "works of love," and so on? Is it not also apparent, looking from the present backwards, that Derrida's probing of "the gift of death" and "haunting" by "spirits" in some of his latest studies of responsibility is compelled by a preoccupation with death that runs through Heidegger, Hegel, and many other thinkers as an integral part of their sense of the problem of fundamental motivation?

I cannot try within the bounds of the present inquiry to identify and assess the most important things that can be said about love or death. But I do want to consider the structural connections of love and death with the development of conceptions of what a fundamental orientation is. This will make a good transition to our study of attitude issues in modern religious thought.

1. *Love* is rivaled only by faith and piety as a substantive conception of sovereign attitude in Western culture; like faith and piety, it is an achieved rectification of self in relationship with a supremely important other around whom the world turns. Two Augustinian dicta, "My love is my weight; wherever I am carried, it is my love that carries me there" and "Love, and do what thou wilt," pretty well sum up the descriptive and directive priority that love plausibly assumes for us, whether or not we accept the other Christian elements of Augustine's thought.[225] These propositions also pose questions that can be answered in competing ways. When Kant asks, In what willing do I find my true self? and What willing is always right? he answers that the authentically personal and good will can in no sense be indulgent of, or tugged by, another person or thing. A contingent affection cannot constrain the meaning of my life a priori. The good will must be concerned with other persons, yes, but only in principle and only with all persons alike. The good will is not love as ordinarily conceived, then. In fact, Kant prefers to conceive it in terms of respect and distance-keeping, in a certain antithesis to love and attraction. Schleiermacher, however, accepts the heteronomous and attractive implications of love and radicalizes them in his conception of absolute dependence.

Thus, we could interpret the division of Kant's and Schleiermacher's conceptions of the anthropological center as the outcome of a kind of fission in the core of love's presumption: Kant's ideally active "I" is the self-finding terminus ad quem of love's movement, "I who must move in this way"; Schleiermacher's infinite Being is its terminus a quo, "the one with whom I must be." Because of our familial, friendly, and sexual experiences of interpersonal affirmation, love is our most powerful name for the prospect of relationship between self and other, the dimension in which we ask philosophically whether or how to affirm *Gesinnung*, *Gefühl*, and *Stimmung*.

2. *Death* is a prospect in which the temporal dimension of our existence comes to the fore and a stimulus to orient our conception of orientation in one time-relative way or another. Heidegger introduces the theme of Being-towards-death as the strongest possible way of disclosing the futurity in Dasein's existence *as part of care*—indeed, as the ultimate projection into possibility. The futurity of death lies not merely in its being unknown and not-yet-constituted, but more uncannily still in its being *my* uncontrollable end and *my* utterly inaccessible secret as far as others are concerned.

Death had been handled differently before. Kant held it at arm's length in norming the good will in the pure present tense of practical rule-consistency, only subsequently and conditionally chartering a "rational faith" in immortality for the sake of unrestricted progress in virtue.[226] In a similar spirit, Kierkegaard conceived the anticipation of death and immortality alike as deepenings of inwardness in a Now that is always the headquarters of the synthesis of existence.[227] Schleiermacher held death off by extolling absorption in the infinite—"Strive here already to annihilate your individuality and to live in the one and all."[228] These and similarly motivated thinkers chose *not* to place their orientational chips on the death-shadowed future—not in their anthropological conception, not in what they most cared about. Either they were so much stronger than death that they could afford to spend their force on a greater challenge, or death scared them off.

Heidegger, in contrast, compellingly redrew the horizon of the discussion of the temporality of basic orientation. Post-Heideggerians like Levinas and Derrida may cross the boundary of Dasein's extinction in order to affirm a future of responsibility to Others, but they do it with the inflection of the mortal self's subjection to the possibility of its own impossibility. For Derrida, the deadness of dead others is the condition of a sufficiently difficult version of communal heritage and normative piety, as we are challenged to continue to rectify our ambiguous relationships with those whose time of actuality has been completed but who continue to contribute, somewhat unmanageably, to our reality.[229]

We may take as our point of departure for a consideration of modern religious attitude thinking the issues of orientational structure that lurk in love and death concerns. They are, in brief:

1. The variable of self-other or Here-There relationship: to what extent and in what basic way separation or union is treated as requisite.

2. The variable of temporal reference: to what extent and in what way a basic orientation involves an investment in the ontological contribution of the future (the opening of possibility), the present (the constituting of actuality), or the past (the given constitution of reality) to our existence.

These two variables have to do with the manner of a subject's attitude's *extension*, one might say; articulating the issue of basic orientation in these terms aims us toward the effects or implications of attitude with regard to how matters stand between a subject and other beings or the whole of reality. A complementary way of asking about basic orientation has more to do with the character of the self-definition of the subject's attitude-holding, its *intensity*: In what way is it feasible or desirable to incorporate in the specification of basic attitude a subjective unconditionality of "passion" or "devotion"? How can we rightly be motivated to "plunge" into a way of existing, subjectively realizing unconditionality by responding wholeheartedly to a supreme attitude-appeal (faith, for example) at the expense of others (piety, for example, or reasonableness)? Or how, if at all, would multiple plunging be possible? In this frame of reference, how may the ideals of perfect receptivity ("faithfulness," "readiness," "eagerness") and perfect activity be related?

eight

Attitude Issues in
Modern Theology

It would be possible to document through the last two centuries nearly every conceivable appropriation of philosophical attitude theses by theologians right up to deconstruction. (As explained in chapter 4, I continue to use "theologian" as the imperfect but apparently best term of convenience for all who speak normatively about divinity as representatives of religious communities.) The story I told in chapter 7 of the development of the modern philosophical situation could furnish the main line of a story of modern religious attitude thinking as well. At this point, however, our penetration into basic attitude issues would not be much furthered by tracing this same development through religious literature. Our study of appeal conceptions already served notice of a deep isomorphism in modern philosophy and religious thinking rooted in the Axial Age project of norming the lives of individuals as individuals; attitude thinking forms part of the same project.

Yet we should be open to the possibility that distinctive insights into basic attitude issues are to be obtained from distinctively religious vantage points as a consequence of being occupied with issues specific to devotion as opposed to being occupied merely with the general problematic of grounding meaningfulness or norming. In *reasonable* discussion it is often supposed that insights conditional on actual devotion cannot be universally applicable, since devotion takes a subject out on an orientational limb to a position that must diverge incommensurably from rival commitments out on other such limbs. Devotion means maximal or illimitable concern for something in feeling and in practice; a subject whose life is utterly given to one thing cannot take anything else fully seriously. But at least one category of insights of universal import can *only* be obtained on the premise of going out on such a limb, namely, insights into how subjects' lives are affected by being utterly committed.

In chapter 5 we built up a conception of attitude by considering how to interpret the movements of minnows in a river that is partly dark. A crucial limitation of that procedure was the externality of our view. As long as we are defining basic orientation by what we observe in another being—even if we happen to admire this orientation and want to share in it—we do not touch a distinctively religious qualification of attitude. The minnow that we called "keen" to find food could, of course, have been called "devoted," but the religious sense of that term was not actually available to us. Nor were we in a position to understand "fanatical," an interesting frontier term for a grotesquely consistent, energetic kind of conduct; it points to a quasi-devotional unreasonableness (condemning it from the viewpoint of reasonableness) and a quasi-logical distortion of religiousness (condemning it from the viewpoint of religiousness). What enrichment of our attitude conception would give us access to the sense of devotion? Once our minnows start talking, and some of them claim a religious basic orientation, what new possibility in basic orientation are we asked to allow?

We would expect religious subjects to claim that their basic orientation confers the advantage of a surpassingly valuable aim or power or experience. Treasures have been unlocked. A devout Minnow A might say, "I get aimed in the dark in such a way that I am always able to find and catch the best food." Does Kant not make an analogous claim for moral reverence? Kantian reverence at least resembles religious devotion, and perhaps could even be identified as a species of devotion. But we think there is a tension between Kantian rationalism and the religious attitude as normally realized—a tension that would come out clearly if Minnow A said further, "This food passes all understanding; it is better even than the best conceivable food." Given this qualification, Nietzsche's program of revaluing all values in a mood of ecstatic life-affirmation would come closer to devotion than Kantianism does. In this respect, a Nietzschean can apparently be more religious than a Kantian.

But there is still an imperfect fit between Nietzsche's freelance philosophical guidance and the category of the religious. Those who take Nietzsche's advice and consequently find themselves in possession of a surpassingly valuable aim or power or experience would still not be proper exemplars of devotion in the view of many tradition-committed religious devotion thinkers. On their view—which I will call the strong religious view, since it maximizes the distinctiveness of religious attitude—Minnow A, to be devout, must be able to say something like "Amazing grace, that saved a fish like me—I *have actually been aimed* in the dark in such a way that I am able, as otherwise I would not be, to find and catch the greatest food." From the perspective of devotion, one acknowledges that an actualization of holiness in one's life *by* holiness is a necessary and perhaps also sufficient condition of one's having an effectively rectifying relationship with holiness. It *happened* or *happens* or *will happen* so that all is changed for the best. The decisive vision of reality is seen by the seer, and shared; the formula for moral perfection is embodied or effectively indicated by the sage, and transmitted; the covenant of righteousness and love is pronounced by God's prophets and written in the hearts of God's followers.

The best general term for this event seems to be "inspiration." It is not an inevitable term. Many Buddhists prefer to conceive the advent of holiness as "enlightenment," for example. But to the extent that one minimizes the inspirational element of impartation, so too one minimizes the role of a specifically religious attitude of devotion. Thus, Buddhism is more clearly qualified as a religious path in involving devotion to exemplars of enlightenment than in promoting enlightenment, and "kill the Buddha!" Buddhism deliberately pushes against religiousness.

The holders of a devout attitude feel that they live in a distinctively better way on the strength of their inspired devotion. Taking them at their word, or simply noting their practical tendencies, observers can reckon that these people are "good for" certain actions or qualities of interaction; they can be expected to be more calm or courageous or forgiving, perhaps. The play of a conception of basic attitude and of a particular inspiration and devotion is not separate from the play of persons among persons.

Schleiermacher must figure prominently in any useful story about modern religious attitude thinking, for his reaction to the Enlightenment critique of religion includes a theological development of the strong religious view of religious attitude, and subsequent leaders in theology react to his view in turn. Schleiermacher newly frames the issue of the nature of a religious attitudinal power that is uniquely possessed (along with whatever insights and actions depend on it) by persons just insofar as they are inspired and devout—a devotional proprium—which includes the issue of how the immanent reference of devotion to the condition of the devout subject relates to the transcendent reference of devotion to the holy object of devotion. Schleiermacher also has an important influence on the transmission into modern religious thinking of a long-simmering issue of the relations between divergent types of devotion. I see no better way of exploring the basic design problems of theological anthropology than to draw heavily from him.

The Issue of the Nature of Inspiration
and the Devotional Proprium

Schleiermacher. When we looked earlier at Schleiermacher's claim in *On Religion* that human life is fundamentally and comprehensively rectified by an actual relation between the individual subject and infinite being, we concentrated on his handling of the anthropological midpoint of connection between thought, feeling, and action in the Second Speech. Schleiermacher goes on to argue in the Fifth Speech that religious feeling can be realized authentically only in "positive religions"—never in an artificially formulated universal "natural religion"—since religious feeling is always born in a concrete set of individual life-circumstances and is necessarily linked to a determinate, distinctive world-intuition: "An individual instance of religion such as we are seeking cannot be established other than . . . by making a particular intuition of the universe the center of the whole of religion and relating everything therein to it . . . Only in the totality of all forms that are possible according to this construction can the whole of religion really be expressed."[1] Evidently, Schleiermacher's conception of the religious spectrum is structurally Leibnizian, the monads having prepared metaphysical places of honor for "particular intuitions." One can cite the necessity of a "particular intuition" in religious life to defend one's attachment to a tradition or to confirm one's sense of vocation in it. On this philosophical basis one can even point out inadequacies in world-intuitions and make a case for the superiority of one's own (as Schleiermacher does for Christianity in the last part of the Fifth Speech). But that is not the same as thinking from within the specific determination of one's religious feeling.

Schleiermacher's major exercise in religious thinking proper is his theological treatise *The Christian Faith*, where he attempts to discuss all the main problems of Christian doctrine consistently from the point of view of a subject or community of subjects whose feeling of absolute dependence on infinite being *has been* radically formed by an intuition of God's love as sovereign in Christ. The spiritual fait accompli of being personally bound to God by faith or piety had already been made a criterion of Christian meaningfulness by the Reformers: "Reason does admittedly believe that God is able and competent to help and bestow; but reason does not know whether He is willing to do this also *for us*" (Luther).[2] Christians know the "for us." Now Schleiermacher gives this principle a modernist twist: Christian insight is valid as the accurate self-description of the Christian consciousness of divine love actually overcoming sin rather than as the externally authorized transmission of specially "revealed" information concerning God, Christ, love, or sin.

> Since the feeling of absolute dependence, even in the [Christian] realm of redemption, only puts in an appearance, i.e., becomes a real self-consciousness in time, in so far as it is aroused by another determination of

the self-consciousness and unites itself therewith, every formula for that feeling is a formula for a definite state of mind [*Gemüthszustand*]; and consequently . . . we must declare the description of human states of mind to be the fundamental dogmatic form. (125–26)[3]

Schleiermacher thinks that special insight and power are realized in the Christian self-consciousness because it admits the fullest recognition of the problem of estrangement from divinity, "sin," while at the same time dealing with that problem as overcome through the Redeemer, Christ (§86).[4] This can occur thanks to the *communication* to the Christian of Christ's God-consciousness (§88). The Christic "communication" is understood as our initiation into the necessarily victorious power of divine spiritual activity by the unique example of perfect divine activity in Christ (§98). Christ's action as Redeemer "is best conceived as a pervasive influence which is received by its object [that is, the religious subject] in virtue of the free movement with which he turns himself to its attraction, just as we ascribe an attractive power to everyone to whose educative intellectual influence we gladly submit ourselves" (427); it is a "person-forming" activity that completely alters all perception as well as all action in altering the attitudinal center; it is necessarily mediated by an actual community in history; it is completed in our self-surrendering responsive action of joining the fellowship of grace (§100).

> We can know the fellowship of the Redeemer only in so far as we are not conscious of our own individual life; as impulses flow to us from Him, we find that in Him from which everything proceeds to be the source of our activity also—a common possession, as it were. This too is the meaning of all those passages in Scripture which speak of Christ being and living in us, of being dead to sin, of putting off the old and putting on the new man. But Christ can only direct His God-consciousness against sin in so far as He enters into the corporate life of man and sympathetically shares the consciousness of sin, but shares it as something he is to overcome. This very consciousness of sin as something to be overcome becomes the principle of our activity in the action which He evokes in us. (425–26)

Such a Christology implies a pneumatology: "As individual influences no longer proceed directly from Christ, something divine must exist. This something we call accordingly the Being of God in it, and it is this which continues within the Church the communication of the perfection and blessedness of Christ." The being in question is nothing other than "the vital unity of the Christian fellowship as a moral personality . . . its *common spirit*" (535). Like any community, the Christian church must be animated by a common spirit to which individual "impulses" are subordinated; but to subordinate the personal *religious* impulse of redeemed life to anything on the communal level other than that very same impulse is out of the question for a Christian. There is a true Christian community, and therefore there is a Holy Spirit (536). One of its expressions is that "all who are living in the state of sanctification feel an inward impulse to become more and more one in their common co-operative activity and reciprocal influence" (560). Christians blessedly energize each other by the mediation of their shared impulse. The impulse points beyond the existing limits of the church:

> We recognize it for the most authentic expression of the Holy Spirit as a consciousness of the need to be redeemed that is alike in all, and of the capacity, alike in all, to be taken up into living fellowship with Christ; and the universal love of humanity we know only as one and the same thing with the will for the Kingdom of God in its widest compass . . . In this sense . . . the common spirit of the Christian Church, and every Christian's universal love for men as a love alike for those who have already become citizens of the Kingdom of God and for those to whom this experience is yet to come, are the same One Holy Spirit. (565)

Note that Schleiermacher's "universality" here is forward-looking; the specifically Christian inspiriting is *not* to be identified with other actions of spirit that are described in the Bible, such as prophetic inspiration (§§123, 132). Rather than accept a broad-front agenda of biblical pneumatological thinking, Schleiermacher emphasizes that the spirit of the Christian community—truly inward, truly universal—differs decisively from its Jewish predecessor.

The fruit of one's connection with Christ, "sanctification," is explained thus: "[T]he natural powers of the regenerate are put at [Christ's] disposal, whereby there is produced a life akin to His perfection and blessedness" (505). Each Christian's life forms a unique, indispensable part of an organic whole, the life of the body of Christ (580).

Schleiermacher does not make provocatively transrational claims. He does not imply that Christians can leap tall buildings on the strength of their Christian piety. His salvation conception is not otherworldly; "we cannot ascribe the same value" to the traditional doctrines of future life, he says, as to the central doctrines of moral reconciliation through grace (703). Schleiermacher's mild, even minimal description of religious life flows from his concentration not on power but on attitude, the principle governing the aim and meaning of power. He believes that the systematic theologian's chief task is to exhibit and enforce the specific character of a pious attitude as the criterion of authenticity in the discourse of that piety. He contends that theology must in general take a middle way "between a magical view, which destroys all naturalness in the continuous activity of Christ [by appealing ad hoc to supernatural interventions], and an empirical [view], which reduces it altogether to the level of ordinary daily experience, and thus does not make its supernatural beginning [in relationship with the eternal] and its distinctive peculiarity the fundamental thing in it" (434). Schleiermacher calls his middle way "mystical," but soberly. It involves esoteric experience only in the sense in which people who implement a new political vision and thereby gain a distinctive sense of political fulfillment also have an esoteric experience (429). The category of the "mystical" should not mislead us: Schleiermacher's primary concern is not an experience at all, but a principle of experience (as well as of thinking and acting)—a "primordial impulse or tendency" or attitude.[5]

Barth. One hundred years later, as part of dialectical theology's turn toward the Wholly Other appeal of divine revelation, Schleiermacher's anthropological approach to theology is condemned. A summons model of God-relation is set against a contact or attunement model. According to Brunner's hostile interpretation of the category of the mystical, the essentially monistic, mystical theology of religious interiority or "experience" is diametrically opposed to the orientation to exteriority of the authentic scriptural and Reformation theology of the divine "word." Brunner claims that the faith-propositions of Schleiermacher's theology of feeling are radically deceptive: "they say 'God' but mean 'I'."[6] Barth rejects what he calls the "Cartesianism" of Schleiermacher's centering of theology in the Christian self-consciousness: "God as the metaphysical extension of our impulse to live . . . is anything but God."[7] The essence of Barth's objection is that any appeal to a subjective variable as a condition of religious meaning involves a failure to recognize the utter lostness of humanity apart from the self-revelation of the wholly Other God; it amounts to a sinful reassertion of human independence. The true *Christian appeal* is to *God's appeal.*

In the first edition of his commentary on Paul's letter to the Romans, Barth takes swipes at all attitudinal formulations of Christianity.

> "Freed from sin, you have become 'slaves' of righteousness (I speak in human concepts because of the weakness of your flesh)" [Romans 6.18–19] . . . Your own freedom, revealed in your wills as the beginning of new world- and life-conditions, you have translated into 'absolute dependence' . . . an inept, inadequate expression indeed. For in the realm of grace there are no slaves. Grace is freedom. Those who are under grace are children, not slaves [Romans 8.15] . . . With your obedience, with your entry into freedom, something positive and irreversible has happened and not . . . only the attainment of a new world-insight and a new life-feeling. Righteousness is, even to a higher degree than sin, a *power*. Not a changeable "disposition" [*Gesinnung*], but an unchangeable *meaning* [*Sinn*] of life that now holds for your lives. Not a mood [*Stimmung*] with higher and lower temperatures, but a *determination* [*Bestimmung*] that has now been pronounced on you. A force that has now made you its own. A lordship under which you now *stand.*[8]

But it is plain here that Barth is fighting fire with fire. The issue having been defined as one of attitude, Barth endeavors to replace a self-regarding and self-validating attitude with an attitude of responsiveness to divine summons and to transcendent possibilities. He has no choice but to use the language of pose and poise, calling on us to be oriented by being-determined and standing-under. Still, from Barth's point of view it would be perverse to enshrine the attitude of responsiveness to God as the Christian norm—that would be to proceed formally in the same manner as Schleiermacher. So Barth relentlessly invokes the appeal of God and the objective "meaning" of relationship with God, elucidating the attitude of responsiveness to transcendent appeal *en passant*.

We will see in a moment why Barth does not use the potentially apt category of piety in this connection. First, let us see what he does with faith. Barth's propositions about faith proceed from his need to confront Schleiermacherian immanentism with a transcendentism—that is, to interpret the paradigmatic Christian position of being grasped by grace primarily in terms of the divine grasping rather than the human graspedness. Thus faith, stipulated as the necessary subjective qualification of Christian existence, must be defined as a principle of meaning-formation that can never be within our own interpretive or practical power. It must refer to the actuality of God's giving of divine knowledge or power without being a generally interesting intellectual commodity. Anthropologically, it must be inscrutable, having in common with other conceptions of basic orientation only the formal principle that it represents that point in a person's life where "all the difference" is made.

> Our faith is God's deed in us . . . One cannot *have* faith, but must always attain it freshly, receiving it as a gift. (1919)[9]

> Faith is awe in the presence of the divine incognito; it is the love of God that is aware of the qualitative distinction between God and man and God and the world; it is the affirmation of resurrection as the turning-point of the world; and therefore it is the affirmation of the divine "No" in Christ, of the shattering halt in the presence of God . . . Faith is the faithfulness of God, ever secreted in and beyond all human ideas and affirmations about Him, and beyond every positive religious achievement. There is no such thing as mature and assured possession of faith: regarded psychologically, it is always a leap into the darkness of the unknown, a flight into empty air. (1922)[10]

> Christian life is man's actual life in the Holy Ghost; man is accounted as righteous through the Word, or for Christ's sake; man's righteousness is by faith on his part, seen in repentance and trust . . . Man's own obedience to his own true reality as one being sanctified is in the Holy Ghost, and is only actual when it responds to the Holy Ghost. (1929)[11]

> We may quietly regard the will and conscience and feeling and all other possible anthropological centers as possibilities of human self-determination and then understand them in their totality as determined by the Word of God which affects the whole man . . . [while on the other hand] the act of acknowledging the Word of God, so far as its immanence in the consciousness can be established from outside, historico-psychologically, by observation of ourselves or others, cannot even be characterized unequivocally as this act, let alone known in its relation to the Word of God. (1932)[12]

> In faith man is no longer in control at his center. Or rather, at his center, he is outside himself and therefore in control . . . [the believer] can no longer

fix his "heart" on other things (even the most important) or on other persons (even the dearest and most indispensable). At the center of his being he is no longer here or there, but at this very definite place outside himself which cannot be exchanged for any other . . . He is lifted above himself, but in the only direction in which this can take place. (1953)[13]

Barth appealed from time to time in his *Church Dogmatics* to the principle of the "analogy of faith" between human and divine meanings, according to which the human terms of a theological statement—for example, "lordship" adduced in an assertion of God's lordship—could conform to their proper divine meaning just in the event of faith (and could count as theologically valid as so conforming).[14]

Barth's thinking about faith, often stated as some variation on the theme that rectification must be achieved by an exterior Rectifier, also often proceeds from a conception of freedom. The freedom of the divine creator, reconciler, and redeemer being the superlative freedom, true human salvation would consist of graciously enabled participation in *this* freedom, which would involve a freeing *from* the limitations of purely human freedom (subjectively registered as a mortification of pride) *for* peace (in a subjective vivification).[15] So the higher freedom meets us as a uniquely necessary responsibility:

> To have our master unavoidably in Jesus Christ means always to have found someone over against us, from whom we can no longer withdraw. We can withdraw from everything else that is over against us, whether it is the world or men. It is at once our misery and comfort, the source of our most serious aberrations and the help of which we simply must avail ourselves from time to time, that again and again we can withdraw to an inward solitude. The outpouring of the Holy Spirit makes this withdrawal impossible, at any rate in relation to the Word of God.[16]

Following the traditional structure of Christian theology, Barth continually weaves together the themes of faith and the Holy Spirit. Barth wonders at the end of his life whether Schleiermacher's best intentions and his own could be pursued together in the form of pneumatology: "Isn't God . . . essentially Spirit . . . , i.e., isn't he the God who in his own freedom, power, and love makes himself present and applies himself?"[17] Thus, Barth's attention moves toward the actual hinging of the religious transformation of existence. This pneumatology cannot be an anthropology. It must acknowledge an objective, transcendent divinity in contrast to the subjective, immanent ground of meaning adopted by liberal theology. That will always be a bone to pick with Schleiermacher.[18] Schematically, however, the interesting development is that Barth looks finally toward a midpoint between his objectivist approach and what he takes to be Schleiermacher's subjectivism—as though he is headed toward another iteration of the logic that led Schleiermacher to focus on a midpoint of feeling between knowing and willing, a logic not merely of conciliation but of the most basic formation of meaning as a unity of its basic conditions. So we can see that Schleiermacher and Barth share a concern with the authentic formation of the meanings of Christian life in the integral union of a distinctive attitude and a distinctive appeal, even if they are destined as historical figures to represent opposed primacies of attitude and appeal within the attitude-appeal complex.

Political and liberation theology. In the later twentieth century, liberal theology is attacked by theologians whose primary concern is social justice and whose worries about theology owe more to the Marxian critique of religious ideology than to the Barthian critique of religious anthropocentrism.[19] Whereas Barth's problem with liberal theology's concentration on religious subjectivity had to do with the status of God, the great problem for this next generation of theologians is the status of the world. Their variously formulated "secular," "political," and "liberation" theologies recast the attitudinal proprium of Christianity as a distinctive power of participating in world-shaping. Schleiermacher too had maintained that redemption is collective and world-forming. In fact, he attacked all teachings that would allow individuals to be "individually and independently enlightened" on the basis of a mere idea of Christ, "perfectly complete" in themselves, outside of actual connection with the historical fellowship of Christians and the historical Christ, and he insisted "that Christianity must develop as a force in history."[20] He recognized the social mediation of sinfulness as well.[21] But in the last analysis, Schleiermacher always understands collectivity and world monadologically, as a gathering of individual subjective centers rather than as a dynamic system of interacting social forces determining outcomes of good and evil.[22] The newer thinkers want to incorporate social dynamics in the synthesis of faith.

For the Roman Catholic theologian J. B. Metz, authentic faith is the acceptance of the world as given a greater "specific gravity" by its eternal creator's affirmation of its creaturely reality (27).[23] Responsibility to God cannot be separated from responsibility to the world, since the essence of responsibility to God is imitation of God's acceptance of the world. The same point holds for historical process, with the specific determinations of its past and present and its open future:

> Our faith, then . . . is the response to a unique event in history. God for us is . . . Emmanuel, the god of an historical hour. Transcendence itself has become an event. It does not just simply stand above and beyond history, but is what is still to come in history; it is the future of man. God is no longer merely "above" history, he is himself "in" it, in that he is also constantly "in front of it" as its free, uncontrolled future. (22–23)

The prescribed acceptance of the world is "eschatological" and yet "not automatically optimistic": because the separation of the world from God is always an estrangement, faith involves suffering, "not *although* we accept [the world's] secularity, but precisely *because* we accept it in faith; and [the world] places itself within the center of our act of faith, in this acceptance that we ourselves cannot see, as something painfully strange" (45–46). Because Christians have been oriented by God's utterly unrestricted acceptance of the world in the event of Jesus Christ (crucified), they are better able than anyone else to see and deal with the world as it really is "without invoking new gods of [human] understanding of the world" (47). Christian faith is not an ideology but rather the supreme position from which to carry out ideology critique.

Historically oriented faith must address an open future and "prove its fidelity as hope" (56). Metz is influenced by the philosopher Ernst Bloch's argument in *The Principle of Hope* for the normative sovereignty of hope, a point of attitude anthropology that features prominently also in Jürgen Moltmann's early work.[24] Bloch develops in an atheistic but attitudinally religious way an ontology in which possibility is credited as the matrix of reality-formation together with a corresponding anthropology of always-still-to-be-defined, experimental human being. The attitude of hope responds to the appeal of possibility in expressions ranging from daydreaming to artistic creation to utopian politics.[25] Moltmann locates the peculiarly great power of Christian hope in its accepting, courageous confrontation with a *concretely* ultimate, ultimately bitter "negative":

> The creative power of God is seen in Isaac's sacrifice, in the abandonment of Job, in Christ crucified, in nothingness, and in the total annihilation of all hope . . . Even where the force of the negative puts an end to all possibilities of man and nature, trust is placed in God, for God is the power of a future which proves itself creative over against total nothingness. This power is not identical with the power of present reality or of the future's open possibility. It is believed and hoped in at that precise point where people come face to face with the negative.[26]

For Moltmann, the God of Christianity is not merely a humanly hopeful projection of a most-adequate cognitive referent, but rather an appellant whose *promises* humans may respond to most-hopefully. This appellant speaks from the future as well as in the present: "I will be who I will be" (Exodus 3:14).[27] The divine promise is directed first to those neediest of hope and to the rest of the world through them, as indicated by Jesus' solidarity with the poor.[28]

Metz's and Moltmann's affirmations of Christian responsibility for shaping the world's future are marked by deep concern not to betray the distinctive meaningfulness of Christian claims by pitting a supposedly Christian political ideology against others.[29] Moltmann asserts that the Christian negation of the world as it is cannot be fit into a world-historical dialectic.[30] But this approach risks keeping Christian responsibility too abstract, too little engaged with real circumstances calling for definite actions, for the sake of maintaining an ideally robust proprium of Christian devotion.[31] South and North American liberation theologians, in contrast, tend to make the most of the premise that an actual struggle for social justice is already determinative of authentic Christian devotion. Since the foremost divine concern attested by the great biblical appeals is to rescue the oppressed from dehumanization, the true Christian proprium is an empowering unity of awareness and trust of divine promises of freedom—a uniquely encouraging promise made through the history of Israel and the death and resurrection of Jesus Christ. Part of this commitment is cognitive: thinking is to be guided by interpretive approaches that expose facts and structures of oppression. As Frederick Herzog puts it:

> Once man grasps corporate freedom he is on the way to becoming man . . . Only through liberation from the concealment of privatism can we be set on the road to becoming human. This occurs in the unconcealed one who uncovers the new direction of our destiny toward a new future: "So if the Son liberates you, you will be free indeed" (John 8.36) . . . Jesus appears as the counterself, the true self, the open man . . . "I am the vine, you are the branches" (John 15.5). Important in Jesus' metaphor is its corporate implication . . . Jesus in standing by the lost and joining their struggle replaced the organization church of the Old Covenant . . . The one who follows Jesus thus does not find the church in the religious establishment, but . . . in liberation, in the fact that God liberates man. Where this libera-tion takes place should not be difficult to see: in the struggle for freedom among the oppressed . . . We have to be gifted the ability to act in these new ways: we have to receive strength from "the vine." The disciple is compelled to persevere in the love with which Jesus loved him long before the disciple knew him (John 15.10).[32]

The empowerment is not automatic for Christians nor is it exclusively Christian, cautions José Miguez Bonino. It is not a license for a crusade; nevertheless, it is the core of Christian life:

> A Christian can offer his praxis to the fire of [socially engaged] criticism totally and unreservedly on the trust of free grace just as he can offer his body [to the liberation struggle] totally and unreservedly in the hope of the resurrection. That so many nonbelievers do these things and so many Christians do not belongs to the mystery of grace and the mystery of evil. But the fact that this freedom is offered to faith at every moment is the very center of the gospel.[33]

A Christian attitude of faith or freedom might be spliced together with an *élan* of the oppressed group, like black "soul" or feminine biophilia.[34] Or it might be claimed that a peculiar Christian power of acting gratefully in acknowl-edgement of divine grace can only be realized in encounter with and commit-ment to the most needy persons.[35]

Liberation theologians commonly adopt or imply a weak view of the devotional proprium of Christianity. They bring us back to Kantian religion insofar as the essential lines of the struggle for social justice, like the essential requirements of the Kantian moral law, can be adequately and more safely articulated without an explicitly Christian grounding. The idea of a distinctive Christian "spiritual" power, accomplishment, or horizon *apart from* the actual liberation struggle in solidarity with the poor is the great temptation of an alienated pie-in-the-sky religious consciousness—a false appeal. Christianity is rectified and proves its value in aligning with liberation work, not vice versa. But to say this is not to impugn the religious authenticity of Christian liberationism, for liberationism generally, like Kantian and neo-Kantian value thinking, draws directive power from the same fundamental attitude-appeal complex as do the biblical religions.

The discussions surrounding political and liberation theology might make it seem that a strong view of the devotional proprium can only apply to private life—the logic being that a peculiar bond with Jesus Christ can be transformative only of the individual subject who receives and responds to that appeal intellectually and emotionally—while effective motivations in public life cannot depend on a special religious backing. We only get this impression, however, because of the weakened credibility and social impact of Christian churches since the Enlightenment and the popularity of theologies of subjectivity. Notwithstanding the communicative primacy of the individual, the orientation of an individual to a religious appeal (and the effective sovereignty such an orientation may have) is not necessarily of greater structural importance than the orientation of a community. A strong view of the devotional proprium could be applied to the activity of the community of followers of Jesus Christ, for example (whether or not their church-building relates positively to world-building), and on this basis, purely personal claims of inspiration could be seen as auxiliary or even as suspect insofar as they are conditioned more by generic psychological factors than by the specific work of the church. Or a collective orientation might be the necessary means of overcoming alienation between differently pointed forms of devotion—a problem to which we will now turn.

The Issue of Divergent Basic Kinds of Devotion: Piety, Faith, and Love

Moltmann sketches large-scale historical shifts in the relative importance in Christianity of different basic attitudes:

> The key factor in medieval theology and sacramental life of the church was the supernatural *reality of love*. The Reformation shifted the focus to the *power of faith* and the congregation. When we come to the peculiar trends of modern times, we speak of secularization, emancipation, and enlightenment. But why did Kant believe that religion is supposed to answer the fundamental question, *What may I hope for?* . . . Only with the beginning of modern times did the *primacy of hope* seem to alternate with the primacy of faith and love.[36]

If a shift like this did occur, one might suppose that medieval Christian life must have differed from modern Christian life in a most profound way, the weight of a present reality pulling the medieval heart more strongly than the magnetism of future possibility. Moltmann assumes, however, that the theologian may construe these attitudes as properly complementary, or even coinherent. Hope is "the essential theme of Christian faith and of that love which in the modern context . . . ever has to be worked out . . . It encourages faith so that it does not degenerate into faintheartedness. It strengthens love so that it does not remain enclosed within itself and with those who are like it."[37] A fuller conception of revelation is demanded by hope: "The revelation of Christ cannot then merely consist in what has already happened in hidden ways being unveiled for us to see, but it must be expected in events which fulfill the promise that is given with the Christ event."[38] Since hope occupies the position of sovereign attitude in Moltmann's proposal, any difficulties in making the intellectual, emotional, and practical implications of hope agree with the implications of other attitudes must be ironed out in principle.

Moltmann presents hope as a *rival qualification* of faith especially in relation to what he calls the transcendental subjectivism of Bultmannian theology, which concentrates on the present moment of summons by God's Word and decision with respect to one's existence in light of that Word.[39] It would not be within the rules of normal Christian discourse to pit hope against faith as a *rival basic attitude*. In fact, the implicit project of this, as of all other attempts to round out an ideal portrait of the sovereign religious attitude, is to *synthesize* the basic valid forms of devotion. In Christian discourse, faith is the category in which this is usually done. But the use of this category is deceptively pacifying insofar as it disguises the depth of Moltmann's disagreement with Bultmann. (The use of a common-denominator concept of "devotion," like Wilfred Cantwell Smith's "faith" in the comparative study of religion, likewise disguises the depth of divergence among traditions and styles of religion.)[40] There is no formal reason why Moltmann should not make a fundamental recommendation of hope and present it as hopeful faith or faithful hope. But if Moltmann fails to accommodate the full force of attitudes other than hope in his proposal—and if Christians go on deepening their responsibility divergently in responding to differently formulated attitude appeals— what then can be said normatively about the devotional character of Christianity? A theologian can warn of the dangers involved in heeding one attitude appeal in preference to another, as Moltmann warns against socially irresponsible theologies of privatized faith or romanticized love.[41] But warnings motivated by the claims of the future can be warned against, in turn, on the basis of the claims of the present, or past, or eternity.[42]

Moltmann usefully opens up the question of relations among alternate formulations of the sovereign religious attitude—that is, those alternatives that are formed along the axis of time. He shows that religious pluralism pertains not only to differences among the cognitive stabilizations of devotion (religious doctrines and beliefs) but also to dispositions of the heart. We will think in the next section about how to relate such rival forms of devotion. If we are to have an adequate map of the major rivals, however, there is at least one other reference point to consider besides those that appear in Moltmann's theology of hope: piety.

* * *

James Gustafson has recently made a notable argument for giving piety priority over faith, an argument that is of particular interest here because, in daring to speak theologically against faith, it disrupts the normal categorical dominance of faith in Christian discourse.[43] To appreciate what might be at stake in a new retrieval of piety, it is well to be aware of the implicit debate on this attitude between Kant and Schleiermacher, reflecting in turn issues of attitude priority already introduced by the Reformers and still simmering in twentieth-century theology.

In *Religion within the Boundaries of Mere Reason*, Kant defines authentic religion as that which purely expresses or nurtures the good will. His ideal religion is not built in a vacuum; he reads it into actual Christianity as the principle that makes the best Christian beliefs and practices affirmable and others condemnable. However, two of the religious attitude ideals that are generally most important for Christians, faith and piety, are evaluated by Kant quite differently than they are in mainstream Christianity.

Faith is an ideal that Kant uses positively only when qualified as moral or rational (in contrast with a historically specified, morally unreliable "ecclesiastical" faith). The expectation of a complete rectification of life by God is subordinated to the requirement that one be continuously devoted to moral self-perfection and to making oneself worthy of the happiness one wishes. Faith is only licit because there is a circumspect way of formulating it that leaves the priority and centrality of the moral law's demand uncompromised. It is the good will itself that is the great adventure of life; faith is but a subjectively necessary completion of the conscientious person's thoughts. Faith as belief-in-X will attach to various objects in the actual history of religions, so that we will find ourselves confronted with a variety of faiths, none of which can be valid a priori in its particularity; the good will, however, is universal (102–108).[44] Kant condemns the "fetish-faith" that God will save us as a consequence of our doing anything other than exerting ourselves morally (193).[45]

About piety, Kant has nothing good to say. He criticizes under that name "the principle of conducting oneself passively in view of the divine blessedness expected through a power from above" (184, n. 1). He gives this description of a piety-dominated style of religion:

> Human beings are yet not easily persuaded that steadfast zeal in the conduct of a morally good life is all that God requires of them to be his well-pleasing subjects in his Kingdom. They cannot indeed conceive their obligation except as directed to some *service* or other which they must perform

> for God—wherein what matters is not the intrinsic worth of their actions as much as, rather, that they are performed for God to please him through passive obedience, however morally indifferent the actions might be in themselves. (103)

To prove their obedience, the pious are liable to use extravagant means, like festivals and sacrifices, that have no necessary connection with moral worth (169).

Kant could see both good and bad fruits of the Pietist movement, an important part of the German religious atmosphere in which he and Schleiermacher both grew up.[46] But the strictly negative associations of piety in Kant's *Religion* show the magnitude of the challenge Schleiermacher accepts in adopting the category of piety, first to explain religion to its cultured despisers, and later to formulate Christian theology in the public square.

Of no less importance than Pietism as an influence on Schleiermacher in this connection is his theological affiliation with the Calvinist Reformed churches, for Calvin had made the concept of piety the centerpiece of a normative psychology of religiousness.[47] Calvinist piety is a counterpoint to the audacious optimism of faith that is Luther's most characteristic theme. The distinctive priorities of piety—all expressing a scrupulous cognizance of what is *owed* the ground of goodness—are on brilliant display in this passage from Calvin's *Institutes*:

> The pious mind does not dream up for itself any god it pleases, but contemplates the one and only true God. And it does not attach to him whatever it pleases, but is content to hold him to be as he manifests himself; furthermore, the mind always exercises the utmost diligence and care not to wander astray, or rashly and boldly to go beyond his will. It thus recognizes God because it knows that he governs all things; and trusts that he is its guide and protector, therefore giving itself over completely to trust in him. Because it understands him to be the Author of every good, if anything oppresses, if anything is lacking, immediately it betakes itself to his protection, waiting for help from him. Because it is persuaded that he is good and merciful, it reposes in him with perfect trust, and doubts not that in his loving-kindness a remedy will be provided for all its ills. Because it acknowledges him as Lord and Father, the pious mind also deems it meet and right to observe his authority in all things, reverence his majesty, take care to advance his glory, and obey his commandments. Because it sees him to be a righteous judge, armed with severity to punish wickedness, it ever holds his judgment seat before its gaze, and through fear of him restrains itself from provoking his anger. And yet it is not so terrified by the awareness of his judgment as to wish to withdraw, even if some way of escape were open. But it embraces him no less as punisher of the wicked than as benefactor of the pious. For the pious mind realizes that the punishment of the impious and wicked and the reward of life eternal for the righteous equally pertain to God's glory. Besides, this mind restrains itself from sinning, not out of dread of punish-

ment alone; but, because it loves and reveres God as Father, it worships and adores him as Lord. Even if there were no hell, it would still shudder at offending him alone . . . Here indeed is pure and real religion: faith so joined with an earnest fear of God that this fear also embraces willing reverence, and carries with it such legitimate worship as is prescribed in the law. And we ought to note this fact even more diligently: all men have a vague general veneration for God, but very few really reverence him; and wherever there is great ostentation in ceremonies, sincerity of heart is rare indeed.[48]

Clearly, Calvin means to rule out the extravagant expressions of piety that Kant condemned. Perhaps it is less clear that his brand of religion is free from what Kant considered servility. In any case, his emphasis comes down heavily on *determined good*, good that *has been done* (God is regarded as the creator of a world, a moral scheme, and a "predestination" that are all in place) and so has generated objectively specifiable duty and an ideal subjective maximum of cognizance of debt and duty, gratitude, joy in communing with this established being, and obedience. Because the discourse of *pietas* (like the Greek *eusebeia*) has characteristically revolved around these issues, "piety" is a good term to mark the distinctively reverent style of devotion. Pious inspiration, considered dynamically, is the dilation of a subject's reverence as the impact on the subject, via cognizance of a supreme appellant's glory, of a good surpassing anything of the subject's own making, even anything imagined as *possible* —hence, of a good *reality*. This cognizance makes the subject secondary, de-centered; the spiritual stimulation centers in the greatness of the reality rather than in the "for me!" of Lutheran faith. As determined reality, the referent of piety is characteristically located in the past, so that the weakness likeliest to be associated with piety is blindness to the peculiar goods of present action or occurrence and futural anticipation. The pious subject experiences, acts, expects, and hopes all on a solid platform of cognizance of an achieved supreme good.

As for Kant, I think it can plausibly be argued that Kantian reverence is conceived, not as anti-pious, but as a pure piety vindicated against pathological expressions of piety. Though Kant stands in horror of pious demonstrations and superstitions, his imperative is centered on a framework of rule-making that he treats as a reality. His mind is filled "with ever new and increasing admiration and awe, the oftener and more steadily" he reflects on the moral law within him.[49] It is of course possible to be a not-very-pious Kantian whose moral stimulation comes mainly from the ever-fresh challenges of situations that call for moral response—not so much for figuring out what valid moral rules *are*, but for *making* valid moral rules—and whose religious devotion is eschatological.[50] But Kant himself seems often to model the pose and poise of the subject-coming-after-the-good and to set a tone of obedience. Kant's rational religion requires hopeful subjects so to act as to render themselves "worthy of happiness"; and "worthiness to be happy" is most readily interpreted as a satisfaction of determinate duty—although the ideal *could* be given a futural twist by making it depend on discoveries of possible harmony among subjects.

Calvin's piety motif reappears in Schleiermacher's appeal to the essential religious feeling, *Frömmigkeit,* German discourse on the *fromm* having taken over the main points of the Latinate discourse on piety, including its characteristic concern with sorting out duties of indebtedness to family, state, and God.[51] With the piety appeal comes the Calvinist emphasis on honoring and debt, as Schleiermacher makes our absolute "dependence" on God the foremost theme of religious awareness. The Calvinist *reserve* returns as well: just as Calvin warned against attributing anything to God beyond God's own clear authorization, Schleiermacher holds back from making any assertion that cannot be derived from the given actuality of Christian self-consciousness. In this important way Schleiermacher is Calvinist even in giving his liberal twist to the doctrine of predestination:

> The self-consciousness we possess as regenerate persons . . . is one with our feeling of absolute dependence not only in so far as we are conscious of our activity in the Kingdom of God as an activity divinely produced by means of Christ's mission, but also in so far as the course of each man's progress is one with the position assigned him in the general context of human relationships. The natural expression for this fact is to say that the ordinance according to which redemption realizes itself in each life is one and the same thing with the carrying out of the [eternal] divine government of the world in respect of that person . . . But as regards those we find outside the fellowship of Christ—they cannot so affect us as to give us reasonable cause to make any statement about them in this connection . . . by this path we can never arrive at the idea that for them, or some of them, there is a foreordination of an opposite kind. That "many are called and few are chosen" holds true at every particular turn in the preaching of the Kingdom of God . . . and so one has always a right to say that the majority are *not yet* to be regarded as chosen.[52]

The distinctive charge of the ideal of piety falls in well with Schleiermacher's realism, and even with his subjectivism—for the pious mind is a scrupulously self-examining mind that stands in relatively great danger of getting caught either in complacency with its dutifulness (one could call this the temptation of Job) or in despairing dissatisfaction with itself (as in the case of the unhappy young Luther).

Barth, another Reformed theologian, sees in Schleiermacher the distortion of pious complacency. He very much wants to insist, like Calvin, on pious deference to God's self-revelation and command, but he also wants to avoid the trap of a self-absorption and pride in piety. So he refuses to pin theology to the "pious mind" as anything like an independent principle. Schleiermacherian theology has so badly compromised this category that he cannot work with it. For the sake of asserting that respect for the divinely given is incompatible with treating devotion itself as a given, Barth pits faith against piety:

> Faith, therefore, is never identical with "piety," however pure and however delicate. In so far as "piety" is a sign of the occurrence of faith, it is so as the dissolution of all other concrete things and supremely as the dissolution of itself. Faith lives of its own, because it lives of God (1922).[53]

> Behind the German word "*Frömmigkeit*," which many like to use, is hidden more or less ashamedly or unashamedly the confession that the modern human no longer dares, in principle and primarily and with a raised voice, to speak of God.[54]

Gustafson, an American Reformed theologian less burdened than Barth by *Frömmigkeit*'s history in German-language theology, is determined to make a point complementary to Barth's by pitting piety against faith. According to Gustafson, "faith, as excessive trust, puts God primarily in the service of humans," whereas piety, encompassing awe, reverence, and gratitude, is a more properly theocentric attitude; pious subjects realize that the world is not run exclusively for their benefit.[55]

Gustafson's turn to piety has another motive that is distinctly out of step with Barth. He wants the religious attitude of cognizance of God's greatness to be seen on a continuum with reverence for goods of all kinds. The aspect of Calvin's understanding of piety that Barth most mistrusts, the idea of a "natural" (that is, "created" and still somehow reliably effective) capacity of humans to perceive and act rightly apart from the direct, actual reception of God's self-revealed command, is expanded by Gustafson to provide for a positive relationship between Christian piety, "natural piety," and more generally affirmable duties. Gustafson can make a "pious mind" argument for ecological concern that is not specifically Christian: "We are deeply and inexorably dependent upon aspects of the natural world for human survival and flourishing. For these we are grateful, since we did not bring them into being. They deserve our respect, for without them we could not be. We recognize a duty to care for them."[56] There is a distinctive Christian completion of the understanding of such debts and duties, but this understanding is properly established *through* cognizance of our real living conditions: "The ultimate power that sustains us and bears down upon us is experienced through the particular objects, events, and powers that sustain us, threaten our interests, create conditions for human action, or evoke awe and respect."[57] Piety is a sovereign attitude for Gustafson because it enables the whole range of appropriate responses to goodness. The emphasis on piety is especially in order at a time of ecological crisis inasmuch as the piously de-centered subject is better able to overcome anthropocentrism in responding to nonhuman beings. Gustafson has adapted the religiously conservative argument that we can only stay in touch with the ground of the greatest goodness in our lives through the mediation of established traditions and institutions to expand responsibility beyond the more narrow, exclusivist boundaries that are usually drawn by conservatives.

* * *

We have seen forms of devotion diverge in relation to the basic ontological difference between the already-constituted and the yet-to-be-constituted, between the real and the possible, between the past and the future. The reality-oriented form of devotion, piety, has a characteristic emotional tonality and set of emphases by which it differs markedly from possibility-oriented hope or hopeful faith. Piety has a strong affinity with sobriety and reasonableness, for example—it wants to take everything duly into account—while faith readily dramatizes its difference from reason for the sake of the boldest optimism. Piety does not leap into the dark. Piety is more naturally specified as the "feeling" or "attunement" kind of attitude. A person who lacks proper reverence or gratitude is felt by others not simply to have made a wrong choice but to *be* intentionally defective—a monster of ingratitude, for instance, a compass needle that won't come right—while faith is more naturally specified as the "disposition" kind of attitude, more the sort of thing we exhort people to shoot for.

It is a little hard to follow Gustafson in thinking of faith in contrast with other forms of devotion, given that the term "faith" has standardly been defined by Christians to comprehend all requirements and excellences of devotion. There is, however, a noticeable tilt to possibility in the pattern of appeals to faith in Western religious discourse, reflecting a tilt to a heavenly future in Christianity. (Other religious positions with a similar orientation, such as messianic Islam and Pure Land Buddhism, also make a great deal of faith as sovereign attitude.) Thus, "faith" seems the best single term for future-oriented devotion. Invoking hope can call attention to the purely attitudinal and futural aspects of faith, as distinct from a faith's belief-contents, but a *religious* hope is one that is essentially related to specific expectations—just as a religious gratitude is one that is related to a specific claim of debt and subordination—and the term "faith," roughly symmetrical with "piety," reminds us of this. Hopefulness as such requires only the weakest and haziest expectations.[58]

The clue of temporality and tense prompts us to ask: Is there a distinctive form of devotion oriented to the *present*, to constitut*ing*, that can differ from piety and faith as much as they differ from each other? Is there an ideal of devotion that stands out from alternatives as clearly as Buber's orientation to the presence of You-saying stands apart from the philosophical piety of Heidegger and the philosophical hope of Derrida?

The religious ideal of a maximal subjective commitment to present constituting has been designated in various ways. One apt term for it is *islam*, often translated with pious overtones as "submission" but perhaps better understood as loving "surrender."[59] In Western religious literature, the term most often used to draw attention to the action of the present is "love." We must be careful to maintain love's relevant specification in this context, for it is an over-rich category of attitude and appeal—more inherently unwieldy, it seems to me, than any other we have dealt with. While no popular attitude category fits entirely within the frame of pure orientation as such, some fit better than others. Hope, for example, is commonly understood as more purely attitudinal than faith, because faith as commitment to some projected value or state of affairs must always carry a significant amount of cognitive baggage. Love fits even less well than faith in the category of orientation because it is of compelling interest to us as a kind of *action* and also in connection with some sort of *consummation*, such as the union of lovers. Nevertheless, a considerable part of the interest of love and the source of its ultimate directive force lies in its attitudinal aspect as the attunement or disposition to act for the good of some being or other beings in general. Since it essentially involves movement toward the other, love naturally overflows its banks and can be found or stipulated wherever devotion goes—not only in ardently hopeful faith but even in respectful piety, as we saw in Calvin's description of the pious mind.

Robert Neville derives from "theological analysis" the conclusion that love "consists of righteousness, piety, faith, and hope combined."[60] But love's distinctive edge is in the affirmation of the other being and the direct impulsion to participate in the good of the other being as the other being *is*—or, more precisely, as the other being *is being*. For the pious mind, love can be too forward, presuming too much on possibilities of joint flourishing; for the mind of faith, love can be too backward, too much weighted down by actuality. But for the loving mind, it is a priority to be *directly attentive* to the other being and not to be guided merely by a conception of the other being as a good either real or possible. As an attitude, love is most naturally specified as a "bearing" or "comportment" in which receptive and active aspects of the subject's orientation are held in a balance.

Sallie McFague picks out this aspect of love with great clarity in *Super, Natural Christians*. In our review of appeal motifs in ecologically oriented theology we took note of McFague's turn to Buber and the ideal of what she calls "subject-subjects relation." Her argument revolves as much around a loving attitude ideal as around a pointing to actual beings, for she is concerned with a fundamental *how* question: "*Should* we love nature? My answer is a resounding Yes. Christians should because the Christian God is embodied . . . God does not despise physical reality but loves it and has become one with it . . . But *how* should we love nature? That is the more difficult and interesting question" (26).[61] Her answer is that we should take an attitude of loving attentiveness. We should be ready to become self-forgetfully absorbed in "the sheer, alien pointless independent existence" of beings we encounter (28). A certain aesthetic detachment is desirable for the sake of letting the other being declare itself independently of our prejudices (114).

247

This love-aestheticism can blend dangerously with an intellectualism: McFague thematizes the contrast between the "loving eye" and the "arrogant eye" as an alternative of "models" by which a being is "seen as" a fellow subject or as a manipulable object, thereby shifting the matter out of the heart (Schleiermacher's midpoint of "feeling") and into the head ("knowing").[62] Yet McFague unmistakably appeals to us on a different wavelength when she characterizes her "subject-subjects" model as one of friendship (38).[63] For in friendship the primary point is to *be* friends, and only for the sake of this to *see* oneself and the other *as* friends. The divine way of being a friend, she claims, is one of embodied solidarity with all other beings, as a Christian is given to understand by the model of Christ.

McFague's formulation of love in *Super, Natural Christians* is well suited to what exists external to the subject simply as it presents itself "naturally," free of the past of preconception and the future of wish. The account applies less well to fellow beings as joint participants in a long-running and ever-unfolding *story* that constantly requires rehearsals and anticipations—the sort of temporally extended existence that human beings share in the frameworks of family, state, and church.[64]

Love can play as crucial a role in a politically oriented theology as in a theology of ecological responsibility, but in a political context it must be presented as part of a synthesis of human action on the large scale. Jon Sobrino's *Spirituality of Liberation* makes crucial appeal to love and hope in combination, rooting optimism in the action of the present and relating the perception of the present to an ideal becoming:

> Whatever direction reality takes, it calls on us to have hope. But the hope it calls for is an active impulse, not the passive hope of mere expectation. It is a hope bent upon helping reality become what it seeks to be. This is love . . . We may hope for the life of the world only if we are willing to bestow life on the world . . . Jesus devoted himself to the humanizing of human beings, to the realization of the *homo vivens, gloria Dei*, as Christians would later say. His point of departure was the *pauper vivens*, the living indigent, and the life that he offered flowed from this starting point to all other human beings as well. (19–20)[65]

The synthesis of love and hope in personal "holiness" corresponds, according to Sobrino, to a synthesis in theological representation of the dynamic actuality of the present, "history," with divine reality: "We are called on to 'make history,' and make it 'according to God'" (73). Love is the hinge of liberationist devotion because it responds directly to actual need and is essentially concerned with the efficacy of actions taken to meet need (64).[66] The loving subject is stuck so firmly to present action as to be unable to evade persecution; in the perfection of devotion, a lover is willing to accept even martyrdom. "With this love, one corresponds to the ultimate loving and saving reality of God [as known through Christ]" (95). The claim is not that Christians are uniquely able to love devotedly, but that people "correspond to," and so find, the Christian God in loving devotion. Nevertheless, in a model of spirituality designed to guide a Christian life, it is proper to derive all right thought, feeling, and action from God's initiative (64).

The theme of integration or synthesis has a uniquely strong affinity with the basic loving attitude. Love can leave nothing alone; it reaches out and receives illimitably. We can think of a lover either as overflowing into past and future (wanting to know everything about the personal history of a human beloved, for instance, and wanting to plan future actions together) or as being flooded by past and future however they become knowable. The pious subject, too, will be concerned with all things under the aspect of piety—for example, with fashioning new practices that comport well with the honor of ancestors, or with imagining a "Well done, faithful servant" moment of ultimate vindication. And the subject of faith will revere a seminal past occasion of promising and infer present duties from it. Each type of devotion takes responsibility in its own way for all sides of time. But the site of the actual gathering of temporal considerations is the present, which is salient for love as it is not for piety and faith.

The pious mind will object to excessively valuing the actual as opposed to the real: in its view, the proper "gathering place" of all considerations is in the real, where everything of any consequence *ends up*, having become what it truly is and deserves to be. Faith will insist on a center of gravity always ahead of us in a synthesis necessarily greater than any yet achieved, a future centering that forms the ultimate condition of meaningfulness of everything remembered and directly experienced. Love has the advantage of being able to appreciate both of these kinds of affirmation more than either can appreciate the other, for love presides over the transition of possibility to reality in the present of actualization and so can balance and blend the appeals of achieved good and surpassing good, cherishing the beloved as having become wonderful and having wonderful potential. The corresponding danger in love, the madness of present-mindedness, is to be concerned with all things present, past, and future *only* in their present representation, flying by the seat of one's pants. Mystics who deliberately pursue this state separate it carefully from the main network of human actions (as in a Sufi circle or Buddhist monastery).

* * *

We have now assembled a strong prima facie case, I think, for the existence of a central religious issue of divergent types of devotion. At least three main types of devotion have strong and quite distinctive attitudinal profiles, and the literature shows that it is possible for leading thinkers to advance a religious cause by pitting the types against each other or by working out the terms of synthesis for some or all of them. I propose now to take the measure of this issue's difficulty in greater depth.

The Problem of the Plunge and the
Prospect of a Devotional Synthesis

Devotion as a religious ideal involves more than merely the subjective maximum of affirmative attention such as anyone might cultivate unaided. It involves an extraordinary, divinely gifted power of affirming. Devoted human beings are, in principle, like bodies no longer weighted by ordinary earth gravity alone, but gripped by an infinitely dense and massive core of reality toward which they are now infinitely accelerating. We use the phrase "taking the plunge" to express our anxiety and excitement about unleashing a possibly uncontrollable movement; accordingly, I will refer to a plunge of devotion. The knowing, willing, and feeling of those who take the plunge of devotion are stretched to match an infinitely expanded breadth and depth in experience, so that they can see the most massive evils as still overshadowed by good, can give up their lives for love of strangers and enemies, and can seriously hope that wolves will one day live with lambs. With these expanded ingredients, the attitudinal synthesis of knowing, willing, and feeling is exceptionally energized. There is an ideally open, instantaneous readiness to get involved with anything devotion proposes. There is an ideally high availability of energy, an effervescence of eagerness, and a zeal that will brook no opposition. There is an ideally trustworthy loyalty that will cling to the projects sanctioned by devotion, no matter what. Devout subjects will wholly dedicate themselves to these projects as a matter of principle and life-plan, according to the ideal of vocation.

The excess over ordinary affirmation in devotion gives rise to two problems corresponding to two major concerns of religious attitude thinking that we reviewed earlier:

(1) The ideal of a religious "inspiration" and devotional proprium creates worries about whether the devout will be responsible to the rest of us: will they be fanatics, "enthusiasts," exempting themselves from the moral regulation of everyday relations as they take their plunges of affirmation?

(2) It seems as though plunges would not submit to the superimposing and harmonizing by which requisite attitudes are commonly brought together in a single subject. Are the subjects of piety, love, and faith fated to separate from each other in their affirming, fated to live in different religious universes, in spite of the optimistic pasting together of the great attitudes that might be ventured by theologians? Or is there indeed a coherent attitudinal structure within which divergent types of devotion can coexist?

1. *Inspiration and responsibility.* The devotional answer most readily given to the worry about responsibility is that any responsible person is bound to respond to whichever appellant most exigently demands response according to the true possibilities of meaningful response—let the chips fall where they may. Barth's answers to Harnack in 1924 are exemplary. Rather than make

Christian theology conform to generally accepted norms of rationality, Barth argues, the task of Christian theology is to make everyone aware of the ultimate futility of their thinking in separation from God (the "crisis" of humanity) and aware also of the terms of their ultimate rectification in relation to God.[67] Barth's approach is high-handed, of course, but it points up how *any* attempt to enforce a standard of responsibility presumes *something* about superordinate appeals and tenable basic attitudes, and that different presumptions are possible; a fair definition of responsibility cannot preclude divergence in identifying the reference points and standards of responsibility.

Schleiermacher thinks he defuses this issue by locating the essence of religion in feeling rather than knowing or willing. For the most part, people clash in what they take to be their responsibility by upholding cognitive or volitional commitments that cannot in themselves be religiously essential. The only responsibility-related difference between persons that does involve the essence of religion is the difference between those who sense and affirm their union with the universe and those who do not—but that is just the difference between those who are deeply responsible, ready to take specific responsibilities seriously, and those who are not. On this view, Schleiermacher can confidently harmonize Christianity with other elements of human culture. Barth's work shows, however, that the question of the identity of the supreme appeal and the problem of rivalry among appeals cannot be set aside as religiously inessential.

The neo-Kantian philosopher Georg Simmel argues that religiosity cannot conflict with a rational attitude because religion and science are general forms for experience rather than debatable contents within it:

> What makes a person religious is the particular way in which he reacts to life in all its aspects, how he perceives a certain kind of unity in all the theoretical and practical details of life . . . Religiousness thus can be seen . . . as a form according to which the human soul experiences life and comprehends its existence—a form, incidentally, that is subject to the kind of strict demands and ideals, beyond the subjective, which a more naive mind would associate only with some externally imposed code. Seen in this way, however, there clearly can be no conflict whatever between religiosity and science . . . both religiosity and science are able to perceive and interpret life in its entirety, and the two are just as incapable of conflicting with each other, or even of crossing paths, as are cognition and matter in Spinoza's system, because each already expresses the whole of existence in its own particular language.[68]

Simmel's main concern here is to show that religion's real vitality lies in its attitudinal root (a permanent human possibility) rather than in any particular cognitive objectivation. As a by-product of this point, he offers a reassurance much like Schleiermacher's: of all basic attitudes, religiosity is the one least capable of causing responsibility problems, since its essential vision or aim is the unity of all things. But this formulation only reminds us how bad our problems are. It is precisely the totalitarianism of the religious and scientific attitudes that makes their approaches to particular things and situations impossible to mediate. The unity-oriented religious soul is liable to feel protective of a living animal, for example, that the scientific soul would very much like to consume in an experiment. Although the scientific soul may give lip service to religion in calling the destruction of the animal a "sacrifice," it really has no clue to the fundamental religious valuation of communion of beings; nor does the religious soul share in a scientist's commitment to empirical curiosity.

A dominant trend in modern theology is to unite devotion with worldly responsibilities rather than aim it toward a separate religious frame of reference. The trend is now more pronounced than ever. Religious unworldliness is blamed (rightly) for contributing to personal immaturity, social injustice, and environmental degradation. Continuity in our responsibilities is a major thrust of Gustafson's piety argument as it was also of the "worldly" Christianity movement inspired by Bonhoeffer.[69] Political engagement based on up-to-date social analysis and collegiality with all who work for the oppressed are main features of liberation theology. There are analogous emphases in ecological theology. Moltmann criticizes Barth for conceiving divine revelation and spirit as discontinuous with worldly experience and being and for thus unduly limiting the Holy Spirit, which should be understood as a universally life-giving power.[70] These thinkers are careful to articulate a valuational framework in which the problem of inspiration's divergence from nondevotional forms of responsibility will not arise; theology's contribution is to enhance right valuation with imaginative and emotional intensity drawn from a religious heritage, ideally from a divine impartation.

Devotion's answer to the responsibility challenge will differ according to the kind of devotion that speaks. A crucial part of Gustafson's argument for piety is that the pious are cognizant of reality and goodness in all forms and that their senses of things can all be woven together into a single larger fabric of responsible life, so that "piety cannot be contrasted with reason" as faith can.[71] It is more characteristic of faith to argue (boldly) for a complete makeover of the challenge's terms of reference, as Barth does in his exchange with Harnack, trusting that the superiority of faith's approaches will become more and more fully manifest. It is more characteristic of love to derive justification, as Sobrino does, from the sincerity of the devout person's actual engagement with other beings, including a vulnerability of the lover in those relations. Love's primary invitation to others is to *meet*—and insofar as a conception of the situation is involved, to commune in forming and revising that conception rather than merely to define and transmit it—on the premise that the crucial evidence of rectification of relations will be produced in actual encounter and in actual rectifying.

2. *Divergence of devotions*. A convenient way to sketch the rival priorities of faith and piety is to set some of the most characteristic utterances of the two leading Protestant Reformers, Luther and Calvin, against each other. These

differences of devotional emphasis can plausibly be linked with important differences in the doctrine and conduct of the churches they have respectively founded. In doctrine, for example, it is a characteristic expression of the "for us!" fervor of Lutheran faith to insist on a whole revelation of God's Word in Christ, while the reverent reserve of Calvinism insists that God may not be so limited (in the doctrine called the *Extra Calvinisticum*).[72] In practice, we might cite the relative political complacency of Lutherans (whose faith looks toward an unworldly "kingdom") and the activism of Calvinists (jealous for the Creator's honor and glory).[73] But it is also true that Calvin has a way of saying virtually everything of theological importance that Luther says, and vice versa. Both of these "major" theologians offer nourishment and guidance to all sorts of devout people in connection with a full range of religious questions. How then should we generally expect to locate devotional divergence and gauge its effects, and how seriously should such divergence be taken by normative religious psychology?

It seems clear, firstly, that plunges do occur, with normative force. We recognize that certain people are "very devout," that with utter sincerity they "go all out" in affirming what they take to be divine and that their attitude is paradigmatic for religiousness. In sounding out the devotion represented by any such individual, we need to consider all the positive attitudinal maxima we can think of (reverence, zeal, loyalty, etc.) to see which apply. In the communities of the world religions it is typically not necessary for every member to take a devotional plunge, but it must be possible for anyone to take one, inasmuch as the subjective benchmark of the community's devotion has been established by people who did take it. (On Indic views, an auspicious rebirth may be required.) If no one in a religious community takes such a plunge, the whole community suffers from loss of a crucial rectifying relationship with the divine.

Secondly, it also seems eminently possible that the plunge be taken with contrasting emphases—in an innerworldly way or in an otherworldly way, in the manner of the "healthy-minded" or of the "sick soul," concentrating on inward contact with the divine or on objectively strict application, with sectarian sharpness or with catholic hospitality, or in the time-relative directions of piety, love, and faith that we have ideally distinguished here.[74] In relation to the temporal constitution of being, is it *necessary* that a religious plunge be taken in just one of those directions? Or is it possible to be subject to an infinite acceleration toward the divine in present actualizing of loving association *and* in pious cognizance of constituted reality *and* in hopeful envisioning of a still-unrealized future? It is intuitively hard to see how persons who live passionately for a future possibility toward which the world as we know it must change can also be passionately grateful for the world as it has already been given; or how persons utterly awed by the reality they have seen can set their heart on something never yet seen; or how persons passionately engaged in loving relations in the present could have any genuinely religious enthusiasm left

253

over for a conception of reality or possibility that stands independent of present action; or how persons passionately committed either to a holy reality or a holy possibility could surrender themselves to present give-and-take with full devotion.

A fully convincing answer to this question requires a full review of religious symbolizations and embodiments. I mean only to launch that review here, but to power the launch I will offer my own hypothesis based on the prominent appeal to faith in Luther and to piety in Calvin. But distinct appeals to piety, love, and faith may be found in either writer. Here, for example, is a "pious mind" passage in Luther's lectures on Genesis:

> [On Ham's dishonoring his father, Noah, in Genesis 9:20–22:] Ham had given up his devotion toward God and his father when he came to believe that he could rule the church better. Secretly he either laughed at or condemned his father. Now he makes such an exhibition of himself that he displays also before others his wicked and disrespectful attitude toward his father . . . though he was preserved with the few during the Flood, [Ham] forgets all piety. Still it is profitable to consider carefully how this fall happened to him. The outward sins we commit with the body must first take form in the heart. That is, before one sins by an act, the heart departs from the Word and the fear of God; it does not know and seek God, as the psalm states (14.2). After the heart gets to the point that it pays no attention to the Word and despises the ministers and prophets of God, there follow ambition and pride; those whom we see standing in the way of our desires we overwhelm with hatred and defamation, until finally our abusive language even brings on murder.
>
> Hence let those who are to rule either churches or states strive with all zeal to remain humble.[75]

By "love," Luther customarily refers to the work of serving one's neighbors, but here, commenting on Romans 8.3, he addresses the loving attitude:

> [Human nature] knows nothing but its own good, or what is good and honorable and useful for itself, but not what is good for God and other people. Therefore it knows and wills more what is particular, yes, only what is an individual good. And this is in agreement with Scripture, which describes man as so turned in on himself that he uses not only physical but even spiritual goods for his own purposes and in all things seeks only himself.
>
> This curvedness is now natural for us, a natural wickedness and a natural sinfulness. Thus man has no help from his natural powers, but he needs the aid of some power outside of himself. This is love, without which he always sins against the Law "You shall not covet," that is, turn nothing in on yourself and seek nothing for yourself, but live, do and think all things for God alone.[76]

Thus we do find in Luther a pious admonition to act always in fear of God and a love-invitation to act for others. Yet these appeals are made with Lutherish faith-twists. The referent of piety is not the Creator or creation but the

Word; Luther's preferred teaching is that we not put our own "ambition" before the stupendous *promise* that God has made. And the supreme referent of love is not "others" generally but "God alone," seen Lutheranly as the amazing savior. Elsewhere, Luther is explicitly at pains to subordinate love to faith, making faith the true principle of devotion and love its worldly consequence.[77]

Calvin, for his part, says this about faith:

> Wherever [Christian] faith is alive, it must have along with it the hope of eternal salvation as its inseparable companion. Or rather, it engenders and brings forth hope from itself. When this hope is taken away, however eloquently or elegantly we discourse concerning faith, we are convicted of having none . . . hope is nothing else than the expectation of those things which faith has believed to have been truly promised by God. Thus, faith believes God to be true, hope awaits the time when his truth shall be manifested.[78]

And about love:

> [The Eucharist] gives us a vehement incitement to holy living, and above all to observe charity and brotherly love among us. For since we are there made members of Jesus Christ, being incorporated into him and united to him as to our Head, this is good reason . . . especially that we have to one another such charity and concord as members of the same body ought to have. To understand properly this benefit, we must not suppose that our Lord only warns, incites and inflames our hearts with the external sign. For the chief thing is that he cares for us internally by his Holy Spirit . . . seeing that the virtue of the Holy Spirit is joined to the sacraments when they are duly received, we have reason to hope they will afford a good means and assistance for our growth and advance in sanctity of life and especially in charity.[79]

But Calvin's understanding of faith's hope depends on his pious interpretation of divine election. Christians hope to learn when "the truth is manifested" that they are among the creatures whom God has already destined for glory, according to the awesome reality of God's plan. As for love, Calvin is just as zealous as Luther to contradict the priority given to love by the Scholastics:

> "Does the essence of righteousness lie more in living innocently with men than in honoring God with piety?" Not at all! But because a man does not easily maintain love in all respects unless he earnestly fears God, here is proof also of his piety . . . It is certain that the Law and the Prophets give first place to faith and whatever pertains to the lawful worship of God, relegating love to a subordinate position.[80]

Both Luther and Calvin know the range of religiously powerful appeals that *can* be made in Christian theology, and both are capable of fashioning an attitudinally comprehensive theology for the whole church. When they do make devotional appeals different from their preferred appeals, there is no good reason to suppose that they are insincere or that they are not themselves deeply moved by those appeals. Nevertheless, Luther sounds most like Luther when he goes on boisterously about the amazing implications of Christian faith, and it seems that the better we get to know him, the more apparent his faith-bias becomes in virtually everything he writes. Our sense of the Calvinish, similarly, reflects Calvin's chronically reverent, sternly disciplinary manner. We use them in this way; they deploy themselves in this way. Whether the distinctively Lutherish and Calvinish effects flow from the innate temperaments of the two individuals or are more a function of the different polemical exigencies and opportunities they happened to encounter is of secondary importance. What is of primary importance is that a potentially decisive point about supreme meaningfulness *can* be made, at times, by sharpening the edge of a possibility-oriented faith or a reality-oriented piety. What can be gained in this way is intensity of devotion, together with any cognitive referents that can be attached to devotion. The appeals of piety and faith are vivid in religious imagination and pull sharply on devotion. Whereas a whole Lutheran curriculum or liturgy may effectively sustain a balanced portfolio of devotions, the religious attention-getter or engine of inspiration in it at a given moment is likely to be the Lutherish appeal to faith.

From the possible dominance of a devotional type in the life or work of an individual, we can see how a devotional type could dominate or be seen as dominant in an entire community or tradition, particularly in its rhetorically acute phases of evangelizing or polemic. It seems a good heuristic rule in religious studies generally to expect that any reasonably durable or inclusive religious community will express every important possibility of religious life in some way. That is a rule of plenitude and balance with regard to devotional alternatives. But we can expect also that in many situations a religious ideology will gain advantage by contrasting itself with attitudinal alternatives. We can see the contrast principle working on the very largest scale: *all* the Axial Age religious movements shared the revolutionary character of appealing in some way to faith against piety. Thus was the prospect of a radical end of suffering preached by Buddhism and the prospect of personal intimacy with God urged by bhakti Hinduism against the Brahmanist system of karma and dharma; thus was the "new covenant" of exilic Judaism formulated with reference to a messianic future; thus was the eschatology of Christianity opposed to Roman civic piety; and thus even the piety-minded Confucians asked for belief in idealized possibilities of piety in contrast to a perpetuation of ancient ways sheerly for the sake of fulfilling a duty to reality. The contrast principle works also within traditions, defining subtraditions and schools: faith-oriented Mahayana Buddhism divides from reverential Theravada; within Mahayana, faith-oriented Pure Land divides from reverential Tiantai; and so forth. Ethically, aesthetically, and mystically oriented movements in all communities advance by appealing to a love ideal.

There are many different possible characterizations of the attitudinal base of religious changes, to be sure, but it is amply evident that the identities of religious movements are established in part contrastively and that the contrasts are grounded in part in attitudinal issues of this fundamental form. Insofar as we understand religious movements as defined by these contrasts, they will not be practically reconcilable. (Whether or for what purposes religious movements *must* be defined by these contrasts is, however, always open to discussion.) Religious pluralism at the level of devotional meaning-formation should be expected to renew itself continuously. And we should expect to come upon ideally or actually stable systems of energetically symbiotic rivals who thrive in mutual contrasting, like the Western European system of faith-Lutheranism, piety-Calvinism, and love-Catholicism, or the Islamic system of faith-Shi'ism, piety-Sunnism, and love-Sufism.

Let us turn back now to the most difficult side of the question of devotional divergence as it concerns the religious psychology of individuals. It is not hard to see how individual members of a religious community might differ in attitude, perhaps "temperamentally," along the lines of devotional type. Two Christians, for example, may follow a shared creedal formula and declare that they "believe in the resurrection of the body" yet mean vastly different things—the one envisioning a future marvelous state, the other a fulfillment in everyday worldly encounters. They may in fact argue or talk past each other even as the shared language of Christian doctrine and the practical harmony of church life keeps the nature of their disagreement obscure. It seems desirable from a normative Christian point of view that each of these individuals be in lively relation with the goods associated with the other's attitude. The concept of attitude implies that either individual can *change* devotional type. But could an individual take the devotional plunge in different ways *simultaneously*, as the *same* religious subject? Could a Christian really bank on a future reconstitution of glorified human flesh at the same time that he or she really banks on embodied solidarity with fellow beings in the present? The combination of attitudes can be figured in discourse; a theologian can appeal to Christians to do this, and such an appeal is impressive in a specifically theological way, at once logically structured and amazing. Thus, Sobrino writes:

> [Appeal to piety:] In the resurrection we find God's definitive sanction of Jesus as *the* human being. [Appeal to love:] But the truth of Jesus' being-human appears only in his history. In the resurrection we have God's guarantee that the genuine human being appears in Jesus' love and surrender . . . [Appeal to faith:] In the resurrection God declares that there will be a new sky and a new earth, and that the risen Christ constitutes the first fruits of that new creation. [Appeal to love:] But in Jesus' preaching of the reign of God we see the basic element of this eschatological novelty in our very history, and we hear the demand that we not only look forward to that reign, but actually construct it. [Appeal to faith:] In the resurrection we behold how God fulfills history, reconciling the seeming irreconcilables of history. [Appeal to love:] But in the proclamation of the reign we see how to fulfill history gradually, maintaining to the hilt poles so difficult to reconcile

historically—justice and mercy, indignation and forgiveness, gratuity and effectiveness, universality and a preference for the poor, structure and person, and so on.[81]

But can a human subject actually hold the complex attitude implied by all these religious desiderata, even with divine empowerment?

What matters in principle for theological anthropology is that the appellate subject is *called upon* to be maximally devout. Schleiermacher shows a way of representing the possibility of this schematically. *The Christian Faith* posits an "immediate self-consciousness" at a midpoint between our receptivity and our activity, a type of consciousness that hosts a more primordial intentional integration than everyday consciousness is capable of. In his *Dialectic*, however, Schleiermacher appeals to the more purely functional notion of a *crossing* point between knowing and willing, thinking more in terms of a coordination of knowing and willing in alternation.[82] We can conceive the religious subject's center also as a crossing point between devotional plunges. When a theologian leads us across this crossing point—as when Sobrino declares that hope and love are two sides of one coin—a bond is proposed between the movements made on either side of the crossing: we are instructed that our maximizing of affirmation in the future realm of possibility gives needed aim and energy to our maximizing of affirmation in the present realm of actualizing, and vice versa. The movement we are called on to make is something like swinging on a swing, where a higher backswing leads to a higher swing forward, and vice versa, even though the two swings are opposite. Just as one cannot swing out either backward or forward without returning to a midpoint, so one cannot go off in any of the prime directions of devotion without coming back to a point of meeting with the other spheres, the analogue of gravity or equilibrium in this case being the ontological indissociability of reality, actualizing, and possibility—or, in valuational terms, the absurdity of honoring without loving or hoping, or of loving without honoring or hoping, or of hoping without honoring or loving.

Another pertinent implication of the swing analogy is that even though a forward swing implies a backward swing, a swinger cannot ordinarily pursue or experience the two phases of the swing in the same way. A swinger faces forward and deliberately gathers force on the backward upswing and forward downswing and conducts the other phases of the swing more passively. When a theologian appeals to me to be aimed in piety, love, and faith all at once, it is like asking me to twirl and strain on a swing with exceptional adroitness. If a theologian appeals just to piety, or to love, or to faith, I can respond with a quasi-kinesthetic happiness of single aim. Then I have a strong sense of where *I* am headed and what *I* am about. As a "knight of faith," for example, I go boldly forward on the strength of a promise. But when my prescribed aim is more differentiated, my sense of functioning as a constituent in a larger system becomes proportionally greater and my sense of a particular mission becomes less vivid. Fulfillment comes more in realizing my microcosmic correspondence to the workings of the larger system than in achieving distinction. The character of centering changes, and with it the normative meaning of self.

There are clues in Schleiermacher for interpreting such variation in the meaning and force of selfhood in devotion. For Schleiermacher has pointed to a complexity in religious selfhood by making his anthropological point of union of knowing and feeling—also a crossing point—coincide with an ontological and cosmological point of union between an individual being and universal being—also a crossing point. What happens to the self in crossing between realizing the individual and realizing the universal? Louis Roy notes that Schleiermacher's famous "immediate self-consciousness" is misleadingly labeled, since it is actually specified as consciousness of the unity of being prior to distinctions among beings, that is, as a realization of universal being as such. Whereas Schleiermacher customarily distinguishes just between immediate self-consciousness and reflective, objectivating consciousness, Roy reconstructs his account to accommodate three phases of consciousness and self-distinctness.[83] Roy calls the primal consciousness of universal being "Consciousness A." In each subject's experience there must also be an apperceptive "Consciousness B" that implicitly relates all experience to a self, unifying it as the experience of that subject. Finally, there is a reflective "Consciousness C" for which the self may be an object among others.

The Schleiermacherian subject is a development of the Leibnizian monad whose perception represents the whole universe and whose unique perspective enriches the universe. The perception of Consciousness A is universal; it is our attunement to being as such, to the proximally graspable possibilities of all things, and to the ultimate reality of all things. (To illustrate the sense of the last part of the claim, I may say that although I am not presently aware of events transpiring on the far side of the moon, I know myself to be part of a fundamental being-event and world-system that includes those events, so that I know that I *am* affected *with* them and *could* at any time be affected *by* them.) The perception of Consciousness B belongs to a particular "here"/"now"/"mine" perspective on the universe. In Consciousness C, universality and particularity are united; definite mental objects are given in an aspect and order bound to a particular perspective but are also construed in the free-ranging perspective of rational thought, according to which the chair I see before me is *a chair*, the idea of noncontradiction I now entertain is *the* ever-applicable principle of noncontradiction, and I myself am one of numerous social-historical entities named Smith.

We may apply the pattern of this analysis to devotion by shifting its reference from awareness to affirmation. Let *affirmation* be defined as that kind of apprehension that combines the impression a subject receives from a being with a putting forth of the subject's own energy in support of that being—perhaps simply in a momentarily vivid representation of the being, most immediately, but in larger frames of reference acting so as to maximize the being's flourishing as that flourishing is understood by the subject *under appeal*, that is, in discovering and following the being rather than in exploiting it. We may define *devotion* descriptively as maximized affirmation, and prescriptively as illimitable affirmation. Now Schleiermacher's "immediate self-consciousness" or Consciousness A is already clearly a devotional ideal at the same time that it is a privileged state of awareness; it is an affirming plunge into the bosom of the Infinite, a limitless enthusiasm for being in the most inclusive sense. We can call it, in this aspect, Devotion A. Since Devotion A must be unlimited, we should conceive it as embracing piety, love, and faith in principle. Corresponding to apperceptive Consciousness B is a B-aspect of devotion, essentially personal. Consciousness B is the preeminent here/now/mine type of awareness, though not to the exclusion of concern with past reality and future possibility. Accordingly, Devotion B can take on the intensely futural character of the faith type, or be piously oriented to already-established reality, or be lovingly engaged in the work and play of the present. Our attention spontaneously inclines and focuses in those ways, usually in a stirring of desire for possession or fear of loss. Thus Devotion B is our usual image of devotion, whereas Consciousness C, not B, is our usual image of consciousness—the reason for this difference being that devotion does not have as immediately and directly enforceable a requirement of universal sharability as does consciousness, with its task of world-representation. We can, however, conceive a reflective, objectivating, and potentially synthesizing Devotion C, which, like Consciousness C, can be relatively impersonal: a commitment not simply to cherish a particular thing in the finite subject's particular relation to it, but to participate in any available way in the affirming of a being or a class of beings.

This Schleiermacher-inspired model of devotion places the most acute divergences of piety, love, and faith in the sphere of Devotion B, the possibility of harmonizing the devotional types in the sphere of Devotion C, and the radical possibility of actually unified devotion in the sphere of Devotion A.

Note that although we have important empirical motives for adopting a scheme like this—for we are faced with manifest psychological, social, and historical developments in religious thinking that the scheme helps to analyze—the scheme can be inferred from what we find to be the ultimate exigencies of meaningful experience in principle. That gives it a transcendental aspect, in the Kantian sense. The question of the basic structure of meaningful experience does have to be addressed in this way insofar as our prescriptive intentions go beyond the plane of empirical experience. We are not free not to worry about how to reconcile our most intense and necessarily more concrete devotion with a fully inclusive, fully adequate devotional mise-en-scène. Transcendental inference is a means of figuring a solution. But transcendental argument is, of course, peculiarly questionable in that it claims to derive the implications of supreme requirements governed by no others and yet can never guarantee that it has done this correctly, since it cannot appeal to higher requirements for validation. Thus, if we are serious about making a case for a scheme of meaning-formation, we must not content ourselves with one intellectually plausible inference, but instead must test every possible claim of superordinacy against every other to make out, as best we can, where the most compelling superordinacy lies.

If, as I have maintained, the ultimate exigencies of meaning-formation are to be identified with the exigencies of rectification of relationships among beings, then the priority of relationship issues to issues of consciousness formation as such requires a pneumatological amendment of the consciousness-based Schleiermacherian model of devotion. This amendment can be stated simply, though it drastically enlarges the horizons of devout meaning-formation: what is required is to affirm that different devout meanings—such as pious reverence for one's ancestors, or hope for heavenly salvation, or hope-and-love in synthesis in a liberation struggle—are formed, and are to be formed, in the rectifying of relationships, superordinately in relationships with fellow intenders. To the extent that devout meanings are formed in a subject's consciousness according to the ontological, cosmological, or empirical exigencies of the *existence* of consciousness, these meanings are ultimately qualified as devout, not by conformity to a consciousness ideal taken in abstraction from the rectifying of relationships, but rather in the spiritual qualifying of that consciousness by the rectifying of relationships.[84] I say that the horizons of devout meaning-formation are greatly enlarged by this amendment because, on the one hand, it allows that rectification is a function not merely of conscious intentions but of the whole unfolding of life, in a community and in the world-system as well as individually; and on the other hand, it allows us to appreciate the work of a variety of spiritual initiatives, language foremost among them, that lead and outrun consciousness. It is possible to express meanings of respect, love, hope, and amazing combinations of these attitudes that go beyond what one can coherently represent to oneself.

Given the pneumatological specification of conditions of supreme meaningfulness, theology cannot decline to conform to that standard; thus, a theology always is a pneumatology—or to put it the other way around, "pneumatology" is a formal indication of what a theology always is. From theology's own point of view, no experience can tell against the fulfillment of a theologically proper specification of the conditions under which relationships *are* ultimately rectified. Religious inspiration will supply anything essential that experience lacks. To grant this license to religious proposals (or rather, to observe that they must claim it for themselves) is not to rule out the possibility that religious thinking is crazy or confused. Few would deny that some religious appeals, at least, are worthy of rejection. But religious appeals can be quite strangely *excessive* and still be worthy of acceptance in a community insofar as they are found to provide superior spiritual guidance and nourishment. The synthesis of piety, love, and faith might be a psychologically excessive yet imperatively edifying ideal.

In pneumatological perspective, Devotion A is the ideal of an enabling primordial event of commitment to affirming relationship; Devotion B is the ideal of the most concretely fervent personal attachment; and Devotion C is the ideal of fully mediated, collegial, comprehensive affirmation. The problem of the synthesis of divergent devotional types (now located more precisely as Devotion B types) is addressed—one might even think, or hope, "solved"— in the sphere of Devotion C, which takes over realizations of Devotion B for its own purposes. In a given religious service I may be directed to sing first a song of pious praise, then a song of solidarity with those who suffer, then a song of heavenly longing, as though I were wholly invested by turns in honoring divine Creation, in loving my fellow beings in the luminance of divine Revelation, and in yearning for divine Redemption.[85] The leader of this observance might be given a privileged role as a realizer of full devotion, an authoritative religious subjectivity.[86]

Let us return now to the idea that a more complex devotional prescription changes the sense—somehow assumable or imputable—of the subject's selfhood. The filling out of Devotion C toward comprehensiveness can be thought of as the work of the community in distinction from the work of the individual—consisting partly of a work of the community *in* the heart of the individual, constituting the individual as more than merely individual. In fact, the difference between individual and communal possibilities does assume major importance in religious discourse: the Jewish "Israel," the Christian *ekklesia*, the Buddhist *sangha*, the Islamic *ummah*, and the social systems of realized piety and dharma honored by Confucians and Hindus are all credited with distinctive salvific powers. The positive correspondence between individual and community is important too: as it is historically evident that a community most energetically launches itself in making a sharp attitudinal appeal to *this* direction of devotion, *not that*—to the eschatological future rather than the ways of the ancestors, for example, or to an amazing justification in faith rather than a sweet sanctification in works—it is correspondingly true that the maximum of attitudinal energy for an individual at any moment is achieved in the movement in a certain direction, such as toward the transcendent or toward the future. But there is a limit to this correspondence in the fact that an individual can survive and flourish within the limits of a pointed devotion in a way that a reasonably inclusive and durable religious community cannot.

In the sphere of Devotion C, we can stipulate for the individual a simultaneous affirmative attention to reality, actuality, and possibility. This attitude could be designated eternity-mindedness, meaning by eternity the supersession of the normal division of time's dimensions. Against this, however, it could be maintained *normatively* that individuals cannot rightly be expected to be comprehensively devout, since an individual differs from a community precisely in not realizing that kind of wholeness. As Leibniz and Schleiermacher emphasized, the ultimate purpose, as well as the ontological limitation, of being an individual is to relate to the universe from a unique perspective within a totality of perspectives—to take up the vocation of realizing a particular aspect of the whole. A distinctive power and interest of a community in comparison with an individual is that it collates and harmonizes these realizations and so draws out their universal meaning. (A community also plays the role of an individual in its relations with other communities, as Schleiermacher notes; thus, every community has the two aspects of partiality and universality.)[87]

An individual may yet aspire to universal awareness and sympathy. Following the model of the ideal community, an individual can indeed arrange a sequence of initiatives and experiences to pursue that universality. Indeed, a "major" thinker or "great" leader achieves this in his or her work—work that may serve as the charter of a community. Any individual can continually gain in effective responsibility by acquiring new forms of response. All the mature members of a community are expected to have the universality of basically understanding and being able to explain any principle, cognitive or practical, that the community considers essential to a well-lived life. And ordinary reasonableness on anyone's part involves being able to mediate between individual and universal horizons of experience. Nevertheless, the reality of the individual *as* an individual, corresponding to the affirmable contribution of the individual as an individual to the life of a community, involves playing one part in the orchestra, not all the parts—a clarinet, for example, which is in the woodwinds—analogically, a Lutherish faith or a Calvinish piety, or a Lutherish way of navigating from a faith affirmation to a love affirmation to a piety affirmation, interestingly different from a Calvinish way of moving from a piety affirmation to a faith affirmation to a love affirmation.

If religious individuals psychologically or ontologically cannot and normatively should not realize a perfectly inclusive and balanced synthesis of piety, love, and faith, then religious axiologies are irreducibly plural in a most important way. For the distinctive valuations of piety, love, and faith must be recognized and weighted differently by every subject. A common axiological universe will remain a necessary figure of discourse, but diversity and volatility in religious history and psychology will always be the basic order of the day.

But if it is unreasonable to expect of any individual subject a full flowering of devotion or a full-fledged intention to perfect a basic attitude along all possible lines at once, it is still possible to indicate a genuinely personal attitudinal correlate of the larger project and demand of devotion. This attitude differs from readiness or eagerness or practical zeal, all of which may be completely taken over by a particular devotion to the exclusion of others. The inherently inclusive attitude is one of appreciative openness toward all valuational possibilities, even especially toward strange ones, which as mere deference we call humility but as active appreciation we call *wonder*. Wonder is characteristically expressed in questioning. The community's interest in sustaining the most vital participation in a complex devotional life is well served by eliciting and sustaining an attitude of wonder, which relates to the plunging fervor of devotion as a balloon's helium relates to its sandbags—with similar navigational advantages.[88]

The Impossible Attitude of Complete Openness to Radical Transformation

The wondering attitude opens an individual subject to unexpected, dazzling possibilities, but it is not itself outlandish. It is to be distinguished from the extreme ideal of complete openness to radical transformation—an ideal that could be held up as one of the ultimates of attitude thinking, since it makes the most of the basic attitude principle of a momentous changeableness in a subject's way of living. But the ideal of complete openness to radical transformation cannot straightforwardly be maintained without self-contradiction. For it is contradictory to affirm a change that cancels the basis of the affirmation, that says something like "There must be no necessity" or "Words are meaningless"; and holding myself agreeable to a radical change of orientation seems to negate the basis of *my* being meaningfully oriented at all.

Radical transformation of self is a religiously popular ideal in familiar ways: religious subjects ask to be given a new heart free of sin or even a new freedom from selfhood itself, hoping that a divine life-principle will constitute for them a life as different from their unredeemed life as good is different from evil. The new life could be implemented through faith, through loving submission, or even through piety, as in a penitent assumption of burdens of history.[89] Devotional plunges are dramatic and infinitely consequential because the life-changing stakes of attitude adjustment are so high. Frederick Streng's widely used definition of religion as "a means of ultimate transformation" is well warranted.[90] The apparent contradiction of aiming to be something other than oneself is overcome by appeal to the actual arrival of the glorious new life-principle (Spirit or dharma or Way) in the self, making it let itself go. Thus it may be said that the basis of the orientation to cancel one's former self is really the newer life's self-affirmation. Yet an orientation to be wholly transformed in a certain way, sustained by a particular principle of a best existence, is not the same as an orientation to be transformed in *any* way, according to *who knows what* principle of existence. When trust becomes infinite, it becomes delirium.

Religious mystics have pushed against this limit of attitudinal possibility by ecstatically giving themselves up to a divine reality that can in no way be prefigured to accord with their human expectations. Their surmise is that perfect being must be radically other than the existence they know; thus, in aiming toward holiness, they hurl themselves into a perfect darkness and disequilibrium as far as their worldly selfhood is concerned. The worldly face of their ecstatic orientation is weird, unaccountable behavior, like the wildness of Majnun while he longed for Layla. It is rightly argued that these mystical adventures are always interpreted by the mystics themselves and by those whom they inspire within a particular, articulated devotional frame-work.[91] The mystic's experience is a case study in perfecting relationship with an *identified* divinity; the radical openness is *to* that god, that love, that bliss, or that freedom, even if the mystic's apprehension of the divinity is supposed to change infinitely. In *being* mystical, however, the mystic is positioned on a psychologically risky and equivocal boundary between a recognizably oriented devotion and an utterly wild, implicitly nihilistic or suicidal adventure.

Some participants in interreligious dialogue push against this attitudinal limit in a comparable way. Raimundo Panikkar writes about his experience in India:

> A decade ago, after fifteen years' absence from the European literary scene, the plainest and yet the most searching question to ask me was: How have I fared? And although my human pilgrimage was not yet finished, I used to give a straightforward—obviously incomplete—answer: I "left" as a Chris-tian, I "found" myself a Hindu and I "return" a Buddhist, without having ceased to be a Christian. Some people nevertheless wonder whether such an attitude is objectively tenable or even intelligible.[92]

How could he have been, how can he now be *that* inwardly open? We may note that Panikkar's spiritual journey is far from picaresque. He was not a ready-for-anything blank slate randomly imprinted by Hindu and Buddhist forms of devotion; he consciously sought to deepen his Christian faith by engaging Hindus and Buddhists. By drawing a distinction between "faith" and "belief," he is able to talk of a purposeful perfecting of a definite faith commit-ment even as his beliefs are held open to revision. His faith is in "the truth," he says, positing that access to *the* truth could never be limited to one person or one finite community. He is under an obligation to collate his apprehensions of truth with everyone else's, which he can accomplish only if he takes others' views with full seriousness, seeing and valuing truth as they do. The ground of his confidence and the focus of his orientation is transcendent. He trusts Reality to be somehow good, life to be somehow worth living.[93] As a Christian, he trusts that he is in a redeeming relationship with this transcendent ap-pellant in holding a devotional focus on Christ, but the ultimate appellant is not the Christ-focus itself, it is the Reality that Christ brings to a focus. The ultimate appellant is not even "truth," Panikkar provocatively admits, given that another person's faith could be expressed in the proposition "Truth does not exist."[94] Panikkar's orientation is to *whatever* can be taken with full serious-ness by a human subject. He makes and answers an appeal to human soli-darity, to not leaving any of one's human fellows out in forming one's world-intuition; and that appeal is seen as coinciding with the Christian ideal of intertwined God- and neighbor-love.[95]

The interreligious learner is given a definite agenda by the concrete forms of devotion that are or may be realized by human beings, and a particular devotional commitment of his or her own may remain in a leading position. As in mystical ecstasy, the adventure is structured; but as also with the mystics, there is an impossibly challenging wild frontier in the adventure insofar as the subject is *really* open to *any* change, and awareness of this impossibility animates some of the objections that an interreligious learner will face.

Panikkar concedes that "not everyone is called to such an undertaking, nor is everyone capable of it."[96] But I suggest that it would be a mistake to think of the attitude of radical openness—or the capacity to adopt that attitude, or momentarily to adopt a more radical version of an open, curious, trusting attitude—as very exceptional, the exclusive province of the mystic or the intrepid interreligious pioneer. To *sustain* such an attitude devoutly is the hard and exceptional thing, but to *adopt* it boldly, or have it come over one crazily, might be as common as jumping into the proverbial swimming pool: the challenge of taking up a new task, a new game, or a new relationship offering who-knows-what roles can touch any of us in this dimension on any given day, bringing as much inward upheaval as we can stand.

We often find that the greater changes in ourselves have occurred as the cumulative result of a series of incremental changes that we were more modestly oriented to seek and accept at each step. One can open oneself curiously and trustingly to a *possibly* unlimited *progression* of change without directly facing the apparent madness of radical transformation; and readiness to go any distance on a path of change can be revolutionary in the end. Many are drawn by stages into a commitment of love, vocation, or religion that changes everything. Religious teachers have created paths—a series of observances, poems, images, koans—to exploit our willingness at many moments to try yet another adjustment.

***

Religion makes the strongest of all directive claims and involves commensurately serious attitudinal difficulties. The idea of right attitude, essential in the world religions, is stretched to the limits of feasibility and intelligibility by the maximally ambitious appeals of religious leaders. There is a great religious challenge not only in representing a greatest Appellant but also in harmonizing the possibly divergent poses and poises of devotion—corresponding to real, actual, and possible aspects of divinity, for example. This is the hardest form of the broader problem we all face of harmonizing diversely requisite attitudes. The hardest form of a problem can be the most revealing in some ways. Once I have seen that I would have to be a self differently in fulfilling the ideals of faith, love, and piety together than in fulfilling any one of these ideals alone, I see more readily how in everyday attempts to combine playfulness, friendliness, and critical reasonableness I am likewise submitting to different centerings of my existence and not merely tuning my autonomous intent. Similarly, mysticism and interreligious engagement present us with a difficult and revealing form of the general problem of our openness to transformation.

Religion makes the strongest directive claims in principle, but religion might not actually make the strongest claims on a particular subject. That kind of supreme appeal might not register; that kind of inspiration might not occur. Nevertheless, in the life of any responsive subject, superordinate appeals of relationship *will* register, and a prompting of right attitude *will* occur. The purpose of the next chapter is to distill the general import of our appeal and attitude inquiries into a characterization of life as spiritual.

nine
A Frame for Pneumaticism

The preceding chapters sought to develop a strategically revealing mise-en-scène for our two most articulate and explicitly ambitious forms of directive thinking, the philosophical and the religious, as we have practiced them and as we may practice them. This final chapter offers a synthesis of implications of what has been revealed, relying on a guiding pneumatological principle and placing that principle in our larger picture.

Fundamental Evaluation in Pneumatological Perspective: The Logical and Historical A Priori

The point of a philosophical study of a matter is to achieve a fundamental evaluation of it. The philosophical ambition par excellence is to evaluate fundamentally our fundamental evaluating.

To evaluate is to determine how a matter stands in relation to an affirmable order. One evaluates how something stands in relation to the order of one's own program and also how one's own intentions and actions relate to a larger order. To do this, it is necessary to understand the relevant larger order.

Suppose a ball rolls up to my feet unexpectedly. What is going on? To determine what to do with the ball, I need to know . . . that I am being included in a game of soccer, as it happens, so I need to know how soccer is played and how the teams are set up in the present game.

A priori evaluation is the determination of how matters stand in relation to an order that must obtain *in any case* as far as we can understand. The first means of a priori evaluation that we normally think of in philosophy are forms that must impose their order in any case whatsoever due to an inescapable logic in the rational analysis of cases. For example, a Kantian a priori evaluation of my situation with the soccer ball at my feet determines that (a) theoretically, the ball's movement had a phenomenal cause (since if this condition were not satisfied, experience could not form a coherent system), and (b) practically, my action with respect to the ball will be right only if I act on a universalizable maxim (since apart from this condition there could be no distinctively moral justification of an action). (The pneumatological expansion of the sense of [b] is that my action with respect to the ball will be superordinately meaningful just insofar as I address therein the issue of rectifying my relations with the ball and other beings.)

But there is another sense of "in any case," one deriving from factually necessary continuities between what is already determined and what is still to be determined, in which I am now bound in any case to respond to the ball's arrival. Whether I decide to pass the ball or try to score on my own, whether I accept or reject involvement in the game, in any case I will live henceforth within an order shaped by this incident. This is my historical a priori. The larger network of actions with which my action is to be linked may be described in quite different ways (a prank rather than a soccer game, an accident rather than an invitation), and any characterization of my historical fate can meaningfully be challenged; nevertheless, the relevance of history to my life is inescapable. No one who acts seriously with respect to other beings can think of starting on an absolutely new line with them or of completely escaping the consequences of actions that affect them. (The appealing depth of this factual necessity of practice is the spiritual datum that the relationships a subject is called upon to participate in rectifying are with *these* beings in *these* situations.)

Evaluating involves affirming an order, and affirming an order involves subjecting experience and practice to it, making it a norm. Norming is an activity; a particular evaluative determination usually belongs to a larger ongoing process. The meaning of an evaluation depends on the norming in which it takes part. Thus, a manager's decision about an employee's rate of pay is either good or bad in one important way according to whether it fulfills or fails to fulfill a communally maintained policy on pay; the meaning of the decision depends also on the character of the policy. Conversely, a normative order is inflected by the particular judgments and actions that express it. Imagine, for example, that the sexism of one community differs concretely from the sexism of another in the relatively more arrogant and dismissive way in which its managers pay women less than men. This is an a priori evaluative consideration not only historically, in defining the practical situation in which members of that community are bound to operate, but also logically, inasmuch as the ideal of fair treatment is intuitively and argumentatively accessible in this community only through the mediation of its members' actual evaluative performances. Thus, a treatise on women's rights written in this community will have a different spiritual texture from its counterparts in other communities.

The most radical evaluation involves examining critically or renegotiating the most basic norming. To do this, it is necessary to identify the factors that function as a priori. We must try to identify the logical a priori in what seem to be the inherently strongest conceptions by which experience and practice may be interpreted; and we must come to terms somehow with the historical a priori in the totality of actions that our own actions are to join. We bring out the logical a priori in an analysis (seeing what we can achieve on the rational attitude's premise that the solution we want is completely accessible at a given moment) and the historical a priori in a story (admitting that we are always on a way).

Philosophy, the project of fundamental evaluation as a human individual's initiative, came into culturally effective existence in the Axial Age, and we cannot conceive it apart from its two great poles of reference in the individual determinandum (figured by such notions as "soul," "mind," and "heart") and the transindividual determinans ("reality," "reason," "value"). The most basic possibility of making the individual subject "right" in relation to the transindividual is grasped through the concept of *attitude*, while the most basic possibility of registering the transindividual as "good" in relation to the individual is grasped through the concept of *appeal*. To interpret experience outside the categories of attitude and appeal would be to deny any depth of vis-à-vis in relations between beings. Reality would be a spectacle for an utterly detached observer or the stuff of blissful satisfaction—either way, no longer a directive concern.

Evaluation and norming are realizations of appeal and attitude in conjunction. Appeal is the stimulus of evaluation, attitude the response. Appeal and attitude are the correlative object- and subject-poles of a field of possibility of meaningful experience and normativity. (Conceptions that approach adequate indication of those poles can bring our thinking into fruitful relation with them but can also impair clarity—for example, in grounding meaningfulness on the abstracted commodity of "value" or on an arbitrary "will" or "desire.") *An evaluative argument needs both an appeal and an attitude as anchors of directive exigency; otherwise, an affirmation of order will make no relevant claim and carry no relevant conviction. But appeals and attitudes in themselves elude incorporation in any graspable order.* (1) This is true of appeals because it is the nature of an appeal to interrupt experience. One can never take an appeal as given. Even in referring to an existing appeal, as a moralist invokes a familiar moral ideal or a religious believer cites a historic revelation, one is *appealing* to it again (a fresh appeal in its own right, with its own volatility) and one is citing it *as an appeal*, letting it speak anew. That an appeal will actually superordinate itself to other claims on its audience's attention cannot be guaranteed; if the status of the appeal were wholly predetermined, it would not have the life-enriching eventfulness that makes it compelling. (2) Attitudes cannot be resolved in a graspable order because it is the nature of a basic attitude to underlie any definite intention. Thus, attitude is a contingency affecting the sense of an argument that the argument's own contrivances can never master. I may address the contingency by appealing directly to an attitude; for instance, I may conclude a justice argument by appealing to you to be reasonable, citing a standard of fairness that I know cannot be contradicted. Still, the meaning of my arguing and the meaning of your response will be determined by our fundamental orientations, and our fundamental orientations involve unfathomable, effectively unique mixtures of reasonable balancings and unreasonable unbalancings of self- and other-regard. Our interintentional action continually proves that full intentional concurrence can never be taken as assured, even given a massive commonality of language and reason; when we approximate to perfect concurrence, we celebrate it as a blessing.

Elusive though they are, appeals and attitudes impinge on our lives with infinite relevance. We are caught in the attitude-appeal relationship like bits of metal between the poles of a magnetic field. Attitude is not sheer freedom; it is orientation *to the world* in which *these* appeals are made. Appeal is not sheer transcendence; it is a call *upon a subject* premised on that subject's capacities of response. The directive force generated by the attitude-appeal relationship is always the charge of a concrete life and a tellable story. We vividly experience gradients of beauty and obligation; we are swept up in the power of the corresponding ideals and the eloquence of normative discourses. In this sea of unfairness we know unbearably well what Justice means, even though we can never accept any one formula of justice or picture of righteousness as a directive last word. We must be vitally interested in the historico-political characterization of our larger actions as adventures of Justice (or as "experiments with truth-force," in Gandhi's potent phrase).[1]

In attempting a fundamental evaluation of fundamental evaluation itself, then, we cannot expect to define pure criteria that would precisely measure our actual or conceivable normative intentions or resolve specific normative issues. Any criteria we could define would be outflanked by imponderably underlying attitudes and potentially insurgent appeals. We can, however, indicate the conditions of fundamental evaluation that are in force in our lives by tracking the vividness and eloquence of the norming that basic attitudes and superordinate appeals have generated and are generating. This will require not only an abstractable analysis of meaning types and conditions applicable to any conceivable case, but also a historically and politically valid story to represent what we have done and are doing, which bears inescapably on any actual future case. For this reason I have formed the present discourse as a contribution to an intellectual and spiritual story. The fundamental motivation for this storytelling is the spiritual exigency of rendering the prospects of action perspicuous for the sake of attending to the rectifying of relationships.

Storytelling is never innocent. It is easy to show that a story always represents beings unfairly and creates a cognitive package that is dangerously manipulable. But abstaining from storytelling altogether is neither socially nor spiritually feasible.

One might take the view that what has actually gone on among beings in the world does not essentially affect the meaning of our appellative and attitudinal points of reference in norming. One might hold, for example, that the ideal meaning of pursuing justice in Paris in 1789 is necessarily the same as the ideal meaning of pursuing justice in Paris in 1968—that the experience and action occurring between the two situations makes no difference to the pure normative content of the ideal of justice. While I do not deny that a vastly important common ground is shared by the activists of 1789 with those of 1968, I do deny that the available, effective ideals of justice can be exactly the same in the two situations. Like Hegel, I affirm that the unfolding of actual history gives an ideal new complexities of momentum and prospect. Like Hegel, I tie this claim to the idea of a spiritual framework in which the full realization of any meaning whatsoever is determined by a superordinate principle, a principle that is also a process.

Against Hegel, however, I define the spiritual as pertaining to the negotiated rectification of relationships among beings rather than to the movement of consciousness into freedom and self-possession. On my view, 1968 justice means something new in relation to 1789 justice, not merely because actual events in the interim have articulated new possibilities of existence and new forms of meaning that can be comprehended by a knowing mind, but more crucially because persons have been trying, through irreversibly consequential actions, to rectify their relationships with each other, participating in a larger endeavor in which we too participate, their various partial failures and successes contributing to the specification of our later position of responsibility.

The concept of the spiritual indicates an essential relationship between the logical and historical apriorities of norming. It is because right order in any conceivable case is ultimately grounded in the *active* rectifying of relations between beings that the history of the *actual* rectifying actions of beings is of essential directive relevance now and in the future. I cannot orient myself rightly while leaving out of account what my fellow beings have been up to. I must understand what has been going on in order to understand what we are all doing now; and I must see how the larger story goes in order to contribute to it with a sense of what will constitute integrity and progress in future actions. Avoiding oversimplifying and violent assumptions about how the story hangs together— like the assumptions of the all-unifying idealist Spirit, perhaps, against which Derrida has staged encounters with "spirits" that are haunting ghosts—I nevertheless must find out what belongs (or *can* or *may* belong) to this story.[2] I must rehearse and extend my fellowship with beings so as to amplify our dedication to mutual flourishing. To do this I must be ready to affirm every ideal I can make affirmative sense of.

Fundamental Alternatives to Pneumatology

This study has been guided by a pneumatological evaluative program that has enabled us to identify and assess the deepest directive currents in our thinking without rejecting any, even though we have found divergences and dramatic oppositions between rival philosophical and religious paths. Finally, we arrive at the ideal of the inclusion of *all* tenable appeals and attitudes. *Can* the root ideal of spiritual existence, the ideal of a commanding qualification of all meanings by the active rectifying of relations among beings, accommodate all potentially valid ideals? We will know we are at the limits of the pneumatological program's accommodation if we can identify fundamental alternatives to it based on radically different principles of evaluation.

The pneumatological interpretation of a priori norming is offered as the interpretation most fully cognizant of and responsible to the conditions of directive meaning, given the foregoing elucidation of those conditions in the framework of appeals and attitudes. What alternative interpretation of a priori norming could be sustained? Two main kinds of alternatives are possible: those that affirm a priori directive meaning on a different premise, and those that reject a priori meaning. The first possibility is represented by rational idealism and divine command fideism. The second possibility is represented by positivist, relativist, noncommittalist, and absolute nondualist approaches (the latter aiming to supersede the structure of appeal and attitude altogether).

1. Alternatives that Affirm A Priori Normative Meaning

A. *Rational idealism* is an apt label for any view that separates forms of directive meaning from the relating actions of beings and that attributes normative force to these abstracted ideals by virtue of the purity and spatiotemporal unrestrictedness they seem to have in their ontological detachment. For rational idealism, actual beings share in the perfection of ideal forms to the degree that they are guided by them; the force of norming is an ontological ennoblement or general procedural advantage. Among the greatest strengths of such a view are that it protects the freedom of evaluating subjects from biasing by particular circumstances, and that it gives as much orientation in planning possible futures as in interpreting the historical past. The great weakness of such a view is that it is committed to identifying the supreme appeal with an abstraction. Since it does not recognize that abstract forms hold directive force for us superordinately only insofar as they effectively relay the appeals and frame the attitudes of concrete beings, it fosters the insensitivity and disingenuousness of legalism.

Rational idealism claims to make possible an extension of normative meaning across all situations, but as I argued for the example of 1789 and 1968 justice, it does this oversimply and reductively in comparison with a more sensitive account that can be given. The pneumatological interpretation leaves out no positive directive meaning that rational idealism adduces—it does not deny the commensurability of 1789 and 1968 justice or the freedom of agents—but it considers in addition the differences that relating actions make to the meaning of agents' choices. Neither does the pneumatological view interfere with our freedom and responsibility in relation to the future, for it implies that our directive intelligence and ambition can gain in strength as our historical experience in norming grows. When Martin Luther King Jr. quoted Amos on the subject of righteousness ("Let justice roll down like waters, and righteousness like a mighty stream"), he did something vastly different than apply a timelessly valid criterion with rational certitude; he generated new inspiration by knitting together an ancient Israelite prophetic project and the American civil rights project into a larger story.[3]

A postmodernist inversion of idealism can be created by making a supreme appeal of the sheer absence of governing form—a firm norm of normlessness.

B. *Divine command fideism.* Another way to ground a priori norming is to make it depend on a "revealed" appeal rather than on an intellectually abstracted principle. The normative force of the supreme principle then inheres in the experienced impressiveness, that is, the "greatness" (or "holiness") of the manifest being. One is swept off one's feet by a divine command and confesses that it has become impossible to follow any other standard. This situation can be invoked as an irrefutable fact. But both idealist and pneumatological critics can fault the divine command fideist for short-circuiting the humanly essential work of thought, perception, and response. Divine command fideism seems disingenuous, moreover, in that it tacitly draws authorization from intellectual abstraction, without which its holy center could not be understood as a universal principle, and on spiritual responsiveness, apart from which the presentation of the holy could not register as an appeal. Suppose, however, that the intellectual and spiritual conditions of life under the divine command are acknowledged but rigorously subordinated to the unaccountable fact of the command's revelation. Then a positivism or relativism takes over, in effect a dismissal of a priori norming, and no authentically a priori claim can be made.

2. Alternatives that Reject A Priori Normative Meaning

A. A priori directive meaning can be dismissed by a *positivist* on the grounds that such a meaning-force is never objectively demonstrable or specifiable. But anyone who advances a positivist worldview in public discourse with any thoughtfulness or practical seriousness must self-contradictorily make a claim upon conviction and to that end must at least tacitly mobilize a story of superordinate appeal and basic attitude, perhaps a story of scientific rationality (like Comte's account of the human mind's growing up to positivist maturity) or hedonism or faith in a peremptory divine command; and this story will inevitably be bound to a superordinate story of rectifying relations just insofar as the handling of the positivist's contention is an active collective concern.[4]

B. *Cultural relativists* are caught in the same self-contradiction as positivists, claiming a priori the impossibility of an a priori claim, unless they are brave enough to make their own normative appeals sincerely and strictly within what they regard as norming's feasible frame of reference, their particular culture alone. But they can carry this through only by refusing to admit the influence of cultures on each other and the ongoing construction of larger cultures insofar as people have wider cultural horizons. They have to fight cosmopolitanism with isolationism, and yet their isolationism must always seek justification before a relatively cosmopolitan bar.

C. A sophisticated cousin of relativism is *noncommittalism,* the view that norming is most acceptably performed within concretely human-scaled limits, modestly ad hoc, in various ways in various contexts, without any presumption of fixing determinate, universally valid results. From this perspective the very idea of a priori or universal norming has too great an affinity with fascism and fanaticism. A sane, humane life includes humble reserve and even an admixture of subjective indifference. Negatively, this position rejects any categorical imperative or plenary meaning claim; positively, it protects the good of letting diverse ways of life be followed.

Classical prototypes of noncommittalism can be found in various skeptically inclined teachings, including Zhuangzi's: "You have only to rest in inaction and things will transform themselves . . . return to the root and know not why."[5] "My will is vacant and blank. I go nowhere and don't know how far I've gotten. I go and come and don't know where to stop. I've already been there and back, and I don't know when the journey is done."[6] "Don't listen with your ears, listen with your mind. No, don't listen with your mind, listen with your spirit [*qi*]. Listening stops with the ears, the mind stops with recognition, but spirit is empty and waits on all things. The Way gathers in emptiness alone."[7] The ideally "empty" subject is not "oriented" in the usual way; an orientation would get in the way of the supremely flexible, opportunistic responsiveness that is desired. Clearly Daoist flexibility *is* a prescribed orientation, and a sovereign one at that, recognizably similar in both design and ambition to other life-rectifying disciplines; but it fixes on no *axis mundi* other than itself.

Like Zhuangzi, contemporary philosopher Charles Scott is angling for an ideal subjectivity that isn't stuck on itself and for a wholly open field of appeals —but in an utterly decentered, less ambitious, and more worldly way. With a carefully light touch, he commends an attitude of "lightness" that "seems" advantageous:

> An overbearing seriousness often comes sooner rather than later in our tradition . . . Weighty seriousness gravitates by centering, by fixing a center. It often seems either to engender or to arise from an obsessive interest in a stable center for things in their variations and mobile borders; it seems unable to free itself for its own dispersions and vicissitudes . . . lightness does seem to be without a need to spend energy to justify or redeem its occurrences and to be able to predispose a perceiver toward singular differences with singular clarity . . . such clarity appears to me to make less dangerous compassion and community, to unburden compassion and community of a measure of weight in some mythological and metaphysical purposes and justifications, to make possible alertness to dimensions of occurrence that are difficult, if not impossible to see when our recognitions are in the service of weighty Truth, Nature, or other capital meanings.[8]

Scott also returns to the Daoist idea that human insistence on value-schemes, as in the "tampering" "way of man" promoted by the Confucians, tends inherently toward cruelty and destructiveness.[9] (His nearer point of reference is Nietzsche's account of Western moral values as poisonously concocted by resentment and world-denial.) "In addition to being morally responsible creatures we must be free of moral responsibility by thinking unresponsibly if we are not to be overcome by the cruel suppressions that deeply and silently compose moral responsibility."[10] "Unresponsibility" is a way of expressing an ultimate (non-)definition of a (non-)principle of humane release from human presumption in assigning natures and causal relations to things.

Both unresponsible and responsible: Scott's position is actually on the border between noncommittalism and pneumatology. He revives an old skeptical appeal on behalf of subjective indifference, yet his "light" justifications lead back to the appeals of beings. To the degree that his discourse resolves into an appeal for beings and for commitment to affirming relations with beings, it becomes pneumatological; but insofar as it refuses to resolve into an objectively centered or subjectively anchored appeal, it wanders outside the arenas of philosophy and religion, posing a challenge to a priori norming only in its equivocal state of being a potential, necessarily not actual, rival norming program—that is, a stance in which at any moment a subject might or might not commit to a certain degree to a certain way of relating to other beings.

D. The most radical challenge to any positive interpretation of a priori norming is *absolute nondualism*, a view that enters fully into the ambiguity and suffering of the relating actions that constitute spiritual life and emerges (it thinks) on the far side of that realm, having realized the ultimate unreality of individual subjects and transindividual appellants. This view, classically rooted in Upanishadic thought, is taken most articulately by some Buddhists and Hindus. (I do not identify either Buddhism or Hinduism wholly with absolute nondualism, however, nor do I mean to obscure important differences in how Buddhists and Hindus formulate and apply nondualism; I leave open the question of how the principles I discuss here relate to various Buddhist, Hindu, and other analogous positions that I do not discuss.[11] Finally, I do not wish to reinforce an over-simple opposition between a robustly ethical "Western" and world-denying "Eastern" religious type.[12])

Unlike the other alternatives I have canvassed, absolute nondualism cannot be refuted or absorbed by pneumatology. The subjective anchor for absolute nondualism is tranquility, and tranquility is the one great Axial Age attitude ideal that is not other-regarding—or rather that projects a surpassing of its genuinely attitudinal form, in which relationships with other beings are indeed accepted and addressed with calm benignity, by a non-attitudinal perfect freedom from practical issues. Absolute nondualism centers on the goal of a perfection of subjective receptivity in enlightenment, whereas spiritual ideals are geared to a perfection of activity in responsibility.

For absolute nondualism, the divergences among beings and actions are to be superseded by an actual unity, not merely ordered in a functional harmony: the center of one's subjective existence is to be the center of being itself rather than to be one irreducibly unique centering among others oriented by a more comprehensive centering. From absolute nondualism's perspective, pneumatology remains unenlightened because, in affirming a real plurality of beings and actions, it binds itself to the root cause of illusion and suffering. In pneumatological perspective, however, tranquility is only a conditional good. Even if the spirit of peace ranks high among spirits, there must be a continuing tension in it, as in any spirit, insofar as an active relating of beings is essential to it. Spiritual storytelling may necessarily envision a happy ending, a final victory of reconciliation, but it pushes this end off into an eschatological distance so as not to spoil the storymaking meanwhile.

Absolute nondualism can be attacked as a form of positivism: anyone who presumes to act on the basis of a cognitive ascertainment that excludes a priori directive issues must contradict that perspective in making any communicative claim for it. But nondualists acknowledge that their communicative appeals belong to the fabric of illusion and suffering. Their teachings and practices are of merely instrumental value; one is advised to climb these ladders toward superior insight and then, in enlightenment, cease to rely on them.

Absolute nondualism can also be construed as a form of rational idealism that goes as far as possible in distinguishing ideal reality from actual beings. But unlike other forms of rational idealism that can be embarrassed by calling attention to how they enfeeble our affirmation of actual beings, absolute nondualism does not ultimately affirm finite beings as such and so cannot be convicted of failing to deal justly with beings or failing to represent the truth of beings adequately.

Pneumatology affirms interactive life as intrinsically rewarding, and worldly action as conscientiously necessary. Thus it is always inclined to model reality as a game or job. But absolute nondualism declines to play or work at this level. Reality is to be identified only with a pure consummation of consciousness. What the absolute nondualist carries into practical life from this realization is perfect serenity, which the fundamental premises of pneumatology must always disturb.

It is important to admit that spiritual life has its own kind of discomfort with the premises of appeal and attitude. "Appeal" unavoidably takes one or both of two alienating senses: a sense in which any appeal, once identified, is detached from the event of a solicitation of attention and becomes a commodity (as most notoriously in the advertising value called "sex appeal"), and a sense of violent domination of the subject by the appellant, appeal working as insistence ("I *appeal* to you!"). "Attitude," once thematized, is always "taken" and "held," and so is maintained as a sort of screen between the subject and other beings instead of existing purely as a qualification of the subject's most basic responsiveness to other beings. These are distortions of the spiritual ideal of a perfect togetherness or attunement of the individual with the trans-individual—typically represented as perfect sincerity and love. For the sake of this ideal, the most robust pneumatology involves a continual supersession of identifiable appeals and attitudes, an avoidance of all imposing and posturing. (In Christian theology, "grace" is the self-undoing appeal, and "humility" is the self-undoing attitude; the equivalents in contemporary philosophy are alterity and responsibility.) In this respect there might seem to be a convergence between spiritual and nondualist evaluation. But the dissolving of subject-object separation in absolute nondualism is fundamentally different from the pneumatological discounting of detachable appeal- and attitude-meanings. It may be presented in a spiritually attractive aspect as a path of sincerity and love, but it is always really aimed beyond relation, as can be seen in this advice from the Buddhist Sogyal Rinpoche:

> You can have no greater ally in this war against your greatest enemy, your own self-grasping and self-cherishing, than the practice of compassion. It is compassion, dedicating ourselves to others, taking on their suffering instead of cherishing ourselves, that hand in hand with the wisdom of egolessness destroys most effectively and most completely that ancient attachment to a false self that has been the cause of our endless wandering in samsara. That is why in our tradition we see compassion as the source and essence of enlightenment, and the heart of enlightened activity.[13]

It is possible that this appeal, in which compassion is portrayed as instrumental to enlightenment, is itself instrumental to a highest good of compassionate worldly solidarity with fellow beings (that at least would be a common Mahayana understanding). But the cutting edge of the appeal taken on its own terms is the absolute nondualist ideal of ceasing to wander in samsara, that is, in worldly existence.

Absolute nondualism seems the ultimate Other of pneumatology. It can make a qualified affirmation of the orientation to rectifying relations among beings insofar as this is conducive to reaching enlightenment. Pneumatology can make a qualified affirmation of nondualism insofar as the orientation to overcome ontological separation is conducive to response to appeal. Nondualism is bound to acknowledge spiritual meanings, among others, for the sake of a perfect nondiscriminatory consciousness. Pneumatology must include nondualism in its assemblage of strategies for harmonizing lives. But neither approach can fully accommodate the other.

Any attempt at a fundamental pneumatological evaluation of nondualism is bound to go wrong because it will culminate in an objection that begs the question. For example, it has long been a Western commonplace to bemoan a supposed negative basic attitude, pessimism, in the nondualist rejection of real plurality. But this criticism assumes a world-affirmation that nondualists do not make. Nondualists are in fact infinitely optimistic in their orientation to an achievable eternal bliss.[14] Moreover, they argue for a carryover of the joy of perfected consciousness to worldly living: "As abiding by the flow of [the clear mind] becomes a reality, it begins to permeate the practitioner's everyday life and action, and breeds a deep stability and confidence."[15] Nor does it make sense to accuse nondualism of a fundamental selfishness when the prime object of nondualist strategy is precisely to end all the problems connected with finite selfhood and the purport of testimonies of nondual experience is a disappearance of finite selfhood.

The real pneumatological objection, or rather regret, concerning nondualism is simply that its transindividual supreme good differs in the most basic structural way from spiritual good. In their production of ideals for the overcoming of strife and loss, pneumatology and nondualism swerve apart at the last step into different affirmations, so that their adherents are evaluatively lost to each other. The appeals that have authority in spiritual life are understood by nondualism as temptations to remain estranged from absolute consciousness; a nondualist critic can see the spiritual mind as clinging to the exteriority of appellants so as always to have a notional prospect of a greater plenitude of being than any that could be realized in a consciousness—a prospect enjoyed, like fantasies generally, in a mental feigning that substitutes for reality. Meanwhile, the bliss ideal of nondualism can be diagnosed pneumatologically as a tempting release from the tension of actively negotiating relationships, enjoyed, like a drug, in a felt elevation and repletion—a realized fantasy of problem-free good.

The least regretful, friendliest characterization of nondualism from a pneumatological perspective might run along these lines: (1) In nondualism, the subject-object and attitude-appeal separation of ordinary directive thinking is canceled precisely by the *absolutely attractive appeal* of infinitely rich Being and the *absolutely adequate attitude* of infinitely receptive consciousness. Ordinary directive thinking is reaffirmed, after all, by placing the extreme implications of nondualist experience in continuity with it. Finite appeals and attitudes can be interpreted as ambiguous worldly manifestations or indications of absolute appeal and attitude. (2) In nondualism, what spiritual stories necessarily envision as a happy ending of peace is realized as the removal of all barriers between beings whatsoever; nondualist enlightenment involves *relating* this experience of monist peace to ordinary pluralist experience, just as a spiritual subject must continually relate the experience of the spiritual adventure to the ideal of its conclusion.

One would expect to find more penetrating discussions of nondualism issues among Hindus and Buddhists than in Western circles, since nondualist forms of Hinduism and Buddhism have become fully institutionalized rivals of dharma- and bhakti-oriented approaches. If there is more for a spiritual evaluator to say about the nondualist alternative than to note regretfully its ultimate difference, it is likeliest to be said by one who shares essential points of devotional reference with absolute nondualism—as the qualified nondualist Ramanuja, for example, shares Vedantic (Upanishadic) points of reference with his absolute nondualist rival Shankara.[16] The chief point in Ramanuja's classic attack on the absolute nondualist interpretation of Vedanta is that we cannot coherently conceive or "prove" or be scripturally informed about a consciousness that has no object, that reposes in no plurality whatsoever. But Shankara's position is that absolute Self-consciousness is indicated by scriptural revelation and actually realizable in "knowledge of Brahman" as *other* than the ordinary subjects and objects of thought and discourse, all of which are founded in our ignorance of the radical unity of being. The disillusioned mind recognizes illusion, while an illusioned mind does not recognize disillusion; thus, the difference between Self-consciousness and ordinary consciousness can be registered *from* the knowledge of Brahman, while it cannot meaningfully be registered from the position of ordinary consciousness (the position that Ramanuja's critique insists on maintaining). Knowledge of Brahman does not provide the "justification" that Ramanuja demands according to the principle that "all means of right knowledge have for their object things affected with difference"; it is not "right knowledge" at all.[17]

Insofar as motivation is at issue, the deep point here is that Ramanuja's attitudinal priority is devoted address of a sublime Lord-Other, while Shankara's equivalent priority is to realize the tranquil being of the sublime Lord-Self.[18] But if the fundamental issue is supposed to be not motivation but simply the inherent character of the Upanishadic "knowledge of Brahman," then the issue can be adjudicated only by entering into the indicated life, holding the guide-ropes of its rival descriptions and finding out which one fits best. For the power of discourse to shape life is evidently sufficient to sustain rival supreme experiences as long as rival interpretive approaches can be kept going. The existing literature implies that some great rivalries of this nature can be sustained indefinitely. If there is to be any adjudication *between* supreme specifications of life, it can only come in an active rectifying of relations between the proponents. To pneumatologists it seems that absolute nondualist experiencers always remove themselves from the rectifying frame of reference at the last step of discussion. So we must abandon hope of a final pneumatological adjudication. But that is not to say that the relating of these alternatives cannot continue, with meaningful results, in a community's spiritual life.

Pneumaticism and the Appeal and Attitude Horizons

A substantial answer can be framed to the question, What is the best life? only in a conjunction of appeal and attitude. (This point can be allowed by nondualists as valid for worldly existence.) A way of life must present itself to us most compellingly, and we must be able to determine that we are most centrally attuned to it, disposed for it, and bearing with it. These two conditions are tied together. We become sure of the power of an appeal by gauging the depth and power of our orientation to it, and we become sure that we are rightly oriented when we appreciate a rewarding relationship that our orientation sustains. Very often it is possible to judge on some working criterion or other that a particular way of thinking, feeling, acting, or being is best without taking explicit account of attitude or appeal issues, but any such determination really depends on a more fundamental addressing of those issues. An approach may be embraced for the sake of "rational consistency," for example, which is an easily wielded, well-accepted standard; but rational consistency is ultimately compelling only in the context of a world-intuition of a publicly accessible, sharable universal order to which the reasonable individual subject is wholeheartedly attuned, finding therein a self-transcendence that is at the same time a sustainable poise.

For the most part, the analysis and narrative of the present study have moved within the ambit of the Axial Age presumption that the question of appeal and attitude is ultimately best addressed by identifying a supreme appeal ("divine revelation" or something normatively equivalent) and forming a sovereign attitude ("faith" or something normatively equivalent). By now, however, we have brought into view enough deep diversity in the identification of superordinate appeals and the formation of basic attitudes that we are compelled to reconfigure the question of supreme appeal to include the question of right relationship *among* exigently superordinate appeals and to reconfigure the question of sovereign attitude to include the question of right relationship *among* controllingly basic attitudes—or, to put it differently, to shift our focus from the prospect of a single concretely decisive supreme appeal or sovereign attitude to the *appeal horizon* and the *attitude horizon* addressed by practical (spiritual) questioners. Axial Age proposals set the table for questioning on this understanding but do not explicitly identify or recommend it. It is an axis hidden within the Axial Age attitude-appeal axis. This other axis is first allowed to come to the fore by the modern Diltheyan program of responsible participation in a temporally unlimited, pluralistic shaping of generally acceptable answers to the ever-fresh question of how best to live.

The Diltheyan program goes beyond a merely positivistic mapping of determinate "world-intuitions." It initiates us into an active (though not controlling) relation with the most fundamental potentialities of practical meaning. Although reflection and public discussion alike may drive in the short term toward limited world-intuitions for the sake of graspable, usable determinacy—and these pictures will indeed hold us captive—in the long term both reflection and public discussion must open toward more inclusive and complex ways of addressing the attitude and appeal horizons. This movement is manifest in the last two centuries of Western thought, as it also was in more complex Axial Age texts like the *Bhagavad Gita*. The spaciousness of the attitude and appeal horizons is the ultimate cause and justification of normative pluralism.

I will designate as *pneumaticism* a maximally affirming orientation to the appeal and attitude horizons. I draw here on the conception of the spiritual as the relationship-directed vitality of our vitality. I use this term to shift my focus from pneumatological assessment of ideas according to their bearing on the rectifying of relations between beings to a proposal for a way of life, an active maximizing of lively relationship that requires the most inclusive identification of terms of relationship and the most open agenda of mutual flourishing. Pneumaticism is the life-program that corresponds to pneumatological evaluation. It plays the normative role of sovereign attitude without purporting to be realizable as a psychological attitude. *Being* a "pneumatic" is an extraordinary possibility; the term has not unfairly been used to warn against presumptuous religious fanaticism (though we sometimes meet an extremely receptive, benevolently experimental, compellingly pneumatic "great-souled" individual like Gandhi). Normally, one *participates in* pneumaticism on the basis of a specific inspiration, one's concrete valuing being more narrowly channeled by a dominant attitude.

Pneumaticism is properly a qualification more directly of a communal than of an individual way of life, and always superordinately the way of a more inclusive community with a more ambitiously affirmative program. Pneumaticism figures also as a supreme philosophical appeal—coordinating, not displacing, the concretely attention-centering appeals to which individuals and communities actually respond. Our relationship to it is most palpable, not in personal decision making, where we are measuring states of affairs against our own ideals (founded on our own identification of a superordinate appeal and our own holding of a governing attitude), but in feeling our way toward collective decisions on communal policy—placing our own ideals (or our "values," as we conveniently say in this context) "into the mix" of public consideration. Our inspiration by pneumaticism is logically parallel to what we have called Devotion C, the more complex devotion-system maintained by a religious community.

The historical life of a religious community will not necessarily be among the richest examples of pneumaticism in action, but it is likely to be among the most self-consciously articulate. For the devout understand themselves to be subject to an inspirational sourcing, prompting, and ruling that exceeds the scale of ordinary practical deliberation, and they accordingly see their history as a manifestation of the work of their divine spirit. Any historically developed religious community has access through its tradition to a collection of perspectives on salvation that are not perfectly reconcilable intellectually or devotionally in the life of any one believer but that nevertheless function together as a more adequate guide for the community as a whole.

To note that members of a community can experience pneumaticism in it is to settle almost nothing about how a spiritual life will work and what it will include. Nor would demonstrations of the feasibility of understanding, say, Christian theology or European history as spiritual stories prove the feasibility of "world theology" or "world history." The general recipe for pneumaticism leaves almost everything yet to be determined as regards the perception of beings and spirits (notably the perception of flourishing and "greatness") and as regards the strategies of expression and interpretation that make up the content of livable spiritual life. World theology and world history face great difficulties in collating the essential constituent perceptions and meaning frameworks in the requisite way. In this study we have drawn the main lines of the fundamental *motivation* of spiritual life, in which a motivation of global culture is inherent.

The fundamental evaluation of fundamental evaluation proceeds most lucidly and responsibly when it most greatly amplifies cognizance of the appeal-and-attitude framework of norming—given that what is most worth seeing *are* appeals and what is most worth having *are* attitudes. Pneumatology follows this structure in making the advent of the other being and the subject's disposition toward the other being pivotal in the formation of superordinate meaning. If the program of pneumatological interpretation is to be carried out pneumatically, then the ideal discourse on norming must be enlivened by a fair representation of the various relating moves that have contributed significantly to our larger story of rectification. For this reason, philosophy of religion, having accepted a responsibility to think through various moves of reason and devotion together, can be a site of especially powerful fundamental evaluation of fundamental evaluation. At any rate, the present study looks forward hopefully to richer fulfillment of its aims in a philosophy of religion.

We have been concerned with three major programs of devotion: the Axial Age formation of "world religions"; the Enlightenment renewal of that project, subject to the norm of rational faith; and the contemporary project of "world theology" in the double sense of a theology inclusive of the insights and concerns of existing religious traditions, and a theology responsible to all the beings of the world, including nonhumans.[19] We have understood these programs as actions in which we are to some extent actually involved and in which we are invited to participate wholeheartedly. All three programs have been affirmed to the degree that they are congruous with the pneumatological conditions of fundamental evaluation.

The three devotional programs have other aspects as well, however, in principle and in their various implementations, which might not be ideally affirmable. Two basic structural problems that they all share, intimately related to their defining ideals, are (1) a *universalistic* way of presenting a supreme appeal that can be insufficiently sensitive to the specific characters and contexts of subjective attitude-holding, and (2) an *individualistic* way of construing the appellate subject that can be insufficiently responsive to the specific characters and contexts of appeals. But the normatively paramount status of pneumaticism in each of the programs implies that fruitful critiques of each program will move toward explicitly pneumatological reconstruction involving a strengthened affirmation of actual rectifying moves, often necessarily with cultural concreteness. Thus, for example, the recent wave of attention in Roman Catholic theology to the "inculturation" of the putatively universal Christian church proceeds from fuller cognizance of the actual rectifying moves that are made by the mediation of ethnically rooted cultures.[20] In relation to the disguised reductiveness and bias of Enlightenment rationalism, female and non-Western philosophers press in a similarly pluralistic way for an expanded cognizance of contexts of directively significant experience.[21] Even "world theology," although it is dedicated to heeding every ideal, comes in for criticism from serious pluralists who warn against an imperialist expropriation of exhibits for a sort of world religion museum; such exhibits would be misleading tokens of the religious cultures they represent and would offer themselves to a falsely unrestricted, spiritually deracinate (late-modern Western) subject.[22]

But the presumptions in favor of universality and individuality cannot ultimately be dismissed. Once we have encountered diverse contexts of compelling appeal and response, we cannot turn aside from the challenge of incorporating these in a more spiritually adequate global context.[23] We are caught up in this situation insofar as we communicate. Once we have begun to answer as individuals to appeals, we can never justifiably submerge ourselves again in a more diffused responsibility—though we may rightly aspire to participate more sensitively and actively in transpersonal spirits, above all in the spirit of pneumaticism. That spirit's embrace of deep pluralism leads us to affirm also that we can never rightly leave a questioning path of wonder.

NOTES

PREFACE

1. Steven G. Smith, *The Concept of the Spiritual: An Essay in First Philosophy* (1988).

1. APPEALS

1. Jean-Luc Marion, *Being Given: Toward a Phenomenology of Givenness*, 266–308. *"Appel"* is "call" in the English translation. For the Levinas precedents, see Marion, "The Voice Without Name: Homage to Levinas," trans. Jeffrey Bloechl, in *The Face of the Other and the Trace of God: Essays on the Philosophy of Emmanuel Levinas*, pp. 224–42. Heidegger is an important appeal-thinker and resource for Marion as well, but I will leave that complication for later.

2. The idea of a primal appeal of Being as such to consciousness and a responsiveness of consciousness purely to Being as such may be warranted—as an interpretation of Aristotle's observation that all subjects spontaneously desire knowledge, for example (*Metaphysics* 980a), or as a religious amplification of experience—but still some hypostatization of the appellant is necessary if the appeal is to play its normal role of offering to make some practical difference in the subject's life.

3. I will leave aside for now the special issues raised by negative contents and references of appeals. It seems evident that an appellant as such is necessarily a positivity—that the limit case of attending to pure negativity must also be the limit case of attending where there is no appeal—and so a negativity can only appeal by virtue of its association with some positive being.

4. Alphonso Lingis plunges deeply into such enjoyments and projections in his account of our "taking direction" from beings in *The Imperative*, placing the decisiveness in an appeal and the objective responsibility in our response to it in a broader continuum of orientational experience.

5. The Beatles, *A Hard Day's Night* (Capitol Records, 1964).

6. Marion makes the complementary point (using the higher-class example of Mozart's *Jupiter* Symphony) that the opening of a musical work manifests the very arriving of a phenomenon, another aspect of its pure appealingness, as distinct from its graspable form (*Being Given*, p. 216).

7. Compare here Charles Scott's work in which a positive value is attached to indifference in subject-object relations for the sake of averting destructive results of subject-object binding, for example, in the perception of trauma ("Trauma's Presentation," paper presented at Millsaps College, April 2003).

8. Efforts have been made to construe as "value" a ground of valuing in that which actually or properly elicits our valuing, often under the rubric of "intrinsic value." But these arguments put the cart before the horse, imposing the form of an appellate subject's reaction to appeal-experience on the initiative of the appellant. (This is, if you will, a version of the *Euthyphro* problem: it cannot be a subject's loving something that makes it lovable.) J. Baird Callicott has tried to work around this problem by invoking a "postmodern," more fundamentally relational and interactive model of experience and being, according to which "intrinsic value" could obtain in much the way I claim meaningfulness occurs. See Callicott, "Intrinsic Value in Nature: A Metaethical Analysis" and "Rolston on Intrinsic Value: A Deconstruction" in *Beyond the Land Ethic*. I think the notion of "value" is fatally burdened for this purpose, but I recognize the tendency of Callicott's argument to converge with mine. The notion of "worth" is sometimes introduced with the aim of pointing beyond this limitation of "value," as by Paul Taylor in *Respect for Nature*.

9. The sense of objects standing against us is so attenuated in the standard modern discourse on subject and object—or, one could say, is so solidly aligned with our experience of beings as falling in with our already-established designs—that Martin Buber replaced the usual German object-word *Gegenstand* with *Gegenüber* ("over-against," "opposite") to refer to the being that confronts us (*Ich und Du*, in *Werke*, vol. 1, p. 87; *I and Thou*, p. 65). I cite the first occurrence in which *Gegenüber* is translated "that which confronts us." Buber opposed the presentness (*Gegenwärtigkeit*) of the *Gegenüber* to the pastness, the having-been-assimilated-in-experience, of the *Gegenstand* (*Ich und Du*, p. 86; *I and Thou*, p. 63). Alternatively, though, one could find independence in the *Gegenstand*'s having-proved-itself.

10. Jocelyn Benoist mobilizes this point but pushes it too far in arguing that "things," insofar as they really are "given," are not "things" at all, but are "events." The conception of "things" here is unjustifiably limited to the objecthood of idealism and empiricism ("Qu'est-ce qui est donné? La pensée et l'évènement").

11. "But if each part [of nature, for instance a butterfly or fly], which has only a particular function and a relative perfection, is capable of delighting with astonishment and admiration those who take the trouble to consider it correctly, how [much finer] must it be for those who know the relations of all the parts and who thereby judge the general harmony and the operation of the whole mechanism?" (Jean-Jacques Rousseau, *Institutions Chimiques*, Book 2, quoted and translated by Patrick Riley in his "Introduction" to Nicolas Malebranche, *Treatise on Nature and Grace*, p. 101). Significantly, Rousseau sets up this point by complaining that operagoers mostly attend to particular elements of a performance and fail to appreciate the whole.

12. Marion, *Being Given*, pp. 296–308.

13. Heraclitus, fragment 196. I use the fragment numbering and translations of G. S. Kirk, J. E. Raven, and M. Schofield in *The Presocratic Philosophers*, 2nd ed.

14. Babylonian Talmud, Tractate Hullin, 108a–109a.

15. Augustine, *On Free Will*, Book 2. A fourteenth-century BCE Egyptian text makes a similar claim, using the vocabulary of polytheism in an interesting way. One passage states that Maat or Truth, a daughter of the Creator-Lord Amon-Re, must be regarded also as his mother: "Thy mother is Truth, O Amon! To thee she belongs uniquely, and she came forth from thee (already) inclined to rage and burn up them that attack thee. Truth is more unique, O Amon, than anyone that exists" ("Hymns to

the God as a Single God," trans. John A. Wilson, in *Ancient Near Eastern Texts Relating to the Old Testament*, p. 372).

16. I say "well-nigh" irresistible because potent counterappeals are offered by skeptics, Nietzscheans, and Dadaists, for example. Whether the rival appeals indeed differ from and overthrow the ideal of truth seems to be permanently contestable.

17. On the "addressed" (*interloqué*), see Marion, *Reduction and Givenness*, trans. Thomas A. Carlson, pp. 200–202; on the "receiver" (*attributaire*) and "gifted" (*adonné*), see *Being Given*, pp. 249, 262.

2. APPEAL IN THE AXIAL AGE

1. All Hebrew Bible quotations are from NJPS (*Tanakh: The Holy Scriptures: The New JPS Translation according to the Traditional Hebrew Text*).

2. *The Complete Works of Chuang Tzu* [*Zhuangzi*], trans. Burton Watson, chap. 33, p. 373.

3. "Leap into the boundless and make it your home!" *Zhuangzi*, chap. 2, p. 49.

4. Karl Jaspers, *The Origin and Goal of History*, trans. Michael Bullock (1953).

5. See *Wisdom, Revelation, and Doubt: Perspectives on the First Millennium* BCE, Special issue, *Daedalus*; and *The Origins and Diversity of the Axial Age*, ed. S. N. Eisenstadt.

6. For an overview of changes in social organization promoted by the use of writing, see Jack Goody, *The Logic of Writing and the Organization of Society*. Goody emphasizes the change in the communicative situation caused by the relative independence of written language from particular interactive contexts.

7. John B. Cobb Jr. makes the point that individuality and freedom in their preeminently meaningful senses come with the shift of the human "seat of existence" to rational, reflective consciousness (see "Axial Existence," chap. 5 in *The Structure of Christian Existence*).

8. Jaspers, *The Origin and Goal of History*, p. 76.

9. Ibid., pp. 2–4.

10. *The Epic of Gilgamesh*, trans. Andrew George, pp. 1–4, 7–9, 15–62, 98–99.

11. Ibid., pp. 77, 80, 83–84.

12. "His companions are kept on their feet by his *contests*, [the young men of Uruk] he harries without warrant. Gilgamesh lets no son go free to his father, by day and by [night his tyranny grows] harsher . . . Though he is their shepherd . . . Gilgamesh lets no girl go free to her bride[groom]" (ibid., p. 4).

13. *Rig Veda* 9.113, trans. Wendy Doniger O'Flaherty, in *The Rig Veda: An Anthology*, p. 134.

14. On the theology of sacred voice and sound, see Guy L. Beck, *Sonic Theology. Hinduism and Sacred Sound*.

15. For the concept of "momentary deities," extraordinarily impressive occurrences that have only a minimal categorical identification (like "*daimon*" in Greek), see Hermann Usener, *Götternamen. Versuch einer Lehre von der religiösen Begriffsbildung* (1896), reviewed by Ernst Cassirer in *Language and Myth*, pp. 15–22.

16. Heraclitus, fragment 196, in *The Presocratic Philosophers*, p. 187.

17. *Daodejing* 16, trans. Arthur Waley, in *The Way and Its Power*, p. 162.

18. Isaiah 43.10–11, adapted from the NJPS.

19. *Chandogya Upanishad* 6, trans. Patrick Olivelle, in *Upanishads*, pp. 152–56 (repeated passim).

20. *Bhagavad-Gita*, 11. My dating of the Gita to the late Axial Age (on the basis of its attitude vocabulary) is on the early end of the current range of estimates, which go as late as the second century CE.

21. *The Egyptian Book of the Dead*, ed. E. A. Wallis Budge, p. cxix.

22. Early speculation, *Rig Veda* 10.129, p. 25: "There was neither non-existence nor existence then; there was neither the realm of space nor the sky which is beyond. What stirred? Where?" On the "search for ultimate objectivity" in the earliest Indian philosophers and the shift from *rita* to *atman* as central explanatory principle, see David Kalupahana, *A History of Buddhist Philosophy*, chap. 1.

23. Thales, fragment 85, and Anaximander, fragment 110, in *The Presocratic Philosophers*, pp. 88–95 and 117–21 respectively.

24. On the early Chinese divinity Di or Shangdi (Lord-on-high), see *Sources of Chinese Tradition*, 2nd ed., ed. W. T. de Bary et al., pp. 10–13, 22–23, 27; on Heaven as a fundamental structure, a concept that becomes a commonplace by the third century BCE, see already *Daodejing* 73 and *Analects* 8.19 and 17.19 (but cf. 5.12).

25. The "Memphite Theology," trans. James B. Allen, in *The Context of Scripture*, ed. William W. Hallo, vol. 1: *Canonical Compositions from the Biblical World*, p. 22.

26. On brahman concepts, see *Sources of Indian Tradition*, 2nd ed., vol. 1, ed. Ainslie T. Embree, p. 6, and *Upanishads*, trans. Olivelle, p. lvi.

27. "The Great Hymn to the Aten," trans. Miriam Lichtheim, in Hallo, vol. 1, p. 46.

28. "King Wen," in the *Classic of Odes*, trans. Burton Watson, in *Sources of Chinese Tradition*, p. 38.

29. Genesis 28.13.

30. Exodus 3.14.

31. Deuteronomy 6.4.

32. Dong Zhongshu, "Luxuriant Gems of the Spring and Autumn Annals," trans. Sarah Queen, in *Sources of Chinese Tradition*, pp. 300–301.

33. *Analects* 3.13, trans. Arthur Waley, in *The Analects of Confucius*, p. 97.

34. Hosea 11.1.

35. *Daodejing* 37, p. 188.

36. *Daodejing* 1, p. 141. This line is often read as *separating* anything we can grasp from a presumed transcendent. But Bo Mou argues on grammatical and transcendental grounds that the line allows a positive relation between any helpful, albeit finite reaching toward the way and the inexhaustible Way ("Ultimate Concern and Language Engagement: A Reexamination of the Opening Message of the *Dao-De-Jing*," pp. 429–39).

37. Heraclitus, fragment 194, in *The Presocratic Philosophers*, p. 187.

38. Isaiah 46.5; 55.9.

39. E.g., *Chandogya Upanishad* 5.3.7, p. 140; see Olivelle's discussion of the significance of these stories of Kshatriyas, rather than Brahmans, possessing the highest wisdom, pp. xxxiv–xxxvi.

40. On the rise and effect of astrology, see Gerardus van der Leeuw, *Religion in Essence and Manifestation*, trans. J. E. Turner, pp. 71–73.

41. A good feminist discussion of this issue will be found in Lorraine Code, *What Can She Know? Feminist Theory and the Construction of Knowledge*.

42. *Chandogya Upanishad* 6.14, p. 155.

43. Heraclitus, fragment 196, in *The Presocratic Philosophers*, p. 187. The conception of "philosophy" as a longing, nonpossessing love of the Good was influentially promoted by Plato in *Symposium* 205–12.

44. *Analects* 4.5, pp. 102–103.

45. 1 Kings 17–19 (Elijah); Hosea 1–2; Jeremiah 27–28; Ezekiel 4; Isaiah 53 (the Suffering Servant).

46. Van der Leeuw discusses Preuss's and Söderblom's concept of the "originator" type of deity in his section on divinity perceived as a "background" power and will (pp. 164–68).

47. Exodus 20.2–3, Deuteronomy 5.6–7.

48. Isaiah 43.26–19.

49. Ezekiel 38–39.

50. Job 38.4.

51. Samples of these views are conveniently found in *Sources of Chinese Tradition*, pp. 44–63 (index p. 44); 174–77 (Kongzi and Xunzi rationalizing the "rites"); 129 (Mengzi on cultivation of the spontaneous human tendency to do good); 205 (Han Feizi on a new formation of the subjects of the state).

52. *Analects* 17.19, *Mengzi* 5.A.5 (*Sources of Chinese Tradition*, pp. 62, 143–44).

53. S. C. Humphreys points out that there is a problem in making the necessary terms of a purportedly universal appeal sufficiently explicit and not too much restricted by the appeal-maker's distinctive social position ("'Transcendence' and Intellectual Roles: The Ancient Greek Case," pp. 112–13).

54. The division created in this way will *not* necessarily coincide with naturally occurring differences of religious temperament or capacity (noted as an "empirical fact" standing "at the beginning of the history of religion" by Max Weber in "The Social Psychology of Religion," in *From Max Weber: Essays in Sociology*, ed. Gerth and Mills, p. 287). It might highlight such differences, but it might also cover them over with its own normative scheme.

55. On Yao, Shun, and Yu in the *Analects*, see, e.g., 8.18–21; on the rites, 3 passim, and Sima Qian's "Life of Confucius" in *The Wisdom of Confucius*, trans. Lin Yutang, esp. p. 60. For the Noachide covenant, see Genesis 6–9; the Abrahamic, Genesis 11.26–22.19; the Mosaic, Exodus 20–24, 32; the Davidic, 1 Samuel 16.1–14, 2 Samuel 7, 1 Kings 2.1–4, 9.1–9.

56. On the preeminence of devotion, see 11.54; on the other three yogas, teachings 3–6.

57. The Pythagoreans come closest; Iamblichus gives the names of seventeen "illustrious Pythagorean women" ("The Life of Pythagoras," in *The Pythagorean Sourcebook and Library*, p. 122). On women in the Upanishads, see Olivelle, *Upanishads*, p. xxxvi.

58. Ibn Rushd (Averroes) argued that what constitutes true belief for a philosopher can be heresy for a non-philosopher and vice versa (*On the Harmony of Religion and Philosophy*, chap. 3, pp. 63–71—note the parable of the skillful doctor on p. 67). A locus classicus in Buddhism for the subjective relativity of religious perspectives is the parable of skillful instructions given by a father to his endangered children in a burning house in the *Scripture of the Lotus Blossom of the Fine Dharma* [*Lotus Sutra*], trans. Leon Hurvitz, chap. 3, pp. 57–64. The notion that souls are reborn into better

lives as a consequence of good actions, and worse as a consequence of worse, appears in the Upanishads—see *Brihadaranyaka Upanishad* 4.4.5 and *Chandogya Upanishad* 5.10.

59. Tacitus complains of Christians' "hatred of the entire human race" (*Annals of Tacitus*, p. 354). Han Yu warns that "the Buddhist doctrine maintains that one must reject the relationship between ruler and minister, do away with father and son and forbid the Way that enables us to live and to grow together—all this in order to seek what they call purity and *nirvana*" ("Essentials of the Moral Way," trans. Charles Hartman, in *Sources of Chinese Tradition*, p. 571).

60. Wisdom of Solomon 13.2–5, probably written in the late first century BCE or early first century CE by a Hellenistic Jew of Alexandria. All quotations from the New Testament and the Apocrypha are from the New Revised Standard Version.

61. John Cowper Powys, *In Defense of Sensuality*, p. 95, quoted by Catherine Madsen in "Revelations of Chaos," 493. In his *Autobiography* (1934), Powys significantly appeals to the Axial Age ideal of coping with life from inner resources—"We *have* the power of re-creating the universe from the depths of ourselves . . . we share the creative force that started the whole process"—but a key exercise of this inner discretion for him is *forgetting* the bad parts of the whole (pp. 331, 343).

62. Donald Redford, *Akhenaten, the Heretic King*, p. 174.

63. Qur'an 6.74–79.

64. Ludwig Feuerbach, *The Essence of Christianity*, trans. George Eliot, chap. 2, p. 34.

65. Euripides, *Trojan Women*, trans. David Kovacs, p. 101, ll. 884–88.

66. *Aitareya Upanishad* 3.3–4, trans. Olivelle, in *Upanishads*, p. 199.

67. *Katha Upanishad* 3.10–11, in ibid., p. 239.

68. *Mundaka Upanishad* 3.1.3–4, in ibid., p. 274.

69. *Bhagavad-Gita* 11.53–54.

70. Iamblichus, "The Life of Pythagoras," p. 70.

71. "In a mirror, dimly," Paul, 1 Corinthians 13.12.

72. Max Weber, "Science as a Vocation," in *From Max Weber: Essays in Sociology*, ed. Gerth and Mills, p. 155.

73. An articulate and not insensitive specimen of this style of thinking about religious meaning is Melford Spiro's "Religion: Problems of Definition and Explanation," in *Anthropological Approaches to the Study of Religion*, ed. Michael Banton, pp. 98–122.

3. THE APPEAL IN MODERN PHILOSOPHY

1. "It is right that what is should not be imperfect; for it is not deficient . . . since there is a furthest limit, it is perfected, like the bulk of a ball well-rounded on every side, equally balanced in every direction from the center" (Parmenides, fragment 299, in *The Presocratic Philosophers*, p. 252).

2. Plato's most pregnant constructive discussion of the truth ideal of eternal forms is *Republic* 475–90, 507–18.

3. Plato, *Parmenides* 130.

4. Aristotle, *Metaphysics* 990a–93a.

5. On the separation of God from the world, see *Metaphysics* 1071b; on the

separation of knowing and human flourishing from the world, *Nicomachean Ethics* 1177a–78a.

6. René Descartes, *Meditations on First Philosophy*, Third Meditation.

7. "*Admirari, adorare.*" Descartes, *Meditationes de Prima Philosophia*, in *Oeuvres de Descartes*, vol. 7, p. 52.

8. Emmanuel Levinas adopted Descartes's "idea of the Infinite" as a conceptual representation of the concretely, ethically infinite appeal of the human Other—see, e.g., "Philosophy and the Idea of Infinity" in *Collected Philosophical Papers*.

9. Immanuel Kant, *Critique of Practical Reason*, Ak. 73, trans. Lewis White Beck, p. 76.

10. Ibid., Ak. 77.

11. Kant, *Critique of Pure Reason*, B 570–86 and *Critique of Practical Reason*, Ak. 119–21, 132; *Critique of Judgment*, Ak. 268; *Religion within the Limits of Reason Alone*, B296–314.

12. *Critique of Practical Reason*, Ak. 79.

13. Alphonso Lingis on Kant: "It is this sense of another locus of the [rational] imperative that makes the other appear to me as . . . a dignity in the field of means—and thus genuinely *other* . . . This is why it is that the feeling of being contested, being summoned, is immediate, coming with the first intuition of being approached by another, and why it is that one is relieved, acquitted, when one begins to see the color and shape of what is there. In the measure that one sees what it was that moved him . . . one dissipates the sense that his law binds me" (*The Imperative*, p. 190).

14. The idea that *collectively* humans *do* have the power to make themselves happy in a morally superordinate sense is indicated by Kant's remark that humans following the moral law together could make a paradise even of an Arctic wilderness (*Lectures on Ethics*, trans. L. Infield, p. 55 [Ak. 27/1, pp. 285–86]; cf. *Critique of Pure Reason*, B 837–38).

15. On this issue in Kant's writings, see my "Worthiness to Be Happy and Kant's Concept of the Highest Good." Kant's central "highest good" argument is in the *Critique of Practical Reason*, Ak. 110–19.

16. On Kant's dialectic of pure practical reason, see *Critique of Practical Reason*, Ak. 106–48. On despair, see especially Søren Kierkegaard, *The Sickness unto Death*, trans. Howard and Edna Hong (1980); on God as the Wholly Other, see especially Kierkegaard, *Philosophical Fragments*, trans. Howard and Edna Hong (1985).

17. Cf. Kierkegaard's analysis of the biblical character Abraham as the type of the "knight of faith" responsive to transrational appeal in *Fear and Trembling*, trans. Howard and Edna Hong (1983). The extent to which fellow human beings are significant appellants in Kierkegaard's thought is much debated; see, e.g., Buber's critique of his "almost monadically intended theistic piety" in "The History of the Dialogical Principle," trans. Maurice Friedman, in *Between Man and Man*, pp. 210–11.

18. It is possible (and, I would say, imperative) to hold that the force of Kantian practical reason's appeal inheres in its representation of concrete appellants, but Kant himself does not offer that sort of social or spiritual interpretation of practical reasonableness. It is implicit in his Rousseauvian respect for human dignity, but repressed: "Rousseau first discovered amid the manifold human forms the deeply hidden nature of man, and the secret law by which Providence is justified through his observations" (quoted in Ernst Cassirer, *Kant's Life and Thought*, p. 89).

19. One clear indication of this perspective comes in Kant's specification of a "world-concept" (*Weltbegriff*): "Philosophy is the science of the relation of all knowledge to the essential ends of human reason, and the philosopher is not an artificer in the field of reason, but himself the lawgiver of human reason . . . but as he nowhere exists, while the idea of his legislation is to be found in that reason with which every human being is endowed, we shall keep entirely to the latter, determining more precisely what philosophy prescribes . . . in accordance with this cosmical concept [*Weltbegriff*], from the standpoint of its essential ends" (*Critique of Pure Reason*, B 866–67). "By cosmical concept is here meant the concept which relates to that in which everyone necessarily has an interest" (B 868n).

20. Weber's view is indicated in "Science as Vocation," in *From Max Weber: Essays in Sociology*, ed. Gerth and Mills, pp. 155–56. On Kantian and neo-Kantian socialism, see Harry van der Linden, *Kantian Ethics and Socialism*. For a Western Marxist linkage with Kant, see Jürgen Habermas's important discussion of the relation between the Kantian conception of reason's essential interest in freedom and the issue of "real freedom" in *Knowledge and Human Interests*, pp. 198–212.

21. A case could be made that "life" functioned patently as an appeal motif in some if not all expressions of *Lebensphilosophie*, but the characteristic prime desiderata in *Lebensphilosophie* are concreteness, wholeness, and integration of thought with experience rather than the appealing-and-heeding relation. Dilthey's conception of a universal mandate of *Verstehen*, particularly as elaborated in Gadamer's hermeneutical theory, especially deserves to be included in a fuller overview of this development. So does the Whiteheadian thematic of "lure" and "persuasion," although Whitehead's metaphysical reconstruction of final causation falls outside the post-metaphysical, exteriority-preoccupied Kantian conversation I am concentrating on. So does neo-Marxist critical theory, although this tradition is obliged to "detour" through neo-Kantianism to avoid the "positivist swamps of vulgar Second International ideology," as Andrew Arato explains in "The Neo-Idealist Defense of Subjectivity," 108–61.

22. Heinrich Rickert, *System der Philosophie*, pp. 102–11. All Rickert translations are mine.

23. Rickert, *Der Gegenstand der Erkenntnis*, p. 225.

24. Ibid., p. 205.

25. Except that Rickert does admit that there is more in real beings than can be known, an "irrational" content (ibid., p. 28).

26. Ibid., p. 186.

27. Rickert, *System*, p. 117.

28. *Gegenstand*, p. 195; *System*, p. 135.

29. *System*, p. 114.

30. Ibid., pp. 348–405.

31. Ibid., pp. 150–51.

32. Martin Buber, *I and Thou*, trans. Walter Kaufmann, p. 58. I agree with Kaufmann's decisions to retain the well-known title *I and Thou* but to translate "Du" in the text as the less archaic "You."

33. Buber, "Aus einer philosophischen Rechenschaft," in *Werke*, vol. 1, p. 1111. He says in *I and Thou* that scientific understanding "should do its work faithfully and immerse itself and disappear in that truth of the relation which surpasses understanding and embraces what is understandable" (91). Meanwhile, he refrains on principle from

making knowledge claims that would be "scientifically" unjustifiable (e.g., concerning a tree [58] and a man [124]).

34. *I and Thou*, p. 65.

35. Ibid., pp. 125–26.

36. Ibid., pp. 53, 78; in *Werke*, vol. 1, pp. 79, 96.

37. Ibid., pp. 127, 57.

38. Rickert, *System*, p. 383.

39. Emmanuel Levinas, "Martin Buber and the Theory of Knowledge," in *The Philosophy of Martin Buber*, ed. Schilpp and Friedman, p. 144. Michael Theunissen argues that Buber's position is limited by its dialectical opposition to the transcendental philosophy to which it is a "counter-project"—as seen in a philosophically sterile appeal to immediacy, for example—and that the I in any case remains central and determinative in Buber's account of meaning (*Der Andere*, pp. 243–329, 483–507; abridged English trans. by Christopher Macann, *The Other*, pp. 257–344, 361–84).

40. Buber, "Replies to My Critics," in *The Philosophy of Martin Buber*, p. 697.

41. Eberhard Grisebach denies that the fully responsive relation with the Other can be construed as an a priori, since an a priori implies an encompassing of its terms within the subject's constituted world of experience (*Gegenwart. Eine kritische Ethik*, p. 481). Buber maintains, however, that "nothing conceptual intervenes between I and You, no prior knowledge . . . and no anticipation" (*I and Thou*, pp. 62–63). The a priori of relation is not supposed to be of the theoretical kind.

42. The focus on the face will be found in Levinas, *Totality and Infinity*, trans. Lingis (1969), and on Saying (*le Dire* in contrast with *le Dit*, the Said) in Levinas, *Otherwise than Being or Beyond Essence*, trans. Lingis (1982).

43. *I and Thou*, pp. 57–59. Buber connects the abstractness of You-saying in relation to the describability of beings with the unknowableness of the real substratum of the sensory object, as attested by modern physics, in "Man and His Image Work," trans. Maurice Friedman, in *The Knowledge of Man*, pp. 156–59. Both sense-perception and description can be normatively described as "faithfulness not to the appearance, but to being—to the inaccessible with which we associate" (159).

44. This point was made in a theological way by Franz Rosenzweig in a 1922 letter to Buber quoted in Rivka Horowitz, *Buber's Way to I and Thou*, p. 208. Creation faith, he says, involves a stronger third-personal meaning of "He [God]-It" than the "crippled" object-reference of modern materialism and idealism to which Buber's It corresponds.

45. Buber, "Aus einer philosophischen Rechenschaft," in *Werke*, vol. 1, p. 1111.

46. Buber, *I and Thou*, pp. 115–17.

47. Martin Heidegger, *The Basic Problems of Phenomenology* (a 1927 lecture course closely related to *Being and Time*), trans. Albert Hofstadter, pp. 297–98. Here, as well as in a similar remark in his 1928 lectures on the *Phenomenological Interpretation of Kant's "Critique of Pure Reason,"* trans. Parvis Emad and Kenneth Maly, p. 214, it appears that Heidegger is commenting, not on Buber's *I and Thou* specifically, but on I-Thou as a new buzzword of the late 1920s (perhaps as popularized by the theologian Friedrich Gogarten).

48. This and subsequent references in the text are to Heidegger, *Sein und Zeit*, 8th ed. (Tübingen: Max Niemeyer, 1957). Except when indicated otherwise, I use the English translation by John Macquarrie and Edward Robinson, *Being and Time*.

49. Ibid., pp. 269, 275, my translations. For *Schuldigsein* (p. 269), I have replaced "Being-guilty" with "Being-lacking."

50. Heidegger, "Postscript" to "What Is Metaphysics?" trans. R. F. C. Hull and Alan Crick, in *Existence and Being*, p. 355.

51. Heidegger, "Letter on Humanism," trans. Frank A. Cappuzzi and J. Glenn Gray, in *Basic Writings*, p. 221.

52. Heidegger, *What Is Called Thinking?* trans. Fred D. Wieck and J. Glenn Gray, p. 242.

53. "Letter on Humanism," p. 228.

54. Buber, "What Is Man?" trans. Ronald Gregor Smith, in *Between Man and Man*, p. 168. Michael Theunissen reviews Grisebach's sharply formulated criticisms of Heidegger along this line in *Der Andere*, pp. 250–51 (*The Other*, pp. 263–65).

55. *Being and Time*, pp. 123, 303, 133.

56. Ibid., §15.

57. Heidegger later moderated the note of Kierkegaardian passion in his discussion of Being's appeal but never, as far as I know, came remotely close to saying "You" to a nonhuman, non-cultural being in the way that Buber modeled in his tree examples. Heideggerians can, however, find this possibility in the theme of "letting-be," for which see, e.g., "On the Essence of Truth," trans. R. F. C. Hull and Alan Crick, in *Existence and Being*.

58. Rickert proposes an ultimate ideal harmony called "value-reality" (*Wertwirklichkeit*), warning against mixing value together with reality in its conception (as had happened in the Platonic ideas) (*System*, pp. 138–39).

59. Buber, *I and Thou*, pp. 68–69.

60. Rickert acknowledges this problem in these terms in "Vom System der Werte," p. 299. His value theory mitigates it by claiming to specify only the largest formal categories of value and value-realization, remaining open to cultural variation and individual preference.

61. The "unconditional act" of Existenz cannot be defined objectively and so must be conceived "merely as an *appeal*, a sign that will not be comprehensible to me unless I translate it into my own being" (Karl Jaspers, *Philosophy*, trans. E. B. Ashton, vol. 2, pp. 256–57). "Existenz can be neither an object nor an objectified subject; it remains an origin that we can subjectively and objectively elucidate only in the form of an appeal. Existential elucidation would be thwarted if we developed it as an ontological doctrine" (ibid., p. 373).

62. Buber, *I and Thou*, pp. 58, 83.

63. Ibid., pp. 55–56.

64. Ibid., p. 85.

65. Walter Kaufmann offers a version of this criticism in "Buber's Failures and Triumph," in *Martin Buber: A Centenary Volume*, ed. Haim Gordon and Jochanan Bloch. Robert Wood responds (in "Oriental Themes in Buber's Work" in the same volume) that Kaufmann overlooks "[Buber's] distinction between *Begegnung* or momentary encounter and *Beziehung* or perduring relation open to the necessary alternation between 'inspiration' and 'work'" (p. 333). That distinction is indeed invoked by Buber later ("Replies to My Critics," in *Philosophy of Martin Buber*, ed. P. A. Schilpp and Maurice Friedman, p. 712), but Kaufmann's point is that *I and Thou* itself does not establish and is not inherently hospitable to it.

66. Nicolai Hartmann gives a provocative and valuable (though not encounter-

centered) analysis of the interdependency of objective and personal spirit in *Das Problem des geistigen Seins*, pp. 61–67, 165–69.

67. Heinrich Rickert, *Die Grenzen der naturwissenschaftlichen Begriffsbildung*, p. 319; abridged translation by Guy Oakes, *The Limits of Concept Formation in Natural Science*, p. 86.

68. An affirmative appreciation of culture is an important element in Buber's writings on Judaism and Israel, e.g., "The Spirit of Israel and the World of Today" in *Israel and the World* (1963). In *I and Thou*, the key general point pertains to the spiritual potentiality of "form," as in this comment on religious tradition: "Form is a mixture of You and It, too. In faith and cult it can freeze into an object; but from the gist of the relation that survives in it, it turns ever again into presence" (167).

69. Heidegger, "On the Essence of Truth," pp. 316–19.

70. Heidegger, *Being and Time*, p. 298.

71. A useful introduction to this issue is Michael Theunissen's discussion of Karl Löwith and Ludwig Binswanger's work bridging the perspectives of Heidegger and Buber in *Der Andere*, pp. 413–76.

72. Heidegger, *Pathmarks*, ed. William McNeill, p. xiii.

73. Heidegger, "Comments on Karl Jaspers's *Psychology of Worldviews*" (1921), trans. John van Buren, in *Pathmarks*, p. 4.

74. François Laruelle, "L'Appel et le Phénomène," p. 27, my translation. Laruelle's main basis for this characterization is the argument for a "third reduction" to "the call as call" in Marion's *Reduction and Givenness* (1990), trans. Thomas A. Carlson, pp. 192–205.

75. Jean-Luc Marion, *Being Given: Toward a Phenomenology of Givenness*, trans. Jeffrey L. Kosky. I will use this translation in quotations but will indicate along the way how it suits my purposes to translate certain key terms differently, notably *donation* as "donation" and *appel* as "appeal."

76. Jean-Luc Marion, "The Other First Philosophy and the Question of Givenness," trans. Jeffrey L. Kosky.

77. This and subsequent references in the text are to Marion, *Being Given*.

78. Marion takes over Derrida's points about the self-contradictions of giving; see Jacques Derrida, *Given Time: I. Counterfeit Money* (1992).

79. For *fond* and *arrière-fond*, see Marion, *Étant donné*, p. 225.

80. For Marion's own view of the Levinas precedents, see Jean-Luc Marion, "The Voice Without Name: Homage to Levinas," in *The Face of the Other and the Trace of God*, 224–42.

81. See Emmanuel Levinas, *Totality and Infinity* and *Otherwise than Being or Beyond Essence*. I abstract in this synopsis from the significant differences in key terms and argumentative strategies between these two works.

82. *Totality and Infinity*, pp. 68–89.

83. On the implications of Levinas's conception of the face for relations with nonhumans, see John Llewelyn, "Am I Obsessed by Bobby? (Humanism of the Other Animal)."

84. Marion argues also that the face's iconic appeal is manifested in religious, erotic, and personally "existential" ways and so is not limited to the category of "ethics" (*In Excess: Studies of Saturated Phenomena*, trans. Robyn Horner and Vincent Berraud, p. 118).

85. *Being Given*, p. 175.

86. "The thesis that Being is evil [is] presupposed [through] the whole length of Levinas's thought" (Didier Franck, "The Body of Difference," trans. Jeffrey Bloechl, in Bloechl, *The Face of the Other and the Trace of God*, p. 24).

87. Page numbers in the text are to this book.

88. The objection cited by Marion is from Dominique Janicaud, "The Theological Turn in French Phenomenology," in Janicaud et al., *Phenomenology and the "Theological Turn*," pp. 64–65.

89. The debate on the allegedly theological character of Marion's philosophy perhaps really turns less on whether Marion is tacitly committed to a certain identification of a supreme *appellant* (i.e., as a *being*, in effect) and more on Marion's aim of making sense *structurally* of a supreme appeal (as a pure possibility of meaning). One might wish to insist that philosophical thinking cannot rightly be *centered* in anything like the way Marion proposes, not without violating necessary methodological scruples (Janicaud) or repressing *différance* with a dogma of presence or unity (Derrida). But to consider *any* centering of the field of appeals "theological" is to obscure the shared orientation that philosophy and religion of the Axial Age type have always had and thus to mistake the character of their divergence and rivalry.

90. John Milbank makes much the same criticism, to which Robyn Horner replies that Marion can sustain his position by: (1) discriminating between coincident but distinct meaning-levels, that of worldly experience with being-content and that of donation as such without determinable content; (2) admitting an ineliminable "risk" in deciding to associate donation with God (or anything benign); and (3) deriving actual religious meaningfulness from the actual seeing of manifested holiness, like a Christian's seeing of Christ. The problem remains, however, that the positive appeal-sense of all experienced appeals has been made to depend on a positive specification of universal donation, which in turn depends for its positive sense (its relevant appellative sense) on an extraphilosophical faith—whether as an arbitrary resolution of an undecidable issue or as a contingent religiously persuasive experience. Supposing that the positive sense of a concrete worldly appeal must differ from the positive sense of universal radical donation, still the relevance of each sense to the other needs to be elucidated. See Milbank, "Only Theology Overcomes Metaphysics," in *The Word Made Strange*, and "Grace: The Midwinter Sacrifice," in *Being Reconciled*, p. 156; Robyn Horner, *Rethinking God as Gift: Marion, Derrida, and the Limits of Phenomenology*, pp. 174–80.

91. Levinas, *Totality and Infinity*, pp. 267–69, 274–80.

92. Marion, *Being Given*, pp. 300–302.

93. Ibid., pp. 40–51; cf. Rickert, *System*, pp. 119–20, and *Gegenstand*, pp. 251–55.

94. This use of Husserl in relation to Heidegger is more fully laid out in *Reduction and Givenness*; see esp. pp. 161–66.

95. Marion, *Being Given*, pp. 20–21; Rickert, *Gegenstand*, pp. 242–43.

96. Marion, *Being Given*, p. 51.

97. Rickert, *System*, pp. xii–xiii.

98. Ibid., pp. 375–83 (*Voll-endung*), 308; Marion, *Being Given,* p. 236.

99. Rickert, *System*, 128.

100. This and subsequent page references are to Buber, *I and Thou*.

101. "We do not find meaning lying in things nor do we put it into things, but between us and things it can happen" (Buber, "Dialogue" [1929], trans. Ronald Gregor Smith, in *Between Man and Man*, p. 36).

102. "On the Psychologizing of the World" [1923], in A *Believing Humanism*, trans. Maurice Friedman, p. 146. Cf. the "ontology of the interhuman" in "Elements of the Interhuman" [1954], trans. Ronald Gregor Smith, in *The Knowledge of Man*, p. 84.

103. On *Denken* as *Danken*, see Heidegger, *What Is Called Thinking?* Part 2, Lecture 3.

4. THE APPEAL IN MODERN THEOLOGY

1. Richard Lovelace, "Lucasta," st. 3.

2. Rudolf Otto, *The Idea of the Holy*, trans. John Harvey (1950).

3. Heidegger, *Being and Time*, §57, pp. 321–22.

4. Franz Rosenzweig, *The Star of Redemption*, Part 2, Book 2, pp. 156–204.

5. "Only in the Word of divine grace is *God's omnipotence* taken seriously. In this Word man's finitude is seen with all its logical implications, as his enslavement to himself . . . Only in this Word is God's holiness taken seriously, as man's finitude is seen in it with all its logical implications as sin . . . Only in this Word is God's *eternity* taken seriously—for as the Word of forgiveness it is the *eschatological* event which renews the world" (Rudolf Bultmann, "The Question of Natural Revelation," trans. James C. G. Greig, in *Essays Philosophical and Theological*, pp. 109–10).

6. See Franz Rosenzweig, *Philosophical and Theological Writings*, ed. Paul W. Franks and Michael L. Morgan, pp. 25–27, for the editors' discussion of the development of the idea that "revelation is orientation" in Rosenzweig's correspondence.

7. Emile Durkheim, *The Elementary Forms of the Religious Life* (1915), pp. 52–57; Mircea Eliade, *The Sacred and the Profane*. For Durkheim, the content of the religious appeal is the felt power of the society as a whole, a power that crackles like electricity when brought to a focus (pp. 240–42).

8. The articulation of concepts of revelation in the world religions—that is, the religious theorizing of the religious supreme appeal—occurs mostly between the two study periods of the present work. Comparative historical work is needed to fill in this picture. For a preliminary overview, see Johannes Deninger's article on "Revelation" in *The Encyclopedia of Religion*, vol. 12. But do not be misled by the preponderance here of Jewish and Christian data; in spite of the strong biblical affiliations of most Western revelation talk, the topic is indeed cross-cultural. Relevant data will be found in Wilfred Cantwell Smith's *What Is Scripture?*

9. Rudolf Bultmann, "Revelation in the New Testament," in *Existence and Faith*, pp. 69–74.

10. Cf. Otto on "creature-feeling," in *The Idea of the Holy*, pp. 8–11. On the "transworthy Other," see Steven G. Smith, *Worth Doing*, pp. 15–20.

11. Diana Eck has written: "In entering into the Hindu world, one confronts a way of thinking which one might call 'radically polytheistic,' and if there is any 'great divide' between the traditions of India and those of the West, it is in just this fact. Some may object that India has also affirmed Oneness as resolutely and profoundly as any culture on earth, and indeed it has. The point here, however, is that India's affirmation of Oneness is made in a context that affirms with equal vehemence the multitude of ways in which human beings have seen that Oneness and expressed their vision. Indian monotheism or monism cannot, therefore, be aptly compared with the monotheism of the West. The statement that 'God is One' does not mean the same thing in India and the West" (*Darshan*, pp. 22–24). But it is evident that the diversity of Hindu forms of

devotion are meaningfully united in the minds of a vast number of devotees by their shared acknowledgment of Vedic revelation.

12. Cf. "What Is Orientation in Thinking?" in Immanuel Kant, *The Critique of Practical Reason and Other Moral Writings*.

13. See esp. *Critique of Practical Reason*, Ak. 110–48 and *Critique of Judgment*, Ak. 447–72. Just how strongly and practically Kant is committed to the ideal of righteousness and happiness combined—due to the presence of a "subjective necessity" in humans of seeking happiness alongside the "objective necessity" of compliance with the moral law imposed by reason—is a matter of extensive debate. Kant dramatized his own moral detachment from concern for promoting happiness in the famous example of refusing to lie to a murderer in "On a Supposed Right to Lie from Altruistic Motives," in *Critique of Practical Reason and Other Moral Writings*.

14. *Critique of Practical Reason*, Ak. 129; *Critique of Judgment*, Ak. 481.

15. *Critique of Pure Reason*, B 847.

16. Ibid., B 845–46 (my translation and emphasis).

17. See note 13 above.

18. *Critique of Pure Reason*, B 612n.

19. Albrecht Ritschl, *The Christian Doctrine of Justification and Reconciliation* (1874), pp. 11, 219. Ritschl and Lotze were colleagues at the University of Göttingen; on their relationship, see Leonhard Stählin, *Kant, Lotze, and Ritschl*.

20. Ritschl, *The Christian Doctrine of Justification and Reconciliation*, p. 398.

21. Ibid., p. 222.

22. Ibid., pp. 24–25, 199–203.

23. Adolf Harnack, *What Is Christianity?* pp. 55–74.

24. Leo Baeck, *The Essence of Judaism* (1922), pp. 35–44, 59–80.

25. Wilhelm Herrmann, *Ethik*, p. 147, my translation.

26. Herrmann, *Systematic Theology*, pp. 33–39.

27. As quoted from Herrmann, *Schriften zur Grundlegung der Theologie*, 2:261, in Simon Fisher, *Revelatory Positivism? Barth's Earliest Theology and the Marburg School*, p. 138.

28. Ibid., p. 145 (*Schriften*, vol. 2, pp. 108–109).

29. Karl Barth quotes a statement by Herrmann to this effect in his *Dogmatik* to make the point that Herrmann never intended that God be absorbed by human subjectivity (Barth, "The Principles of Dogmatics According to Wilhelm Herrmann," in *Theology and Church*, p. 254).

30. Karl Barth, "Moderne Theologie und Reichsgottesarbeit," pp. 317–21.

31. Fisher, *Revelatory Positivism?* pp. 133–43.

32. Barth's dialectical theology develops through a series of wartime and postwar writings collected in *The Word of God and the Word of Man*, as well as in the 1919 edition of *The Epistle to the Romans*. The early links with Herrmann and Schleiermacher are apparent in Karl Barth, "Der christliche Glaube und die Geschichte," *Schweizerische Theologische Zeitschrift* 29 (1912): 1–18, 49–72. For Buber's route to so similar a point, see Maurice Friedman, *Martin Buber's Life and Work: The Early Years 1878–1923*.

33. About Gogarten: Letter of Barth to Eduard Thurneysen of October 27, 1920, reprinted in Barth and Thurneysen, *Revolutionary Theology in the Making*. About Bultmann: Rudolf Bultmann, "Karl Barth's *Epistle to the Romans* in its Second Edition" [1922], in *The Beginnings of Dialectic Theology*, ed. James M. Robinson.

34. Barth, *Epistle to the Romans*, 2nd ed. [1922], trans. E. C. Hoskyns from the 6th ed. (1933)—revelation exterior to experience, pp. 50–51, 60, 92, 109–10, 126, 135, 237, 285, 296, 365–66; transcendent of "value," pp. 63, 68, 111, 322, 463.

35. The "crisis" formula for the revelation situation was introduced by Gogarten in a 1920 talk, "The Crisis of Our Culture," in *The Beginnings of Dialectic Theology*, ed. James M. Robinson, pp. 283–309. The crisis theme was important also in Barth's *Epistle to the Romans*, 2nd ed. (1922), and Brunner's *Theology of Crisis* (1929).

36. Barth, "The Problem of Ethics Today" (1922), in *The Word of God and the Word of Man*, p. 179.

37. Barth, "Church and Culture" (1926), in *Theology and Church*, p. 340.

38. A criticism of Schleiermacher's Romantic view of religious experience (Barth, "Schleiermacher's 'Celebration of Christmas'" (1924), in *Theology and Church*, pp. 156–57). Cf. Emil Brunner's similarly oriented critique in *Die Mystik und das Wort* (1924).

39. Barth, *Epistle to the Romans*, pp. 386–87 (commenting on Romans 10.16–17).

40. Barth, *Die christliche Dogmatik* (1927), pp. 461–62.

41. Adolf von Harnack, "Fifteen Questions to Those among the Theologians Who Are Contemptuous of the Scientific Theology," and Karl Barth, "Fifteen Answers to Professor von Harnack," trans. Keith R. Crim, in *Beginnings of Dialectic Theology*, pp. 166, 169.

42. Ibid.

43. E.g., in George Lindbeck, *The Nature of Doctrine*. Lindbeck's proposal gets off the Barthian track in an instructive way by keying religious faith to general considerations about the priority of "cultural-linguistic form" in the constitution of meaning. He recognizes that cultural-linguistic form being the "leading partner" (i.e., over experience) in religion formation (p. 34) does not entail that a cultural-linguistic form can establish the *religiousness* of the religion (as opposed to its intelligibility and functionality as such), since a cultural-linguistic form becomes religious only with the qualification that it deals with what is in fact "most important" to subjects (p. 32). Similarly (and looking ahead to issues that concern us in the second part), that a cultural-linguistic form can generate a religious attitude (p. 33) does not establish that the form is the source or norm of the attitude's religious meaning; the form may be auxiliary to and religiously redeemed by the attitude, the attitude having the force that it does because of its actual achievements in relating the appellate subject to the supreme appellant.

44. Barth, "No!" in Karl Barth and Emil Brunner, *Natural Theology* (1934; comprising "Nature and Grace" by Brunner and "No!" by Barth), trans. Peter Fraenkel, p. 85.

45. Ibid., p. 123.

46. Brunner, "Nature and Grace," pp. 51–59. On the task of "Christian eristics," a Kierkegaard-inspired campaign of making people aware of their inauthenticity apart from God, see Brunner's "Die andere Aufgabe der Theologie," pp. 255–76.

47. Friedrich Gogarten, "Das Problem einer theologischen Anthropologie," p. 496. For Gogarten's view of the ontological dependence of I upon You and of history as the product and determining context of I-You relation, see esp. "Community or Corporate Society?" (from *Von Glaube und Offenbarung*, pp. 63–83), in *Beginnings of Dialectic Theology*, pp. 328–42; *Ich glaube an den dreieinigen Gott*, pp. 65–126.

48. Gogarten, *Ich glaube an den dreieinigen Gott*, p. 49.

49. Ibid., pp. 68–69. For a Fichtean precedent for this position, see below in chapter 7, pp. 234–37.

50. Personalism against "naturalism," *Ich glaube an den dreieinigen Gott*, pp. 62–63; God as uniquely the absolute You, "Community or Corporate Society?" p. 339. Ferdinand Ebner's book *The Word and the Spiritual Realities* (1921) appeared two years ahead of *I and Thou* with a Christ-centered version of the exteriority argument of I-You thinking and was admired by Gogarten; see Peter Lange, *Konkrete Theologie? Karl Barth und Friedrich Gogarten "Zwischen den Zeiten" (1922–1933)*, p. 382 n. 44.

51. *Ich glaube an den dreieinigen Gott*, p. 177.

52. Not coincidentally, Barth instinctively resisted Gogarten's way of "concretizing" human identity: in a certain seminar in 1930, "this Frau von Tiling in a typical Gogartenish way said to me: 'Herr Professor, who are you really? You are a husband, a son, a father, a professor' . . . To this I replied quite naively: 'Yes, and I'm myself! That is something, too.' But she and Gogarten would not have it. For them everything was determined by an 'ordinance of creation,' according to which a person is a father, a mother, a husband, an official, a Swiss, or whatever . . . [I] said that I could not allow myself to be dissolved into relationships in that way" (a 1964 reminiscence recorded in Eberhard Busch, *Karl Barth: His Life from Letters and Autobiographical Texts*, trans. John Bowden, p. 194). In a letter to Bultmann he characterized Frau von Tiling's approach as "intellectual brutality" (*Karl Barth/Rudolf Bultmann: Letters 1922–1966*, trans. Geoffrey W. Bromiley, p. 53).

53. The "orders of creation" are mentioned in *Ich glaube an den dreieinigen Gott* (206ff.), where Gogarten uses the example that obeying God enables a father to respond authentically to the appeal of his son (cf. the Marion father-son example in *Being Given* noted in chapter 2); see also Gogarten's *Politische Ethik* (1932).

54. For the controversy with liberal theology, see Ernst Troeltsch, "An Apple from the Tree of Kierkegaard," and Gogarten, "Against Romantic Theology: A Chapter on Faith," in *The Beginnings of Dialectic Theology*. For Barth's unhappiness with Gogarten's "system" in *Ich glaube an den dreieinigen Gott*, see his letter of June 12, 1928, to Bultmann in *Karl Barth/Rudolf Bultmann: Letters 1922–1966*, p. 42. For Grisebach's critique of Gogarten, see *Gegenwart*, pp. 155–61, 200–202. I have discussed problems inherent in Grisebach's position in "Idealism and Exteriority: The Case of Eberhard Grisebach," pp. 136–49.

55. On this episode, see Larry Shiner, *The Secularization of History: An Introduction to the Theology of Friedrich Gogarten*, pp. 204–16.

56. Gogarten, "Volkstum und Gottesgesetzt" (1934), quoted in Shiner, p. 212.

57. Gogarten, *Gericht oder Skepsis*, p. 9. Brunner voiced a complementary worry in "Die andere Aufgabe der Theologie" that Barth's "principles and attitude will entice others to speak no longer to the real person—and that always means to speak to today's men and women—and therefore, not to *speak* at all, but rather to *declaim*" (trans. Bruce McCormack, in *Karl Barth's Critically Realistic Dialectical Theology*, pp. 405–406).

58. Liberation theologies do not characteristically make a major argument concerning revelation as appeal—their emphasis is on overcoming any potential of separation between experience of God and the struggle to realize justice and human dignity. "God's self-manifestation, today as all through the course of biblical revelation, is realized only in real history. Accordingly, honesty with and fidelity toward the real are

not only prerequisites for a spirituality, they are the very foundations of that spirituality, and this is what is most basic . . . they express the basic realization of our response to God's word" (Jon Sobrino, *Spirituality of Liberation*, trans. Robert R. Barr, p. 21). From this perspective even Gogarten knows too much (in a free-traveling way) about revelation.

59. McCormack, *Karl Barth's Critically Realistic Dialectical Theology*, p. 392.

60. Barth, *Epistle to the Romans*, p. 82.

61. Barth, *How I Changed My Mind*, p. 44.

62. Barth, *Church Dogmatics*, vol. 4/1, pp. 17–18. I give a documented interpretation of this stage of Barth's theological development in *The Argument to the Other*, chap. 5.

63. Barth, *Church Dogmatics* 2/1, p. 334.

64. Barth, *Church Dogmatics* 1/2, p. 42.

65. Barth commented in 1939, "I have been reproached with having completely withdrawn behind a Chinese wall" (*How I Changed My Mind*, p. 44). Perhaps the most often cited "revelation positivism" charge is that of Dietrich Bonhoeffer in *Letters and Papers from Prison*, pp. 280, 286, 328–29. On the larger picture of Bonhoeffer's relationship with Barth on this issue, see Andreas Pangritz, *Karl Barth in the Theology of Dietrich Bonhoeffer*.

66. "It is clear that *Christ* is revelation and that revelation is the *word*; for these two are one and the same. Christ is not the act of God's love as a fact within the world that one can find some place and demonstrate to be an 'act of love' . . . for the love directed to *me—and* this alone can make me a new creature—cannot be demonstrated by historical observation. It can only be promised to me directly; and this is what is done by the proclamation" ("Revelation in the New Testament," in *Existence and Faith*, p. 102). Bultmann links this resolution of the "historical Jesus" problem in Christian theology to Paul's self-understanding: "Paul has become Christ himself for his hearers—not because he is deified and is gazed upon by them as a pneumatic, but because he preaches to them. 'So we are at work for Christ . . . in such a way that God makes his appeal through us . . .' (II Corinthians 5.20)" (88–89).

67. Bultmann, *Jesus and the Word*, trans. Louise Pettibone Smith and Erminie Huntress, p. 103.

68. Bultmann, *History and Eschatology*, pp. 140–41.

69. Ibid., p. 152.

70. Barth, *Church Dogmatics* 4/1, p. 767. Cf. Barth's "Rudolf Bultmann, An Attempt to Understand Him," in *Kerygma and Myth*, vol. 2; and Bultmann's reply of November 1952 in *Karl Barth–Rudolf Bultmann Letters, 1922–1966*, pp. 87–104. Bultmann argues that the faith-event must not be equated with "experience" as an object of psychology in, e.g., *Jesus Christ and Mythology*, pp. 70–73.

71. Ritschl, *The Christian Doctrine of Justification and Reconciliation*, p. 199.

72. Thoreau, "Walking," p. 18; Dillard, "Teaching a Stone to Talk," p. 33, in *This Sacred Earth: Religion, Nature, Environment*, ed. Roger Gottlieb.

73. See, e.g., Andrew Linzey, *Christianity and the Rights of Animals*, chap. 1.

74. See Don Beck and Graham Linscott, *The Crucible: Forging South Africa's Future*.

75. Thomas Berry and Brian Swimme, *The Universe Story: From the Primordial Flaring Forth to the Ecozoic Era—A Celebration of the Unfolding of the Cosmos*, p. 264.

76. Ibid., p. 263.

77. This and subsequent references in the text are to Rosemary Radford Ruether, *Gaia and God: An Ecofeminist Theology of Earth Healing.*

78. Ruether's direct acknowledgment of Buber comes in connection with this statement: "Encompassing our relation to nature as usable things there must remain the larger sensibility, rooted in the encounter with nature as 'thou,' as fellow beings each with its own integrity" (*Gaia and God*, pp. 227–28).

79. Ibid., pp. 31, 207.

80. Buber, *I and Thou*, pp. 125–26.

81. This and subsequent references in the text are to Sallie McFague, *Super, Natural Christians: How We Should Love Nature.*

82. E.g., Stephen H. Webb, "Should We Love All of Nature? A Critique of Sallie McFague's *Super, Natural Christians*," in *Encounter* 59 (affirming the special claims of higher animals), and Celia Deane-Drummond, review of same in *Ecotheology* 8 (affirming the relevance of ecological information).

83. Herrmann, *Systematic Theology*, p. 37. The German original, made from lecture notes, was published posthumously in 1925.

84. Bultmann, "Liberal Theology and the Latest Movement," in *Faith and Understanding*, trans. Louise Pettibone Smith, pp. 29–30.

85. Barth, "The Word of God and the Task of the Ministry," in *The Word of God and the Word of Man*, p. 190.

86. Subsequent references in the text are to Jay McDaniel, *Earth, Sky, Gods and Mortals: Developing an Ecological Spirituality.*

5. ATTITUDES

1. See, e.g., Philip G. Zimbardo and Michael R. Leippe, *The Psychology of Attitude Change and Social Influence*, pp. 30–36.

2. As first done in L. L. Thurstone's work, *The Measurement of Attitudes* (1929).

3. For a superbly insightful review of the triumphant progress of the concept of attitude in both academic and popular discourse since Darwin first turned it to scientific use, see Donald Fleming, "Attitude: The History of a Concept," in *Perspectives in American History*, ed. Donald Fleming and Bernard Bailyn, 1:287–365.

4. By the late seventeenth century, via Italian and French mutations of *aptitudo*, according to the *Oxford English Dictionary.*

5. J. R. Maze has written a wake-up call, if one is needed, in "The Concept of Attitude." For example: "It commonly happens that potentially very wounding epithets of an essentially moralistic kind ('dirty,' 'greedy,' 'cruel,' etc.) are applied to a child's behavior, or indeed to his own nature ('You dirty boy!') by persons whom he loves and whose respect, affection, and protection he urgently needs" (p. 183).

6. Robert Audi, "A Cognitive-Motivational Theory of Attitudes," p. 79.

7. Nina Bull links the active and static implications of attitude to its twin etymological ancestors *acto* and *apto*. Every action requires postural preparation, she notes, citing the revelatory southern U.S. expression "fixing to [do something]" (*The Attitude Theory of Emotion*, pp. 3–4).

8. For example, Gabriel Marcel criticizes the "optimism" of Leibniz as a pose taken and maintained at a certain distance from things felt, "not drawn from the most intimate and living part" of a person (*Homo Viator*, p. 34). Cf. the classic existentialist

analysis of freedom-betraying "attitudes" in Simone de Beauvoir's *The Ethics of Ambiguity*. Kenneth Burke makes the related observation that "an attitude of sympathy [e.g.] may either lead to an act of sympathy or may serve as substitute for an act of sympathy. It is thus 'potentially' two different kinds of act" (*A Grammar of Motives*, p. 242).

9. In "Shame and Blame: The Self through Time and Change," Jennifer Radden argues that of all emotions, guilt has the strongest implications for conservation of personal identity.

10. Bruno Snell tracks the emergence of these conceptions between Homer and the Attic Enlightenment in *The Discovery of the Mind in Greek Literature and Philosophy*.

11. "In the conception of universal neighborliness, there is a certain group of attitudes of kindliness and helpfulness in which the response of one calls out in the other and in himself the same attitude. Hence the fusion of the 'I' and the 'me' which leads to intense emotional experiences. The wider the social process in which this is involved, the greater is the exaltation . . . I think that the religious attitude involves . . . the carrying-over of the social attitude to the larger world" (George Herbert Mead, *Mind, Self, and Society*, pp. 274–75).

12. *Rasa*, "delight," in Indian aesthetic theory is an objectively specifiable quality of beauty and response to beauty and offers a taste of eternal bliss; see Sneh Pandit, "'Rasa' as a Principle in Art and Aesthetics," chapter 2 in his *An Approach to the Indian Theory of Art and Aesthetics*.

13. Still the most substantially interesting such account is Max Scheler's in *The Nature of Sympathy* (1970), and *Formalism in Ethics and Non-Formal Ethics of Values* (1973). For a recent review of the strengths and difficulties of cognitivist emotion theory, see Kristján Kristjánsson, "Some Remaining Problems in Cognitive Theories of Emotion."

14. Recently, Doret de Ruyter, "The Virtue of Taking Responsibility," *Educational Philosophy and Theory* 34 (2002): 25–35.

15. For more on how our moral evaluation of Jane depends on how thing actually go in the world, see Steven G. Smith, "Worthy Actions," *Journal of Ethics* 5 (2001): 315–33.

16. I am distinguishing "sympathy" from "benevolence" more clearly than David Hume did in the *Treatise of Human Nature*, where "sympathy" does most of the work, or in the *Inquiry Concerning the Principles of Morals*, where "benevolence" comes to the fore. Key passages in the *Treatise* include pp. 575–76 on sympathy as susceptibility to be affected by others, and p. 499 on sympathy as benevolence; in the *Inquiry*, pp. 47–58 and 105 on the sentiment of benevolence or humanity.

17. Friedrich Schleiermacher, *On Religion: Speeches to Its Cultured Despisers*, trans. John Oman, p. 39.

18. Georg Simmel, "Fundamental Religious Ideas and Modern Science: An Inquiry" (1909), in *Essays on Religion*, trans. Horst Jürgen Helle with Ludwig Nieder, p. 5.

6. ATTITUDE IN THE AXIAL AGE

1. Yasna 37.5, trans. J. Darmesteter and L. H. Mills, in *Anthology of World Scriptures*, p. 203.

2. S. N. Kramer, in *Ancient Near Eastern Texts Relating to the Old Testament*, 3rd ed., ed. James B. Pritchard, pp. 589–91, emphasis added. Jacob Klein translates this text

as "Man and His God" in *The Context of Scripture*, ed. William W. Hallo, 1:573–75; the slight differences in Klein's version do not affect my argument.

3. *Daodejing* 22, cited by the chapter number and using the Arthur Waley translation in *The Way and Its Power*, but with updated romanization.

4. Micah 6.8–9; Proverbs 15.33; Matthew 5.5. Hebrew Bible quotations are taken from the New Jewish Publication Society translation; New Testament translations are from the New Revised Standard Version.

5. Pritchard, *Ancient Near Eastern Texts*, p. 5.

6. Snell, *The Discovery of the Mind*, chap. 1.

7. *Brihadaranyaka Upanishad* 3.9.21–22. Upanishad translations are from *Upanishads*, trans. Patrick Olivelle, except as noted.

8. *Brihadaranyaka Upanishad* 3.9.24–26.

9. Kirk, Raven, and Schofield, *The Presocratic Philosophers*, no. 476.

10. See *Timaeus* 30–32, 37, 90, in Plato, *Collected Dialogues*.

11. See, e.g., Diogenes Laertius 7.88, 7.135–39; trans. Brad Inwood and L. P. Gerson in *Hellenistic Philosophy: Introductory Readings*, pp. 136, 96–97.

12. Hesiod, *Works and Days*, ll. 11–24; Heraclitus, nos. 211, 212 (*eris* and *polemos*). I use the fragment numbering and translations of Kirk, Raven, and Schofield in *The Presocratic Philosophers*.

13. Kirk, Raven, and Schofield, *The Presocratic Philosophers*, pp. 232–35, 325–30.

14. Kongzi (Confucius), *Analects* (Lunyu) 7.22, trans. Arthur Waley, *The Analects of Confucius*. All numbering and translations are Waley's except as otherwise noted.

15. John 14.15–17, 25–26.

16. John 3.3–8; 1 John 4.4–6.

17. Pritchard, *Ancient Near Eastern Texts*, p. 380.

18. "I am Hammurabi, noble king. I have not been careless or negligent toward humankind, granted to my care by the god Enlil, and with whose shepherding the god Marduk charged me . . . the great gods having chosen me, I am indeed the shepherd who brings peace, whose scepter is just. My benevolent shade is spread over my city" ("Epilogue," in *The Context of Scripture*, ed. William W. Hallo, 2:351).

19. I derive this idea from Colleen McDannell and Bernhard Lang in *Heaven: A History*, pp. 14–15, 19–20.

20. See, e.g., Holy Roman Emperor Charles V's abdication speech (1555) in *The Western Tradition*, ed. Eugen Weber, 1:432–33.

21. *Works and Days*, ll. 1–2, 6, in *Hesiod*, trans. Hugh G. Evelyn-White.

22. For Yahweh, e.g., Isaiah 2.5–17; for Indra, e.g., *Rig Veda* 2.12.10. The political significance of the story of the humbling god is plainly stated in the *Mahabharata*: "Like disciples humbling themselves in the presence of preceptors or the gods in the presence of Indra, all men should humble themselves before the king" (Book 12, quoted in John Weir Perry, *Lord of the Four Quarters: The Mythology of Kingship*, p. 127).

23. *Mencius (Mengzi)* 2.B.7, trans. D. C. Lau ("Kongzi" for "Confucius").

24. Heraclitus 195, 196.

25. Kongzi (Confucius), *Analects* 13.18. I substitute "Kongzi" for "Master K'ung" and "The Master."

26. For Mengzi it is so obvious that benevolence is fundamental that he gives relatively more emphasis to the need to exercise benevolence intelligently, heeding precedents and laws (e.g., 4.A.1).

27. Some passages seem to point more one way, some more the other: "Believe in God, believe also in me. In my Father's house there are many dwelling places. If it were not so, would I have told you that I go to prepare a place for you? And if I go and prepare a place for you, I will come again and will take you to myself, so that where I am, there you may be also. And you know the way to the place where I am going" (John 14.1–4) vs. "He whom God has sent speaks the words of God, for he gives the Spirit without measure. The Father loves the Son and has placed all things in his hands. Whoever believes in the Son has eternal life" (John 3.34–36).

28. *Bhagavad-Gita* 4.39. All Gita translations are from *The Bhagavad-Gita*, trans. Barbara Stoler Miller, except as noted.

29. *Bhagavad-Gita* 12.8, 19.

30. *The Book of Odes*, "King Wen," trans. Burton Watson, in *Sources of Chinese Tradition*, p. 38.

31. *Daodejing* 25.

32. Zhuangzi, *The Complete Works of Chuang Tzu*, trans. Burton Watson, sec. 1, p. 56.

33. See Robert Eno, *The Confucian Creation of Heaven*, on this class of persons (*ru*, "scholars") generally.

34. A. C. Graham, *Disputers of the Tao*, pp. 18–19.

35. *Analects* 17.6. This passage has the look of the attitude-happy third century BCE or later and is identified as a later interpolation by E. Bruce Brooks and A. Taeko Brooks, *The Original Analects*, p. 180.

36. The "thread," *Analects* 4.15. On *zhong* and *shu*, see A. C. Graham, *Disputers of the Tao*, pp. 20–21.

37. As defined in *The Lore of the Way (Dao Shu)* by Jia Yi of the second century (Graham, *Disputers of the Tao*, 21).

38. *Shu* is translated as "empathy" by Brooks and Brooks, *The Original Analects*.

39. *Mengzi* 2.A.6 argues that all humans have germs of goodness, which if developed will grow "like a fire starting up or a spring coming through." If one fails to develop them, however, one will be morally crippled.

40. *Analects* 6.28—a third century BCE interpolation, according to Brooks and Brooks, *The Original Analects* (there numbered 6.30), p. 176.

41. Graham, *Disputers of the Tao*, p. 22.

42. Graham's interpretation may underrate the distance of goodness from us—in effect, its transcendence. Graham quotes *Analects* 7.30: "Is jen [ren] so far away? As soon as I desire jen, jen arrives." But the point of this passage may be to remind us ironically that true willing of ren is extraordinarily difficult. Consider also the pathos of 8.7: "Master Tseng said, The true Knight of the Way must perforce be both broad-shouldered and stout of heart; his burden is heavy and he has far to go. For Goodness is the burden he has taken upon himself; and must we not grant that it is a heavy one to bear? Only with death does his journey end; then must we not grant that he has far to go?" A more positive reason to think of ren as transcendent lies in the model of lifelong learning that Kongzi promotes (e.g., 7.21, 15.30).

43. *The Classic of Filial Piety*, in *The Sacred Books of Confucius*, trans. Chai and Winberg Chai.

44. Mengzi: "The Way lies at hand . . . If only everyone loved his parents and treated his elders with deference, the Empire would be at peace" (4.A.11).

45. *Analects* 17.21, 11.11; Brooks and Brooks, *The Original Analects*, p. 158.

46. *The Doctrine of the Mean* (*Zhongyong*) 30, giving "Heaven" for *tian*, trans. David L. Hall and Roger T. Ames in *Thinking Through Confucius*, p. 241.

47. *Mengzi* 7.B.25. Hall and Ames comment: "The classical Chinese alternative to the dualism of creator and human creature is this continuum: the human being in striving to realize himself becomes deity" (*Thinking Through Confucius*, p. 242).

48. *Mengzi* 4.B.20.

49. *Daodejing*, trans. Arthur Waley, *The Way and Its Power*, 68. Subsequent references to this source are in the text.

50. On this carver, see chapter 3 of the *Zhuangzi*.

51. *Daodejing* 1. Graham thinks the intent of this couplet is "to smash the dichotomy of desire and desirelessness by contradictory commands" (220). Ames and Hall's rendering suggests balance: "Thus, to be really objectless in one's desires is how one observes the mysteries of all things, while really having desires is how one observes their boundaries" (*Daodejing: A Philosophical Translation*, trans. Roger T. Ames and David Hall, p. 77). However, quenching desire seems to be the main emphasis throughout the *Daodejing*.

52. *Daodejing* 61; Ames and Hall have "equilibrium" instead of "quiescence" for *jing*.

53. Waley, *The Way and Its Power*, pp. 17–39; Graham, *Disputers of the Tao*, p. 95.

54. *Mengzi* 7.A.1–4.

55. *Xunzi* 21.34–39, in Graham, *Disputers of the Tao*, p. 253.

56. Graham, *Disputers of the Tao*, p. 161.

57. Ibid., p. 98.

58. *Mengzi* 4.A.9.

59. *Mengzi* 4.A.10.

60. "I am the one who blows like the wind, embracing all creatures" (10.125, trans. Wendy Doniger O'Flaherty in *The Rig Veda: An Anthology*, p. 63). For an overview of this thought in the Rig Veda and the Atharva Veda, see William K. Mahony, *The Artful Universe: An Introduction to the Vedic Religious Imagination*, pp. 114–16.

61. *Sources of Indian Tradition*, 2nd ed., ed. Ainslie T. Embree, 1:29.

62. *Chandogya Upanishad* 7.26.2.

63. *Chandogya Upanishad* 7.2–8. "Strength," in turn, has conditions in food, water, heat, and space (7.9–12), which have conditions in memory, hope, and life breath (7.13–15); clearly the intent of this discussion is not to segregate the mental from the physical. Cf. *Katha Upanishad* 6.7: "Higher than the senses is the mind, higher than the mind is the essence, higher than the essence is the immense self; higher than the immense is the unmanifest. Higher than the unmanifest is the person, pervading all and without any marks . . . His appearance is beyond the range of sight . . . with the heart, with insight, with thought, has he been contemplated—those who know this become immortal."

64. *Chandogya Upanishad* 8.1.4.

65. As spelled out later in the *Adhyatma Upanishad*: "Wise people should abandon the concept of 'I' and 'mine' in the body and in the senses, which are not really Atman. Having known himself as an embodiment of the Self, the witness of the awakened intelligence and of its activities, one should ever think 'I am That' . . . Thus, one should see Atman as pervading all things and as existing autonomously by itself" (in Mahony, *The Artful Universe*, p. 187). I follow Mahony's translation of the *Katha*

Upanishad 3.13 passage cited here (p. 195). Mahony speaks rightly of a perfection of Vedic sacrifice in the sacrifice *of* the mind (pp. 195–96).

66. In this development one side of Vedic attitude discourse supersedes the other: the prescription to act with a good heart, devotedly, etc. is fulfilled, and the praise of divine generosity, mercy, etc. is eliminated. Thus, the core of a typical Vedic thought such as "King Soma, have mercy on us for our well-being. Know that we are devoted to your laws . . . If we break your laws, O god, have mercy on us like a good friend" (*Rig Veda* 8.48.8–9, trans. O'Flaherty, p. 135) is revealed to be "we are devoted." The *Brihadaranyaka Upanishad* notes wryly, "The gods, therefore, are not pleased at the prospect of men coming to understand this" (1.4.10).

67. As Mahony observes, "The mind thus stands [in the Upanishads] as a pivot of sorts. It can direct its attention and energy outward, thereby entrapping the human spirit in the ephemeral and transient manifold world of multiplicity . . . Or the mind can turn its attention around and direct its energy deeper, toward its unified, sublime source. This latter, inward movement frees one from the frustrations, disappointments, and pain of [the manifold world]" (*The Artful Universe*, p. 195).

68. Olivelle translates *upasana* as "veneration," while the Advaitin Swami Nikhilananda translates it as "meditation" (*The Upanishads*, see comment on p. 282). Many passages obviously bear the meaning *both* of respectfully addressing an external thing *and* forming an inward realization; thus: "He should venerate this Saman [chant] with the thought, 'I am the Whole!'" (*Chandogya Upanishad* 2.21.4).

69. "Those whose intellect has awakened to these four holy truths, and who have correctly penetrated to their meaning . . . they will gain the blessed calm, and no more will they be reborn" (Ashvaghosha, "Nanda the Fair" [*Saundaranandakavya*], in *Buddhist Scriptures*, trans. Edward Conze, p. 113).

70. But cf. the perfected mind "being a single mass of perception; consisting of bliss, and thus enjoying bliss" (*Mandukya Upanishad* 5).

71. "The highest bliss can't be described . . . Does it shine? Or does it radiate? There the sun does not shine, nor the moon and stars . . . Him alone [*Brahman*, the changeless], as he shines, do all things reflect" (*Katha Upanishad* 5.14–15). The imagination-stretching argument that the bliss of the world of *Brahman* is exponentially more than lower forms of "success" and "wealth" (*Brihadaranyaka Upanishad* 4.3.33) either confirms attachment or breaks it. Those who have ears to hear, let them hear.

72. *Chandogya Upanishad* 3.14.1–4.

73. That is, as a theme of the classical literature. Compassion is a major concern of Vedanta spirituality today.

74. *The Book of the Gradual Sayings* [*Anguttara Nikaya*] i.22 (p. 3). Cf. *The Book of the Kindred Sayings* [*Samyutta Nikaya*] i.105 (p. 14). All quotations from the Pali canon in this section are from the Pali Text Society translations. Page numbers in parentheses refer to Harvey B. Aronson, *Love and Sympathy in Theravada Buddhism*, my source for this material.

75. Aronson, *Love and Sympathy*, pp. 14–18.

76. Ibid., pp. 60–77.

77. *Dialogues of the Buddha* [*Digha Nikaya*] ii.251 (p. 71).

78. Aronson, *Love and Sympathy*, pp. 86–94 (here arguing with Winston King's characterization of Theravada Buddhism's ethic as ultimately world-indifferent).

79. From the *Lankavatara Sutra*, in *The Teachings of the Compassionate Buddha*, ed. E. A. Burtt, p. 143.

80. *Bhagavad-Gita* 1.36–44.

81. Snell, *The Discovery of the Mind*, p. 47; all Archilocus fragments are translated by Snell on this same page and are cited by Diehl number, as in *Anthologia Lyrica Graeca*, 3rd ed.

82. Additional line supplied from A. T. Murray's translation of the *Odyssey* in the Loeb series, 2nd ed. (Cambridge, Mass.: Harvard University Press, 1995).

83. Cf. Proverbs 16.1–3: "A man may arrange his thoughts, but what he says depends on the LORD. All the ways of a man seem right to him, but the LORD probes motives. Entrust your affairs to the LORD, and your plans will succeed."

84. Heraclitus 232. This and subsequent references are to fragment numbers in Kirk, Raven, and Schofield in *The Presocratic Philosophers*.

85. Peter Kingsley, in his book *In the Dark Places of Wisdom*, ascribes a quasi-Upanishadic program to Parmenides, stressing the significance of the attitude of stillness (*hesuchasm*) to which he was reportedly led by his teacher. *Hesuchasm* as godlike stillness is a surprisingly important idea in Plato, as Ali Gocer shows in "Hesuchia, a Metaphysical Principle in Plato's Moral Psychology."

86. *Oedipus at Colonus*, ll. 260–62, trans. Lewis Campbell, in *Fifteen Greek Plays*, p. 258; *The Eumenides*, ll. 885–87, trans. Gilbert Murray, in ibid., p. 153. Cf. *Oedipus at Colonus*, ll. 1004–1007, p. 280: "of all lands that yield the immortal Gods just homage of true piety, [Athens in her glory] is foremost"; ll. 1124–27, p. 283: "Only in Athens, only here i' the world, have I found pious thought and righteous care, and truth in word and deed."

87. Plato, *Apology* 19b, in *Euthyphro, Apology, Crito, Phaedo, Phaedrus*, trans. H. N. Fowler. This volume is the source of all *Euthyphro, Apology*, and *Crito* translations used here.

88. *Euthyphro* 9e–11b.

89. *Euthyphro* 12e, 14b.

90. *Apology* 24c–26a; 31a–33a; 28b–30b.

91. *Crito* 49c–d.

92. Aristotle, *Rhetoric* 1378a5.

93. "This it is that my heart biddeth me tell the Athenians, and how that even as ill-government [*dusnomia*] giveth a city much trouble, so good rule [*eunomia*] maketh all things orderly and perfect" (quoted from Demosthenes' *On the Embassy*, in *Elegy and Iambus*, vol. 1, trans. J. M. Edmonds).

94. *Republic* 400d–e.

95. *Republic* 507b, 508b.

96. *Republic* 509a, from Paul Shorey's translation in *The Collected Dialogues of Plato*, ed. Edith Hamilton and Huntington Cairns.

97. *Laws*, Book 10; *Timaeus* 29a–30b.

98. Democritus 594; Kirk, Raven, and Schofield, *The Presocratic Philosophers*, pp. 429–33.

99. Aristotle, *Nicomachean Ethics* 1141b30–1142a10.

100. See Sextus Empiricus, *Outlines of Pyrrhonism*, Book I, Chapters 1–12—e.g., in *Sextus Empiricus: Selections from the Major Writings*, ed. Philip P. Hallie, pp. 31–42.

101. Epicurus, Letter to Menoeceus 128, in Inwood and Gerson, *Hellenistic Philosophy*, p. 24.

102. Cicero, *On Fate* 22–23, in Inwood and Gerson, *Hellenistic Philosophy*, pp. 37–38.

103. Epicurus, Letter to Herodotus, 76b–82a; in Inwood and Gerson, *Hellenistic Philosophy*, pp. 13–15.

104. "The entire cosmos and the heaven are the substance of god . . . nature is a condition (*hexis*) which moves from itself, producing and holding together the things it produces at definite times, according to spermatic principles . . . [and] aims at both the advantageous and at pleasure" (Diogenes Laertius 7.148–49, in Inwood and Gerson, *Hellenistic Philosophy*, p. 97).

105. Martha Nussbaum, *The Therapy of Desire*.

106. Marcus Aurelius, *Meditations* 4.3, 6.24, 10.6, 11.18; cf. 8.17, 9.28, 39. I use the second numbering of the Loeb Classical Library edition.

107. *Meditations* 2.15, 4.3.

108. *Encheiridion* 1, in *Epictetus*, vol. 2, trans. W. A. Oldfather.

109. Chrysippus, reported by Cicero in *De Natura Deorum* (*On the Nature of the Gods*) 2.38, trans. H. Rackham.

110. Cicero, *On the Nature of the Gods* 2.153.

111. Marcus Aurelius, *Meditations* 8.48, 7.28.

112. It seems to be primarily for this reason that Nussbaum feels able to say that the Stoics "in no way subordinate [practical reasoning] to the good of *apatheia* [detachment]" (*Therapy of Desire*, p. 492).

113. Marcus Aurelius, *Meditations* 8.52.

114. Chrysippus quoted in Plutarch, *On Stoic Self-Contradictions*, in Inwood and Gerson, *Hellenistic Philosophy*, p. 154. The possible contradiction in Chrysippus is that he also said that in philosophical studies "we must put the logical first, the ethical second, and the physical third," with theology capping off physics as a "final revelation" (p. 153).

115. See J. J. Scullion, "Righteousness," in *The Anchor Bible Dictionary*.

116. "For three transgressions of Judah, for four, I will not revoke [punishment]: because they have spurned the Teaching of the LORD and have not observed His laws" (Amos 2.4)—possibly a later addition. Tyre is blamed in 1.9 for "not remembering the covenant of brotherhood," but this reads more as an expression of horror at Tyre's inhumanity than as a citation of disobedience. Compare Isaiah of Jerusalem—"Because they transgressed teachings, violated laws, broke the ancient covenant . . . That is why a curse consumes the earth" (Isaiah 24.5–6)—and Second Isaiah: "I the LORD am your God, instructing you for your own benefit, guiding you in the way you should go. If only you would heed my commands! Then your prosperity would be like a river, your triumph like the waves of the sea" (Isaiah 48.17–18). On abuse of the poor, see Isaiah 2.6–7, 4.1, 5.10–12.

117. These words also occur frequently in Proverbs and in the Psalms, generally to announce a connection between God's righteousness, human righteousness, and life: "The Lord is righteous; he loves righteous deeds; the upright shall behold His face" (Psalm 11.7). "The road of righteousness leads to life; by way of its path there is no death" (Proverbs 12.28).

118. Some exceptions to this rule: Israelite scouts are said to exhibit *hesed* during the conquest of Canaan (Judges 1.24), the good kings Josiah and Hezekiah are credited with it (2 Chronicles 32.32, 35.26), and the wicked person is faulted for lacking it (Psalm 109.16).

119. Babylonian Talmud, Shabbat 133b; New Testament, Matthew 5:48.

120. Isaiah 40.18–21, 28, 31. Compare Hosea 14.4: "Nor ever again will we call our handiwork our god, since in You alone orphans find pity!"

121. Especially Isaiah 50.5–6, 53.7.

122. Leviticus 19.3; Isaiah 33.6.

123. There is, however, *hanef*, "profane," translated "impious" in the NJPS version of Proverbs 11.9.

124. Deuteronomy 13—with the significant exception that one's *parent* is not named as a possible offender (13.6). The logic of the ban on idolatry does not really spare parents, but the text refuses to envision this case.

125. *The Septuagint with Apocrypha*, trans. Lancelot C. L. Brenton.

126. Acts 3.12, 10.2.

127. See *eusebes* in *Theological Dictionary of the New Testament*, 7:175–84.

128. Little faith, Matthew 6.30, e.g.; great faith, Matthew 8.10, e.g.

129. Daniel 6.4 ("extraordinary spirit") and chapter 6 generally. The story was a favorite with early Christians.

130. E.g., John 3.31–36.

131. This is part of Martin Buber's thesis in *Two Types of Faith*.

132. According to the Gospel of John, Jesus and his followers are sent by God to redeem the world because of God's great love of the world (3.16), but the world, being dominated by the "evil one," hates them (17.14–18). But cf. 1 John 2.15–17: "Do not love the world or the things in the world. The love of the Father is not in those who love the world; for all that is in the world—the desire of the flesh, the desire of the eyes, the pride in riches—comes not from the Father but from the world. And the world and its desire are passing away, but those who do the will of God live forever."

133. Buber, *Two Types of Faith*, pp. 63–64.

134. Babylonian Talmud, Berachot 17a.

135. The one exception is a Hebrew Bible quotation: 1 Samuel 13.14 at Acts 13.22.

136. *Kardiognostes*, Acts 1.24, 15.8; Paul, 1 Thessalonians 2.4 and 2 Thessalonians 3.5.

137. Deuteronomy 24.1–4, at Mark 10.5.

138. Paul's groaning, Romans 8.26. Abraham Heschel elucidates pathos in Hebrew prophecy in *The Prophets*, vol. 2, esp. chaps. 1, 3–4, 7.

139. *Bhagavad-Gita* 9.30–32.

140. On pagan virtues as splendid vices, see Augustine, *The City of God against the Pagans* 19.25.

141. The idea that will is to grace as horse is to rider is attributed to Augustine by Thomas Aquinas in *Summa Theologica*, First Part of the Second Part, Q. 110, Art. 4, Obj. 1 and by John Calvin in *Institutes* 2.4.1.

142. *Apology* 41c–d; *Analects* 7.22.

7. ATTITUDE ISSUES IN MODERN PHILOSOPHY

1. Also in the work of Jürgen Habermas, among others; but I have chosen to concentrate on Levinas and Derrida among more recent thinkers because of their closer connections to Buber and Heidegger, who are centrally important to my account. There is an appropriate place in the next chapter to consider Ernst Bloch's contribution.

2. According to the *Oxford English Dictionary*, "optimist" and "optimism" were terms introduced in a Jesuit publication of 1737 to characterize Leibniz's position,

deriving from his use of "optimum" for "best" in the *Theodicy* (1710). They were popularized by Voltaire in *Candide ou l'Optimisme* (1759).

3. G. W. Leibniz, *Monadology*, §55, trans. Nicholas Rescher, in *G. W. Leibniz's Monadology*.

4. G. W. Leibniz, "The Principles of Nature and Grace, Based on Reason," §18, in *Philosophical Essays*, trans. Roger Ariew and Daniel Garber, p. 213.

5. For Spinoza's view, see the appendix to *Ethics*, Book 1. Sometimes Leibniz talks as though actual entities come to exist strictly according to an ontological necessity rather than by a god's wise choice: "There is a certain . . . straining toward existence in possible things or in possibility or essence itself [so that] of the infinite combinations of possibilities . . . the one that exists is the one through which the most essence or possibility is brought into existence" (Leibniz, "On the Ultimate Origination of Things," in *Philosophical Essays*, p. 150). The notion of "straining" essences may not really be any different from the idea of essences beckoning to a good and wise God to be realized.

6. Letter of December 1714 to Bourguet, quoted in Georges Friedmann, *Leibniz et Spinoza*, pp. 241–42; my translation.

7. Leibniz, *Discourse on Metaphysics*, §8.

8. Leibniz, *Monadology*, §8. Subsequent references are in the text.

9. On Leibniz's own polemical characterizations of contemporary views as neo Stoic and neo-Epicurean, see Friedmann, pp. 158–59.

10. *Monadology*, §§78–80.

11. Spinoza, *Ethics*, Part 1, Appendix (critique of final causation); Part 5, Propositions 7–20 (blessedness in love of God). In the Preface of Part 4, "good" is defined as usefulness (i.e., in living most actively).

12. *Monadology*, §18.

13. Kant, *Critique of Pure Reason*, B 103, 151.

14. For Hume's view, see *Enquiry Concerning Human Understanding*, §§4–5, 7.

15. Kant, "What Is Orientation in Thinking?" in *Critique of Practical Reason and Other Writings in Moral Philosophy*, trans. Lewis White Beck, p. 298, Ak. 8.139.

16. Kant, *Critique of Practical Reason*, Ak. 5.110.

17. Ibid., Ak. 130–31.

18. Kant, *Groundwork of the Metaphysic of Morals*, trans. H. J. Paton, Ak. 4.394.

19. See, however, his critique of Epicureanism and Stoicism in *Critique of Practical Reason*, Ak. 126–27 (as insensitive, respectively, to the objectively necessary claim of the moral law and to the subjectively necessary claim of the interest in happiness).

20. *Critique of Practical Reason*, Ak. 126. In the era of neo-Kantianism, Georg Simmel most explicitly argues that the religious attitude generates the contents of religious thinking; see his *Essays on Religion*.

21. J. G. Fichte, *The Vocation of Man*, trans. Peter Preuss, p 77

22. Kant, *Groundwork*, Ak. 455–63; cf. *Critique of Pure Reason*, B 570–86, 713.

23. On Humean justice, see Hume's *Inquiry Concerning the Principles of Morals*, Sections 2–3; for Kant's way of thinking about worthiness to be happy, see *Critique of Practical Reason*, Ak. 110.

24. For Hume on benevolence as the basic moral motive, see *An Inquiry Concerning the Principles of Morals*, Section 2; for Kant's critique of benevolent feeling as a moral motive, see *Critique of Practical Reason*, Ak. 82–83.

25. *Groundwork*, Ak. 406, 435 (*Gesinnung* contrasted with "subjective *Disposition*"); *Critique of Practical Reason*, Ak. 71.

26. Kant, *Religion within the Boundaries of Mere Reason,* trans. George di Giovanni, in *Religion within the Boundaries of Mere Reason and Other Writings,* Ak. 6.25; cf. 67, 74.

27. *Critique of Practical Reason,* Ak. 67n.

28. Ibid., Ak. 86–87.

29. Kant, *Groundwork,* Ak. 421, 427–29.

30. Fichte, *The Vocation of Man,* p. 76. On the presentation of the call of conscience by the fellow rational being within a natural system, see also Fichte's *Foundations of Transcendental Philosophy nova methodo* [1796/99], §19.

31. *The Vocation of Man,* p. 109.

32. On the alleged atheism problem in Fichte's philosophy, see F. H. Jacobi's "Open Letter to Fichte, 1799," in *Philosophy of German Idealism,* ed. Ernst Behler.

33. *Critique of Practical Reason,* Ak. 82.

34. *The Vocation of Man,* p. 106.

35. Ibid., p. 107.

36. *Groundwork,* Ak. 439.

37. *The Vocation of Man,* p. 113.

38. *Groundwork,* Ak. 433.

39. In, e.g., his 1806 lectures on *The Way Toward the Blessed Life or the Doctrine of Religion,* in *The Popular Works of Johann Gottlieb Fichte.*

40. "Faith," *The Vocation of Man,* p. 71; compulsion to act, pp. 67–68; predicaments and rights of others, pp. 78–79, 82–85; better world, p. 80.

41. Ibid., p. 80. In another passage, Fichte cites "the mark proper to spirit: constant progress to greater perfection in a straight line which goes on to infinity," p. 122.

42. Ibid., p. 80.

43. In *Wilhelm Dilthey: Selected Writings,* p. 67.

44. J. G. Fichte, *Science of Knowledge* (First Introduction), trans. Peter Heath and John Lachs, p. 16; 1.435.

45. Friedrich Schleiermacher, *Aus Schleiermachers Leben in Briefen,* vol. 2, p. 483, trans. Richard Brandt in his *The Philosophy of Schleiermacher,* p. 12.

46. G. W. F. Hegel, *Lectures on the Philosophy of World History: Introduction,* trans. H. B. Nisbet, p. 48.

47. Schleiermacher, *The Christian Faith,* pp. 8–9.

48. Schleiermacher, *On Religion,* 1st ed., trans. Richard Crouter, p. 102.

49. *Schleiermacher's Soliloquies,* trans. Horace Leland Friess, p. 31.

50. On this issue, see Hans-Georg Gadamer, *Truth and Method,* pp. 162–73, and Richard Palmer, *Hermeneutics: Interpretation Theory in Schleiermacher, Dilthey, Heidegger, and Gadamer.*

51. Schleiermacher, *On Religion,* 1st ed., relation of humanity to the universe, p. 97; religious orientation, p. 105; "sworn enemy," p. 109.

52. See the articles on "Gefühl" in *Historisches Wörterbuch der Philosophie,* vol. 3. Goethe himself is quoted here as appealing to an "original truth-feeling [that] is a synthesis of world and spirit, which gives the most blessed assurance of the eternal harmony of existence" (p. 91, my translation).

53. Kant, *Critique of Pure Reason,* B 383–84.

54. Schleiermacher, *On Religion,* 1st ed., p. 133.

55. Ibid., p. 113.

56. On Schleiermacher's shifting treatment of "intuition" and some problems with the concept, see Richard Crouter's introduction in ibid., pp. 61–63.

57. *The Christian Faith*, p. 13.

58. *On Religion*, 3rd ed., trans. John Oman, p. 103.

59. Ibid., p. 106; cf. *Friedrich Schleiermacher's Reden ueber die Religion: Kritische Ausgabe*, ed. Georg Christian Berhard Pünjer, p. 137.

60. John Hick has developed a "seeing as" account of religious experience in "Religious Experience as Seeing-As," in *Talk of God*, ed. Godfrey Vesey.

61. *On Religion*, 3rd ed., p. 36. "Stirring" is my translation of *Regung* (vs. Oman's "affection").

62. *The Christian Faith*, §4.

63. "A person's virtuosity [in theory or practice] is, as it were, merely the melody of his life; and it remains individual tones if he does not add religion to it. The latter accompanies the former in ever-richer variation with all the tones that are not fully repugnant to it, and thus transforms the simple song of life into a full-voiced and magnificent harmony" (*On Religion*, 1st ed., p. 132).

64. *The Christian Faith*, §5.

65. *On Religion*, 1st ed., p. 79.

66. *The Christian Faith*, p. 27.

67. *On Religion*, 1st ed., p. 163.

68. See especially the Fifth Speech of *On Religion*, 1st ed., pp. 189–223.

69. *On Religion*, 1st ed., p. 129.

70. *The Christian Faith*, pp. 14–15.

71. *On Religion*, 1st ed., p. 102.

72. Ibid., p. 166.

73. Ibid., p. 103.

74. See, e.g., Kant, *Religion within the Limits of Reason Alone*, Ak. 125–27, 167, 184n.; Schleiermacher, *On Religion*, 1st ed., pp. 211–23; and *The Christian Faith*, §§8–10.

75. *The Christian Faith*, p. 81.

76. *On Religion*, 1st ed., p. 108.

77. Søren Kierkegaard, *The Sickness unto Death*, trans. Howard V. and Edna H. Hong, S.V. 11.127.

78. "For an existing person it is impossible to think about existence without becoming passionate, inasmuch as existing is a prodigious contradiction from which the subjective thinker is not to abstract, for then it is easy, but in which he is to remain" (Kierkegaard, *Concluding Unscientific Postscript to Philosophical Fragments*, trans. Howard V. and Edna H. Hong, S.V. 7.304).

79. Schleiermacher, *Aesthetik* [1819], p. 71. He says he would use the word *Gesinnung* had it not taken on a predominantly practical connotation (Schleiermacher, *On the 'Glaubenslehre': Two Letters to Dr. Lücke*, trans. James Duke and Francis Fiorenza, p. 39). These references are courtesy of Louis Roy, "Consciousness According to Schleiermacher," 218.

80. Søren Kierkegaard, *The Concept of Anxiety*, trans. Reidar Thomte, S.V. 4.286n.

81. Ibid., S.V. 288.

82. Ibid., S.V. 422.

83. Kierkegaard, "The Expectancy of Faith" [1843], in *Eighteen Upbuilding Discourses*.

84. "Faith is a marvel, and yet no human being is excluded from it; for that which unites all human life is passion, and faith is a passion" (Kierkegaard, *Fear and Trembling*, trans. Howard V. and Edna H. Hong, S.V. 3.116); on the moment and the need for "spirit," *Concept of Anxiety*, S.V. 4.358; on concentration of all upon a point, *Fear and Trembling*, S.V. 126; on the paradoxical apprehension of the infinite, *Concluding Unscientific Postscript*, S.V. 490–96. Cf. the heroic "movement of infinite resignation" with which Abraham's faith is contrasted in *Fear and Trembling*, S.V. 124–27.

85. *The Concept of Anxiety*, S.V. 414.

86. Ibid., S.V. 415.

87. Ibid., S.V. 417.

88. On the "deeper self," Kierkegaard, "To Need God," in *Eighteen Upbuilding Discourses*, S.V. 5.94–96; on despair and faith, *The Sickness unto Death*, S.V. 128.

89. *Concluding Unscientific Postscript*, S.V. 176.

90. Ibid., S.V. 368.

91. See esp. Friedrich Nietzsche, *The Gay Science*, §§124–25, 343.

92. Arthur Schopenhauer, *The World as Will and Representation*, vol. 2, chap. 46, pp. 581–83.

93. For a helpful sorting out of types of pessimist thesis, see Ivan Soll, "Pessimism and the Tragic View of Life: Reconsiderations of Nietzsche's *Birth of Tragedy*," in *Reading Nietzsche*, ed. Robert C. Solomon and Kathleen M. Higgins.

94. Nietzsche, the "Attempt at a Self-Criticism" attached to *The Birth of Tragedy*, in *The Birth of Tragedy and The Case of Wagner*, §1, p. 17.

95. *The Birth of Tragedy*, §§1–5.

96. Because of the importance of Kant's work on the basic moral *Gesinnung*, it is especially his study of basic aesthetic *Gefühlen* that attracts our attention today in *Observations on the Beautiful and the Sublime* (1764), although Edmund Burke's *Philosophical Enquiry into the Origin of Our Ideas of the Sublime and the Beautiful*, 2nd ed. (1759) is more lucidly disturbing with regard to the affiliation of masculinity with the terrifying power in the sublime.

97. *The Birth of Tragedy*, §18.

98. Ibid., §24.

99. Cf. Nietzsche, *Ecce Homo*, in *The Genealogy of Morals and Ecce Homo*, pp. 271–74.

100. The element of cruelty is studied especially in *The Genealogy of Morals*, Second Essay.

101. Nietzsche, "Attempt at a Self-Criticism," §5, p. 23; cf. *The Genealogy of Morals* (1888), in *The Genealogy of Morals and Ecce Homo*.

102. Nietzsche, *Thus Spoke Zarathustra* (1883–84). Zarathustra praises the "over-rich star" in the Prologue, sec. 1, p. 10.

103. Nietzsche speaks most strongly against following Zarathustra in the Foreword to *Ecce Homo*, pp. 219–20.

104. On the triumphant idea, *The Will to Power*, §1053 et seq., pp. 544–50. On Stoicism as gloomy and self-hardening, see *The Will to Power*, §427, p. 232. Nietzsche did trace the idea of the Eternal Recurrence through Stoicism, however; see *Ecce Homo*, p. 274.

105. *Thus Spoke Zarathustra*, 4.19.10, p. 323.

106. "That *everything recurs* is the closest *approximation of a world of becoming to a world of being*:—high point of the meditation" (*The Will to Power*, §617, p. 330).

107. *On the Genealogy of Morals*, Second Essay, §6, p. 65.

108. Ludwig Klages, *Der Geist als Widersacher der Seele* (1929). For Nietzsche's negative and positive interpretations of *Geist*, see, e.g., *The Will to Power*, §§480, 526, 529 (negative) and 687, 820, 899, 1045, 1052 (positive).

109. Wilhelm Dilthey, *Introduction to the Human Sciences*, Book 6, Sec. 3; *Gesammelte Schriften* (hereafter G.S.) 19.237, p. 439.

110. Ibid., G.S. 1.xviii.

111. For Dilthey's dismantling of the idealist metaphysical approach to the human studies see Book 2 of *Introduction to the Human Sciences*. The leading idea is that experience involves relations with real Others that cannot be cut to the measure of a rational system (G.S. 1.395).

112. Dilthey, "Ideas Concerning a Descriptive and Analytic Psychology," G.S. 5.213; trans. Richard M. Zaner in Dilthey, *Descriptive Psychology and Historical Understanding*.

113. Ibid., G.S. 157.

114. Dilthey, "Breslau draft" of *Introduction to the Human Sciences*, G.S. 19.346–47, trans. Charles R. Bambach in his *Heidegger, Dilthey, and the Crisis of Historicism*, p. 155.

115. Dilthey, G.S. 8.44–45, 80–81, 143–45; see also Otto Friedrich Bollnow, *Dilthey*, pp. 67–71.

116. Dilthey, *The Essence of Philosophy*, p. 35 ("This attitude [*Verhaltensweise*], in which we apprehend the lived and the given, produces our picture of the world, our concepts of reality . . . At every stage of this process inclination and feeling are at work. They are the center of our mental structure; from this point all the depths of our being are stirred"), G.S. 5, xxx.

117. "Ideas," chap. 9.

118. Dilthey, *Die Typen der Weltanschauung und ihre Ausbildung in den metaphysischen Systemen*, G.S. 8.82, my translation.

119. Dilthey, "Traum," G.S. 8.221, my translation.

120. Cf. F. J. Wetz on Dilthey's conception: "*Stimmungen* are more than states of feeling, they are encompassing world-relations in the light of which reality appears to us in various ways. They establish relations not to individual objects but to the whole of my world, which can reach from the near horizon of my neighborhood to the far horizon of the starry heavens. Fundamental attunements remain chiefly hidden and in the background; they are non-objectively general, if not unstable and vacillating" ("Stimmung," in *Historisches Wörterbuch der Philosophie*, vol. 10, p. 174, my translation).

121. This and subsequent references in the text are to Dilthey, *Die Typen*, trans. William Kluback and Martin Weinbaum, in *Dilthey's Philosophy of Existence: Introduction to Weltanschauungslehre*.

122. Dilthey's statement of the point is modeled on the Kantian realization that perennial conflicts in speculative thinking are grounded in the structure of reason.

123. This and subsequent references in the text are to Jaspers, *Psychologie der Weltanschauungen* [1st ed. 1919], 3rd ed., v, 2–7; my translations.

124. Dilthey, *Die Typen*, G.S. 8.82; my translation.

125. Dilthey, *Die Typen*, Chap. 1, Sec. 4 (pp. 24–25 in trans.).

126. The Nietzsche connection is not exploited in *Psychologie*, however. On radical freedom expressed in the "revaluation of all values," see the overview of Nietz-

sche's moves in Walter Kaufmann, *Nietzsche: Philosopher, Psychologist, Antichrist*, pp. 102–18.

127. The philosophical anthropologists include Martin Buber (*I and Thou*), Erich Rothacker (*Geschichtsphilosophie* and *Philosophische Anthropologie*), and Arnold Gehlen (*Man: His Nature and Place in the World*); see G. Funke, "Haltung," in *Historisches Wörterbuch der Philosophie*, vol. 3, p. 991. The "answer" idea is Rothacker's. Jaspers later regards *Haltung* as a provisional necessity of human life but a problem for genuine freedom in purporting to stabilize and complete it. Heidegger views *Haltung* similarly, although in 1929 he is willing to speak of a *Grundhaltung* of Dasein that consists of the letting-occur of Dasein's freedom (*Einleitung in die Philosophie*, p. 397). Reviewing the deployment of attitude terms by philosophers, Otto Bollnow stresses the affiliation of *Haltung* with freedom, "taking one's existence in hand responsibly," choosing the world-relation that in *Stimmung* is immediately registered as an experienced unity. *Haltung* and *Stimmung* are always in a certain balance; the balance may always shift. In degenerate attunements like sentimentality, *Haltung* is overpowered (*Das Wesen der Stimmungen*, pp. 158–60).

128. Heraclitus points in this direction also in his remarks on the essentially hidden and conflictual character of being—nos. 194–96 on the Logos and nos. 211–12 and 208 on conflict and hiddenness, in Kirk, Raven, and Schofield, *The Presocratic Philosophers*.

129. Jaspers, "Myth and Religion," in Karl Jaspers and Rudolf Bultmann, *Myth and Christianity*, p. 38.

130. Ibid., pp. 41, 44.

131. Ibid., pp. 97–98. "And then one became two" is a line from a poem by Goethe.

132. See Jaspers, *Philosophy* [1932], vol. 2, "Communication" [Book 2, Part 1, Sec. 3], and *Reason and Existenz* [1935], Third Lecture, "Truth as Communicability."

133. This is at least a tacit agenda of all his work after *Being and Time*, but see especially "Letter on Humanism," trans. Frank A. Capuzzi with J. Glenn Gray and David Farrell Krell, in Heidegger, *Basic Writings*.

134. See Theodore Kisiel, *The Genesis of Heidegger's Being and Time*, esp. pp. 72–74, 89–93, 112–14 on Heidegger's relation to Schleiermacher.

135. *Being and Time*, trans. John Macquarrie and Edward Robinson, p. 47, citing the pagination of the eighth edition of *Sein und Zeit* (1957); cf. *Einleitung in die Philosophy*, pp. 346–54. For Heidegger's critique of "philosophical anthropology," see *Being and Time*, §10 and also *Kant and the Problem of Metaphysics* (1929), §37. Heidegger mentions "world-intuitions" in *Being and Time* only to assert that his inquiry is on a deeper level; later references are sharply critical, which reflects less on Dilthey and more on what has become of "world-intuition" discourse in the years intervening; see Heidegger, *Contributions to Philosophy (From Enowning)* (1936–38), pp. 18, 26–29.

136. Jaspers's "method of mere observation must evolve into an 'infinite process' of radical questioning that always includes itself in its questions and preserves itself in them" (Heidegger, "Comments on Karl Jaspers' *Psychology of Worldviews*," trans. John van Buren, in Heidegger, *Pathmarks*, p. 38). The use of types "always remains within a surreptitious aesthetic attitude" (in Kierkegaard's broad sense of "aesthetic") and so is estranged from the radical motivation of existential questions (p. 34).

137. On Dilthey and "life," *Being and Time*, p. 46; on Jaspers, "Comments," p. 3.

138. Dangerous also in encouraging looseness in concept formation. Heidegger wants the appropriate kind of "scientific" rigor in first philosophy. He proposes to achieve it, not by deriving ontological concepts from an a priori first principle, however, but by most thoroughly pursuing a phenomenological course of inquiry. Thus in *Being and Time* he is able to uncover a complex network of "equiprimordial" ontological categories, the real relatedness of which is authentically disclosed rather than artificially constructed.

139. This and subsequent references in the text are to *Being and Time*, §18.

140. On *Bewandtnis* in *Being and Time* and the preparation for it, see Kisiel, *The Genesis of Heidegger's Being and Time*, pp. 388–92. Kisiel notes that Heidegger was inspired by Emil Lask to use *Bewandtnis* as an alternative to "form" for the sake of featuring the "how" of the organization of experience (p. 391).

141. On the inspiration of the Augustinian restless heart in this matter, see *Being and Time*, p. 190 n. 1 (in the English trans., n. iv), and Kisiel, *The Genesis of Heidegger's Being and Time*, p. 105.

142. A heroic ethos seems massively important in *Being and Time*, but Heidegger does not appeal to it in those terms except in alluding to "the possibility that Dasein may choose its hero" on p. 385.

143. Romano Pocai argues that this "dimensional" understanding of temporality misleadingly neutralizes the actual negativities of time, in effect privileging a positively valued time-experience of theoretical-aesthetic tarrying; he opposes in general Heidegger's "structuralization" of meaning-possibilities (*Heideggers Theorie der Befindlichkeit*, pp. 234–36).

144. E.g., *Concluding Unscientific Postscript*, S.V. 97–103.

145. *Being and Time*, §56.

146. In *Pathmarks*.

147. Heidegger, "What Is Metaphysics?" in *Existence and Being* (1949); Leibniz, "Principles of Nature and Grace, Based on Reason," §7.

148. "What Is Metaphysics?" pp. 347–48.

149. Heidegger, "On the Essence of Truth," trans. R. F. C. Hull and Alan Crick, in *Existence and Being*, pp. 310–11.

150. Heidegger, *The Fundamental Concepts of Metaphysics*, pp. 59–69.

151. Ibid., p. 75.

152. This and subsequent references in the text are to Heidegger, *Contributions to Philosophy (From Enowning)*.

153. "Letter on Humanism," in *Basic Writings*, p. 221.

154. Heidegger, "The Question Concerning Technology," in *Basic Writings*, p. 317.

155. Michel Henry, "The Power of Revelation of Affectivity according to Heidegger" (from *The Essence of Manifestation*, §65), in *Martin Heidegger: Critical Assessments*, vol. 1,

156. On happier moods, see Ludwig Binswanger, *Grundformen und Erkenntnis Menschlichen Daseins* (1942), especially on love; and Otto Friedrich Bollnow, *Das Wesen der Stimmungen* (1941), on the qualitatively full experience of "elevated" moods. On other ways of seeing the temporal dimensions of moods, see David Wood, *The Deconstruction of Time*, pp. 226–28. On the issue of Heidegger's cultural attunement attributions, see Michel Haar, "Stimmung et pensée," in Franco Volpi et al., *Heidegger et l'idée de la phénoménologie*.

157. Pocai, *Heideggers Theorie*, pp. 37–46.

158. Championing the "positive expectant" attitude of hope, Ernst Bloch condemns Heidegger's mood account for its petit bourgeois desperation (*The Principle of Hope*, 1:105–10).

159. See Nietzsche, *Thus Spoke Zarathustra*, pp. 78–79 (self-irony), 41 (dancing god).

160. Gilles Deleuze and Félix Guattari, *Anti-Oedipus*.

161. "It is characteristic of philosophical writing that relations with an exterior are always mediated and dissolved by an interior, and this process always takes place within some given interiority. Nietzsche, on the contrary, grounds his thought, his writing, on an immediate relation with the outside, the exterior . . . illegitimate misinterpretations [of Nietzsche] all . . . spring from the spirit of seriousness, the spirit of gravity, Zarathustra's ape—that is, the cult of interiority" (Gilles Deleuze, "Nomad Thought," trans. David B. Allison, in *The New Nietzsche*, pp. 144, 147).

162. Dilthey, "Beiträge zur Lösung der Frage vom Ursprung unseres Glaubens an die Realität der Aussenwelt und seinem Recht," G.S. 5.90–138.

163. For these themes in the early Buber, see *Daniel: Dialogues on Realization* (1913). *Daniel's* anticipation of the great dualism of *I and Thou* sheds an interesting light on key terms of our inquiry: "There is a twofold active relation [*Verhalten*] of humans to their lived-experience [*Erlebnis*]: orientation [*Orientierung*] or attitude-taking [*Einstellen*] and realizing [*Realisierung*] or actualizing [*Verwirklichen*]"; p. 22, my trans. (cf. the original in Buber's *Werke*, vol. 1). Orientation and attitude-taking here have the sense of intrasubjective housekeeping and pertain to what *I and Thou* calls the sphere of the I-It, while realizing and actualizing pertain to the sphere of the I-Thou.

164. Martin Buber, *I and Thou* (1923), pp. 67, 113.

165. Ibid., pp. 83–84.

166. Ibid., p. 89.

167. Buber, "What Is Man?" (1938), in *Between Man and Man*, p. 193.

168. Ibid., pp. 203–205.

169. "All actual life is encounter," *I and Thou*, p. 62.

170. "All lines of relation intersect," ibid., p. 84.

171. Ibid., p. 90.

172. See Emmanuel Levinas, *Totality and Infinity*, esp. pp. 123–26, 298–99. Levinas's earliest major statement on the problem of "ontologism" is *On Escape* (1935).

173. For example, in an understanding glance between two strangers in an air-raid shelter, or in the resonance between two strangers listening to a Mozart concert ("What Is Man?" p. 204).

174. *Totality and Infinity*, pp. 302–303.

175. Ibid., pp. 68, 291.

176. Ibid., p. 43.

177. See Levinas, *Otherwise than Being or Beyond Essence*, on obsession and persecution, pp. 86–89; psychosis, p. 142; trauma, p. 111; hostageship, p. 6; hemorrhage, p. 74; substitution, pp. 113–18—the substitutive subject equated with the monad that expresses all other monads at p. 87 n. 24. On responsibility for the responsibility of the Other, see, e.g., "God and Philosophy" in Levinas, *Collected Philosophical Papers*, p. 167.

178. *Otherwise than Being*, p. 14.

179. *Totality and Infinity*, pp. 53–81, 102–105, 172–73; cf. the preparatory work

on the "hypostasis" of subjectivity in *Existence and Existents* (1947), where Levinas claims: "The *here* that belongs to consciousness, the place of its sleep and of its escape into itself, is radically different from the *Da* involved in Heidegger's Dasein. The latter already implies the world. The *here* we are starting with, the *here* of position, precedes every act of understanding, every horizon and all time. It is the very fact that consciousness is an origin, that it starts from itself, that it is an *existent*" (p. 71). Levinas's earliest formulations for this separation of the subject from impersonal Being refer in Heideggerian style to moods like evasion and horror; see *On Escape*.

180. "Atheist" selfhood, *Totality and Infinity*, pp. 53–59.

181. *Otherwise than Being*, pp. 149–52, on "prophecy."

182. Ibid., p. 116.

183. Levinas, "Enigma and phenomenon," in *Collected Philosophical Papers*, p. 73.

184. On the God who has passed by, see Levinas, "Meaning and Sense," in *Collected Philosophical Papers*, pp. 106–107.

185. *Otherwise than Being*, p. 128.

186. *Totality and Infinity*, e.g., pp. 199, 277, 306.

187. The paper in which one finds a pivoting from future-oriented to past-oriented argument is "The Trace of the Other" (1963), in *Deconstruction in Context*, ed. Mark Taylor.

188. Levinas, *Of God Who Comes to Mind*, xiv.

189. Levinas, *Time and the Other* (1947), Part IV, p. 83; cf. pp. 93–94.

190. Buber sides to some extent with Nietzsche on the nature of optimal relationship when he responds to Levinas that "relationship seems to me to win its true greatness and powerfulness precisely there where two men without a strong spiritual ground in common . . . still stand over against each other so that each of the two . . . accepts and confirms the other, even in the severest conflict . . . Levinas, in opposition to me, praises solicitude as the access to the otherness of the other. The truth of experience seems to me that he who has this access apart from solicitude will also find it in the solicitude practiced by him—but he who does not have it without this, he may clothe the naked and feed the hungry all day and it will remain difficult for him to say a true Thou" ("Replies to My Critics," in *The Philosophy of Martin Buber*, ed. Paul Arthur Schilpp and Maurice Friedman, p. 723). In Levinas, the encounter of the "face" is the major motif in *Totality and Infinity*, and "proximity" is an aspect of responsible hostageship in *Otherwise than Being*, pp. 102–18.

191. *Otherwise than Being*, pp. 115–16.

192. Ibid., pp. 181–82.

193. Jacques Derrida's study of Heidegger's hesitations and plunges with German spirit-words in *Of Spirit: Heidegger and the Question* is a good introduction to the risks of vulgarity on the one hand and metaphysical abstraction on the other that would have loomed before Levinas.

194. A useful overview of Levinas and Derrida in relation is Simon Critchley, *The Ethics of Deconstruction: Derrida and Levinas*. For the early Derridean critique of presence, see esp. Derrida, *Speech and Phenomena and Other Essays On Husserl's Theory of Signs* (1967; including "Differance," 1968).

195. In *Writing and Difference*. Subsequent references in the text are to this work.

196. Levinas, *Otherwise than Being*, p. 7.

197. "I have on several occasions spoken of 'unconditional' affirmation or of

'unconditional' 'appeal.' The very least that can be said of unconditionality (a word that I use not by accident to recall the character of the categorical imperative in its Kantian form) is that it is independent of every determinate context, even of the determination of a context in general. It announces itself as such only in the *opening* of context . . . [Although] nothing exists outside of context . . . the limit of the frame or the border of the context always entails a clause of nonclosure" (Derrida, "Afterword," trans. Samuel Weber, in *Limited Inc.*, p. 152).

198. I have analyzed these ideas in *Gender Thinking*, chapters 3–6.

199. Derrida, "Choreographies" in *Points . . . Interviews, 1974–94*, p. 108.

200. Derrida claims that sexual duality as such, but not sexual difference, may be neutralized in Heidegger's *Dasein*, "liberating the field of sexuality for a very *different* sexuality, a more multiple one" ("Women in the Beehive: A Seminar with Jacques Derrida," in *Men in Feminism*, ed. Alice Jardine and Paul Smith, p. 199). For an overview of Derrida's address of sexual difference, see Geoffrey Bennington and Jacques Derrida, *Jacques Derrida*, pp. 204–28.

201. One point of departure being remarks by Nietzsche (see Derrida, *Spurs/ Nietzsche's Styles*).

202. Derrida, "At This Very Moment in This Work Here I Am," in *Re-Reading Levinas*, esp. pp. 40–46.

203. Derrida, "Force of Law: The 'Mystical Foundation of Authority,' " in *Deconstruction and the Possibility of Justice*, p. 15.

204. Ibid., pp. 22–25; cf. Derrida, "The Villanova Roundtable," in *Deconstruction in a Nutshell: A Conversation with Jacques Derrida*, p. 17.

205. "Villanova Roundtable," pp. 18–19.

206. Derrida, "Faith and Knowledge: The Two Sources of 'Religion' at the Limits of Reason Alone," trans. Samuel Weber, in Jacques Derrida and Gianni Vattimo, *Religion*, p. 64.

207. See John D. Caputo's discussion of Derrida's unpublished lectures on "Questions of Responsibility: Hostility/Hospitality," in "A Commentary: Deconstruction in a Nutshell," in *Deconstruction in a Nutshell*, pp. 109–13. The theme runs through "Faith and Knowledge," and cf. Derrida, *Adieu to Emmanuel Levinas*, p. 101, and *Of Hospitality*.

208. The issue is surveyed in Critchley, *The Ethics of Deconstruction*, chapter 5.

209. "Faith and Knowledge," p. 2.

210. Ibid., p. 7.

211. Ibid., p. 19; on the theme of "to come," see Derrida, "On a Newly Arisen Apocalyptic Tone in Philosophy," in *Raising the Tone of Philosophy: Late Essays by Immanuel Kant, Transformative Critique by Jacques Derrida*, ed. Peter Fenves.

212. "Villanova Roundtable," pp. 21–22.

213. Ibid., pp. 22–23; cf. "Faith and Knowledge," p. 17–19.

214. "Villanova Roundtable," pp. 23–24.

215. Cf. "Faith and Knowledge," pp. 5–6; and *Adieu*, p. 141 n. 71.

216. Derrida, "A 'Madness' Must Watch Over Thinking," in Weber, *Points . . . Interviews*, p. 359; cf. Derrida, *The Gift of Death*, pp. 25–26. Note in comparison how a Christian deconstructionist registers this orientation, in a progression of formulae he finds increasingly adequate: "(1) *I do not know who I am or whether I believe in God* . . . [This] is the least grateful and the least responsive way to respond to the secret by which

we are all inhabited and impassioned, the least willing to say yes, to take a risk, to let ourselves be engaged by the momentum in things . . . (2) *I do not know whether what I believe in is God or not . . .* This is better, although one could be a little more passionate. (3) *I do not know what I love when I love my God.* That is to reach full stride, to open the throttle . . . to let life dance . . . to be impassioned by the passion for the impossible" (John D. Caputo, *The Prayers and Tears of Jacques Derrida,* pp. 331–32).

217. Jaspers, *Philosophy,* vol. 3, pp. 192–208; Derrida on "negative theology," "Differance," in *Speech and Phenomena,* p. 134, and *On the Name.*

218. This is the point on which Levinas avows in *Totality and Infinity* (p. 28) his fundamental debt to Rosenzweig, who in *The Star of Redemption* articulated a pluralist counterthrust to "the idea of totality" governing idealism. Derrida's strategy, rather than to declare pluralism in the manner of *Totality and Infinity* (p. 305) or "an-archaeology" in the manner of *Otherwise than Being* (p. 7), is continual deconstructive harassment of any bias toward "gathering together," like Heidegger's *Versammlung* ("Villanova Roundtable," pp. 13–14).

219. "Faith and Knowledge," p. 26.

220. Jan Patočka, *Heretical Essays,* Fifth Essay, "Is Technological Civilization Decadent, and Why?"; Derrida, *The Gift of Death,* chaps. 1–2.

221. *The Gift of Death,* p. 25.

222. Ibid., p. 27.

223. Nietzsche, *The Will to Power,* §§489–92, 524, 526, 532.

224. Nietzsche, *Twilight of the Idols,* trans. Walter Kaufmann, in *The Portable Nietzsche,* p. 500.

225. Augustine, *Confessions,* 13.9, p. 322; "Homilies on the First Epistle of John," 7.8, in *Nicene and Post-Nicene Fathers,* vol. 7, p. 504.

226. On immortality as one of Kant's postulates of pure practical reason, see *Critique of Practical Reason,* Ak. 121–24, where it is presented, not as a "subjectively necessary" concomitant of the hope for happiness, but as part of the morally rigorous demand for self-perfection (although the idea of "endless progress" toward perfection can, as far as pure morality is concerned, be interpreted intensively rather than extensively in time).

227. Kierkegaard, *Concluding Unscientific Postscript,* S.V. 137–47.

228. Schleiermacher, *On Religion,* 1st ed., p. 139.

229. For Levinas, see esp. *Time and the Other,* Parts 3 and 4, and the "Death and Time" course in *God, Death, and Time;* for Derrida on *spectres* and *revenants,* see, e.g., *Specters of Marx.*

8. ATTITUDE ISSUES IN MODERN THEOLOGY

1. Friedrich Schleiermacher, *On Religion,* 1st ed., pp. 199–200.

2. Martin Luther, *Lectures on Jonah* (on Jonah 1.5), trans. Charles D. Froehlich, in *Luther's Works,* vol. 19, p. 54; emphasis added.

3. This and subsequent references in the text are to Schleiermacher, *The Christian Faith,* §30, pp. 125–26.

4. Cf. *On Religion,* p. 213: "The original intuition of Christianity is more glorious, more sublime, more worthy of adult humanity . . . It is none other than the intuition of the universal straining of everything finite against the unity of the whole and of the way

in which the deity handles this striving, how it reconciles the enmity directed against it and sets bounds to the ever-greater distance by scattering over the whole individual points that are at once finite and infinite, at once human and divine."

5. "Primordial impulse or tendency": Schleiermacher, *Introduction to Christian Ethics* (1826/27), pp. 46–48.

6. Emil Brunner, *Die Mystik und das Wort*, p. 117, my translation.

7. Karl Barth, *Die christliche Dogmatik im Entwurf* (1927), p. 389, my translation.

8. Barth, *Der Römerbrief*, 1st ed. (1919), p. 239; translations mine.

9. Ibid., pp. 147, 449.

10. Barth, *The Epistle to the Romans*, 2nd ed. (1922), trans. Edwyn C. Hoskyns, pp. 39, 98.

11. Barth, *The Holy Ghost and the Christian Life* (1929), trans. R. Birch Hoyle, pp. 9–10.

12. Barth, *Church Dogmatics*, vol. 1/1 (1932), trans. Geoffrey W. Bromiley, pp. 202, 223.

13. *Church Dogmatics*, vol. 4/1 (1956), trans. Geoffrey W. Bromiley, p. 743.

14. *Church Dogmatics*, vol. 1/1, pp. 240–44. On the *analogia fidei* in Barth, see the classic interpretation by Hans Urs von Balthasar in *The Theology of Karl Barth*, which makes much of it as a guiding principle, and the rival view of Bruce L. McCormack in *Karl Barth's Critically Realistic Dialectical Theology* (pp. 2–20) emphasizing its subordinate place in the development of Barth's theology.

15. *Church Dogmatics*, vol. 1/1, pp. 771–75.

16. *Church Dogmatics*, vol. 1/2 (1938), trans. G. T. Thomson and Harold Knight, p. 270.

17. Barth, "Concluding Unscientific Postscript on Schleiermacher" (1968), in *The Theology of Schleiermacher*, trans. Geoffrey W. Bromiley, p. 278.

18. Bruce L. McCormack argues in "What Has Basel to Do with Berlin?" that Schleiermacher's true position in *The Christian Faith* differs significantly in this regard from the Troeltschian thoroughgoing anthropologism that Barth was taught to associate with Schleiermacher—notably, that the "feeling of absolute dependence" is intended by Schleiermacher to assure the primacy of transcendent divinity and the absolute particularity of a religious life.

19. Barth himself was greatly influenced by socialism and religious socialist movements, but that is another story, for which see Friedrich-Wilhelm Marquardt's controversial study, *Theologie und Sozialismus. Das Beispiel Karl Barths*, and (in support of quite a different point) McCormack, *Karl Barth's Critically Realistic Dialectical Theology*, pp. 78–125.

20. Schleiermacher, *The Christian Faith*, pp. 492, 583.

21. *The Christian Faith*, §71. The pioneering political theologian Walter Rauschenbusch is able to quote tellingly from Schleiermacher on this subject (*A Theology for the Social Gospel* [1917], pp. 92–93): "The distinctive form of original sin in the individual . . . is only a constituent part of the form it takes in the [social] circle to which he immediately belongs, so that, though inexplicable when taken by itself, it points to the other parts as complementary to it. And this relationship runs through all gradations of community." *The Christian Faith*, §71, p. 288 (this is the Mackintosh translation; Rauschenbusch's translation is different).

22. *The Christian Faith*, p. 427.

23. This and subsequent references in the text are to Johannes B. Metz, *Theology of the World*, trans. William Glen-Doepel.

24. Ernst Bloch, *The Principle of Hope* (1959), trans. Neville Plaice, Stephen Plaice, and Paul Knight, esp. pp. 114–316.

25. Jürgen Moltmann, "Where There Is Hope, There Is Religion," in *The Experiment Hope*, trans. M. Douglas Meeks.

26. Moltmann, "Ernst Bloch and Hope Without Faith," in *The Experiment Hope*, p. 35.

27. Moltmann, "Introduction to the 'Theology of Hope,'" in *The Experiment Hope*, p. 48.

28. Moltmann, "Political Theology," in *The Experiment Hope*, pp. 115–18.

29. See, e.g., Metz, *Theology of the World*, pp. 107–24; and Moltmann, "Political Theology," pp. 115–18.

30. Moltmann, *Theology of Hope*, p. 226.

31. So Gustavo Gutierrez argues, e.g., in his critique of Moltmann and Metz in *A Theology of Liberation*, pp. 216–25.

32. Frederick Herzog, *Liberation Theology: Liberation in the Light of the Fourth Gospel*, pp. 126, 137, 196.

33. José Miguez Bonino, *Doing Theology in a Revolutionary Situation*, p. 100; cf. p. 124: "Christians assume, and participate in, human struggles by identifying with the oppressed. But they have no particularly divine or religious power to contribute. There is no room for crusades, for sacred wars . . . [and] Christians are called to use for this struggle the same rational tools that are at the disposal of all human beings. There is no short-cutting of analysis, ideology, strategy, tactics."

34. Black "soul," James H. Cone, *A Black Theology of Liberation*, p. 60; feminine biophilia, Starhawk, "Witchcraft and Women's Culture," in *Womanspirit Rising*, ed. Carol P. Christ and Judith Plaskow, pp. 263–64.

35. Jon Sobrino, *Spirituality of Liberation*, p. 38.

36. Moltmann, "On Hope as an Experiment: A Postlude," in *The Experiment Hope*, pp. 186–87.

37. Ibid., pp. 187, 189.

38. Moltmann, *Theology of Hope*, p. 228.

39. Ibid., pp. 37–69; cf. Dorothee Soelle's similarly motivated attempt to rescue Bultmann from subjectivism on the strength of the implications of his historical-critical approach in *Political Theology* (1974).

40. For Wilfred Cantwell Smith's conception of the common basis of all religious life as "faith" understood as personal orientation to and involvement in transcendence, see *The Meaning and End of Religion*, chap. 7, and *Faith and Belief*, chaps. 1 and 7. Smith is careful to hold the category of faith open for all qualifications of devotion.

41. Moltmann, *Theology of Hope*, pp. 304–38.

42. "[Barth] had his suspicions of Moltmann's *Theology of Hope*: namely over the 'single line' on which he makes 'the whole of theology end up in eschatology.' 'Salvation comes . . . from the knowledge of "the *eternally* rich God." Compared with this Moltmann's God seems to me to be a bit poor'" (Eberhard Busch, *Karl Barth*, trans. John Bowden, p. 487).

43. James L. Gustafson, *Ethics from a Theocratic Perspective*.

44. This and subsequent references in the text are to Immanuel Kant, *Religion within the Boundaries of Mere Reason*. Pagination in vol. 6 of the Akademie edition.

45. There is an interesting mixture here of a Lutheran rejection of superstitious external works-righteousness and a fundamentally anti-Lutheran call for an inner works-righteousness.

46. For Kant and pietism, see Ernst Cassirer, *Kant's Life and Thought*, pp. 16–18; for Schleiermacher and pietism, see Martin Redeker, *Schleiermacher: Life and Thought*, pp. 8–14.

47. I locate Calvin in the development of the larger Western discourse on piety in "Piety's Problems," *Scottish Journal of Religious Studies* 16 (spring 1995): 5–24.

48. John Calvin, *Institutes of the Christian Religion* 1.2.2, trans. Ford Lewis Battles.

49. Kant, *Critique of Practical Reason*, trans. Lewis White Beck, in *Kant's Critique of Practical Reason and Other Writings in Moral Philosophy*, Ak. 5.161.

50. Moral subjects must regard themselves as *makers* of universal law; "although in the concept of duty we think of subjection to the law, yet we also at the same time attribute to the person who fulfils all his duties a certain sublimity and *dignity*. For it is not in so far as he is *subject* to the law that he has sublimity, but rather in so far as, in regard to this very same law, he is at the same time its *author* and is subordinated to it only on this ground" (Kant, *Groundwork of the Metaphysic of Morals*, trans. H. J. Paton, Ak. 4.433, 440). In interpreting this dignity as a clue to the temporality of Kantian devotion, we must bear in mind also that the *center* of Kantian moral law-making is an *eternal* willing, according to Kant's theory of noumenal freedom.

51. On the history of this discourse, see "Piety's Problems."

52. Schleiermacher, *The Christian Faith*, §119, pp. 546–48. Calvin: "We call predestination God's eternal decree, by which he *compacted* with himself what he *willed* to become of each man. For . . . eternal life is *foreordained* for some, eternal damnation for others. Therefore, as any man *has been created* to one or the other of these ends, we speak of him as *predestined* to life or to death" (*Institutes* 3.21.5, p. 926; emphasis added).

53. Barth, *The Epistle to the Romans*, 2nd ed., p. 40.

54. Barth, "*Unterricht in der christlichen Religion*," vol. 1: *Prolegomena* (1924), pp. 224–25; my translation.

55. Gustafson, *Ethics from a Theocentric Perspective*, 1:164, 201–204. Robert Neville has also revived piety as an ideal of "profound respect and appreciation for the goodness in all components of creation regardless of their measure in the human moral scale of things" (*A Theology Primer*, p. 57).

56. Gustafson, *Ethics from a Theocentric Perspective*, p. 209. Robert Neville argues similarly, but laying greater emphasis on pious *deference to* other beings than on self-referring *gratitude for* them, in *Symbols of Jesus*, pp. 185–90.

57. Gustafson, *Ethics from a Theocentric Perspective*, pp. 208–209.

58. Louis Pojman shows the compatibility of hope even with disbelief in the hoped-for outcome in "Faith without Belief?" in *Philosophy of Religion*, 1998.

59. On the translation of *islam* as "surrender," see Fazlur Rahman, "Islam," in *The Encyclopedia of Religion*, 7:303. Rahman's explanation of *islam*-surrender tilts toward the acceptance of an already-constituted order; it is a main thrust of Sufism, however, to bring *islam* into actualizing, equating it with love. In the canonical definition of Islam as consisting of *iman* (belief), *islam* (practice), and *ihshan* (virtue), *islam* plays a role that "piety" has often played in Christian discourse. See Cyril Glassé, *The Concise Encyclopedia of Islam*, "Ihshan," p. 182.

60. Neville, *A Theology Primer*, p. 61.

61. This and subsequent references in the text are to Sallie McFague, *Super, Natural Christians*.

62. Ibid., chaps. 4–5. Here we must recognize McFague's larger project, extending over a series of previous works, of evaluating cognitive "models" that shape religious thinking. It is fairer to give *Super, Natural Christians* credit for strengthening Mc-Fague's account of the relations between "models" and basic attitudes than to object that it intellectualizes the concept of basic attitude.

63. Cf. McFague's discussion of seeing God as friend in *Metaphorical Theology*, pp. 177–92.

64. This story dimension is present even in biological observation, now that we understand biology evolutionarily. To appreciate what is going on in an anthill, for example, I have to consider, among other things, how certain wasps benefited millions of years ago by abandoning their wings to become ants, and how antlike strategies for collective living are likely to adapt successfully or not to future states of the environment.

65. This and subsequent references in the text are to Jon Sobrino, *Spirituality of Liberation*. On this point cf. p. 122, where love is invoked to fulfill the dimension of action.

66. In this section Sobrino is reviewing proposals by Gustavo Gutierrez in *We Drink From Our Own Wells* (1971).

67. See above, chapter 4, pp. 88–89.

68. Georg Simmel, "Fundamental Religious Ideas and Science: An Inquiry" (1909), in *Essays on Religion*, trans. Horst Jürgen Helle with Ludwig Nieder, p. 5.

69. On "worldly" Christianity, see the contribution of Otto Dudzus to the "world-piety" discussion, "Weltfrömmigkeit Dietrich Bonhoeffers," in *Weltfrömmigkeit. Grundlagen, Traditionen, Zeugnisse*, ed. Anton Zottl.

70. Jürgen Moltmann, *The Spirit of Life*, pp. 6–7.

71. Gustafson, *Ethics from a Theocentric Perspective*, 1:203.

72. See Karl Barth's discussion of the *Extra Calvinisticum* in *Die christliche Dogmatik*, pp. 268–72.

73. For a compact yet nuanced review of the political record of Lutherans and Calvinists, see Roland H. Bainton, *The Reformation of the Sixteenth Century*, chap. 12.

74. On the "healthy-minded" attitude vs. that of the "sick soul," see William James, *The Varieties of Religious Experience* (1902), lectures 4–7. On the inwardly oriented "spirituality of the emergent source" vs. the objectively oriented "spirituality of strict application," see Roger Burggraeve, "The Bible Gives to Thought: Levinas on the Possibility and Proper Nature of Biblical Thinking," in *The Face of the Other and the Trace of God: Essays on the Philosophy of Emmanuel Levinas*, ed. Jeffrey Bloechl, pp. 169–74.

75. Luther, *Lectures on Genesis 6–14*, trans. George V. Schick, in *Luther's Works*, vol. 2, ed. Jaroslav Pelikan, pp. 170–71.

76. Luther, *Lectures on Romans* [8:3], trans. Jacob A. O. Preus, in *Luther's Works*, vol. 25, ed. Hilton C. Oswald, p. 345.

77. For Luther, faith alone can establish the properly supreme love-relationship: "In their books and writings the sacramentarians have pestered us with 'love.' They say to us, 'You Wittenbergers have no love.' But if one asks, 'What is love?' we are told that it means to be united in doctrine and to stop religious controversies. Yes, do you hear?

There are two tables [of the Decalogue], the first and second. Love belongs in the second table. It's superior to all other works there. On the other hand, [in the first table] it is commanded: 'Fear God. Listen to his Word.' The sacramentarians don't bother with this. 'He who loves father and mother more than me is not worthy of me' [Matthew 10.37], said Christ . . . When this 'me' comes, love stops. Accordingly I'm glad to be called obstinate, proud, headstrong, uncharitable, and whatever else they call me. Just so I'm not a participant [in their doctrine]. God keep me from that!" (*Table Talk*, trans. Theodore G. Tappert, in *Luther's Works*, ed. Helmut Lehmann, vol. 54, pp. 463–64, no. 5601). This declaration reflects a remarkably murky mixture of attitudinal, practical, and cognitive issues.

78. John Calvin, *Institutes*, 3.2.42, p. 590.

79. Calvin, "Short Treatise on the Holy Supper," in *Calvin: Theological Treatises*, trans. J. K. S. Reid, p. 149.

80. Calvin, *Institutes* 2.8.53, pp. 416–17.

81. Sobrino, *Spirituality of Liberation*, p. 131. Compare the synthesis proposed by an idealist philosopher: "In inspiration there is a convergence of the memory of the self's crises, the ideas furnished by history or springing from the intellectualization of perception, the energy which is material inasmuch as it results from the situation of the body and spiritual inasmuch as the infinite adds hope to it, and the existential maturing in which the contributions of the will are condensed" (René Le Senne, *Obstacle and Value* [1934], trans. Bernard Dauenhauer, p. 269).

82. Louis Roy brings together evidence of this conception from different editions of the *Dialektik* in "Consciousness According to Schleiermacher."

83. Ibid., pp. 217–32.

84. It is semantically possible to impose these pneumatological qualifications on consciousness to the extent of defining and describing "consciousness" *as spirit*, in the manner of French personalist idealism—as, for example, in René Le Senne—but we are pneumatologically better advised to project outside the Cartesian circle of consciousness-description for the sake of a nonreductive, sufficiently pluralistic affirmation of beings and possibilities that transcend consciousness. The telltale signs of misguidedness in an idealist approach are that all its roads lead to an Absolute that inevitably figures as a super-Self, all hearing of appeals is interpreted as a function of the appetite and movement of this Self, and all fellowship of beings is transmuted into the obtaining of "value."

85. Franz Rosenzweig (*The Star of Redemption*) saw this temporal articulation of religious orientation worked out in the Jewish and Christian liturgical calendars; and see Eugen Rosenstock-Huessy's similarly oriented analyses in, e.g., *Out of Revolution* and "The Penetration of the Cross" in *The Christian Future*, pp. 166–74.

86. Dietrich Bonhoeffer once suggested that the leader charged with proclaiming the Word of God to a Christian congregation is a "sociological" subject—a distinct kind of subject representing the life of the whole church—and a subject of "predicative cognition" transcending the cognition proper to an individual believer (*Act and Being* [1931], trans. Bernard Noble, pp. 147–48). Bonhoeffer also proposed that Christian revelation is essentially given to the church rather than to individuals as such (p. 122). This conception overcomes the stalemate between the "being" and "act" models of revelation: "If the being of revelation is fixed in entity it remains past, existentially impotent; if it is volatilized into the non-objective, its continuity is lost. And so the being

of revelation must enjoy a mode of being which satisfies both claims, embodying both the continuity proper to being and the existential significance of the act. It is as such a mode of being that we understand the person and the community. Here the possibility of existential impact is bound up with genuine objectivity in the sense of a concrete standing-over-against [i.e., of the person vis-à-vis the community]" (pp. 124–25).

87. Schleiermacher, *On Religion*, 1st ed., pp. 192–95; *The Christian Faith*, §10, p. 47.

88. I develop this ideal in "Topics in Philosophical Pneumatology: Inspiration, Wonder, Heart," in *Advents of the Spirit: An Introduction to the Current Study of Pneumatology*, ed. Bradford Hinze and Lyle Dabney.

89. Projecting a new ecumenical Christian life, H. Richard Niebuhr fashioned what in 1955 was an amazingly changed agenda of Christian piety: "There will be no union of Catholics and Protestants until through the common memory of Jesus Christ the former repent of the sin of Peter and the latter of the sin of Luther, until Protestants acknowledge Thomas Aquinas as one of their fathers, the Inquisition as their own sin and Ignatius Loyola as one of their own Reformers, until Catholics have canonized Luther and Calvin, done repentance for Protestant nationalism, and appropriate Schleiermacher and Barth as their theologians" (*The Meaning of Revelation*, p. 119).

90. Frederick Streng, *Understanding Religious Life*, p. 7. The definition allows also for an "ultimate" transformation that is less dramatic and more supportive of continuity —"ultimate" more in the sense of "total" and "final" than of "radical."

91. See Steven T. Katz, "Language, Epistemology, and Mysticism," in *Mysticism and Philosophical Analysis*.

92. Raimundo Panikkar, *The Intra-Religious Dialogue*, p. 2.

93. Panikkar, *Invisible Harmony*, p. 176.

94. Panikkar, *Intra-Religious Dialogue*, pp. 8–9.

95. Ibid., pp. 10–11.

96. Ibid., p. 12.

9. A FRAME FOR PNEUMATICISM

1. Gandhi's autobiography is entitled *The Story of My Experiments with Truth*. He understood political action as an experimentally persistent implementation of an understanding of social justice controlled by the classic attitude of *ahimsa*, a disposition to do no harm.

2. Jacques Derrida, *Of Spirit* (1989) and *Specters of Marx* (1994).

3. See, e.g., the *Letter from Birmingham City Jail* and the final speech, "I Have Seen the Promised Land," in *Testament of Hope: The Essential Writings of Martin Luther King, Jr.*, pp. 297 and 282 [Amos 5.24].

4. Auguste Comte, "The Nature and Importance of the Positive Philosophy," in *Introduction to Positive Philosophy* (1830), ed. Frederick Ferré.

5. Zhuangzi, *The Complete Works of Chuang Tzu*, trans. Burton Watson, chap. 11, p. 122.

6. Ibid., chap. 22, p. 241.

7. Ibid., chap. 4, pp. 57–58.

8. Charles Scott, *The Lives of Things*, pp. 72, 143.

9. Consider the well-meaning assassination of Hun-tun (hospitable Chaos) by

the emperors of the South and North Seas; they did Hun-tun the favor of drilling seven openings in his body so he could function like normal people; *Zhuangzi*, section 7, p. 97.

10. Charles Scott, *On the Advantages and Disadvantages of Ethics and Politics*, pp. 163–64.

11. Madhyamika Buddhism, for example, avoids the categorical denial of the reality of things at the same time that it refrains from affirming an independent reality in any thing (that is, a reality outside of interdependent co-arising). In this perspective, relationship issues can be irreducibly meaningful.

12. A trap into which Arthur Danto may have fallen in *Mysticism and Morality*, where he argues that the nondualist metaphysics of the *Bhagavad Gita* cuts the ground from under its dharma prescriptions.

13. Sogyal Rinpoche, *The Tibetan Book of Living and Dying*, p. 189.

14. Here is an "optimism" defense of nondualism from the end of the nineteenth century, when talk of optimism and pessimism was at its height in the evaluation of religion: "The Vedanta system begins with tremendous pessimism and ends with real optimism. We deny the optimism of the senses but assert the real optimism of the supersensuous. That real happiness is not in the senses but above the senses, and it is in every man. The sort of optimism which we see in the world is what will lead to ruin through the senses" (Swami Vivekananda, *Vedanta: Voice of Freedom*, p. 62).

15. Rinpoche, *The Tibetan Book of Living and Dying*, p. 163.

16. See the selections from Shankara's and Ramanuja's commentaries on the Vedanta Sutras given in *A Source Book in Indian Philosophy*, ed. Sarvepalli Radhakrishnan and Charles A. Moore, pp. 509–55.

17. *Source Book in Indian Philosophy*, p. 543.

18. On Bradley Malkovsky's reading, however, Shankara is actually closer to Ramanuja's position and to bhakti ideals than Ramanuja realizes. See *The Role of Divine Grace in the Soteriology of Samkaracarya* (2001).

19. "World theology" is the designation preferred by Wilfred Cantwell Smith. See his *Towards a World Theology: Faith and the Comparative History of Religion* (1981).

20. A good synopsis of the "inculturation" program is given by Eugene Hillman, C.S.Sp., in *Toward an African Christianity: Inculturation Applied*, chap. 2, "A Radically New Attitude." The key theological principle affirmed in Vatican II documents and newly articulated in the 1990 papal encyclical *Redemptoris Missio* is that the Holy Spirit works through cultures as well as individual hearts (p. 30).

21. See, e.g., Elizabeth K. Minnich, *Transforming Knowledge*.

22. S. Mark Heim, *Salvations: Truth and Difference in Religion*, chap. 4; Kenneth Surin, "Towards a 'Materialist' Critique of 'Religious Pluralism,'" in *Religious Pluralism and Unbelief*, ed. Ian Hamnett. John Hick takes account of important newer criticisms in *A Christian Theology of Religions* (1995).

23. This point does not negate but does qualify Heim's pluralist point that one can only recognize the profundity of the claims of alternative spirits if one is profoundly committed to one's own (*Salvations*, p. 1).

BIBLIOGRAPHY

The Analects of Confucius (Lunyu). Trans. Arthur Waley. New York: Vintage, 1938.

The Anchor Bible Dictionary. Ed. David Noel Freedman. New York: Doubleday, 1992.

Ancient Near Eastern Texts Relating to the Old Testament. 3rd ed. Ed. James B. Pritchard. Princeton, N.J.: Princeton University Press, 1969.

Anthologia Lyrica Graeca. 3rd ed. Ed. Ernst Diehl. Leipzig: Teubner, 1954.

Anthology of World Scriptures. Ed. Robert E. Van Voorst. Belmont, Calif.: Wadsworth,
   1994.

Aquinas, Thomas. *Summa Theologica.* Dominican trans. Notre Dame, Ind.: Ave Maria,
   1981.

Arato, Andrew. "The Neo Idealist Defense of Subjectivity." *Telos* 21 (1974): 108–61.

Aristotle. *Metaphysics.* Trans. Richard Hope. Ann Arbor: University of Michigan Press,
   1952.

———. *Nicomachean Ethics.* Trans. Martin Ostwald. Indianapolis, Ind.: Bobbs-Merrill,
   1962.

Aronson, Harvey B. *Love and Sympathy in Theravada Buddhism.* Delhi: Motilal Banar-
   sidass, 1980.

Audi, Robert. "A Cognitive-Motivational Theory of Attitudes." *Southwestern Journal of
   Philosophy* 5 (1974): 77–88.

Augustine. *The City of God Against the Pagans.* Ed. R. W. Dyson. Cambridge: Cambridge University Press, 1998.

———. *Confessions.* Trans. Rex Warner. New York: Mentor, 1963.

———. "Homilies on the First Epistle of John." Trans. H. Browne. In *Nicene and
   Post-Nicene Fathers,* vol. 7. Ed. Philip Schaff. New York: Scribner's, 1903.

Babylonian Talmud. The Soncino Hebrew-English Talmud. 30 vols. London: Soncino,
   1994.

Baeck, Leo. *The Essence of Judaism.* Trans. Irving Howe. New York: Schocken, 1948.

Bainton, Roland. *The Reformation of the Sixteenth Century.* Boston: Beacon, 1952.

Bambach, Charles R. *Heidegger, Dilthey, and the Crisis of Historicism.* Ithaca, N.Y.:
   Cornell University Press, 1995.

Barth, Karl. *Die christliche Dogmatik im Entwurf.* Zürich: TVZ, 1982.

———. "Der christliche Glaube und die Geschichte." *Schweizerische Theologische
   Zeitschrift* 29 (1912): 1–18.

———. *Church Dogmatics.* 4 vols. Ed. G. W. Bromiley and T. F. Torrance. Edinburgh:
   T. & T. Clark, 1968–78.

———. *The Epistle to the Romans.* 2nd ed. Trans. E. C. Hoskyns. London: Oxford
   University Press, 1933.

———. *The Holy Ghost and the Christian Life*. Trans. R. Birch Hoyle. London: Frederick Muller, 1938.

———. *How I Changed My Mind*. Richmond: John Knox, 1966.

———. "Moderne Theologie und Reichsgottesarbeit." *Zeitschrift für Theologie und Kirche* 19 (1909): 317–21.

———. *Der Römerbrief*. 1st ed. Zürich: TVZ, 1985.

———. "Rudolf Bultmann, An Attempt to Understand Him," trans. Reginald H. Fuller. In *Kerygma and Myth*, vol. 2, ed. Hans Werner Bartsch. London: SPCK, 1962.

———. *Theology and Church*. Trans. Louise Pettibone Smith. London: SCM, 1962.

———. *The Theology of Schleiermacher*. Trans. Geoffrey W. Bromiley. Grand Rapids, Mich.: Eerdmans, 1982.

———. "Unterricht in der christlichen Religion." Vol. 1: *Prolegomena*. Zürich: TVZ, 1985.

———. *The Word of God and the Word of Man*. Trans. Douglas Horton. New York: Harper & Row, 1957.

Barth, Karl, and Emil Brunner. *Natural Theology*. Trans. Peter Fraenkel. London: Bles/Centenary, 1946.

Barth, Karl, and Rudolf Bultmann. *Karl Barth/Rudolf Bultmann. Letters 1922–1966*. Trans. Geoffrey W. Bromiley. Grand Rapids: Eerdmans, 1991.

Barth, Karl, and Eduard Thurneysen. *Revolutionary Theology in the Making*. Trans. J. D. Smart. Richmond: John Knox, 1964.

Beauvoir, Simone de. *The Ethics of Ambiguity*. Trans. Bernard Frechtman. New York: Philosophical Library, 1948.

Beck, Don, and Graham Linscott. *The Crucible: Forging South Africa's Future*. Denton, Tex.: New Paradigm, 1991.

Beck, Guy L. *Sonic Theology: Hinduism and Sacred Sound*. Columbia: University of South Carolina Press, 1993.

The Beginnings of Dialectic Theology. Ed. James M. Robinson. Richmond: Westminster, 1968.

Bennington, Geoffrey, and Jacques Derrida. *Jacques Derrida*. Trans. Geoffrey Bennington. Chicago: University of Chicago Press, 1993.

Benoist, Jocelyn. "Qu'est-ce qui est donné? La pensée et l'évènement." *Archives de Philosophie* 59 (1996): 629–57.

Berry, Thomas, and Brian Swimme. *The Universe Story: From the Primordial Flaring Forth to the Ecozoic Era—A Celebration of the Unfolding of the Cosmos*. San Francisco: HarperCollins, 1992.

The Bhagavad-Gita. Trans. Barbara Stoler Miller. New York: Bantam, 1986.

Binswanger, Ludwig. *Grundformen und Erkenntnis menschlichen Daseins*. 3rd ed. Munich: Ernst Reinhardt, 1962.

Bloch, Ernst. *The Principle of Hope*. Vol. 1. Trans. Neville Plaice, Stephen Plaice, and Paul Knight. Cambridge, Mass.: MIT Press, 1986.

Bollnow, Otto Friedrich. *Dilthey*. 3rd ed. Stuttgart: W. Kohlhammer, 1955.

———. *Das Wesen der Stimmungen*. 3rd ed. Frankfurt-am-Main: V. Klostermann, 1956.

Bonhoeffer, Dietrich. *Act and Being*. Trans. Bernard Noble. London: Collins, 1962.

———. *Letters and Papers from Prison*. Ed. Eberhard Bethge. New York: Macmillan, 1971.

The Book of the Gradual Sayings [*Anguttara Nikaya*]. Trans. F. L. Woodward. London: Pali Text Society, 1951.

The Book of the Kindred Sayings [*Samyutta Nikaya*]. 5 vols. Trans. F. L. Woodward. London: Pali Text Society, 1917–30.

Brandt, Richard. *The Philosophy of Schleiermacher*. New York: Harper, 1941.

Brooks, E. Bruce, and A. Taeko Brooks. *The Original Analects*. New York: Columbia University Press, 1998.

Brunner, Emil. "Die andere Aufgabe der Theologie." *Zwischen den Zeiten* 7 (1928): 255–76.

———. *Die Mystik und das Wort*. Tübingen: J. C. B. Mohr, 1924.

———. *Theology of Crisis*. New York: Scribner's, 1929.

Buber, Martin. *A Believing Humanism*. Trans. Maurice Friedman. New York: Simon and Schuster, 1967.

———. *Between Man and Man*. Trans. Ronald Gregor Smith and Maurice Friedman. New York: Macmillan, 1965.

———. *Daniel: Dialogues on Realization*. Trans. Maurice Friedman. New York: Holt, Rinehart & Winston, 1964.

———. *Ich und Du*. In *Werke*, Vol. 1. Munich/Heidelberg: Kösel/Lambert Schneider, 1962; *I and Thou*. Trans. Walter Kaufmann. New York: Scribner's, 1970.

———. *Israel and the World*. New York: Schocken, 1963.

———. *The Knowledge of Man*. Ed. Maurice Friedman. New York: Harper & Row, 1965.

———. *Two Types of Faith*. Trans. Norman P. Goldhawk. New York: Harper & Row, 1961.

———. *Werke*. Vol. 1. Munich/Heidelberg: Kösel/Lambert Schneider, 1962.

Buddhist Scriptures. Trans. Edward Conze. Harmondsworth: Penguin, 1959.

Bull, Nina. *The Attitude Theory of Emotion*. New York: Nervous and Mental Disease Monographs, 1951.

Bultmann, Rudolf. *Essays Philosophical and Theological*. Trans. James C. G. Greig. London: SCM, 1955.

———. *Existence and Faith*. Trans. Schubert M. Ogden. New York: Meridian, 1960.

———. *Faith and Understanding*. Trans. Louise Pettibone Smith. New York: Harper & Row, 1969.

———. *History and Eschatology*. Edinburgh: Edinburgh University Press, 1955.

———. *Jesus and the Word*. Trans. Louise Pettibone Smith and Erminie Huntress. New York: Scribner's, 1934.

———. *Jesus Christ and Mythology*. New York: Scribner's, 1958.

Burggraeve, Roger. "The Bible Gives to Thought: Levinas on the Possibility and Proper Nature of Biblical Thinking." In *The Face of the Other and the Trace of God: Essays on the Philosophy of Emmanuel Levinas*, ed. Jeffrey Bloechl. New York: Fordham University Press, 2000.

Burke, Edmund. *Philosophical Enquiry into the Origin of Our Ideas of the Sublime and the Beautiful*. 2nd ed. Menston: Scolar Press, 1970.

Burke, Kenneth. *A Grammar of Motives*. Berkeley: University of California Press, 1969.

Busch, Eberhard. *Karl Barth. His Life from Letters and Autobiographical Texts*. Trans. John Bowden. Philadelphia: Fortress, 1976.

Callicott, J. Baird. *Beyond the Land Ethic: More Essays in Environmental Philosophy*. Albany: State University of New York Press, 1999.

Calvin, John. *Calvin: Theological Treatises*. Trans. J. K. S. Reid. Philadelphia: Westminster, 1954.

———. *Institutes of the Christian Religion*. Trans. Ford Lewis Battles. Philadelphia: Westminster, 1960.

Bibliography

Caputo, John D. *The Prayers and Tears of Jacques Derrida*. Bloomington: Indiana University Press, 1997.

Cassirer, Ernst. *Kant's Life and Thought*. Trans. James Haden. New Haven: Yale University Press, 1981.

———. *Language and Myth*. Trans. Susanne K. Langer. New York: Harper and Brothers, 1946.

Charles V. Abdication speech. In *The Western Tradition*, Vol. 1. Ed. Eugen Weber. Lexington: D.C. Heath, 1995.

Cicero. *On the Nature of the Gods*. Trans. H. Rackham. Cambridge, Mass.: Harvard University Press, 1951.

The Classic of Filial Piety. In *The Sacred Books of Confucius*. Trans. Ch'u Chai and Winberg Chai. New Hyde Park: University Books, 1965.

Cobb, John B., Jr. *The Structure of Christian Existence*. Philadelphia: Westminster, 1967.

Code, Lorraine. *What Can She Know? Feminist Theory and the Construction of Knowledge*. Ithaca, N.Y.: Cornell University Press, 1988.

Comte, Auguste. *Introduction to Positive Philosophy*. Ed. Frederick Ferré. Indianapolis, Ind.: Hackett, 1988.

Cone, James H. *A Black Theology of Liberation*. Philadelphia: Lippincott, 1970.

The Context of Scripture. Vol. 1: *Canonical Compositions from the Biblical World*. Ed. William W. Hallo. Leiden: Brill, 1997.

The Context of Scripture. Vol. 2: *Monumental Inscriptions from the Biblical World*. Ed. William W. Hallo. Leiden: Brill, 2000.

Critchley, Simon. *The Ethics of Deconstruction: Derrida and Levinas*. 2nd ed. Edinburgh: Edinburgh University Press, 1999.

Danto, Arthur C. *Mysticism and Morality*. New York: Columbia University Press, 1987.

Daodejing. Trans. Arthur Waley, *The Way and Its Power*. New York: Grove, 1958.

Daodejing: A Philosophical Translation. Trans. Roger T. Ames and David L. Hall. New York: Ballantine, 2003.

Deane-Drummond, Celia. Review of Sallie McFague's *Super, Natural Christians*. *Ecotheology* 8 (2000): 136.

Deconstruction in a Nutshell: A Conversation with Jacques Derrida. Ed. John D. Caputo. New York: Fordham University Press, 1997.

Deleuze, Gilles. "Nomad Thought." In *The New Nietzsche*. Trans. David B. Allison. New York: Delta, 1977.

Deleuze, Gilles, and Félix Guattari. *Anti-Oedipus*. Trans. Robert Hurley, Mark Seem, and Helen R. Lane. Minneapolis: University of Minnesota Press, 1983.

Deninger, Johannes. "Revelation," trans. Matthew J. O'Connell. In *The Encyclopedia of Religion*, ed. Mircea Eliade, vol. 12. New York: Macmillan, 1987.

Derrida, Jacques. *Adieu to Emmanuel Levinas*. Trans. Pascale-Anne Brault and Michael Naas. Stanford, Calif.: Stanford University Press, 1997.

———. "At This Very Moment in This Work Here I Am." Trans. Ruben Berezdivin. In *Re-Reading Levinas*, ed. Robert Bernasconi and Simon Critchley. Bloomington: Indiana University Press, 1991.

———. "Choreographies." In *Points . . . Interviews, 1974–94*, ed. Elisabeth Weber. Stanford, Calif.: Stanford University Press, 1995.

———. "Faith and Knowledge: The Two Sources of 'Religion' at the Limits of Reason

Alone." Trans. Samuel Weber. In *Religion,* ed. Jacques Derrida and Gianni Vattimo. Stanford, Calif.: Stanford University Press, 1998.

———. "Force of Law: The 'Mystical Foundation of Authority.'" In *Deconstruction and the Possibility of Justice,* ed. Drucilla Cornell. New York: Routledge, 1992.

———. *The Gift of Death.* Trans. David Willis. Chicago: University of Chicago Press, 1995.

———. *Given Time: I. Counterfeit Money.* Trans. Peggy Kamuf. Chicago: University of Chicago Press, 1992.

———. *Limited Inc.* Trans. Samuel Weber and Jeffrey Mehlman. Evanston, Ill.: Northwestern University Press, 1988.

———. *Of Hospitality.* Trans. Rachel Bowlby. Stanford, Calif.: Stanford University Press, 2000.

———. *Of Spirit: Heidegger and the Question.* Trans. Geoffrey Bennington and Rachel Bowlby. Chicago: University of Chicago Press, 1989.

———. *On the Name.* Ed. Thomas Dutoit. Stanford, Calif.: Stanford University Press, 1995.

———. "On a Newly Arisen Apocalyptic Tone in Philosophy." Trans. John Leavey Jr. In *Raising the Tone of Philosophy: Late Essays by Immanuel Kant, Transformative Critique by Jacques Derrida.* Ed. Peter Fenves. Baltimore, Md.: Johns Hopkins University Press, 1993.

———. *Specters of Marx.* Trans. Peggy Kamuf. New York: Routledge, 1994.

———. *Speech and Phenomena and Other Essays On Husserl's Theory of Signs.* Trans. David B. Allison. Evanston, Ill.: Northwestern University Press, 1973.

———. *Spurs/Nietzsche's Styles.* Trans. Barbara Harlow. Chicago: University of Chicago Press, 1979.

———. "Violence and Metaphysics." In *Writing and Difference,* trans. Alan Bass. Chicago: University of Chicago Press, 1978.

———. "Women in the Beehive: A Seminar with Jacques Derrida." In *Men in Feminism,* ed. Alice Jardine and Paul Smith. New York: Methuen, 1987.

Descartes, René. *Meditationes de Prima Philosophia.* In *Oeuvres de Descartes,* vol. 7, ed. C. Adam and P. Tannery. Paris: Vrin, 1973. English translation by Elizabeth Haldane and G. R. T. Ross, *Meditations on First Philosophy.* In *The Philosophical Works of Descartes.* Cambridge: Cambridge University Press, 1911.

Dialogues of the Buddha [*Digha Nikaya*]. Ed. T. W. Rhys. London: Pali Text Society, 1920–1921.

Dilthey, Wilhelm. *Descriptive Psychology and Historical Understanding.* Trans. Richard M. Zaner. The Hague: Martinus Nijhoff, 1977.

———. *Dilthey's Philosophy of Existence: Introduction to Weltanschauungslehre.* Trans. William Kluback and Martin Weinbaum. New York: Bookman, 1957.

———. *The Essence of Philosophy.* Trans. Stephen A. Emery and William T. Emery. Chapel Hill: University of North Carolina Press, 1954.

———. *Gesammelte Schriften.* Vols. 1–12. Stuttgart: 1962. Vols. 13–18. Göttingen: Vandenhoeck & Ruprecht, 1961–

———. *Introduction to the Human Sciences.* Ed. Rudolf A. Makkreel and Frithjof Rodi. Princeton, N.J.: Princeton University Press, 1989.

———. *Wilhelm Dilthey: Selected Writings.* Trans. H. P. Rickman. Cambridge: Cambridge University Press, 1976.

Bibliography

The Doctrine of the Mean. In *Confucius: The Analects, The Great Learning, and The Doctrine of the Mean*. Trans. James Legge. New York: Dover, 1971.

Dudzus, Otto. "Weltfrömmigkeit Dietrich Bonhoeffers." In *Weltfrömmigkeit. Grundlagen, Traditionen, Zeugnisse*, ed. Anton Zottl. Eichstätt: Franz-Sales-Verlag, 1985.

Durkheim, Emile. *The Elementary Forms of the Religious Life*. Trans. Joseph Ward Swain. Glencoe, Ill.: Free Press, 1965.

Ebner, Ferdinand. *The Word and the Spiritual Realities*. Trans. Harold Green. Ann Arbor: University of Michigan Press, 1980.

Eck, Diana. *Darshan*. 2nd ed. Chambersburg, Pa.: Anima, 1985.

The Egyptian Book of the Dead. Trans. E. A. Wallis Budge. New York: Dover, 1967.

Elegy and Iambus. Trans. J. M. Edmonds. Cambridge, Mass.: Harvard University Press, 1961.

Eliade, Mircea. *The Sacred and the Profane*. Trans. Willard Trask. New York: Harper Brace, 1959.

The Encyclopedia of Religion. Ed. Mircea Eliade. New York: Macmillan, 1987.

Eno, Robert. *The Confucian Creation of Heaven*. Albany: State University of New York Press, 1990.

The Epic of Gilgamesh. Trans. Andrew George. London: Penguin, 1999.

Epicurus. Letter to Herodotus and Letter to Menoeceus. In *Hellenistic Philosophy: Introductory Readings*, trans. Brad Inwood and L. P. Gerson. Indianapolis, Ind.: Hackett, 1988.

Epictetus. 2 vols. Trans. W. A. Oldfather. Cambridge, Mass.: Harvard University Press, 1925–28.

Euripides. *Trojan Women*. Trans. David Kovacs. Cambridge, Mass.: Harvard University Press, 1999.

Feuerbach, Ludwig. *The Essence of Christianity*. Trans. George Eliot. New York: Harper & Row, 1957.

Fichte, J. G. *Foundations of Transcendental Philosophy nova methodo [1796/99]*. Trans. Daniel Breazeale. Ithaca, N.Y.: Cornell University Press, 1992.

———. *The Popular Works of Johann Gottlieb Fichte*. Trans. William Smith. London: Trübner, 1889.

———. *Science of Knowledge*. Trans. Peter Heath and John Lachs. Cambridge: Cambridge University Press, 1982.

———. *The Vocation of Man*. Trans. Peter Preuss. Indianapolis, Ind.: Hackett, 1987.

Fifteen Greek Plays. Trans. Gilbert Murray et al. New York: Oxford University Press, 1943.

Fisher, Simon. *Revelatory Positivism? Barth's Earliest Theology and the Marburg School*. Oxford: Oxford University Press, 1988.

Fleming, Donald. "Attitude: The History of a Concept." In *Perspectives in American History*, vol. 1, ed. Donald Fleming and Bernard Bailyn. Cambridge, Mass.: Charles Warren Center in American History, Harvard University, 1967.

Franck, Didier. "The Body of Difference," trans. Jeffrey Bloechl. In *The Face of the Other and the Trace of God: Essays on the Philosophy of Emmanuel Levinas*, ed. Jeffrey Bloechl. New York: Fordham University Press, 2000.

Friedman, Maurice. *Martin Buber's Life and Work: The Early Years 1878–1923*. London: Search, 1982.

Friedmann, Georges. *Leibniz et Spinoza*. Paris: Gallimard, 1962.

Gadamer, Hans-Georg. *Truth and Method*. New York: Seabury, 1975.

Gandhi, Mohandas K. *The Story of My Experiments with Truth*. Trans. Mahadev H. Desai. Washington, D.C.: Public Affairs Press, 1948.

Gehlen, Arnold. *Man: His Nature and Place in the World*. Trans. Clare McMillan and Karl Pillemer. New York: Columbia University Press, 1988.

Glassé, Cyril. *The Concise Encyclopedia of Islam*. New York: HarperCollins, 1989.

Gocer, Ali. "Hesuchia, a Metaphysical Principle in Plato's Moral Psychology." *Apeiron* 32 (1999): 17–36.

Gogarten, Friedrich. *Gericht oder Skepsis*. Jena: Eugen, 1937.

——. *Ich glaube an den dreieinigen Gott*. Jena: Eugen Diederichs, 1926.

——. *Politische Ethik*. Jena: Eugen Diederichs, 1932.

——. "Das Problem einer theologischen Anthropologie." *Zwischen den Zeiten* 7 (1929): 493–511.

——. "Volkstum und Gottesgesetzt." *Deutsche Theologie* 1 (1934): 83–88.

——. *Von Glaube und Offenbarung*. Jena: Eugen Diederichs, 1923.

Goody, Jack. *The Logic of Writing and the Organization of Society*. Cambridge: Cambridge University Press, 1986.

Graham, A. C. *Disputers of the Tao*. La Salle, Ill.: Open Court, 1989.

Grisebach, Eberhard. *Gegenwart. Eine kritische Ethik*. Halle: Max Niemeyer, 1928.

Gustafson, James L. *Ethics from a Theocentric Perspective*. 2 vols. Chicago: University of Chicago Press, 1981–84.

Gutierrez, Gustavo. *A Theology of Liberation*. Trans. Sister Caridad Inda and John Eagleson. Maryknoll, N.Y.: Orbis, 1973.

——. *We Drink from Our Own Wells*. 2nd ed. Trans. Matthew J. O'Connell. Maryknoll, N.Y.: Orbis, 1984.

Haar, Michel. "Stimmung et pensée." In *Heidegger et l'idée de la phénoménologie*, ed. Franco Volpi et al. Dordrecht: Kluwer, 1988.

Habermas, Jürgen. *Knowledge and Human Interests*. Trans. Jeremy J. Shapiro. Boston: Beacon, 1971.

Hall, David L., and Roger T. Ames. *Thinking Through Confucius*. Albany: State University of New York Press, 1987.

Harnack, Adolf. *What Is Christianity?* Trans. Thomas Bailey Saunders. New York: Harper & Row, 1957.

Hartmann, Nicolai. *Das Problem des geistigen Seins*. Berlin: Walter de Gruyter, 1933.

Hegel, G. W. F. *Lectures on the Philosophy of World History: Introduction*. Trans. H. B. Nisbet. Cambridge: Cambridge University Press, 1975.

Heidegger, Martin. *The Basic Problems of Phenomenology*. Trans. Albert Hofstadter. Bloomington: Indiana University Press, 1982.

——. *Basic Writings*. Ed. David Farrell Krell. New York: Harper & Row, 1977.

——. *Being and Time*. Trans. John Macquarrie and Edward Robinson. New York: Harper & Row, 1962.

——. *Contributions to Philosophy (From Enowning)*. Trans. Parvis Emad and Kenneth Maly. Bloomington: Indiana University Press, 1999.

——. *Einleitung in die Philosophie*. Ed. Otto Saame and Ina Saame-Speidel. Frankfurt am Main: V. Klostermann, 1996.

——. *Existence and Being*. Trans. Douglas Scott, R. F. C. Hull, and Alan Crick. Chicago: Regnery, 1949.

——. *The Fundamental Concepts of Metaphysics*. Trans. William McNeill and Nicholas Walker. Bloomington: Indiana University Press, 1995.

335

———. *Kant and the Problem of Metaphysics.* Trans. James S. Churchill. Bloomington: Indiana University Press, 1962.

———. *Pathmarks.* Ed. William McNeill. Cambridge: Cambridge University Press, 1998.

———. *A Phenomenological Interpretation of Kant's "Critique of Pure Reason."* Trans. Parvis Emad and Kenneth Maly. Bloomington: Indiana University Press, 1997.

———. *Sein und Zeit.* 8th ed. Tübingen: Max Niemeyer, 1957. English translation by John Macquarrie and Edward Robinson, *Being and Time.* New York: Harper & Row, 1962.

———. *What Is Called Thinking?* Trans. Fred D. Wieck and J. Glenn Gray. New York: Harper & Row, 1968.

Heim, S. Mark. *Salvations. Truth and Difference in Religion.* Maryknoll, N.Y.: Orbis, 1995.

Hellenistic Philosophy: Introductory Readings. Trans. Brad Inwood and L. P. Gerson. Indianapolis, Ind.: Hackett, 1988.

Henry, Michel. *The Essence of Manifestation.* Trans. Girard Etzkorn. The Hague: Martinus Nijhoff, 1973.

———. "The Power of Revelation of Affectivity according to Heidegger." In *Martin Heidegger: Critical Assessments*, vol. 1, ed. Christopher Macann. London: Routledge, 1992.

Herrmann, Wilhelm. *Dogmatik.* Gotha-Stuttgart: F. A. Perthes, 1925.

———. *Ethik.* 4th ed. Tübingen: J. C. B. Mohr, 1909.

———. *Schriften zur Grundlegung der Theologie.* 2 vols. Munich: Christian Kaiser, 1966–67.

———. *Systematic Theology.* Trans. Nathaniel Micklem and Kenneth A. Saunders. New York: Macmillan, 1927.

Herzog, Frederick. *Liberation Theology: Liberation in the Light of the Fourth Gospel.* New York: Seabury, 1972.

Heschel, Abraham. *The Prophets.* 2 vols. New York: Harper & Row, 1962.

Hesiod. Trans. Hugh G. Evelyn-White. Cambridge, Mass.: Harvard University Press, 1914.

Hick, John. *A Christian Theology of Religions.* Louisville, Ky.: Westminster John Knox, 1995.

———. "Religious Experience as Seeing-As." In *Talk of God*, ed. Godfrey Vesey. London: Macmillan, 1969.

Hillman, Eugene, C.S.Sp. *Toward an African Christianity: Inculturation Applied.* New York: Paulist Press, 1993.

Historisches Wörterbuch der Philosophie. Ed. Joachim Ritter et al. Basel: Schwabe, 1971–

Homer. *The Odyssey.* 2 vols. Trans. A. T. Murray. Cambridge, Mass.: Harvard University Press, 1995.

Horner, Robyn. *Rethinking God as Gift: Marion, Derrida, and the Limits of Phenomenology.* New York: Fordham University Press, 2001.

Horowitz, Rivka. *Buber's Way to I and Thou.* Philadelphia: Jewish Publication Society, 1988.

Hume, David. *An Enquiry Concerning Human Understanding.* Ed. Eric Steinberg. Indianapolis, Ind.: Hackett, 1977.

——. *An Inquiry Concerning the Principles of Morals.* Indianapolis, Ind.: Bobbs-Merrill, 1957.

——. *A Treatise of Human Nature.* Oxford: Oxford University Press, 1888.

Humphreys, S. C. " 'Transcendence' and Intellectual Roles: The Ancient Greek Case." In *Wisdom, Revelation, and Doubt: Perspectives on the First Millennium* BCE, Daedalus 104, 2 (1975). Cambridge, Mass.: American Academy of Arts and Sciences.

Iamblichus. "The Life of Pythagoras." In *The Pythagorean Sourcebook and Library*, ed. Kenneth Sylvan Guthrie. Grand Rapids, Mich.: Phanes, 1987.

Ibn Rushd (Averroes). *On the Harmony of Religion and Philosophy.* Trans. George F. Hourani. London: Luzac, 1967.

James, William. *The Varieties of Religious Experience.* New York: Modern Library, 1936.

Janicaud, Dominique, et al. *Phenomenology and the "Theological Turn."* Trans. Bernard G. Prusak. New York: Fordham University Press, 2000.

Jaspers, Karl. *The Origin and Goal of History.* Trans. Michael Bullock. New Haven, Conn.: Yale University Press, 1953.

——. *Philosophy.* 3 vols. Trans. E. B. Ashton. Chicago: University of Chicago Press, 1969–71.

——. *Psychologie der Weltanschauungen.* 3rd ed. Berlin: Julius Springer, 1925.

——. *Reason and Existenz.* Trans. William Earle. New York: Noonday, 1955.

Jaspers, Karl, and Rudolf Bultmann. *Myth and Christianity.* New York: Noonday, 1958.

Kalupahana, David. *A History of Buddhist Philosophy.* Honolulu: University of Hawaii Press, 1992.

Kant, Immanuel. *The Critique of Practical Reason and Other Moral Writings.* Trans. Lewis White Beck. Chicago: University of Chicago, 1949.

——. *Groundwork of the Metaphysic of Morals.* Trans. H. J. Paton. New York: Harper & Row, 1964.

——. *Immanuel Kant's Critique of Pure Reason.* Trans. Norman Kemp Smith. New York: Macmillan, 1929.

——. *Immanuel Kants gesammelte Schriften* [the "Akademie" edition]. Berlin: G. Reimer, 1902–

——. *Lectures on Ethics.* Trans. Louis Infield. London: Methuen, 1930.

——. *Observations on the Beautiful and the Sublime.* Trans. John Goldthwait. Berkeley: University of California Press, 1960.

——. *Religion within the Boundaries of Mere Reason and Other Writings.* Ed. Allen Wood and George di Giovanni. Cambridge: Cambridge University Press, 1998.

Katz, Steven T. "Language, Epistemology, and Mysticism." In *Mysticism and Philosophical Analysis*, ed. Steven T. Katz. New York: Oxford University Press, 1978.

Kaufmann, Walter. *Nietzsche: Philosopher, Psychologist, Antichrist.* 4th ed. Princeton, N.J.: Princeton University Press, 1974.

Kierkegaard, Søren. *The Concept of Anxiety.* Trans. Reidar Thomte. Princeton, N.J.: Princeton University Press, 1980.

——. *Concluding Unscientific Postscript to Philosophical Fragments.* Trans. Howard V. and Edna H. Hong. Princeton, N.J.: Princeton University Press, 1992.

——. *Eighteen Upbuilding Discourses.* Trans. Howard V. and Edna H. Hong. Princeton, N.J.: Princeton University Press, 1990.

———. *Fear and Trembling*. Trans. Howard and Edna Hong. Princeton, N.J.: Princeton University Press, 1983.

———. *Philosophical Fragments*. Trans. Howard and Edna Hong. Princeton, N.J.: Princeton University Press, 1985.

———. *The Sickness unto Death*. Trans. Howard and Edna Hong. Princeton, N.J.: Princeton University Press, 1980.

King, Martin Luther, Jr. *Testament of Hope*. Ed. James Melvin Washington. New York: HarperCollins, 1986.

Kingsley, Peter. *In the Dark Places of Wisdom*. Inverness, Calif.: Golden Sufi Center, 1999.

Kisiel, Theodore. *The Genesis of Heidegger's Being and Time*. Berkeley: University of California Press, 1993.

Klages, Ludwig. *Der Geist als Widersacher der Seele*. Leipzig: J. A. Barth, 1929.

Kristjánsson, Kristján. "Some Remaining Problems in Cognitive Theories of Emotion." *International Philosophical Quarterly* 41 (2001): 393–410.

Lange, Peter. *Konkrete Theologie? Karl Barth und Friedrich Gogarten "Zwischen den Zeiten" (1922–1933)*. Zurich: TVZ, 1972.

Laruelle, François. "L'Appel et le Phénomène." *Revue de Métaphysique et de Morale* 96 (1991): 27–41.

Leeuw, Gerardus van der. *Religion in Essence and Manifestation*. Trans. J. E. Turner. Gloucester: Peter Smith, 1967.

Leibniz, G. W. G. W. *Leibniz's Monadology*. Trans. Nicholas Rescher. Pittsburgh, Pa.: University of Pittsburgh Press, 1991.

———. *Discourse on Metaphysics, Correspondence with Arnauld, Monadology*. Trans. George Montgomery. La Salle, Ill.: Open Court, 1902.

———. *Philosophical Essays*. Trans. Roger Ariew and Daniel Garber. Indianapolis, Ind.: Hackett, 1989.

———. *Theodicy*. Ed. Austin Farrer. London: Routledge & Kegan Paul, 1951.

Le Senne, René. *Obstacle and Value*. Trans. Bernard Dauenhauer. Evanston, Ill.: Northwestern University Press, 1972.

Levinas, Emmanuel. *Collected Philosophical Papers*. Trans. Alphonso Lingis. The Hague: Martinus Nijhoff, 1987.

———. *Existence and Existents*. Trans. Alphonso Lingis. The Hague: Martinus Nijhoff, 1978.

———. *God, Death, and Time*. Trans. Bettina Bergo. Stanford, Calif.: Stanford University Press, 2000.

———. "Martin Buber and the Theory of Knowledge." In *The Philosophy of Martin Buber*, ed. Paul Arthur Schilpp and Maurice Friedman. La Salle, Ill.: Open Court, 1967.

———. *Of God Who Comes to Mind*. Trans. Bettina Bergo. Stanford, Calif.: Stanford University Press, 1998.

———. *On Escape*. Trans. Bettina Bergo. Stanford, Calif.: Stanford University Press, 2003.

———. *Otherwise than Being or Beyond Essence*. Trans. Alphonso Lingis. The Hague: Martinus Nijhoff, 1982.

———. *Time and the Other*. Trans. Richard A. Cohen. Pittsburgh, Pa.: Duquesne University Press, 1987.

——. *Totality and Infinity*. Trans. Alphonso Lingis. Pittsburgh, Pa.: Duquesne University Press, 1969.

——. "The Trace of the Other." Trans. Alphonso Lingis. In *Deconstruction in Context*, ed. Mark C. Taylor. Chicago: University of Chicago Press, 1986.

Lindbeck, George. *The Nature of Doctrine*. Philadelphia: Westminster, 1984.

Linden, Harry van der. *Kantian Ethics and Socialism*. Indianapolis, Ind.: Hackett, 1987.

Lingis, Alphonso. *The Imperative*. Bloomington: Indiana University Press, 1998.

Linzey, Andrew. *Christianity and the Rights of Animals*. New York: Crossroads, 1987.

Llewelyn, John. "Am I Obsessed by Bobby? (Humanism of the Other Animal)." In *Re-Reading Levinas*, ed. Robert Bernasconi and Simon Critchley. Bloomington: Indiana University Press, 1991.

Lovelace, Richard. *The Poems of Richard Lovelace*. Ed. C. H. Wilkinson. Oxford: Clarendon, 1968.

Luther, Martin. *Luther's Works*. Ed. H. T. Lehmann et al. St. Louis: Concordia, 1955–

McCormack, Bruce L. *Karl Barth's Critically Realistic Dialectical Theology*. Oxford: Clarendon, 1995.

——. "What Has Basel to Do with Berlin?" *Princeton Seminary Bulletin* 23 (2002): 146–73.

McDaniel, Jay. *Earth, Sky, Gods and Mortals*. Mystic, Conn.: Twenty-Third, 1990.

McDannell, Colleen, and Bernhard Lang. *Heaven: A History*. New Haven, Conn.: Yale University Press, 1988.

McFague, Sallie. *Metaphorical Theology*. Philadelphia: Fortress, 1982.

——. *Super, Natural Christians*. Philadelphia: Fortress, 1997.

Madsen, Catherine. "Revelations of Chaos." *Cross Currents* 41 (1991/92): 484–505.

The Mahabharata of Vyasa. 12 vols. Ed. P. C. Roy. Calcutta: Bharata, 1884–1896.

Mahony, William K. *The Artful Universe: An Introduction to the Vedic Religious Imagination*. Albany: State University of New York Press, 1998.

Malkovsky, Bradley. *The Role of Divine Grace in the Soteriology of Samkaracarya*. Leiden: Brill, 2001.

Marcel, Gabriel. *Homo Viator*. Trans. Emma Craufurd. New York: Harper & Row, 1962.

Marcus Aurelius. *Meditations*. Trans. C. R. Haines. Cambridge, Mass.: Harvard University Press, 1953.

Marion, Jean-Luc. *Étant donné*. 2nd ed. Paris: Presses Universitaires de France, 1998. English trans. by Jeffrey L. Kosky, *Being Given: Toward a Phenomenology of Givenness*. Stanford, Calif.: Stanford University Press, 2002.

——. *In Excess*. Trans. Robyn Horner and Vincent Berraud. New York: Fordham University Press, 2002.

——. "The Other First Philosophy and the Question of Givenness." Trans. Jeffrey L. Kosky. *Critical Inquiry* 25 (1999): 784–800.

——. *Reduction and Givenness*. Trans. Thomas A. Carlson. Evanston, Ill.: Northwestern University Press, 1998.

——. "The Voice without Name: Homage to Levinas." Trans. Jeffrey Bloechl. In *The Face of the Other and the Trace of God: Essays on the Philosophy of Emmanuel Levinas*, ed. Jeffrey Bloechl. New York: Fordham University Press, 2000.

Marquardt, Friedrich-Wilhelm. *Theologie und Sozialismus. Das Beispiel Karl Barths*. Munich: Christian Kaiser, 1972.

Martin Buber: A Centenary Volume. Ed. Haim Gordon and Jochanan Bloch. New York: KTAV, 1984.

Maze, J. R. "The Concept of Attitude." *Inquiry* 16 (1973): 168–205.

Mead, George Herbert. *Mind, Self, and Society.* Chicago: University of Chicago Press, 1934.

Mencius [Mengzi]. Trans. D. C. Lau. Harmondsworth: Penguin, 1970.

Metz, Johannes B. *Theology of the World.* Trans. William Glen-Doepel. New York: Seabury, 1969.

Miguez Bonino, José. *Doing Theology in a Revolutionary Situation.* Philadelphia: Fortress, 1975.

Milbank, John. *Being Reconciled.* London: Routledge, 2003.

———. *The Word Made Strange.* Oxford: Blackwell, 1997.

Minnich, Elizabeth K. *Transforming Knowledge.* Philadelphia: Temple University Press, 1990.

Moltmann, Jürgen. *The Experiment Hope.* Trans. M. Douglas Meeks. Philadelphia: Fortress, 1975.

———. *The Spirit of Life: A Universal Affirmation.* Trans. Margaret Kohl. Minneapolis: Fortress, 1992.

———. *Theology of Hope.* Trans. James W. Leitch. New York: Harper & Row, 1967.

Mou, Bo. "Ultimate Concern and Language Engagement: A Reexamination of the Opening Message of the *Dao-De-Jing.*" *Journal of Chinese Philosophy* 27 (2000): 429–39.

Neville, Robert Cummings. *Symbols of Jesus.* Cambridge: Cambridge University Press, 2001.

———. *A Theology Primer.* Albany: State University of New York Press, 1991.

Niebuhr, H. Richard. *The Meaning of Revelation.* New York: Macmillan, 1955.

Nietzsche, Friedrich. *The Birth of Tragedy and The Case of Wagner.* Trans. Walter Kaufmann. New York: Vintage, 1967.

———. *The Gay Science.* Trans. Walter Kaufmann. New York: Vintage, 1974.

———. *The Genealogy of Morals and Ecce Homo.* Trans. Walter Kaufmann and R. J. Hollingdale. New York: Vintage, 1967.

———. *Thus Spoke Zarathustra.* Trans. Walter Kaufmann. London: Penguin, 1966.

———. *Twilight of the Idols.* Trans. Walter Kaufmann. In *The Portable Nietzsche,* ed. Walter Kaufmann. New York: Viking, 1968.

———. *The Will to Power.* Ed. Walter Kaufmann. New York: Vintage, 1967.

Nussbaum, Martha. *The Therapy of Desire.* Princeton, N.J.: Princeton University Press, 1994.

The Origins and Diversity of the Axial Age. Ed. S. N. Eisenstadt. Albany: State University of New York Press, 1986.

Otto, Rudolf. *The Idea of the Holy.* Trans. John Harvey. Oxford: Oxford University Press, 1950.

Palmer, Richard. *Hermeneutics: Interpretation Theory in Schleiermacher, Dilthey, Heidegger, and Gadamer.* Evanston, Ill.: Northwestern University Press, 1969.

Pandit, Sneh. *An Approach to the Indian Theory of Art and Aesthetics.* New Delhi: Sterling, 1977.

Pangritz, Andreas. *Karl Barth in the Theology of Dietrich Bonhoeffer.* Grand Rapids, Mich.: Eerdmans, 2000.

Panikkar, Raimundo. *The Intra-Religious Dialogue.* New York: Paulist Press, 1978.

———. *Invisible Harmony*. Ed. Harry James Cargas. Minneapolis: Fortress, 1995.

Patočka, Jan. *Heretical Essays*. Trans. Erazim Kohák. Chicago: Open Court, 1996.

Perry, John Weir. *Lord of the Four Quarters: The Mythology of Kingship*. New York: Paulist Press, 1991.

Perspectives in American History. Vol. 1. Ed. Donald Fleming and Bernard Bailyn. Cambridge, Mass.: Charles Warren Center in American History, Harvard University, 1967.

Philosophy of German Idealism. Ed. Ernst Behler. New York: Continuum, 1987.

The Philosophy of Martin Buber. Ed. Paul Arthur Schilpp and Maurice Friedman. La Salle, Ill.: Open Court, 1967.

Plato. *The Collected Dialogues of Plato*. Ed. Edith Hamilton and Huntington Cairns. Princeton, N.J.: Princeton University Press, 1961.

———. *Euthyphro, Apology, Crito, Phaedo, Phaedrus*. Trans. H. N. Fowler. Cambridge, Mass.: Harvard University Press, 1914.

Pocai, Romano. *Heideggers Theorie der Befindlichkeit. Sein Denken zwischen 1927 und 1933*. Freiburg: Karl Albert, 1996.

Pojman, Louis. "Faith Without Belief?" In *Philosophy of Religion*, 3rd ed., ed. Louis Pojman. Belmont: Wadsworth, 1998.

Powys, John Cowper. *Autobiography*. New York: Simon & Schuster, 1934.

———. *In Defense of Sensuality*. New York: Simon & Schuster, 1930.

The Presocratic Philosophers. 2nd ed. Ed. G. S. Kirk, J. E. Raven, and M. Schofield. Cambridge: Cambridge University Press, 1983.

Qian, Sima. "Life of Confucius." In *The Wisdom of Confucius*, trans. Lin Yutang. New York: Random House, 1938.

The Qur'an. Trans. M. A. S. Abdel Haleem. Oxford: Oxford University Press, 2004.

Radden, Jennifer. "Shame and Blame: The Self through Time and Change." *Dialogue* 34 (1995): 61–74.

Rauschenbusch, Walter. *A Theology for the Social Gospel*. Nashville, Tenn.: Abingdon, 1945.

Redeker, Martin. *Schleiermacher: Life and Thought*. Trans. John Wallhausser. Philadelphia: Fortress, 1973.

Redford, Donald. *Akhenaten, the Heretic King*. Princeton, N.J.: Princeton University Press, 1984.

Rickert, Heinrich. *Der Gegenstand der Erkenntnis*. 6th ed. Tübingen: J. C. B. Mohr, 1928.

———. *Die Grenzen der naturwissenschaftlichen Begriffsbildung*. 5th ed. Tübingen: J. C. B. Mohr, 1929. Abridged English trans. by Guy Oakes, *The Limits of Concept Formation in Natural Science*. Cambridge: Cambridge University Press, 1986.

———. *System der Philosophie*. Tübingen: J. C. B. Mohr, 1921.

———. "Vom System der Werte." *Logos* 4 (1913): 295–327.

The Rig Veda: An Anthology. Trans. Wendy Doniger O'Flaherty. London: Penguin, 1981.

Riley, Patrick. "Introduction" to Nicolas Malebranche, *Treatise on Nature and Grace*. Trans. Patrick Riley. Oxford: Clarendon Press, 1992.

Ritschl, Albrecht. *The Christian Doctrine of Justification and Reconciliation*. Trans. H. R. Mackintosh et al. Clifton: Reference Book, 1966.

Rosenstock-Huessy, Eugen. *The Christian Future*. New York: Scribner's, 1946.

———. *Out of Revolution*. New York: William Morrow, 1938.

Rosenzweig, Franz. *Philosophical and Theological Writings.* Ed. Paul W. Franks and Michael L. Morgan. Indianapolis, Ind.: Hackett, 2000.

———. *The Star of Redemption.* 2nd ed. Trans. William W. Hallo. Boston: Beacon, 1971.

Rothacker, Erich. *Geschichtsphilosophie.* Munich: Oldenbourg, 1934.

———. *Philosophisches Anthropologie.* 5th ed. Bonn: Bouvier, 1982.

Rousseau, Jean-Jacques. *Institutions chimiques.* Ed. Bruno Bernardi and Bernadette Bensaude Vincent. Paris: Fayard, 1999.

Roy, Louis. "Consciousness According to Schleiermacher." *Journal of Religion* 77 (1997): 217–32.

Ruether, Rosemary Radford. *Gaia and God: An Ecofeminist Theology of Earth Healing.* San Francisco: HarperCollins, 1992.

Ruyter, Doret de. "The Virtue of Taking Responsibility." *Educational Philosophy and Theory* 34 (2002): 25–35.

Scheler, Max. *Formalism in Ethics and Non-Formal Ethics of Values.* Trans. Manfred S. Frings and Roger L. Funk. Evanston, Ill.: Northwestern University Press, 1973.

———. *The Nature of Sympathy.* Trans. Peter Heath. Hamden: Archon, 1970.

Schleiermacher, Friedrich. *Aesthetik.* Ed. Rudolf Odebrecht. Berlin: Walter de Gruyter, 1931.

———. *Aus Schleiermachers Leben in Briefen.* 4 vols. Berlin: G. Reimer, 1858–63.

———. *The Christian Faith.* 2nd ed. Ed. H. R. Mackintosh and J. S. Stewart. Edinburgh: T. & T. Clark, 1928.

———. *Friedrich Schleiermacher's Reden ueber die Religion.* Ed. Georg Christian Berhard Pünjer. Braunschweig: C. A. Schwetschke, 1879.

———. *Introduction to Christian Ethics.* Trans. John C. Shelley. Nashville, Tenn.: Abingdon, 1989.

———. *On the 'Glaubenslehre': Two Letters to Dr. Lücke.* Trans. James Duke and Francis Fiorenza. Chico, Calif.: Scholars Press, 1981.

———. *On Religion.* 1st ed. Trans. Richard Crouter. Cambridge: Cambridge University Press, 1988.

———. *On Religion: Speeches to Its Cultured Despisers,* 3rd ed. Trans. John Oman. New York: Harper & Row, 1958.

———. *Schleiermacher's Soliloquies.* Trans. Horace Leland Friess. Chicago: Open Court, 1957.

Schopenhauer, Arthur. *The World as Will and Representation.* 2 vols. Trans. E. F. J. Payne. New York: Dover, 1969.

Scott, Charles. *The Lives of Things.* Bloomington: Indiana University Press, 2002.

———. *On the Advantages and Disadvantages of Ethics and Politics.* Bloomington: Indiana University Press, 1996.

———. "Trauma's Presentation." Paper presented at Millsaps College, April 2003.

Scripture of the Lotus Blossom of the Fine Dharma [*Lotus Sutra*]. Trans. Leon Hurvitz. New York: Columbia University Press, 1976.

Scullion, J. J. "Righteousness." In *The Anchor Bible Dictionary,* ed. David Noel Freedman. New York: Doubleday, 1992.

The Septuagint with Apocrypha. Trans. Lancelot C. L. Brenton. Peabody: Hendrickson, 1992.

Sextus Empiricus. Selections from the Major Writings. Ed. Philip P. Hallie. Indianapolis, Ind.: Hackett, 1985.

Shiner, Larry. *The Secularization of History: An Introduction to the Theology of Friedrich Gogarten*. Nashville, Tenn.: Abingdon, 1966.

Simmel, Georg. *Essays on Religion*. Trans. Horst Jürgen Helle with Ludwig Nieder. New Haven, Conn.: Yale University Press, 1997.

Smith, Steven G. *The Argument to the Other: Reason Beyond Reason in the Thought of Karl Barth and Emmanuel Levinas*. Chico, Calif.: Scholars Press, 1983.

———. *The Concept of the Spiritual: An Essay in First Philosophy*. Philadelphia: Temple University Press, 1988.

———. *Gender Thinking*. Philadelphia: Temple University Press, 1992.

———. "Idealism and Exteriority: The Case of Eberhard Grisebach." *Journal of the British Society for Phenomenology* 20 (1989): 136–49.

———. "Piety's Problems." *Scottish Journal of Religious Studies* 16 (1995): 5–24.

———. "Topics in Philosophical Pneumatology: Inspiration, Wonder, Heart." In *Advents of the Spirit: An Introduction to the Current Study of Pneumatology*. Ed. Bradford Hinze and Lyle Dabney. Milwaukee, Wis.: Marquette University Press, 2001.

———. *Worth Doing*. Albany: State University of New York Press, 2004.

———. "Worthiness to Be Happy and Kant's Concept of the Highest Good." *Kant-Studien* 75 (1984): 168–90.

———. "Worthy Actions." *Journal of Ethics* 5 (2001): 315–33.

Smith, Wilfred Cantwell. *Faith and Belief*. Princeton, N.J.: Princeton University Press, 1979.

———. *The Meaning and End of Religion*. New York: Macmillan, 1963.

———. *Towards a World Theology: Faith and the Comparative History of Religion*. Philadelphia: Westminster, 1981.

———. *What Is Scripture? A Comparative Approach*. Minneapolis: Fortress, 1993.

Snell, Bruno. *The Discovery of the Mind in Greek Literature and Philosophy*. Trans. T. G. Rosenmeyer. New York: Dover, 1982.

Sobrino, Jon. *Spirituality of Liberation*. Trans. Robert R. Barr. Maryknoll, N.Y.: Orbis, 1988.

Soelle, Dorothee. *Political Theology*. Trans. John Shelley. Philadelphia: Fortress, 1974.

Sogyal Rinpoche. *The Tibetan Book of Living and Dying*. Ed. Patrick Gaffney and Andrew Harvey. New York: HarperCollins, 1992.

Soll, Ivan. "Pessimism and the Tragic View of Life: Reconsiderations of Nietzsche's *Birth of Tragedy*." In *Reading Nietzsche*. Ed. Robert C. Solomon and Kathleen M. Higgins. New York: Oxford University Press, 1988.

A Source Book in Indian Philosophy. Ed. Sarvepalli Radhakrishnan and Charles A. Moore. Princeton, N.J.: Princeton University Press, 1957.

Sources of Chinese Tradition. 2nd ed. Ed. William Theodore de Bary et al. New York: Columbia University Press, 1999.

Sources of Indian Tradition. 2nd ed. Ed. Ainslie T. Embree. New York: Columbia University Press, 1988.

Spinoza, Baruch. *The Ethics and Selected Letters*. Ed. Seymour Feldman. Indianapolis, Ind.: Hackett, 1982.

Spiro, Melford. "Religion: Problems of Definition and Explanation." In *Anthropological Approaches to the Study of Religion*, ed. Michael Banton. New York: Praeger, 1966.

Stählin, Leonhard. *Kant, Lotze, and Ritschl*. Trans. D. W. Simon. Edinburgh: T. & T. Clark, 1889.

Starhawk. "Witchcraft and Women's Culture." In *Womanspirit Rising,* ed. Carol P. Christ and Judith Plaskow. San Francisco: Harper & Row, 1979.

Streng, Frederick. *Understanding Religious Life.* 2nd ed. Belmont, Calif.: Wadsworth, 1976.

Surin, Kenneth. "Towards a 'Materialist' Critique of 'Religious Pluralism.'" In *Religious Pluralism and Unbelief.* Ed. Ian Hamnett. New York: Routledge, 1990.

Tacitus. *The Annals of Tacitus.* Trans. Donald R. Dudley. New York: New American Library, 1966.

Tanakh: The Holy Scriptures. Philadelphia: Jewish Publication Society of America, 1986.

Taylor, Paul. *Respect for Nature.* Princeton, N.J.: Princeton University Press, 1986.

The Teachings of the Compassionate Buddha. Ed. E. A. Burtt. New York: New American Library, 1982.

Theological Dictionary of the New Testament. Ed. G. Kittel and G. Friedrich. Trans. Geoffrey W. Bromiley. Grand Rapids: Eerdmans, 1964–74.

Theunissen, Michael. *Der Andere.* 2nd ed. Berlin: Walter de Gruyter, 1977. Abridged English translation by Christopher Macann, *The Other.* Cambridge, Mass.: MIT Press, 1984.

This Sacred Earth: Religion, Nature, Environment. Ed. Roger Gottlieb. New York: Routledge, 1996.

Thurstone, L. L. *The Measurement of Attitudes.* Chicago: University of Chicago Press, 1929.

The Upanishads. Trans. Swami Nikhilananda. New York: Harper & Row, 1963.

Upanishads. Trans. Patrick Olivelle. Oxford: Oxford University Press, 1996.

Urs von Balthasar, Hans. *The Theology of Karl Barth.* Trans. John Drury. New York: Holt, Rinehart and Winston, 1971.

Usener, Hermann. *Götternamen: Versuch einer Lehre von der religiösen Begriffsbildung.* Bonn: F. Cohen, 1896.

Vivekananda, Swami. *Vedanta: Voice of Freedom.* Ed. Swami Chetanananda. St. Louis, Mo.: Vedanta Society of St. Louis, 1986.

Voltaire. *Candide ou l'Optimisme.* Trans. John Butt. London: Penguin, 1947.

Webb, Stephen H. "Should We Love All of Nature? A Critique of Sallie McFague's *Super, Natural Christians.*" *Encounter* 59 (1998): 409–19.

Weber, Max. *From Max Weber: Essays in Sociology.* Ed. H. H. Gerth and C. Wright Mills. New York: Oxford University Press, 1946.

Wisdom, Revelation, and Doubt: Perspectives on the First Millennium BCE. Special issue, *Daedalus* 104, no. 2 (1975). Cambridge, Mass.: American Academy of Arts and Sciences.

Wood, David. *The Deconstruction of Time.* Atlantic Highlands, N.J.: Humanities, 1989.

Xunzi. Trans. Burton Watson. New York: Columbia University Press, 2003.

Zhuangzi. *The Complete Works of Chuang Tzu.* Trans. Burton Watson. New York: Columbia University Press, 1968.

Zimbardo, Philip G., and Michael R. Leippe. *The Psychology of Attitude Change and Social Influence.* Philadelphia: Temple University Press, 1991.

INDEX

A priori: logical, 269–70; historical, 269–70
Abraham, 33, 36, 153, 156–58, 218, 314n84
Actualization, 248–49
Advaita. *See* Nondualism
Aeschylus, 24
Ahimsa, 327n1
Akhenaten, 25, 35–36
Alterity. *See* Other
Ames, Roger T., 306nn47,51
Amos, 153, 218
Analects (of Kongzi), 30, 131
Anamorphosis, 62, 67–68, 93, 103
Anaxagoras, 122, 145
Anaximander, 24
Anschauung, 181–82
Anthropocentrism, 54, 94–95, 245
Anti-foundationalism, 214
Anxiety, 188–89, 203, 205
Appeals and appealing, x, 2–18, 52–58, 60–
    61, 63–64, 68, 71, 73–74, 85, 86, 97–98,
    100–101, 103–104, 107, 221, 236, 267,
    283; absolute, 279; abstractness, 35–37;
    as action, 19; aesthetic, 191; alienated,
    278; answering intentions, 8; being-
    appeal, 81; call-appeal, 81; communica-
    tive, 12–15, 21, 28, 57, 74; competition,
    74; conjunction with attitudes, 281; con-
    solidation, 23–24; divine, 177; enforced
    by attitude, 220; ethical, 63, 177; and fu-
    ture, past, and present, 72, history, 19;
    horizon, 281–82; inclusiveness, 34–35;
    incontinence, 14; in inspiration, 123; in-
    tellectual, 23–24, 27–28; interruptive,
    270; Jaspers on, 56; in monadic agency,
    122; ontological location and relation to
    time, 31, 93; philosophical, 150–51, 282;
    pluralism, 37; political, 24–28; power,
    13–16; religious, 63, 74–77, 79–80, 82–
    83, 85–87, 90–93, 96, 100, 233, 246,
    261; selection (quasi-Darwinian), 14;

subjectivity, 17, 30, 37, 44, 57, 66, 91,
    284; by subjects, 79–80, 90; supreme, x–
    xii, 20, 22–39, 42–44, 60, 65, 72, 74–76,
    78, 80, 82–83, 87, 89–92, 96, 100, 164,
    176, 210, 214, 218–20, 273, 282, 299n43;
    and transcendence, 271; as veils, 9–10; in
    a Way, 122–23; and world structure, 10
Aquinas, Thomas, 327n89
Aranyakas, 137
Arato, Andrew, 292n21
Archilocus, 143–44
Arguments, 6; evaluative, 270; transcendental,
    260
Aristotle, 41, 56, 109, 114–15, 145, 148–49,
    285n2
Arjuna, 143
Ashvaghosha, 307n69
Astrology, 29
Atheism, 177, 190, 221, 237
Atman. See Self, Upanishadic
Attitude and attitudes, 103, 105–17, 137, 149,
    151, 153–54, 156, 181, 197, 222, 224,
    236, 251, 267, 270, 283; absolute, 279; as
    adhered to rather than embodied, 160;
    and aiming, 108–109; appealing, 118,
    125, 160–61, 226, 240; Apollinian, 191,
    208, 223; as approach, 196; in art, 106;
    authenticity, 197; as changeable, 106,
    108–109, 114, 136, 160–61; claims as
    manipulative, 106; collapse of distinc-
    tions between cognition, will, and feel-
    ing, 162–63; and communication, 110–
    11; conjunction with appeals, 281; and
    desire, 110–11; determined by reaching
    understanding, 197; Dionysian, 191, 208,
    223; and emotion, 113–14; of enthusi-
    asm, 168; and experience, 116–17, 139,
    185; formalization, 198; and freedom,
    271; and happiness, 107; harmonizing,
    266; horizon, 281–82; impossible, 217; as

Index

347

Index

Index

Index

Index

Steven G. Smith has taught philosophy and religious studies at Millsaps College since 1985. He is the author of *The Argument to the Other: Reason Beyond Reason in the Thought of Karl Barth and Emmanuel Levinas* (1983), *The Concept of the Spiritual: An Essay in First Philosophy* (1988), *Gender Thinking* (1992), *Worth Doing* (2004), and journal articles in philosophy of religion, ethics, and aesthetics.